KEYS OF POSTTRAUMATIC COPING
Resilience, Posttraumatic Growth, Religious Coping, and Second Corinthians

Luis Cruz-Villalobos, PhD

KEYS OF POSTTRAUMATIC COPING

Resilience, Posttraumatic Growth, Religious Coping, and Second Corinthians

Luis Cruz-Villalobos, PhD

•;•

Independently
Academic

Key of Posttraumatic Coping. Resilience, Posttraumatic Growth, Religious Coping, and Second Corinthians.
© Luis Cruz-Villalobos (2020).

Original title: *Practical Theology of Posttraumatic Coping. Hardiness, Resilience, Posttraumatic Growth, and Second Corinthians.* PhD dissertarion, Vrije Universiteit Amsterdam (2020).

ACADEMISCH PROEFSCHRIFT: ter verkrijging van de graad Doctor of Philosophy aan de Vrije Universiteit Amsterdam, op gezag van de rector magnificus prof.dr. V. Subramaniam, in het openbaar te verdedigen ten overstaan van de promotiecommissie van de Faculteit Religie en Theologie op maandag 22 juni 2020 om 13.45 uur online Vrije Universiteit, De Boelelaan.

Promotor: prof. dr. R.R. Ganzevoort. Copromotor: dr. C. van Engen.

Gratitud to Issachar Fund for the scholarship granted to carry out the 'Writer's Retreat' in the city of Grand Rapids (Michigan, USA), from January to March 2016, to make progress in the writing of this dissertation. Project hosted by the research area of Medical Care and Human Dignity.

All Scripture quotations were taken from the *New International Version* (1995) of the Bible. Grand Rapids, MI: Zondervan.

Cover image: Hugo Godoy (2017).

© Independently Academic
First Edition
Maule, Chile, 2020

ISBN: 9798662675568

Book printed in the United States of America.

This work is dedicated with deep gratitude
to trinitarian trill *and to my wife and children.*

INDEX / TABLE OF CONTENTS

LIST OF DIAGRAMS:

LIST OF TABLES:

LIST OF BOXES:

Summary

The present research is a study on posttraumatic coping in some paragraphs of the second letter to the Corinthians of the Apostle Paul. As a research in the field of practical theology, in methodological terms, this thesis follows the steps of the hermeneutical arc proposed by Ricoeur (1976, 2002, 2016), from the perspective of the Psychological Biblical Criticism (Rollins 1983, Kille, 2001, 2004; Ellens, 2012).

In the first part of this study a detailed review of current research on posttraumatic coping in the field of psychology is made. Then we examine exegetically four selected texts from 2 Corinthians that describe the ways in which Paul faced various traumatic events in his life. Each paragraph is analyzed looking for the texts to show their world and their own sense, to then identify the hermeneutical keys of coping that are observed in them.

After a careful analysis, eleven keys of coping present in the selected Pauline texts were categorized: 1) Paradoxical identity that marks the experience of the Apostle as a phenomenon of self-understanding that incorporates the awareness of fragility and constant vulnerability to hardship, but simultaneously united to the perception of itself as triumphant to adversity, thanks to its unconditional link with the sacred, manifested in Jesus as the Messiah; 2) Experience of faith understood as fidelity and perseverance, especially in the midst of tribulations, in such a way that resisting, overcoming and even growing out of suffering is described as an expression of authentic faith and genuine affection for Jesus as Lord; 3) Resignification of death and traumatic events, as circumstances of a negative nature that is relativized and whose harmful effects are not perceived as chronic; 4) Coping associated with an altruistic practice towards his brothers and sisters in faith; 5) Coping with a marked character of eschatological type; 6) Explicit and habitual expression of the traumatic events experienced, which implies taking charge of them, without denying nor evading them; 7) Detachment from the material or visible things, considering these aspects of life as facets of reality that are not definitive, but as manifestations of a preliminary plan that will disappear; 8) Identification with Jesus as a model of coping with extreme adversities; 9) Thanksgiving or gratitude, as a permanent practice, in both favorable and unfavorable circumstances; 10)

Perception of the consoling presence of God constantly in the midst of suffering; and 11) Prayer described as a personal and community behavior of concrete beneficial influence in life.

Finally, a conversation between these findings and the current psychological contributions on positive coping of trauma, allowed us to corroborate the significant similarities between the approaches of Paul regarding coping in extreme adverse events and the outcomes of this research on hardiness, resilience, posttraumatic growth and positive religious coping.

Among the main conclusions reached in this investigation, we can highlight that Paul offered, in the analyzed texts of 2 Corinthians, coping modalities that showed a permanent search for "sense of coherence" (Antonovsky, 1979, 1984, 1987, 1993), which involves the comprehensibility, manageability and meaningfulness of adverse events, but in his case, from a fundamentally theological framework ("sense of theological coherence"). In addition, it was found, when looking for common factors in the coping keys observed in the Pauline texts, that these can be synthesized in the so called "theological virtues": faith, hope and love, besides the concept of identity in Christ, which function as dispositions that allow the religious/spiritual articulation of traumatic events, both on a personal and community level.

The present study sought to develop a practical theology (defined as theological understanding of Christian praxis) of posttraumatic coping in a Pauline perspective. We believe that this study has achieved a significant understanding of hardiness, resilience, posttraumatic growth and positive religious coping modalities, from a theological perspective, which can contribute to the development of new practices of pastoral care, especially in contexts of adversity.

Chapter 1
Introduction

To suffer
What is its shape and head?
To pain
Wich nuances accompany it?
With what eyes does sadness look for us?
With what color did it pain its strange peace?
How does sadness walk?
Speak up, he who knows its homeland.
Who defines it, where does it live?
Wich woman had those entrails?
Silvio Rodríguez[1]

In March 1974, in Santiago, Chile, a young socialist militant was arrested by agents of the DINA (National Intelligence Directorate) and sentenced to be confined to sinister torture centers. She managed to resist for five months, but when facing threats directed at her family, she decided to collaborate. She disclosed names, provided left wing movement charts, established love relationships with her captors, until one year after her capture she was officially recruited as a DINA official. Her testimony in the first person is included in her story called *El Infierno* (Arce, 2017). "Here is a truth that hurts and I have struggled not to transform it into a knife" (Ibíd., p. 16).

> The priest José Luis de Miguel, in the prologue, says:
> Although fine tuned in recent years, *El Infierno* owes its gestation to an earlier period, in which the author needed to relate, as a personal catharsis, her experience during the dictatorship. This, in order to be able to personify her own unique and inalienable experience, not in general terms nor as experiences seen by outsiders. By then, she had already had

---

[1] "Que levante la mano la guitarra" (song of album: "Erase que se era", 2006), translated by R. Flanders for this document. In Spanish: "Sufrir, ¿qué forma tiene, qué cabeza? Al dolor, ¿qué matices lo acompañan? ¿Con qué ojos nos busca la tristeza? ¿De qué color pintó su paz extraña? ¿Cómo camina la tristeza? Hable quien conozca su patria. Quién la define, dónde vive ¿Qué mujer tuvo esas entrañas?".

what she calls her reencounter with the Lord. I find this to be decisive for the future of Luz and, I dare to say, for the gestation and publication of this work. According to her, she would find, in the Lord, in her roots, the union between the meaning of life, also of her life; and the sense of redemptive pain. "Pain —she says— makes siblings survivors", which would mean being truly free (Ibíd., p. 12)[2].

This hard case of a compatriot of the author of the present investigation is a good illustration of the subject that we will research in this thesis dealing with human suffering, violence, torture, the confrontation of evil, faith, hope and posttraumatic growth.

Since ancient times, poets have been wondering about the nature of human pain and the meaning of suffering, and in their songs have searched for consistency and significance amidst personal, communal, and national adversity. In the same way, in the fields of philosophy, religion, medicine, and the social sciences, interest in explaining and understanding how human beings deal with adverse or traumatic experiences[3] has been increasing in ever greater quantity and depth.

The most common psychological, psychopathological, and clinical approaches to trauma have almost exclusively focused on the

---

[2] In Spanish: "Si bien afinado en estos últimos años, El Infierno debe su gestación a un período anterior, en el que la autora necesitaba relatar, a modo de catarsis personal, su experiencia durante la dictadura para poder personar y personarse, no en términos generales o sobre experiencias ajenas, sino a partir de su propia vivencia, única e inalienable. Para entonces, ya había tenido lo que ella llama su reencuentro con el Señor. Encuentro decisivo para el futuro de Luz y, me atrevo a decir, para la gestación y publicación de la presente obra. Según ella constataría, en el Señor, en sus raíces, el reencuentro con el sentido de la vida, también de su vida; con el sentido del dolor redentor. 'El dolor —dice— hace hermanos a los sobrevivientes', lo que significaría ser libre de verdad".

[3] In this dissertation when referring to the term trauma, we will make the distinction between traumatic event, traumatic experience and trauma itself. We will use the concept of *traumatic event*, operationalizing it in the way it is established in the diagnosis for PTSD in the DSM-5 (APA, 2013, p 274), to delimit its polysemy and limit it to particularly disruptive events, where the person is exposed, directly or as a witness, to death or the possibility of serious damage to personal integrity. We will use the notion of *traumatic experience* to understand the disruptive and unadaptative response to a traumatic event. We will talk about the *trauma itself* when a traumatic experience occurs before a traumatic event.

negative effects that adverse events have on people that experience them. They especially concentrate on the development of mental disorders, such as Posttraumatic Stress Disorder (PTSD). The presence of PTSD has been viewed as the expected response to traumatic events, to such a point that positive and asymptomatic coping responses to extremely stressful episodes are seen as exceptional and even clinically suspicious.

By focusing exclusively on the harmful effects of adverse events in the human being has often created the impression that the person suffering from traumatic event normally develops some sort of irreversible damage or pathology. However, from some current perspectives, human beings have begun to be observed as active agents, possessing important personal, social, and contextual resources for coping with adverse situations. They are viewed as having the potential to develop a capacity to resist and rebuild despite and/or because of adversity, even in extreme situations.

Most people face significant loss or experience potentially or effectively traumatic events at some point in their lives. However, many continue to have positive emotional experiences and show minimal or transitory changes in their capacity to grow and develop. Much of the knowledge about how people deal with loss and trauma has come from individuals who sought treatment after experiencing intense discomfort in their response to an adverse event, and because of this, all forms of positive posttraumatic coping have been seen as strange, or simply pathological.

Concepts such as hardiness (Kobasa, 1979, 1982; Eschleman, Bowling & Alarcón, 2010; Maddi, 2005, 2013), resilience (Garmezy, 1993; Du Plessis, 2001; Fletcher & Sarkar, 2013; Wu, et al., 2013; Kent, Davis & Reich, 2014; Southwick, et al., 2014) and posttraumatic growth (Calhoun & Tedeschi, 1999, 2004a, 2004b, 2006, Zoellner & Maercker, 2006; Berger, 2015) present a real alternative to concepts that only include pathological responses to adversity, and describe positive coping modes that seem to occur more frequently than formerly thought (Bonanno, 2004; Almedom, 2005).

These concepts are framed within what is called Positive Psychology, which seeks to understand the dynamics and resources that underlie human beings' strengths and virtues, and is becoming a new discipline focused on positive subjective experience, preventing pathologies that arise when life is sterile and meaningless, and when the individual, social, and institutional traits may allow for an improved quality of life (Seligman & Csikszentmihalyi, 2000).

Recent results from longitudinal research suggest that Nietzsche's aphorism, "that which does not kill us makes us stronger[4]", seems to be true in some cases. A widespread assumption is that exposure to adverse life events is related to negative effects on the mental health and wellbeing of people in such a way that adversity becomes a kind of predictor of negative results in the lives of individuals. However, it has been observed that adverse experiences can also foster the capacity to recover from subsequent adverse events, with resulting benefits for mental health and wellbeing. In a significant number of cases, people with a history of adversity have shown better indicators of mental health and greater life satisfaction over time compared to those who do not have a history marked by adversity (Seery, Holman & Silver, 2010).

This observation that humans can grow when facing adversity is in fact not a new one. Religious traditions since long have described this and even offered modes of healing and growth in the face of adversity. To date, however, there is only scarce research into the relation between the wisdom of these traditions and the clinical observation. The present work is an interdisciplinary research project within a practical theological framework referring to posttraumatic coping. It seeks to develop a theological understanding that integrates the main contributions present in the Apostle Paul's writings (especially in the second letter to the Corinthians) with research on positive coping with trauma in the field of psychology, especially surrounding the concepts of hardiness, resilience and posttraumatic growth.

One of the topics that has attracted the most interest throughout the history of humanity has been the understanding of suffering, especially extreme suffering, and the search for positive ways

---

[4] Original: "Was mich nicht umbringt macht mich stärker". The saying comes from of Nietzsche's book, *Twilight of the the Idols* (1888). He used later a similar sentence in *Ecce Homo* (written 1888, published 1908). In the chapter entitled "Why I Am So Wise", he wrote that a person who has "turned out well" from an adverse situation could be recognized by certain attributes, such as a knack for exploiting bad accidents to his advantage. Regarding such a man, Nietzsche said: "What does not kill him makes him stronger." ("Was ihn nicht umbringt, macht ihn stärker")

to cope with it. From the prespective of different religions, philosophies, and modern scientific disciplines, answers have been sought to the questions raised by the harsh reality of encountering or witnessing life threatening or severely damaging events. In theological terms, we can see that traumatic experiences and ways of coping with them are themes found throughout the Bible, particularly in the death and resurrection of Jesus Christ. However, reflection on evil and on extremely adverse experiences has been done primarily from the perspective of theodicy (Laato & de Moor, 2003; Berthold, 2004; Neuhouser, 2008; Theide, 2008; Poma, 2013) and less so from the perspective of trauma or growth. There are of course exceptions. Liberation theology, for example, seeks to not only theologically understand the suffering of the oppressed, but also to promote ways of transforming the political-economic structures that sustain it, but not from the perspective of trauma or growth (Gutiérrez, 1975; Boff, 1986; Boff & Boff, 1986; Berryman, 1987; Dussel, 1887).

In this sense, religion, and particularly the experience of the Christian faith, is presented in this project as a reality bonded to the complex phenomenon of trauma and coping, a reality that requires extensive theological articulation to account for the deep ambiguities, difficulty of expression, symbols, social and cultural connotations, demands for justice, and possibilities for hope.

Today, from some perspectives, the effects of extreme adversity and ways of coping with it, as they relate to the human experience, are considered fundamentally as hermeneutical phenomena, that is, a set of singular interpretive experiences of the person who lives them, personally, in a community, or nationally (Bracken, 2002). Within this context, this research aims to provide a current review of major research on positive coping with trauma, addressing concepts such as resilience, memory, forgiveness, social support, and posttraumatic growth (Almedom, 2005; Vera, Carbelo & Vecina, 2006; Acero, 2008).

Religion and spirituality as positive physical and mental health factors have been quite thoroughly discussed in the literature, and certain practices and lifestyles associated with religion and spirituality have been observed to have an overall positive contribution (Koenig & Cohen, 2002; Huguelet & Koenig, 2009; Koenig, 1998, 2012, 2015). In particular, the study of posttraumatic growth seeks to identify factors that determine adaptation or 'healing' from maladaptive or psychopath-logical responses. And one of these principal factors seems to be the wisdom of religion and the practices of spiritual traditions (Pargament, 1997; Calhoun & Tedeschi, 2004a, 2004b, 2006; Ano & Vasconcelles, 2005; Prati & Pietrantoni, 2009).

The experiences of extreme adversity associated with transformation are not new topics. In fact, they are central to the biblical tradition and indeed to all religious traditions. The different religious and wisdom traditions reveal the great number of different interpretations given to situations of suffering. Such interpretations form an important part of the coping modes used at the moment of experiencing a traumatic event. Suffering is one of the key experiences that leads to the creation of religious meaning and the Bible contains many examples of transformation from extreme adversity (Riggs, 2006; Villega Besora, 2006; Eisen & Laderman, 2007). This thesis will investigate the hermeneutical connections between the biblical text and the human experience, connections that may contribute to a pastoral theology that offers positive coping responses to traumatic events and experiences. Specifically, we will study some biblical texts that deal with the topic of coping with extreme adversity. We will look for correlations, distinctions and possible integrations with the results of a study of the main hermeneutical keys present in the writings of the Apostle Paul regarding extreme adversity and positive coping, specifically in 2 Corinthians. We have chosen this letter for various reasons: a) It is one of the authentic Pauline writings that is more experiential and emotional in nature; b) It is the Pauline letter that addresses the subject of coping with adversity the most number of times; c) It is a text with important sections that we can consider in an applied pastoral theology; d) It allows us to focus on a major text (selected from many others found in the Bible) so as to not overextend the research; and e) Of all Pauline writings, this letter contains the highest number of comments and interpretations of Paul's adverse experiences.

The main research question for this thesis is: What insights regarding coping with adversity can we find in the writings of the Apostle Paul (particularly in 2 Corinthians) and in recent research on positive coping with trauma for the purposes of building a practical theology of posttraumatic coping?

To answer this question, the present study will be an investigation in a practical theological framework that seeks to develop a multidisciplinary approach. Methodolo-gically, practical theology begins with the concrete and local. There are many methods in which scholars and ministers have analyzed the dynamics of theology and faith in practice. The diferent methods are a means to connect theory and practice in academy, church, and society (Ganzevoort, 2009a; Miller-McLemore, 2012).

Methodologies in practical theology have been developed from several perspectives, for example, through the use of the following.

a) The inductive method of reviewing human experience defined by the three phases of review developed by the French *Young Christian Workers* (Meza, 2002; Prentiss, 2008): seeing, judging, and acting. This method has proposed an analysis that starts from the visible and concrete facts of life (*socio-analytical mediation*, in Liberation Theology), then turns to Scripture as a revelation of creation and restoration's projection (*hermeneutic mediation*), and ends with the concrete experience of Christian commitment (*practical mediation*).

b) An empirical and critical method that is somewhat similar to the above by having three phases, defined as *kairological* (analysis or appraisal of the situation), *projective* (identification, from a model of Church, that being objectives or goals for achieving a renewed praxis) and *strategic* (moving from a given situation to a desired one) (Floristan, 1998; Midali, 1991).

c) The method of pastoral praxis that begins with pastoral observation (in a systematic and rigorous way that tries to answer the descriptive and comprehensive issues of real life), pastoral interpretation (content analysis and deduction of a meaning that attempts to verify Christian authenticity in context), and pastoral planning (as a transformative process that responds to the immediate future and involves joint participation) (Floristán, 1998).

d) The method of practical theology as a science of action that takes as its form of departure elements of Christian and ecclesial praxis, then turns to the Christian tradition to establishe what the praxis should be, and susequently, out of the confrontation of the two previous steps, extracts some directives for action (Neira, 1994).

There are important theoretical and empirical develop-ments that have had different emphases about practical theology when understood as an empirical discipline whose broad object of study is the link between praxis and the sacred (Heimbrock, 2004; Van der Ven, 2004; Ganzevoort, 2004a, 2004b, 2010; Ganzevoort & Roeland, 2014)[5]. Several methodlogies which have been used in practical theology share three fundamental steps[6]: begin from reality, move to Scripture, and then go back to reality (somewhat along the lines of hermeneutic circularity, and particularly the *hermeneutic arc* proposed by Ricoeur (1976, 2002, 2016), which shall be a important perspective we will use in this research).

We will apply these steps in our research by starting from an observation of the reality of suffering, extreme adversity, and positive coping patterns, then introduce an emblematic example found in Scripture of coping with adversity (passages from 2 Corinthians), and finally arrive at some key concepts that will be used to develop contributions toward a practical theological understanding of posttrau-matic coping.

Starting from the proposition that "the ancient texts can be opened and illumine contexts unseen by the original author" (De Wit, 2002, p. 9), this study will seek to find keys on the topic of posttraumatic coping from important readings in the biblical text, taken as a hermeneutical product of a paradigmatic and normative nature but open to reinterpretation in light of new developments (Croatto, 1994). Thus, with a serious exegetical methodology, the approach to the biblical text will seek to ascertain and respect the meaning and original content of Paul's writings, but also allow the reader to be a producer of meaning (Croatto, 1994; Ricoeur, 1976, 2002, 2016; De Wit, 2002, 2010). In the passages of 2 Corinthians that

---

[5] If we consider acommon ground of practical theology as 'hermeneutics of lived religion' (as that marks the distinction from social sciences of religion on the one hand and other theological disciplines on the other), the forks in the road have to do with how broad the object is defined (as ordained ministry, church, faith, religion, culture, or society), how praxis and theological theory are related methodologically (as object, source, telos, field, or forum), how the researcher is positioned vis-a-vis the object (as player, coach, referee, or commentator), and how the primary audience is to be understood (as academy, church, or society) (Ganzevoort, 2009a).

[6] Parallels the Liberation Theology-method (Gutiérrez, 1975; Boff & Boff, 1986).

explicitly relate to coping with adverse experiences, we will search for interpretive keys in the writings of the Apostle Paul that can be correlated with the current findings of psychological research on positive coping with trauma. This process will respect the difference between the two fields and their epistemic approaches, but will aim to find their meeting point in the fact that the hermeneutical act is essential for both disciplines.

Practical Theology, in our perspective, is understood as "a hermeneutics of Christian praxis" (Hoch, 2011, p.76) and "theological discernment in human action" (Brown, 2012, p. 113) in two ways. First, it helps the church interpret Scripture and apply it to current context by bringing Scripture to life in a way that goes beyond the time and place in which it was spoken or transcribed. Second, it presents itself as a theological discipline whose task is to ensure that the church keeps pace with the changing world in which it lives, requiring an understanding of current society in its complexity, with the particular help of the social sciences (Floristán, 1998; Hoch, 2011).

This investigation, therefore, will seek to maintain a hermeneutic articulation between the psychological field of research on positive coping with trauma and relevant Pauline writing (of 2 Corinthians) in such a way that the interpretive theory may provide epistemological orientations, along with a methodological framework, that contribute to the development of a practical theology of posttraumatic coping. We seek not only to describe and analyze the ecclesial praxis, but also to improve it (Brown, 2012; Ganzevoort & Roeland, 2014).

To achieve our research objectives mentioned, within a hermeneutical methodological framework, we will work from the perspective of Psychological Biblical Criticism, which is a field within biblical criticism that seeks to examine the psychological dimensions of Scripture through the use of behavioral science. As the name implies, here is "the intersections of three fields: psychology, the Bible, and the tradition of rigorous, critical reading of the biblical text" (Kille, 2001, p. 3).

As one of the pioneers in this field, Rollins argued that Psychological Biblical Criticism was interested in:

[...] texts, their origination, authorship, modes of expression, their construction, transmission, translation, reading, interpretation, their transposition into kindred and alien forms, and the history of their personal and cultural effect, as expressions of the structure, processes, and habits of the human psyche, both in individual and collective manifestations, past and present (1999, pp. 77-78).

Unlike many other forms of biblical criticism, Psychological Biblical Criticism is not a particular method of interpretation, but rather a perspective of an approach to the biblical text that seeks to complement studies on cultural, sociological and anthropological influences on writing, but discussing the psychological dimensions of the authors of the text, the material they wish to communicate to their audience, and the reader's reflections and meditations (Rollins, 1983, Kille, 2001, 2004).

The use of psychological theories in the study of ancient texts have been met with the obstacle of temporal and cultural distance between the analyst and the writers/authors. Psychological Biblical Criticism seeks not to be a reductionist tool, but a particular perspective that uses the traditional methods of historical and cultural criticism, illuminating aspects of purpose, meaning, and cognitive and affective processes present in the author when writing the text, being very careful not to try to reach something beyond what the text allows us (Kille, 2001).

Psychological Biblical Criticism also seeks to understand the effect of the text on the contemporary reader, as indicated by Rollins (1983, p. 98):

[...] we often come to Scripture with the question 'What is this book?', but discover that this book asks us, 'Who is this that reads it?'... Each of us carries... a set of values, a list of personal problems, a well seasoned worldview, and a large dose of humanity, wherever we go and to whatever task we undertake. When we approach Scripture we come with the same baggage. It is not possible to come in any other way.

In this way, the interest is not exclusively in the psychology of the writer, nor in the original meaning of the text and the characters exposed, but also in how the reader can use, interpret, and be changed by the text; how the text is relevant to the personal lives of readers in such different contexts (Rollins 1983, Kille, 2001, 2004).

Regarding our choice of this methodological perspective, it is worth mentioning that we have considered it specifically for the type of subject we are dealing with, which corresponds to a psychological phenomenon (positive coping with traumatic events), associated with the sacred in the case of the Apostle Paul. We have also chosen, when exegetically addressing the biblical text, the use of resources in a critical-historical line, instead of adopting more current approaches such as, for example, narrative or canonical criticism, especially for reasons that we will indicate next and which are related to the character of 2 Corinthians and of passages selected:

Second Corinthians is a text that belongs to the epistolary genre, written with a marked style of diatribe, not as a continuous literary narrative. It also has evident breaks in the discourse that require a reordering of the texts to achieve minimum psychological coherence and to be able to leave, in turn, the selected passages in their precise chronological contexts within the relational dynamic of Paul with the Corinthians which allows these writings to be better understood.

On the other hand, the chosen paragraphs are autobiographical testimonies explicitly related to coping with high stress events, which will be studied in terms of the meaning of their specific declared contents, but also, later on, in terms of the psychological dynamics they reveal (particularly in reference to factors associated with psychological hardiness, resilience, and posttraumatic growth), in other words, as phenomena of positive coping with traumatic events. All this with an eye on the light that these writings can shine on adverse circumstances for contemporary readers, both on a personal as well as community/ ecclesial level. In short, it seems to us that Psychological Biblical Criticism, used as a heuristic perspective under the methodological use of the *hermeneutical arc* (we see this in more detail in a section referring to the hermeneutical methodological framework) allows us to adequately address the Apostle Paul's coping with extreme adversities, understanding "practical theology as hermeneutics of lived religion" (Ganzevoort, 2009a, p.1).

The study of written testimony of traumatic experiences and the coping mechanisms employed by survivors has been a relevant field of research, especially after World War II. Many people who experienced traumatic events left their memories in writings that are now seen as sources for different types of valuable studies (Levi, 1976; Appelfeld, 1983; Patruno, 1995; Améry, 1998; Budick, 2005; Wolf, 2007; Brudholm, 2008; Alford, 2009; Magavern, 2009; Sodi & Marcus, 2011; Weindling, 2015; Levi & De Benedetti, 2015).

In the field of trauma psychology, the testimony of victims, including their personal experience, has been researched (Frankl, 1992, 2000). Most studies on resilience and posttraumatic coping are based on field studies and trauma survivors' self-reporting (Garmezy, 1993; Calhoun, L. G. & Tedeschi, 1999, 2004a, 2004b, 2006; Fletcher & Sarkar, 2013; Wu, et al., 2013; Kent, Davis & Reich, 2014; Berger, 2015).

Psychological studies on the written testimony of people who have passed away are very relevant, although not abundant. Among these studies, we can highlight the introduction to a book by Pérez-Sales (2006), who examined the written testimony of Nazi concentration camp survivors (P. Levi, J. Améry, and V. Frankl), focusing his analysis on the differences in their writings related to: a) characteristics of the traumatic event; b) the consequences of the event; c) the elements of resistance described by each author; and d) how these writings can inform perspectives on clinical care.

Moreover, while attempts have been made to interpret the life of the Apostle Paul, his writings, and his theology from a psychological perspective (Theissen, 1987; Callan, 1990; Beck, 2002; Rollins & Kille, 2007), our study of several paragraphs from 2 Corinthians will be fundamentally hermeneutical at the outset, to later discuss psychological contributions for understanding positive coping with traumatic events.

Our approach to studying Paul's writings begins with a *naïve* reading rooted in the curiosity inspired by positive coping to extreme events like those described by Paul in the texts. The texts are selected based on the primary concern apparent in concrete references to traumatic events, along with implicit and explicit examples of coping with them. We will perform a general exegetical analysis[7] of these

---

[7] We will explore the contextual and linguistic richness of the texts. However, this will not be done with the same rigor that would be demanded in research in the field of biblical studies, obviously, since our analysis will be framed within Practical Theology as

writings, which contain interesting psychological content, while taking care not to directly appropriate them or impose our own insights about the topic and thus impose our own world on the text. We will put aside our comprehensive categories and models developed out of recent research on trauma and coping in order to conduct a broader exegesis that will let the text speak for itself ("its thing" in the word of Ricoeur), so that it can reveal to us today its wealth of meaning and guide us towards legitimate interpretive possibilities (Ricoeur, 1976; Croatto, 1994).

However, we will read with intention, selecting specific paragraphs that reference coping with traumatic events, and we will pay attention to dynamics that are pertinent to this phenomenon. Nevertheless, our objective will be to seek a clearer understanding of what Paul's texts show us about his own experience of coping with the extremely adverse events described in 2 Corinthians. This pursuit will allow us to begin a discussion about these findings and those resulting from current research in the field of positive psychology, especially related to concepts like resilience and posttraumatic growth. In this way, we will be able to critically read Paul's writings in a broader and more contemporary light, while at the same time allow these texts to open up their reserve of meaning in order to evaluate our current Christian praxis in this specific field through a new theological lens.

In short, methodologically we will follow the steps of the hermeneutic arc posed by Ricoeur (1976, 2002, 2016). We will begin with a detailed review of current research on positive coping with trauma in the field of psychology, and some of its links with religion and spirituality. We will examine the texts of 2 Corinthians that deal with the topic of coping with adversity, focusing especially on examples of positive coping with extreme situations described by Paul. However, instead of appropriating texts directly, and immediately comparing them with the results of current research, we will make a wide detour that will allow us to let the text speak for itself and reveal its world. This will ensure that our re-reading is not based in our own assumptions, thus imposing our world on the world of the text. Rather

---

a central discipline of this paper. Instead, we will work from a perspective of Psychological Biblical Criticism, whose exegetical rigor allows for legitimate interdisciplinary dialogue.

we seek to let the text itself guide us. Finally, in the last part of this dissertation, we will seek to understand the Pauline texts about positive coping with extreme adversity found in 2 Corinthians in a way that takes into consideration current research on this type of behavior and attitudes, so that we can re-read these writings in a broader, contemporary setting that lets the texts again deploy new meanings that inform new perspectives on our present Christian praxis.

Chapter 2
Adversity, Coping, and Trauma

Human life, like that of any other living organism, develops in a complexly configured way so that equilibriums necessary for life can be maintained. However, every living being is continuously subjected to innumerable factors and variables that attack its internal equilibrium and put its life at risk.

The human being is one of the most adaptive organisms in terms of environmental diversity, having inhabited terrains from the frozen coasts of Greenland and the Beagle Canal to the arid Sahara and Atacama deserts. Humans face a greater variety of adversity than other living organisms. In addition to demanding circumstances that are a natural part of life (e.g., looking for food, protecting against predators, and facing natural disasters), humans create situations for themselves that demand physical as well as psychosocial adaptation and recovery, with great implications (e.g., wars, terrorist attacks, rape, and torture).

In the course of their lives, everyone will be exposed to stressful experiences that demand adaptive coping responses, of varying degrees. Below, we present some aspects of those involved in the processes of coping with stress.

2.1. Stress and Coping

Stress first began to be studied in the field of physiology in a way that the first perspectives on the topic conceptualized stress as a fundamentally *physiological response* (Reeve, 1994; Jaureguizar & Espina, 2005).

If we take a historical look, the physiologist Walter Cannon (1932) was the first to introduce the concept of stress in the field of health, along with the term "homeostasis", which began to be closely related to stress. Homeostasis was defined as the tendency of an organism to maintain a constant state that allows for an optimal level of functioning in such a way that, for example, the organism would tend to react to stressful situations by trying to restore equilibrium or its "normal" prior state.

Selye (1936, 1956, 1976) later connected Cannon's notion of "homeostasis" and "General Adaptation Syndrome" with a series of stress responses (alarm, resistance, and exhaustion). These responses were defined as a set of nonspecific physiological responses (of the sympathetic nervous system as well as the adrenocortical and adrenal medullary neuroendocrine systems) to external or internal physical stimuli. For Selye, there is a prototypical stress response that is indistinctly produced by any stressful stimulus, a response that we will describe later when referring to the specific physiological consequences of stress.

Mason (1968), completing Selye's approach, added that all neuroendocrine systems and subsystems, not just the adrenocortical and adrenal medullary systems, were involved in the physiological response. He also proposed that physiological responses would present peculiarities that depend on the specific type of stimulation where the type of situation that provoked the stress would not be as important as the severity, duration, and instability of the resulting physiological response produced.

Another perspective of stress is one that sees it as a *stimulus event* that requires the individual to adapt (Holmes, 1979) to the point that any circumstance, particularly exceptional ones that require the individual to change his habits would be considered stressful.

Contrary to the perspective of stress as stimulus, Lazarus and Folkman (1984, cf. Biggs, Brough & Drummond, 2017), suggest that stress cannot be understood simply as a physiological response, since there are many factors involved in increasing activity in the autonomic nervous system that do not necessarily correspond to stressful events. Further, the same physiological response could be interpreted in various ways, depending on the person and his/her biography, immediate context, and culture, to highlight some factors. For this reason, the authors mentioned propose a different approach to stress, defining it as a *process* that involves individual cognitive aspects as well as interaction between individuals and their environment.

Lazarus and Folkman (1984) identify three phases in understanding stress as a process: a) the anticipation phase, in which the person prepares himself or herself before the stressor, thinking about what it will be like and what consequences it could have; b) the waiting phase, in which the person awaits feedback about how adequate his/her coping responses are; and c) the results phase, in which the person exposes himself or herself and reacts to the success or failure of his/her coping response to said stressful circumstance. On the other hand, two concepts that play a very important role in understanding stress as a process: a) Cognitive appraisal, which the individual performs to determine whether or not the stressor is important for his/her wellbeing and, if so, if it is potentially good or bad; b) The coping response, which is be the cognitive, behavioral, and/or emotional effort the individual makes to manage the stressor (Jaureguizar & Espina, (2005).

Folkman, Lazarus, Gruen & Delongis (1986) identify two types of cognitive appraisal: primary-spontaneous appraisal as to whether the stimulus poses some risk; and secondary appraisal, appraisal as to whether or not something can be done, and if resources are available to adapt to or control the stressor.

According to Lazarus and Folkman (1984), when the individual faces an event, which could be an important vital experience, an everyday inconvenience, or a chronic vital circumstance, then, the individual does a *primary appraisal* of the perceived stimulus, where the personal meaning of the event is evaluated to determine whether or not it is relevant for his/her own physical and/or psychological wellbeing. If the stimulus is considered irrelevant, then no changes occur in the autonomic nervous system (ANS) and, therefore, it is not necessary to employ any particular coping mechanism. If, on the contrary, the event is considered relevant for personal wellbeing, it could be evaluated as a challenge or as a threat. Evaluating the stimulus as a challenge would lead to hyperactivity in the ANS with an impulse to approach it. In contrast, evaluating it as a threat would lead to an impulse to avoid the stimulus.

According to the authors mentioned above, the activation of the ANS would lead to a secondary analysis: the individual would determine if he/she possess sufficient strategies, resources, and abilities to successfully cope with the challenge or threat. Specifically, secondary appraisal involves: a) searching for behavioral and cognitive coping options; and b) predicting the possibilities for each coping option to be successful. After evaluating personal strategies, abilities, and capacities, voluntary and strategic coping responses are presented. These responses will seek to manage the stressor as much as possible, so that it ceases to be a threat or challenge, thus diminishing ANS activation. If the coping response fails, the ANS will continue to be activated until the stressor is terminated, the coping responses are successful, or the ANS fails from exhaustion. In this way, the level of stress will be a function of the lack of adequacy between the environmental demands and the organism's resources, the discrepancies between the organism's demands and the way in which the individual could respond to them, or the individual's perception of his/her own ability to manage the situation (Jaureguizar & Espina, 2005).

For various authors (Zajonc, 1984; Amigo, Fernández & Pérez, 1998; Guidano, 1987, 1991; Maturana, 2001; Arciero & Bondolfi, 2009; Pruessner, Wuethrich & Baldwin, 2010; Arciero, Bondolfi, & Mazzola, 2018), this perspective puts too much emphasis on cognition, thus downplaying the emotional process, that would play a primary role in a pre-reflexive evaluation of threatening events. This view also neglects the insights of neurosciences regarding responses to overwhelming effects, responses that are equally prereflective. We will review this topic later.

2.1.1. Consequences of Stress

The consequences of stress on people are varied, as recent studies such as Fink (2010) and Contrada and Baum (2011) have shown in detail. Here we will mention only some of the most important consequences:

Physiological consequences: The Autonomic Nervous System (ANS) controls the activity of internal organisms responsible for maintaining optimal vital conditions that are not consciously controlled by the individual[8]. General activation of the organism

---

[8] The ANS is divided into the Sympathetic Nervous System (SNS) and the Parasympathetic Nervous System (PNS). Both are complementary, with the SNS being responsible for activating the organism's basal or rest levels so it can act in required situations, and the PNS being responsible for reducing sympathetic activity to return to the basal level. In regards to stress, it is worth highlighting that the SNS also acts on the adrenal glands, which releases two hormones, adrenaline and noradrenaline, that are carried throughout the body through the bloodstream. Similarly, the hypothalamic-pituitary-adrenal (HPA) axis plays an important role in physiological stress response. First, corticotrophin-releasing hormones (CRH) are made in the hypothalamus gland out of a group of neurons from the periventricular nucleus, which are then transported to the pituitary gland. In the pituitary gland, CRH stimulates secretion of adrenocorticotropic hormone (ACTH), which is distributed throughout the whole body. ACTH acts primarily in the adrenal cortex, where it promotes the release of glucocorticoids in the bloodstream, which has various effects on the organism, among them its roll in favoring glucose

produced as a consequence of stress was described by Selye in his classical theory of General Adaptation Syndrome (GAS). According to the extensive research conducted by Selye (1976, 1980), when sympathetic activity is sustained, hyperactive hormones and viscera provoke physiological alteration. Accordingly, he proposed three stages of physiological stress response:

a) Alarm Stage: When faced with a stressful situation the ANS mobilizes a defense response in the organism for fight and/or flight by means of a series of changes, such as an increased heart rate; contraction of the spleen and release of a large number of red blood cells; redistribution of the blood from less relevant areas (skin, viscera) to increase supply to the muscles, brain, and heart; an increase in respiratory capacity: dilation of the pupils; and an increase in blood coagulation and lymphocyte count. If the stressor disappears, parasympathetic activation occurs and the body recovers from the alarm reaction.

b) Resistance Stage: In this stage, the organism adapts to or confronts the stressor's demands. Therefore, this stage not only implies that the person is suffering as in the alarm stage, but is also fighting to maintain hormonal balance. Priority is given to activating the hypothalamic-pituitary-adrenal axis. In this stage saving energy stored in the organism is essential. Nevertheless, this hyperactive state is limited and, if the ANS cannot meet the stressor's demands, it will move to the third phase;

c) Exhaustion Stage: The organism in which it falls below its normal capacity due to a lack of energy and resources to adapt to the situation's demands. In this stage, the organism suffers major damage from overload, which in the most extreme cases can lead to death (Berczi & Szelenyi, 1994). As a specific case, some research has shown that the early severe stress produces a cascade of neurobiological events that have the potential to cause enduring changes in brain development. These changes occur on multiple levels, from neuro-

---

production and its anti-inflammatory and immunosuppressant effects (Anisman, Kokiinidis & Sklar,1985; Veith-Flanigan & Sandman, 1985; Armario, 2000; Sandi, 2000).

humoral to structural and functional[9] (Teicher, et al., 2003; cf. Derks, et al., 2017).

Emotional consequences: Stress generates significant emotional distress, resulting mainly in irritability, anxiety, fear, excitement, anger, depression, guilt, and resignation (Horowitz, et al., 1980; Zautra, 2003; Mollica, 2012). However, antecedents indicate that there are different affective styles, as well as the individual's own traits and the context, that determine the ways in which stress is responded to emotionally (Arciero & Bondolfi, 2009; Arciero, Bondolfi, & Mazzola, 2018).

Cognitive consequences: At this level, memory, attention, and concentration problems, as well as difficulty in making decisions, are exhibited (Cohen, 1980; Mandler, 1982; Keinan, 1987). In equal measure, primary personal and contextual elements also exist that influence cognitive stress response or consequences (Meichenbaum & Turk, 1982; Arciero & Bondolfi, 2009).

Motor consequences: Behavioral stress response has been mainly described in four general types: flight, fight, avoidance, and passivity. Despite the fact that stressful experiences provoke an automatic nervous system response that prepares the body to react to the danger and demand, the emotional, cognitive, and contextual factors are fundamental to the final behavior exhibited by the individual in response to environmental stress, in such a way that all of these areas mentioned here are complexly interconnected (Contrada & Baum, 2011).

2.1.2. Coping

The ways in which human beings respond to and deal with stressful events has been called coping, which corresponds to the set of

---

[9] The major structural consequences of early stress include reduced size of the mid-portions of the corpus callosum and attenuated development of the left neocortex, hippocampus, and amygdala. Major functional consequences include increased electrical irritability in limbic structures and reduced functional activity of the cerebellar vermis. There are also gender differences in vulnerability and functional consequences. The neurobiological sequelae of early stress and maltreatment may play a significant role in the emergence of psychiatric disorders during development (Teicher, et al., 2003). For a more comprehensive study of the subject the following arerecommended: Baum & Contrada (2010), Conrad (2011), and Cooper & Quick, 2017).

responses that attempt to reduce the negative or adverse qualities of a stressful situation.

Coping could be understood as the effort, adaptive or not, conscious or unconscious, to prevent against, eliminate, or weaken the sources, triggers, or maintainers of stress, or to tolerate stress effects in the least harmful way (Reeve, 1994, p. 406). It could also be defined as follows:

> Constantly changing cognitive and behavioral efforts made to manage specific external and/or internal demands determined to surpass or overwhelm the individual's resources (Jaureguizar & Espina, 2005, p. 35, translated by the author[10]).

Various classifications of the different types of coping responses have been made: Lazarus (1966): active/passive response; Folkman and Lazarus (1980): problem-focused coming/emotion-focused coping; Valdés & Flores (1985): adaptive fight or inhibition mechanisms; Reeve (1994): direct coping methods and defensive coping methods. Rodríguez Marín (1995) proposes a classification that integrates these varying perspectives about the different types of coping responses.

We can classify coping responses in this way:

According to the focus: responses aimed at the problem (attempting to control the cause of the stress) and the emotion (which seeks to control the affective response caused by the stress), and responses aimed at the situation (trying to directly modify the source of the stress), at the representation (trying to change the problem's cognitive representation) and the evaluation (trying to act on the relative valence).

According to the method: approach or active (direct confrontation or flight responses) and avoidance or passive responses (responses where all action is omitted).

According to the process: behavioral (which imply concrete behaviors aimed at dealing with the stress situation) and cognitive responses (predominant use of cognition in coping).

---

[10] In Spanish: "Esfuerzos cognitivos y conductuales constantemente cambiantes que se desarrollan para manejar las demandas específicas externas y/o internas que son evaluadas como excedentes o desbordantes de los recursos del individuo."

According to the moment: anticipatory (before the event in attempts to prevent it) and reparative responses (after the event in attempts to adapt).

According to its amplitude: global (used in a wide range of stressful situations) or specific responses (used in very specific situations).

Jaureguizar and Espina (2005) conclude the following from a literature review: a) Coping is a complex process: Each person uses all types of coping strategies, although some less than others; b) The coping response and the appraisal of the situation are closely linked: When the appraisal is positive, coping strategies are largely problem-focused, whereas strategies are focused on the emotion when the appraisal is negative; c) The coping style tends to vary in function of the situation's demands; d) Each person tends to have relatively stable coping styles: Thus, cognitive re-evaluation or self-control are two fairly stable strategies, and are used in a wide range of situations; e) Coping is an important mediator of emotional responses: Positive emotions are associated with certain strategies, while negative emotions are associated with other strategies; f) A coping strategy's usefulness will vary according to the specific situation or the individual's personality; g) Generally, ineffective coping mechanisms are related to strategies such as avoidance, confrontation, and self-blaming, whereas strategies like problem resolution planning tend to have more satisfactory effects; h) It could be said that there are certain "coping styles" that characterize each person.

Therefore, it is important to highlight that in coping with stressful events, an individual evaluates the meaning of what is happening in relation to him/herself and his/her environment, and assesses the stressors' possible positive or negative impact on his/her personal wellbeing, and measures his/her resources to effectively manage the stressful event's demands. The evaluation and ideographical significance of the event and the possibilities for coping are fundamental (Cheavens & Dreer, 2009).

2.2. Posttraumatic Responses

Next we will see some general aspects of the responses to traumatic events and we will stop at some detail in Posttraumatic Stress Disorder.

2.2.1. General Aspects

The systematic study of human response to adversity in the medical and psychosocial disciplines, although having its origins in ancient religious and philosophical texts, dates back to 1889, when Pierre Janet published his first text, *L'Automatisme Psychologique*, which dealt with how the human brain processes traumatic experiences. Later, he would be the first to clearly and systematically describe syndromes such as dissociation, which he considered to be the most common psychological defense response to overwhelming traumatic events (Johnson, 2009).

However, as proposed by Benyakar (1997), it was mainly Freud who incorporated the concept of "Trauma" in the field of psychology, placing great emphasis on it in his theories of psychic functioning. Freud adopted the Greek concept of "Trauma" from traditional medicine to refer to a wound or break in the psychic apparatus, considering it to be the backbone of the etiology of neurosis.

Just as Vetö (2011) explains, starting in his first proposals dealing with trauma (although initially focused substantially on sexuality), Freud highlights the retroactive element present in trauma. This is where the effects of the event do not unfold until later on, since the event is not processed or incorporated at the moment it occurs in the continuity of the experience, the identity, or the consciousness. This happens to the point that one could say that the event is not experienced in the present, rather only having a memory trace that would be fundamentally unconscious. The memory behaves in the individual's experience as if it were itself an actual event (Freud, 1896, in Vetö, 2011, p. 131). In this sense, that which is traumatic is not the experience itself, but rather the relived memory, which, according to Freud, corresponds to the psychic reality as such.

Trauma then occurs when an event hits this protective barrier hard and in a surprising way (a *sine qua non* condition) and breaks through it. This concept of trauma in effect recovers the old medical meaning of the term, likened to a surgical wound consisting in the rupture of the skin or the body's protective covering (Leys, 2000, p. 19), but in this case the body is no longer biological but rather historical-social (Vetö, 2011, p.132, translated by the author[11]).

Although trauma was a foundational concept in psychoanalysis[12], it has transformed into a not very specific term, resulting in professionals facing a wide range of often contradictory theoretical and clinical positions and proposals (Benyakar, 1997).

After World War I, many clinical descriptions were made outlining traumatic experiences mainly of combatants or surviving civilian victims. But it was not until after World War II when the study of psychological trauma acquired greater attention in the clinical world.

Psychological trauma has been described as a consequence of exposure to an unavoidable event that overwhelms an individual's coping capacity. Some authors have proposed (Backen, 2002; Johnson, 2009; Morris, 1996, 2015) that no two individuals exposed to the same event would react identically, since the capacity of a person to deal with a traumatic event is associated with an important number of factors, such as the person's belief system; prior traumatic experiences; history of stressful experiences; level of social support; the perception of his/her capacity to deal with the event; coping modalities; and other stress factors in his/her life at the moment of the event.

Despite how idiosyncratic the response to a high-stress event can be, we can conceptualize trauma in the psychosocial sense, as we find in Pérez Sales (2006), who studied narrative testimonies of people who had experienced extreme adversity, such as surviving a concentration camp, genocide, or natural disasters:

---

[11] In Spanish: "El trauma sobreviene entonces cuando un acontecimiento golpea fuertemente y de manera sorpresiva (condición *sine qua non*) esta barrera protectora, perforándola. Esta concepción del trauma recupera, en efecto, la antigua significación medica del término: "una herida quirúrgica, concebida de acuerdo al modelo de la ruptura de la piel o de la envoltura protectora del cuerpo..." (Leys, 2000, p. 19), pero un cuerpo no ya biológico sino histórico-social"

[12] For a more comprehensive study of the subject it is recommended: Herman (1992) and Morris (2015).

Concept of Trauma (Pérez Sales, 2006, p. 51):

1. An experience consisting in a threat to the individual's physical or psychological integrity. Frequently associated with chaotic and confusing experiences during the event, fragmentation of the memory, absurdity, horror, ambivalence, or bewilderment.

2. Which is characterized as being:
   – Unspeakable, uncountable
   – Incomprehensible for others

3. Which breaks one or more basic assumptions that constitute human beings' reference points for security, and especially the belief in invulnerability and control over one's own life.
   – Trust in others, their good nature, and predisposition to empathy
   – Trust that the world is controllable and predictable

4. Which questions the constructs of oneself and of oneself against the world.

According to the same author, a definition of the traumatic event's psychological consequences should consider at lease the following elements:

Phenomenology of the response to traumatic situations (Pérez Sales, 2006, p. 52):

1. Feeling of alienation from those who have not experienced the trauma. Isolation.

2. Emotional and affective withdraw.

3. Questioning oneself and one's position in the world:
   – Facing experiences of personal responsibility and guilt.
   – Facing feelings of humiliation or shame, or questioning personal dignity.

4. Questioning basic presumptions about:
   – The goodness of human beings and their friendly nature.
   – The world's predictability.
   – The capacity to control one's own life.

5. The need to reconstruct what happened and fill in the gaps in attempts to seek meaning or a new ending.

6. Which involves processes of personal life reformulation and integration of the experience and the elements of posttraumatic growth that unfold.

2.2.2. Posttraumatic Stress Disorder

Responses to traumatic situations or events vary, but from the perspective of clinical psychology some symptomatic patterns characteristic of individuals with trauma have been discovered and have been characterized in what is known as Posttraumatic Stress Disorder (PTSD).

As proposed by Rosen (2004), in contrast to almost all mental disorders found in psychiatric manuals (especially the DSM), diagnosing Posttraumatic Stress Disorder requires an etiological specification[13]: exposure to a traumatic stressor. If a person has not been exposed to a stressor deemed "traumatic", then such a diagnosis cannot be made, independent of the presence of symptoms related to this disorder. Therefore, how we define the traumatic stress factor is fundamental, as well as the trauma itself in its psychological acceptance, given its relativity in relation to different individuals.

According to DSM-III (1980), in order for a stressor to be qualified as traumatic it should "evoke significant symptoms of distress in almost everyone" (APA, 1980, p. 238). DSM-III (1980) qualifies events such as rape, torture, and earthquakes as traumatic. Already in the 1987 revision of DSM-III, the authors included witnesses (family or friends) that had been exposed to great danger, without needing to have directly experienced them.

In editing DSM-IV, the PTSD committee estimated that an excessively rigorous definition of what was considered a traumatic event would exclude many people that suffered this type of disorder and would require specialized treatment to cope with it. Thus, there was discussion as to whether a subjective judgment of an event as being

---

[13] Although not in a strict sense, since it does not correspond to an explicative etiology as such.

46

traumatic should or should not be included in the definition of a traumatic stress factor.

According to Rosen (2004), the possibility of removing Criteria A was discussed, eliminating the reference to an etiological event (the traumatic event) for diagnosis of the disorder. But, given the possibility of an eventual over-diagnosis of PTSD, with its respective forensic and scientific problems, in DSM-IV the requirement that it be "an event that is outside the range of usual human experience" (APA, 1987, p 250) was omitted, since what constituted "usual" human experience and what was "common" about traumatic events (such as assaults, automobile accidents, etc.) was not clear, particularly in specific contexts. The DSM-IV committee therefore established that a person exposed to a traumatic stressor would be one who "the person experienced, witnessed, or was confronted with an event or events that involved actual or threatened death or serious injury, or a threat to the physical integrity of self or others", as long as " the person's response involved intense fear, helplessness, or horror". In this way, a traumatic stress factor is not only defined by external criteria, considering, as in DSM-III, that witnessing or knowing about the misfortunes of others is traumatic for the witness or receiver of this information, without needing to be family members or friends, in the case of DSM-IV and DSM-5.

In summary, we can call trauma both an event that deeply threatens the wellbeing or life of an individual as well as the exposure of individuals to the account of said experience, as a consequence of this event on the experience of the person.

The most current diagnostic criteria for PTSD in DSM-5 (APA, 2013) introduce some changes in respect to DSM-IV (APA, 2000), particularly moving it from the category of anxiety disorders to a new class referred to as "trauma and stress related disorders". All conditions included in this classification require exposure to a traumatic or stressful event as a diagnostic criterion. The main reason for creating this new class was based on clinical recognition of variable expressions of distress as a result of the traumatic experience. And more importantly, it acknowledges the explicit influence of adverse events on mental health and disorders.

PTSD diagnostic criteria include a history of exposure to a traumatic event that meets specific stipulations and symptoms from each of the four symptom groups: intrusion, avoidance, negative changes in cognition and mood, and changes in arousal and reactivity. The sixth criterion refers to the duration of symptoms, the seventh to functional development, and the eighth stipulates that symptoms not be attributable to substances or co-occurrence of a medical condition.

Two specifications are indicated, including delayed expression and a dissociative subtype of PTSD, which is new in DSM-5 (pp. 274-271). In both specifications, diagnostic criteria for PTSD must be met for justified application.

Criterion A: stressor

The person was exposed to: death, threatened death, actual or threatened serious injury, or actual or threatened sexual violence, as follows: (one required)

1. Direct exposure.

2. Witnessing, in person.

3. Indirectly, by learning that a close relative or close friend was exposed to trauma. If the event involved actual or threatened death, it must have been violent or accidental.

4. Repeated or extreme indirect exposure to aversive details of the event(s), usually in the course of professional duties (e.g., first responders, collecting body parts; professionals repeatedly exposed to details of child abuse). This does not include indirect non-professional exposure through electronic media, television, movies, or pictures.

Criterion B: intrusion symptoms

The traumatic event is persistently re-experienced in the following way(s): (one required)

1. Recurrent, involuntary, and intrusive memories. Note: Children older than six may express this symptom in repetitive play.

2. Traumatic nightmares. Note: Children may have frightening dreams without content related to the trauma(s).

3. Dissociative reactions (e.g., flashbacks) which may occur on a continuum from brief episodes to complete loss of consciousness. Note: Children may reenact the event in play.

4. Intense or prolonged distress after exposure to traumatic reminders.

5. Marked physiologic reactivity after exposure to traumarelated stimuli.

Criterion C: avoidance

Persistent effortful avoidance of distressing trauma-related stimuli after the event: (one required)

1. Trauma-related thoughts or feelings.

2. Trauma-related external reminders (e.g., people, places, conversations, activities, objects, or situations).

Criterion D: negative alterations in cognition and mood

Negative alterations in cognitions and mood that began or worsened after the traumatic event: (two required)

1. Inability to recall key features of the traumatic event (usually dissociative amnesia; not due to head injury, alcohol, or drugs).

2. Persistent (and often distorted) negative beliefs and expectations about oneself or the world (e.g., "I am bad," "The world is completely dangerous").

3. Persistent distorted blame of self or others for causing the traumatic event or for resulting consequences.

4. Persistent negative trauma-related emotions (e.g., fear, horror, anger, guilt, or shame).

5. Markedly diminished interest in (pre-traumatic) significant activeties.

6. Feeling alienated from others (e.g., detachment or estrangement).

7. Constricted affect: persistent inability to experience positive emotions.

Criterion E: alterations in arousal and reactivity

Trauma-related alterations in arousal and reactivity that began or worsened after the traumatic event: (two required)

1. Irritable or aggressive behavior,

2. Self-destructive or reckless behavior,

3. Hypervigilance.

4. Exaggerated startle response.

5. Problems in concentration.

6. Sleep disturbance.

Criterion F: duration

Persistence of symptoms (in Criteria B, C, D, and E) for more than one month.

Criterion G: functional significance

Significant symptom-related distress or functional impairment (e.g., social, occupational).

Criterion H: exclusion

Disturbance is not due to medication, substance use, or other illness.

Specify if: With dissociative symptoms.

In addition to meeting criteria for diagnosis, an individual experiences high levels of either of the following in reaction to trauma-related stimuli:

1. Depersonalization: experience of being an outside observer of or detached from oneself (e.g., feeling as if "this is not happening to me" or one were in a dream).

2. Derealization: experience of unreality, distance, or distortion (e.g., "things are not real").

Specify if: With delayed expression.

Full diagnosis is not met until at least six months after the trauma(s), although onset of symptoms may occur immediately.

The main differences in PTSD diagnostic criteria between DSM-IV and DSM-5 are (APA, 1980, 1997, 2000, 2013; Friedman, et al., 2011; Miller, et al., 2012; Lanius, et al., 2012; Scheeringa, Zeanah & Cohen, 2011):

The 3 groups of symptoms in DSM-IV are divided into 4 groups in DSM-5: intrusion, avoidance, negative alterations in cognition and mood, and changes in arousal and reactivity. Criterion C in DSM-IV, avoidance and numbing, was separated in to two criteria: Criterion C (avoidance) and Criterion D (negative alterations in cognition and mood). The reason for this change was based on factorial analysis studies, and a diagnosis of PTSD now requires at least one avoidance symptom

Three new symptoms were added: Criterion D (negative alterations in cognition and mood): Persistent distorted blame of self or others, and persistent negative emotional state. Criterion E (changes in arousal and reactivity): imprudent or destructive behavior.

Other symptoms were revised to clarify symptom expression, such as Criterion A2 (which required fear, helplessness or horror to occur immediately after the trauma) which was removed in DSM-5, given that research suggested that this criterion did not improve diagnostic precision.

In DSM-5 a clinical subtype was added: "with dissociative symptoms". This subtype is applicable to individuals that meet criteria for PTSD and have additional symptoms of depersonalization and derealization.

One important difference between DSM-IV and DSM-5 is the new inclusion of an independent diagnosis, as a subtype for children 6 years of age or younger (preschool subtype).

Based on initial analysis of DSM-5 criteria, the prevalence of PTSD is similar to DSM-IV, being greater in women than in men, as also seen in the exposure to multiple traumatic events (Miller, et al., 2012).

According to DSM-5, the prevalence of PTSD:

In the United States, projected lifetime risk for PTSD using DSM-IV criteria at age 75 years is 8.7%. Twelve-month prevalence among U.S. adults is about 3.5%. Lower estimates are seen in Europe and most Asian, African, and Latin American countries, clustering around 0.5%-1.0%. Although different groups have different levels of exposure to traumatic events, the conditional probability of developing PTSD following a similar level of exposure may also vary across cultural groups. Rates of PTSD are higher among veterans and others whose vocation increases the risk of traumatic exposure (e.g., police, firefighters, emergency medical personnel). Highest rates (ranging from one-third to more than onehalf of those exposed) are found among survivors of rape, military combat and captivity, and ethnically or politically motivated internment and genocide (DSM-5, 2013, p. 276).

As these prevalence data show, most of the research indicates that[14], despite the fact that the great majority of people are exposed to traumatic events during their lifetimes, only a minority develop PTSD, although it must be considered that other disorders could develop as a response to traumatic situations, or partial PTSD. Nevertheless, a majority of coping responses present few symptoms and involve positive adaptation (Mollica, 2012).

A variable group of people would exist in which symptoms become chronic. In this subgroup, symptoms would remain unchanged for an extended time after the traumatic event, causing the individual's ability to adapt in his social and work environments to be incapacitated. On the other hand, in studies up until now, it is not clear if the initial response to traumatic events predicts the individual's ability to adjust in the future. Additionally, it has been observed that PTSD is among the disorders with greatest comorbidity of those addressed in DSM-IV, especially associated with depressive, obsessive-compulsive, and substance abuse disorders (Pérez Sales, 2006; Johnson, 2009).

With regard to comorbidity, it has been observed that PTSD is mainly associated with alcohol abuse in men (51.9%), major depression (48%), conduct disorders in men (43.3%), simple phobia (30%), social phobia (28%), alcohol abuse in women (27.9%), and agoraphobia in women (22.4%), with no statistical significance in other diagnoses (Kessler, et al., 1995).

---

[14] Helzer, Robins & McEvoy, 1987; Breslau, et al., 1991; Kessler, et al., 1995; Breslau, et al., 1998; Davidson, et al., 1991; Norris, 1992; Resnick, et al., 1993; Rioseco, et al., 1994; Breslau, et al., 1997; Perkonnig, et al., 2000; Rosen, 2004; Rosen & Frueh, 2010; Norris & Slone, 2014; Atwoli, et al., 2015.

2.3. Explanatory Perspectives on Trauma and Coping

At the present time, there are various models for explaining the posttraumatic phenomenon. Here we offer a brief review[15] of some of the most relevant theoretical perspectives that have been developed and are applied in the field of clinical psychology.

2.3.1. The Experimental and Biochemical Perspectives

One classic psychological study, called "Inescapable shock and learned helplessness", corresponds to the experimental work of Seligman (1991), who used dogs as the subjects of his experiments. Upon receiving electric shocks they could not escape or predict, the dogs would enter into a deep state of depression and apathy, characterized by a) a marked difficulty to escape from new stressful situations; b) reduced motivation to learn new responses that could lead to escape; c) decreased exploratory behavior; e) biological evidence of stress; and f) immunological deficit and an increase in tumor generation.

In experimentation with animals, it has been observed that when subjected to prolonged isolation animals exhibit aggressive behavior and experience behavioral deficits that in many ways are similar to the learned hopelessness resulting from inescapable shock. In some cases self-mutilation behavior can develop, which is not rare in the case of wild animals put in captivity when they are adults (Morris, 1970).

Furthermore, in experiments with monkeys, it has been observed that early separation from the attachment figure is associated with symptoms similar to those present in PTSD, with a two-stage response: first with aggressive protest, and then depression (similar to what Bowlby (1973, 1980, 1999) observed in children separated from their mothers). Later as adults, monkeys that were separated from their mothers early on showed high vulnerability and exaggerated response to social stimuli, quickly beginning to behave in a disorganized manner in new situations, with a significant amount of aggressive responses. In neurotransmitters, lower basal levels of noradrenaline are observed, as

---

[15] For reasons of space and scope, this work will only give a brief overview of the different perspectives, highlighting some of their fundamental models and/or aspects.

53

well as exaggeratedly high noradrenaline responses to small stress situations, social stimuli, or separation, along with chronically low levels of serotonin.

As living organisms, human beings are constantly exposed to internal changes (in the body), and external changes (in the environment) and they use a lot of energy for the purpose of maintaining her equilibrium. When exposed to a new situation (that which is not recorded in memory), human beings develop strategies that require different levels of energy expenditure, with the goal being adaptation. If this goal is not achieved, the stress reaction appears.

The organism is exposed daily to uncountable stressors that attack homeostasis, thus finding itself permanently between two physiologically opposite situations: potential for harm versus protection and removal of the damage. Hormonal regulation of stress is handled by the adrenal gland, which releases glucocorticoids and adrenaline in response to stress. The main stimulus for secreting glucocorticoids is pituitary ACTH (adrenocorticotropin), which is in turn regulated by the hypothalamic CRF (corticotrophin-releasing factor), a central mediator released in stress situations (hypothalamic-pituitary-adrenal axis, HPA). While the HPA is the central system for mediating biological stress responses, it does not act alone, since there are also other systems that participate in this process, such as the sympathetic system (adrenergic system), the release of central catecholamines and excitatory neurotransmitters (CNS), and the production of pro-inflammatory cytokines. In return, the parasympathetic nervous system counteracts the sympathetic nervous system, reducing the release of pro-inflammatory cytokines. Similarly, Dehydro-epiandrosterone (DHEA) counters the effects of cortisol. In this way, each function has its counterpart, in the system's attempt to maintain homeostasis. All of these systems interact according to complex and non-linear models. Imbalance in this network of functions could have repercu-ssions on principal organic functions (cardiovascular, cerebral, metabolic, and immunological) (D'Alessio, 2010, p. 20).[16]

Although the majority of people who are exposed to traumatic events do not develop psychopathology, trauma has often been associated with increased vulnerability to psychiatric disorders. In addition, alterations in the HPA-axis have been demonstrated in patients with trauma-related psychiatric disorders. Some researchers have raised the hypothesis that trauma causes dysregulation of the HPA-axis, especially in cases of early life stress (Klaassens, van Veen & Zitman, 2007; Copeland & Gorey, 2012).

Pain, in neurophysiological terms, is one of the most complex sensations, since many areas of the brain are involved in processing it (Moore, 2012). The brain is the main organ responsible for adaptive responses in the environment and is in charge of regulating the individual's neurobiological and psychological mechanisms connected with the response to various stress-generated demands, which could be defined as an organism's set of response to changes and stimuli that attack homeostasis (dynamic equilibrium).

Although stress constitutes a necessary adaptive physiological mechanism, alterations in the brain and functioning of the organism can be generated, especially during the acute stress, prolonged stress, or

---

[16] Translated by the author. In Spanish: "El organismo está expuesto diariamente a un sinnúmero de estresores que atentan contra la homeostasis, por lo que se encuentra permanentemente entre dos situaciones fisiológicas opuestas: potencialidad de daño versus protección y remoción del daño. La regulación hormonal del estrés está a cargo de la glándula adrenal, que libera glucocorticoides y adrenalina en respuesta al estrés. El principal estímulo para la secreción de glucocorticoides es la ACTH hipofisaria (adrenocorticotrofina), que a su vez es regulada por el CRF (factor liberador de corticotrofina) hipotalámico, un mediador central que se libera en situaciones de estrés (Eje Hipotálamo-Hipófiso-Adrenal, EHHA). Si bien el EHHA es el sistema central en la mediación de respuestas biológicas al estrés, no actúa solo, ya que también hay otros sistemas que participan en este proceso, como por ejemplo el sistema simpático (sistema adrenérgico), la liberación de catecolaminas centrales y neurotransmisores excitatorios (SNC) y la producción de citoquinas proinflamatorias. Como contrapartida, el sistema nervioso parasimpático contrarresta la acción del sistema nervioso simpático, disminuyendo la liberación de citoquinas proinflamatorias. En forma similar, la dehidro-epiandrosterona (DHEA) se opone a los efectos del cortisol. De esta manera, cada función tiene su contraparte, en un intento del sistema de mantener la homeostasis. Todos estos sistemas interactúan siguiendo modelos no lineales y complejos. El desequilibrio de esta red de funciones podría tener repercusiones en las principales funciones orgánicas (cardiovascular, cerebral, metabólica e inmunológica)".

chronic stress stages. The concept of allostasis arises in this context (McEwen & Wingfield, 2003), introduced to refer to the active process through which:

> The organism responds to daily changes, maintaining homeostasis or dynamic equilibrium. When the magnitude of the changes surpasses the system's adaptive capacity (an increase in allostatic load), the brain and the body suffer deleterious consequences at the level of physiological, psychological, and behavioral functions (D'Alessio, 2010, pp. 12-13).

As demonstrated by Kart & Werner's meta-analysis (2006), the fifty main investigations on PTSD's relation to variations of specific parts of the brain (particularly the hippocampus and the amygdala), carried out between 1990 and 2005, have come to conclusions that suggest there would be a significant negative correlation between exposure to a traumatic event and the size of the hippocampus. There would be two alternative explanations for this: 1) the hippocampus of individuals exposed to trauma, independent of their diagnosed condition (with or without PTSD), may have a smaller premorbid size (before the trauma) compared to non-exposed individuals, with an even smaller hippocampus associated with severe PTSD cases; or, 2) independent of the diagnosis, exposure to trauma itself is associated with a reduction in the hippocampus' size, which would be seen along a continuum of PTSD severity.

The conclusions of Kart & Werner's meta-analysis (2006) are as follows (comment in parenthesis at the end added): The results of our study provide reliable evidence that: 1) trauma exposure (regardless of diagnostic status) is associated with smaller hippocampal volumes that appear to be moderated by age and gender; 2) in comparisons with trauma exposed controls, severe PTSD in un-medicated, adult samples is associated with smaller hippocampal volumes; 3) for all comparisons, effect sizes increase with PTSD severity; 4) volumetric differences are not restricted to the hippocampus; and 5) adults and minors exhibit different types of structural abnormalities (adults in the hippocampus and left amygdala, children and adolescents in frontal areas).

It has been observed that long term administration of antidepressant medication is associated with an increase in the hippocampus' size, as well as improvements in PTSD symptoms and memory performance, which could lead to difficulties in interpreting that a smaller hippocampus is exclusively due to genetic factors. Nevertheless, there would not be a result that supports the possibility that chronic administration of antidepressants could compensate for some type of congenital biochemical anomaly that affects the size of the hippocampus in adults. With respect to whether or not a smaller hippocampus is the result of premorbid vulnerabilities or interaction with the effects of trauma exposure, new research is still needed (Kart & Werner, 2006).

These are very significant results, considering the functions the amygdala and hippocampus are observed to have, as proposed by LeDoux (1991, 1993), who indicated that the amygdala would play an important role in the memory of emotionally relevant events (due to short circuits that do not pass through the neocortex). Even more significant is the correlation between the smaller size of the hippocampus in people exposed to traumatic events (especially in individuals with sever PTSD). This is because, as the same author indicates, this limbic cerebral structure would be key in recording and assigning meaning to perceptive guidelines and with respect to memory and different contexts, which could be related to some cognitive models that suggest the relevance of the loss of contextualization of the traumatic event suffered by people with PTSD (Ehlers & Clark, 2000).

2.3.2. The Psychodynamic Perspectives

Understanding traumatic processes from the psychodynamic perspective, as we present it, started with Freud who assigned trauma a central function in the majority of the mental disorders he described.

Historically, after World War II, many authors borro-wed the term "trauma" from psychoanalysis and defined it to mean a break in defenses caused by internal and/or external stimuli that provoke a temporary inability in the self. Some focused on the stimuli's characteristics and particularities, while others considered that the specific nature of the stimulus, while itself not being vitally important, emphasized the self's incapacity to maintain its defenses when facing extreme stimuli (Benyakar, 1997).

Freud's perspective does not describe memory as a reliable record of the past but rather as a novel story, where fantasy plays an important role in modifying what happened. To understand the memory of an individual you have to know his biography in a broad way, because while a person lives, the days to come are changing the record of the past. In his writing *Studies on Hysteria* of 1895, written with J. Breuer, Freud tried to explain the neurosis by placing his cause in a traumatic childhood experience that was unconsciously repressed. In this way, he concluded that if the traumatic past was recovered and brought to consciousness, then it could be stripped of its destructive component and would achieve the recovery of the patient, his cure (Freud & Breuer, 1996). However, some time later, he would find that his patients' story was not necessarily a reliable description of what happened. Trauma could no longer be understood as the result of a fact, but of a given meaning. Instead of a traumatic event, there was a fanciful record that related the subject especially to his desire. Even if there was a real aggression on the victim, for Freud that aggression is never stored in memory as a clear event, but always ends up in constructions where imagination or fantasy plays an important role unconsciously (Freud, 1994). Thus, the condition for an experience to have the condition of being traumatic is related to the traumatic force it possesses, provided it acquires a subjective significance such that the discharge of affection is impeded, or cannot be integrated with other existing representations. Trauma, which remains a foreign body in psychism, can return or manifest itself through different symptoms (Corrales, 2002).

On the other hand, for Lacan, it is only when language appears in the subject that events can acquire the state of trauma, which can occur long after the event (or perhaps it will never happen). The trauma is understood, therefore, as repression, but in such a way that the repressed always comes from the future, from its integration through language, from the symbolic universe of each individual that gives it some meaning (Lacan, 1988).

In order to explain the psychological consequences of war, psychoanalytic contributions in the existentialist vein were made by authors such as Brüll (1969) and Frankl (2000), among others. Brüll proposes that, during war, the self's inability to perceive the flow of time, or the relationship between a before and an after, creates an unbearable situation. According to him, the individual then faces a change in his life's meaning due to a sudden confrontation with death. For his part, Frankl, in telling about his experience in concentration camps during World War II, emphasizes that developing a meaning for life is what can keep an individual mentally healthy, thus avoiding psychological trauma.

Within this approach we can also highlight, Weiss (1993) who situates early and unconscious lessons learned at the base of posttraumatic symptomatology, which should be explored psycho-therapeutically in order to compare them to the individual's reality. Horowitz (1976), on the other hand, asserts that what relevant and potentially traumatic events have in common is the fact that, in one way or another, they deal with loss or the danger of loss that questions the individual's internal, material, and social world and puts it at risk. Thus, the way the individual adapts to the new reality depends on situational, cognitive, affective, and social factors.

2.3.3. Behavioral and Cognitive Perspectives

In the broad context of behavioral theories focused on conditioning processes, the primary model for explaining PTSD is Mowrer's bifactorial theory (1960) that describes the acquisition of this disorder's symptoms through classical conditioning. Here, the unconditioned adverse situation is associated with a series of neutral stimuli that then acquire conditioned properties, in order to later be maintained by avoiding said conditioned stimuli. This is done using operative conditioning mechanisms, where the avoidance response is negatively reinforced by distancing from the conditioned adverse situation.

According to the theories focused on information processing, the individual that suffers traumatic events stores complex memories of the traumatic event that crystalize as threatening cognitive schemes. These would later be activated in other situations, awakening the same emotions and images associated with events that do not appear to be related. From this perspective, posttraumatic symptoms are manifest-tations of anxiety that the fear memory will be activated, which possess a specific neural network with multisensory mnemonic elements in response to subsequent real or symbolic stimuli (Foa, Keane & Friedman, 2003).

From a similar perspective within the cognitive models, trauma has been proposed to be a break in the frames of reference which is to say that the important factor is the way in which the traumatic event changes the individual's vision of himself and of the world. One class of cognitive models proposes a worldview comprised of underlying assumptions about the self and the world that are undermined, or shattered, by the experience of trauma. In her "shattered assumptions" theory, Janoff-Bulman (1992) articulates the role of the worldview in psychological efforts to retain and enhance perceptions of control and stability after traumatic events. Individuals develop fundamental, yet unarticulated, assumptions about the world and themselves that allow for healthy human functioning. The most important assumptions include beliefs in a just, benevolent, predictable world in which the individual possesses competence and worth. The worldview's primary function is to provide the individual with meaning, self-esteem, and the illusion of invulnerability.

According to shattered assumptions theory, when individuals experience an event that damages their worldview, the subsequent state of defenseless, terrifying, and confusing awareness of personal vulnerability gives rise to the anxiety and physiological reactivity that characterize PTSD. Importantly, it is not only that worldviews are undermined, but that individuals become intensely aware of their own mortality when those beliefs are stripped away (Janoff-Bulman, 1992; Ganzevoort, 2009b; Edmondson, et al., 2011).

According to this approach, we as individuals have a series of cognitive biases that permit us to live in an adaptive way, such as: a) the illusion of control (the future is predictable); b) the illusion of goodness (people are good and bad things do not occur frequently); c) the illusion of invulnerability (nothing bad will happen to me, only to others). These biases come to function as basic schemes of organizing experience, very much in line with the individual's worldviews. In response to a traumatic event, these schemes are disorganized in such a way that the individual experiences his world as a random and unpredictable reality, where one cannot have security, since the world is characterized by evil and selfishness (especially in the cases of premeditated violence, such as terrorist attacks, rape, etc.). In this way, live is disorganized and loses its meaning, not being able to be integrated in a coherent whole of past, present, and future (Pérez Sales, 2006).

There are a great number of models within the cognitive approach that vary in complexity as well as explanatory and therapeutic capacity[17], but in very general terms they propose that PTSD becomes chronic when individuals cognitively process trauma in a way that they develop a feeling of serious and permanent threat, where said feeling arises as a consequence of excessively negative assessments of the trauma and/or its aftereffects and disturbances on autobiographical memory characterized by poor elaboration and contextualization (Ehlers & Clark, 2000).

2.3.4. Constructivist and Narrative Perspectives

Constructivism, unlike the approaches presented thus far as explanatory perspectives, is seen as a meta-theory framed within the philosophical branch of epistemology and distinguishes itself from: a) the idealist position, which supposes that no external reality exists, therefore declaring that knowledge is always a pure invention of the individual, and that the knowledge-reality relationship is mere coincidence; as well as b) the realist perspective, which affirms that an external reality exists that is knowable and independent of the observer, thus understanding knowledge as a reflection of reality, and that the relation between them is of correspondence (Botella, Herrero & Pacheco, 1997; Hessen, 2007).

> As an alternative to both positions, constructivist epistemology starts from the premise that, whether or not a reality exists that is external to the observer, its meaning is only accessible through constructing dimensions of interpret-tation. Knowledge is understood as construction, and its relation with reality is adaptive, understood as viable [...] constructivism starts from the fundamental epistemological premise that individuals as well as groups of individuals proactively construct models for attributing meaning to the

---

[17] For an extensive and detailed review that goes beyond our interest in these particular models, refer to Dalgleish (2004).

world and to themselves, models that vary widely from one to the other and that evolve in function of experience. These meaning attribution models are not understood as mere "filters" of continuous experience, but rather as active creators of new experiences that determine what the individual will perceive as "reality" (Botella, Herrero & Pacheco, 1997, p. 4).

According to Mahoney (2005) the constructivist perspective of human experience emphasizes the action of generating meaning through personal development in one's social environment. In this way, aspects such as human beings' continuous proactivity are highlighted, especially with respect to the processes of ordering and assigning meaning, which would be socio-symbolically mediated. Additionally, the process of self-organizing the experience will simultaneously occur on two levels: a) the immediate experience level and b) the level of its linguistic ordering. The first level is tacit, emotional, and continuous, while the second level is explicit, cognitive, and discontinuous. Nevertheless, both levels would be subjected to the experience's narrative structure, which is where narrative approaches from constructivist perspectives are frequently integrated (Neimeyer & Mahoney, 1998; Gonçalves, 2002; Miró, 2005).

In accordance with recent meta-analyses carried out on the use of narrative perspective in psychotherapy, results have been found indicating that most of the models incorporate a constructivist epistemological approach that adopts a representative view of language and focuses mainly on micro-narratives of the patient. A smaller group of models takes an approach framed within social constructivism, with a functional view of language, emphasizing aspects linked to social interaction and more extensive sociocultural narratives (Avdi & Georgaca, 2007).

Human beings' sensory and affective experience is measured from the beginning of language by narrations (representations, metaphors, images in temporary dynamic connection) about our past and what we imagine our future will be (based on our experiences). In constructivist terms (although cognitive terms as well), traumatic events act on a prior beliefs system, which in turn is composed of preexisting elements of vulnerability derived from the types of affective links created during infancy and from the forms of organizing meaning that arise from them and subsequent events, particularly traumatic ones (Crittenden, 2002; Guidano & Liotti, 2006).

From the constructivist and narrative perspective, in order to be able to help someone overcome the memory of traumatic events (that no longer exist in a concrete sense, but do as a present or available narrative), the construction (or reconstruction) of new narratives of the events (or remembered / interpreted "events") must be facilitated that present healthy alternatives to prior accounts and consist of reconceptualization of the self and the self's existence.

For some authors, all pain can be bearable if you place it in a story, or tell a story, about it. This is because human life seeks a narrative, as it tries to discover a pattern that enables it to deal with chaos and confusion in cases of loss or traumatic experiences (Mena, 2006). Therefore, personal narrative is fundamental as a resource for dealing with traumatic events, even more so if we consider that in recent decades cognitive psychological researchers have observed that human beings have two basic modes of processing information: a digital mode, called *paradigmatic* or *logico-scientific* by some, and another analog, or narrative, mode (Bruner, 1997).

Cyrulnik (2003), suggests that a traumatic experience causes harm, but it is the representation or interpretation of said experience that causes the trauma, since pain is experienced in human beings as the perception of pain, as interpretation. Pain itself lacks specific meaning, being a biological signal transmitted to the brain that can even be blocked. However, this signal acquires meaning based on the cultural and historical context of each person, and by attributing meaning to the painful event we modify what is experienced (Cylurnik, 2002).

In this way, the idiosyncratic aspect plays a large role in coping with adverse events, as indicated by Vásquez, Crespo & Ring (2000). They suggested that, in response to traumatic events, it has been observed that: a) the majority of people do not exhibit clinical depression; b) grief reactions are not necessary and individuals that do not show grief do not necessary develop problems in the future; and c) the majority of people seem to adequately recover after a long period of time after the traumatic event occurred.

In general terms, a comprehensive model of traumatic experience from a constructivist and constructionist-narrative perspective could be summarized in the following points (Neimeyer, Keesee & Fortner, 1997; Botella, et al., 1997): a) Traumatic experience, like any other event, could validate or invalidate the assumptions that form the base upon which we live, or could become a new experience for which we do not have constructions for understanding or that provide us coherence; b) Traumatic experience is a process that is personal, idiosyncratic, and inseparable from the meaning we attribute to who we are; c) Traumatic experience is something in which we are active subjects, it is not something that we receive or that happens to us passively; d) Traumatic experience can be coped with by way of actions that affirm or reconstruct a personal world of meaning that has been challenged by the trauma; e) Feelings have a function and should be understood as signs of our efforts to give meaning to the events; f) We all construct and reconstruct our identity as survivors in response to a traumatic event in negotiation with others, always situated in a social and cultural context.

For Sluzki (1995) narratives are self-regulating semantic systems that have a plot, characters, and a setting, which gives the story cohesion at the same time they are maintained by the story, preventing possible alternative explanations that exceed said implied or explicit narrative coherence. In a narrative approach to trauma, any alteration in the content of the story, the way it is told or interpreted, becomes fundamental, since it will cause changes in the plot, characters, and content, in a way that "any important change in dominant stories will affect the way in which the problems are conceived, perceived, described, explained, judged, and represented. Such a change would provide access to new solutions" (Fernandez & Rodríguez, 2001, p. 244).[18]

2.4. Critical Approach on Trauma Perspectives

So far we have exposed, very briefly, some of the main perspectives that explain trauma and its effects. However, it is important to dwell on some critical approaches to the usual understanding of trauma that

---

[18] Translated by the author. In Spanish: "cualquier cambio importante en los relatos dominantes afectará la manera en que se concibe, perciben, describen, explican, juzgan y representan los problemas. Tal cambio proporcionaría el acceso a nuevas soluciones."

arise from recent studies on neurophysiology of memory, which align with the constructivist perspective, as previously mentioned, and, in a very particular way, with the recent theoretical developments of the hermeneutic phenomenology applied to psychology and psychotherapy (Arciero & Bondolfi, 2009, Cruz-Villalobos, 2014a, Arciero, Bondolfi & Mazzola, 2018).

2.4.1. Neurophysiology of Memory and Trauma

Memory is not a true copy of the world.
Foster (2009, p.14)

Without memory there is no trauma. Some authors describe trauma as the past that bursts painfully into the present (Mann & Cunningham, 2009). The way in which we understand memory, as a complex neurocognitive function, will determine the way to understand the trauma. For this it is important to focus on the knowledge developed at present from the neurosciences, especially if we consider that most explanatory perspectives have not sufficiently emphasized, or have simply left out, the understanding of the neurophysiological processes of human memory when trying to explain the traumatic phenomena (Bracken, 2002; Cruz-Villalobos, 2014b).

From an evolutionary perspective the brain has functioned as a complex virtual emulator of reality whose objective would be the prediction and modification of the conditions of the organism and / or the environment, which guarantee adaptation and survival. In the case of the human being, high complexity processes stand out, within which memory is one of the most relevant (Edelman & Tononi, 2000).

Memory processes correspond to the reactivation of groups of neurons that fire together in a pattern similar to that generated by the experience that triggered them for the first time. Memories are necessarily associative processes, never identical to the original experience (Buzsáki, 2006, Agren, 2012). The human brain, obviously, cannot retain all the experiences that are in a day; the vast majority of events are forgotten. What begins to consolidate as a memory can be done through various means. Nowadays, it has been observed that the dream[19] plays a very important role in the process of selecting what is forgotten and what is remembered, by means of processes that involve the integration into existing dynamic networks or mnemic nuclei, where common patterns can be found that allow establishing new memories based on the similarity with those already present, usually excluding discordant information or that is not relevant in terms of adaptation and survival. This is the fundamental criterion of brain functioning at the level of memory, since the brain "is not interested" in authentically reproducing reality or original experiences, but in allowing adaptation and survival of the organism (Diekelmann, Born & Wagner, 2010; Stickgold & Walker, 2013).

Particularly as a result of studies related to neurological pathologies as the result of brain injuries, we verified that there are multiple memory systems in humans which involve neuronal systems in extensive areas of the cerebral cortex in connection with important subcortical areas which would work as a set of parallel, complex and specialized memory systems (Eichenbaum, 2002)[20].

---

[19] There is evidence that indicates that sleep after learning is critical for the subsequent consolidation of memory. It has been observed that a single night without sleep produces a significant deficit in the activity of the hippocampus during the memory coding process, producing the consequent lack of retention. It has also been found that certain prefrontal brain regions predict the success of coding in individuals deprived of sleep compared to what they normally sleep on. These results demonstrate that the absence of sleep is a substantial compromise in terms of neuronal and behavioral capacity for the formation of new experiences in memory (Yoo, et al., 2007).

[20] In general terms, human memory has been divided into two large systems, starting with short-term memory, which is subdivided into: sensory memory corresponding to the shortest (<1 sec.) And which is associated with experience immediate sensory and working memory (<1 min.), which allows continuity in the performance of various tasks. The other great system corresponds to the long-term memory that in turn involves two independent and complementary memory systems: the declarative memory, responsible for the memory of events and events, divided in turn in the episodic and semantic memory; and procedural or procedural memory, responsible for remembering skills and developing tasks or procedures. In addition to this classification, it has also distinguished between explicit memory, which corresponds to the memories that are acquired in a conscious way, and implicit memory, which involves experiences or knowledge whose acquisition is not conscious. These different classifications are independent, because we can be aware of acquiring a new motor skill, such as driving a car (explicit-procedural), as it is also possible not to be aware of the acquisition of a new skill, such as the handling of grammar rules. a new language (implicit-procedural). In the same way, we can be aware of learning a new set of concepts or vocabulary (explicit-declarative), but unconscious of subliminal messages that deliver advertising and affect our behavior as consumers

With regard to trauma, it is more important to refer to long-term memory systems: declarative memory ("know what") and procedural memory ("know how"). These types of long-term memory are considered different mnemonic systems especially because they are stored in different regions of the brain and undergo quite different neurophysiological processes[21].

To understand memory and, especially, traumatic phenomena, it is important to keep in mind that memories of events are not acquired in a definitive and stable way, but rather they undergo a gradual process of dynamic stabilization over time. The consolidation of a new synaptic trace of memory at the cortical level occurs slowly through the repeated and coordinated reactivation of the hippocampal and cortex networks in order to progressively increase the strength and stability of the aforementioned connections. general, to the original experience. When memories have been consolidated, after days or weeks, the role of the hippocampus gradually decreases, allowing cortical areas to sustain memories permanently and mediating their recovery independently (Andersen, et al., 2007; Lesburguères, et. al., 2011).

(implicit-declarative) (Edelman & Tononi, 2000; Eichenbaum, 2002; Mann & Cunningham, 2009).

[21] Declarative memories are 'encoded' by the hippocampus, the entorhinal cortex, and the perirhinal cortex (all within the medial temporal lobe of the brain), but they are consolidated and stored in the temporal cortex and elsewhere. The procedural memories, on the other hand, do not seem to involve the hippocampus, and are mainly consolidated in the cerebellum, putamen, caudate nucleus and motor cortex, all of which are involved in motor control. The learned motor skills are associated with putamen; instinctive actions to the caudate nucleus and the cerebellum, which is involved with the synchronization and coordination of bodily abilities. In this way, without the medial temporal lobe (the structure that includes the hippocampus), a person may be able to form new procedural memories, but can not remember the events during which they occurred or were learned. The formation of new long-term memories requires the participation of the temporal medial hippocampus region, which functions in conjunction with the cortex. Important structures for declarative memory include areas of association of the neocortex, the cortical regions surrounding the hippocampus, and the hippocampus. The formation of a long-term memory requires complex biological processes involving the activation of genes, new synthesis of proteins and the growth of new synaptic connections, associated with neuronal assemblies that imply information that continues to change for many years and that can finally arrive to be independent of the medial temporal region, particularly the hippocampus, which would not store the memories, but would be a kind of classification system that filters new associations, distinguishing information as to its degree of relevance for the maintenance of the organism (Squire & Kandel, 2000).

In neurophysiological terms, declarative memory[22] is a reconstruction of a network of synaptic connections distributed over wide areas of the brain, such that tens or hundreds of millions of synaptic connections are involved and the specific location of synaptic connections is never accurate. Each time a trace of memory is recovered, a different neuronal set could be activated, along with the original synaptic connections involved in the experience being recalled. In turn, newly consolidated memory traces could modify the synapses used by older traces. That is why a memory is always something different every time we remember it, in such a way that the information that we ultimately remember from an experience is not a "high resolution copy" of the lived experience, but rather an "low resolution edition", in which much of the content and original context has been lost forever (Eichenbaum, 2002, Gazzaniga, 2009).

Research shows that after the reactivation of "stable" memories (already consolidated cortically) these can become sensitive to significant modifications, which would require another phase of subsequent stabilization, called reconsolidation. Experimentally it has been observed that after multiple reactivations the memories remain sensitive to important modifications during several hours (Fuster, 1999, Edelman & Tononi, 2000, Wichert, Wolf & Schwabe, 2013).

The process of consolidation and reconsolidation of the declarative memory, fundamental for the understanding of the trauma, we must see it, therefore, as a process of constructive (or reconstructtive) character, by means of a selective neural activation of a memory trace, that is to say, of a pattern of synaptic networks that are reconstituted approximately to the last time in which said network was activated. A reconsolidated memory is, therefore, an edition of the last edition that said trace of memory represents, which, in turn, is also an edition that goes back to the original activation (generated by the event and the initial experience that is remembered). This is so because the memory systems, rather than the precise reproduction of the events,

---

[22] This type of memory system would be composed of two sub-types: the episodic and the semantic. Episodic memory is responsible for recording the specific events that have been experienced, and that are located in a specific space and time. Semantic memory refers to information or knowledge learned about specific and independent subjects, such as grammatical knowledge, philosophical ideas, mathematical procedures or recognition of places (Squire & Kandel, 2000, Eichenbaum, 2002, Gazzaniga, 2009).

perform a recovery process based on fragments, which when reconstructed omit and add information, as well as completing the missing data in an associative manner. "Memory is a repetition of neural response patterns suitable for performance, not a sequence of specific details" (Fuster, 1999; Edelman & Tononi, 2000, p. 98; Agren, 2012; Cruz-Villalobos, 2014a).

Therefore, all perspectives that insist on seeing the traumatic event as a static event or "stored" in the mind of an individual, which requires a process of "psychological archeology" of the past for its treatment, forget that our memory systems are far from being a reliable record of the original experience[23].

Reconsolidation, understood as the evolution of previously consolidated memories that become labile through the reactivation of the mnemic trace, is an active process that allows maintaining, strengthening, weakening and / or modifying the memories that are in the long-term memory (Sara, 2000; Dudai, 2004; Tronson & Taylor, 2007; Roediger, Dudai & Fitzpatrick, 2007).

Examples of the lability in which "memories are remembered" have been demonstrated through the study of conditioned fear where it has been discovered that a memory of consolidated fear becomes labile and vulnerable to significant modification during the next six hours after the reactivation of memory, entering a changing state that requires new protein synthesis, which are associated with the possibility of mnemic consolidation (Debiec, et al., 2006)[24].

---

[23] An additional category that is sometimes distinguished from declarative memory is called autobiographical memory, although in reality it can only be considered as an area of episodic memory. This memory system involves the recording of episodes of a person's own life, ordered spatially and temporally, often based on a combination of episodic memory (personal events, places and people) and semantic memory (general knowledge and facts about the world). Within this mnemic system, we also speak of a particular case that is known as "flash memory", which corresponds to an "instant" activation of a memory trace associated with a very specific event that is remembered in detail and an exceptionally vivid form that had a high emotional load, particularly stress or fear. These types of memories are present in PTSD and seem to be very resistant to oblivion, although it has also been observed that memories of this type (flashbacks) are not particularly accurate, despite being apparently experienced with great vividness and clarity (Kandel, 2007; Fuster, 2008; Foster, 2009).

[24] Although there would be a specific biochemical distinction between the processes of initial consolidation and subsequent reconsolidation. For both consolidation and reconsolidation can be blocked by pharmacological agents (for example, by inhibiting the

On the other hand, recent investigations on the reconsolidation of memory (Alberini, 2013, Alberini & LeDoux, 2013), have significantly changed our understanding of memory processes and the recovery of memories, offering a well-founded explanation of the dynamic nature of memory, which leads us to understand it as a phenomenon that, in addition to allowing the relative conservation of experience (learning), also collaborates in behavioral and cognitive adaptation, allowing flexibility in coping with changing environments or traumatic events. This is so, mainly, because these new knowledge disconfirms the traditional way of conceiving memory from static metaphors, as "storage of things", and proposes an understanding of trauma as a dynamic phenomenon and open to multiple reconsolidations, since "the memories can only rarely, if ever, be stored in a truly stable, non-modifiable form" (Nader, et al., 2013, p. 34)[25].

In the light of these considerations, the act of remembering has been likened to the task of a paleontologist who constructs a dinosaur from an incomplete set of bones, but who possesses a great deal of general knowledge about dinosaurs. In this analogy, the past event leaves us with access to an incomplete set of bones (with occasional 'foreign' bones that are not derived from the past event at all). Our knowledge of the world then influences our efforts to re-assemble those bones

---

synthesis of the anisomycin protein) and both require the protein transcription factor CREB. However, recent research on the amygdala suggests that the BDNF protein, which acts as a growth factor in the family of neurotrophins associated with nerve growth factor, is necessary for consolidation, but not for reconsolidation; whereas the transcription factor and Zif268 gene is required for the reconsolidation but not for the consolidation (Debiec, et al., 2006).

[25] The processes of reconsolidation have been found in a great variety of types of memories (explicit and implicit, aversive and reinforcing, simple and complex) and in many types of organisms (from invertebrates to humans). It has been clearly demonstrated that the consolidation of the memory is not a unique process of stabilization that occurs at a single time for each memory. Memories can be reconsolidated after recovery, and this can happen many times. The long-term memories are stabilized labile, because then they are destabilized and re-stabilized according to the continuous processes of reactivation of the relatively similar traces of memory, never equal to the original experience. Hence, memories suffer, therefore, many cycles of reconsolidation in the course of their existence. The 'storage' (term, therefore inaccurate) of the memory is a dynamic process and a consolidated memory is far from being fixed and stable (Alberini & LeDoux, 2013; Nader, et al., 2013).

into something that resembles the past episode. The memory that we assemble may contain some actual elements of the past (i.e. some real bones), but –taken as a whole– it is an imperfect re-construction of the past located in the present (Foster, 2009, p. 14).

The theoretical and practical relevance of the issues so far raised regarding the neurophysiology of memories and their possible implications for an understanding of the trauma and its coping, are evident in an emblematic recent research experimentally found that even the new strong memories are susceptible of interruption and modification if new information is added during its recovery. In a series of experiments carried out by a research team from Iowa State University it was shown that it is possible to significantly change a memory, shortly after recalling it, if different information is given, belonging to the same context of the original memory. For this intervention it was observed that the time spent after the recovery of the memory was key, since the susceptibility to future changes of a trace of reactivated memory (particularly declarative) must occur closely, since it was found that new information has no effect on the original memories when it is presented 48 hours later of the remembrance. This would be so because our memory would open a kind of door after recovery (or remembrance), and this would be open for about six hours. After that period of time, the original memory has been reconsolidated, with a relative degree of stability, until the mnemic trace is activated again and another subsequent reconsolidation is generated (Chan & LaPaglia, 2013).

The scope of this type of research for the field of treatment of victims of traumatic events, are extremely significant. The trauma from this perspective is presented as a dynamic and dynamic mnemic phenomenon, open to a more adaptive or healthy reconsolidation.

2.4.2. Trauma as a Hermeneutical Phenomenon

The approaches just discussed regarding the neurophysiology of memory, have an important critical character towards all perspectives that address the trauma from a static perspective. On the other hand, the hermeneutic phenomenological approach applied to trauma is fully aligned with an understanding of trauma and its confrontation as a dynamic phenomenon and subject to significant and permanent mnemic reconsolidations. Next, we will review this perspective briefly, and we will also use it as an introduction to the topic of positive coping of trauma, which is the approach we have chosen in this work and from which we will approach our main object of study: the Pauline texts on coping with the adversity of 2 Corinthians.

Pain is a much deeper and complex state than simple physical discomfort, because in pain human beings seek an answer, we want to understand the meaning of torment, beyond its cure or analgesia, which without a doubt is also fundamental. Pain requires interpretation; it involves us in hermeneutical debates, which can take us from the extreme of total lack of meaning to full meaning, or vice versa. In all cultures pain has been understood as a phenomenon that requires interpretation, which challenges a search for meaning, not only on a personal level, but also on a community level (Morris, 1996).

Human beings live their lives normally with the feeling that the world we inhabit is significant, coherent, because they perceive a certain pattern that allows us to have the impression of harmony and meaning. This coherence and underlying order is at the basis of everyday life and provides a certain matrix in which relationships, projects, pleasures and pains are given. The usual thing for people is that the meaning of the world is inherent, because they live their lives without having reasons to question it normally. However, there are times when the meaning and coherence of the world is lost. Moments in which it seems that the checkered board has been removed. The pieces remain in place, but their connection to each other becomes arbitrary. Moments in which we do not perceive any sense or direction under our feet and our lives come to lack direction and purpose. These moments give rise to emotions that range from anxiety to pure terror. In those instances we can say that we are facing a traumatic event, characterized by a deep struggle with the search for meaning, particularly when confronted drastically with our mortality condition (Bracken, 2002).

A traumatic event is one that has the potential to cause a confrontation in the foundational understanding of our world, a disarticulation of our being-in-the-world, as is often indicated by the words of the survivors, for whom the traumatic event has a profound impact on fundamental assumptions about the world (Janoff-Bulman

1992). Thus, the immediate effect of a traumatic experience is the confrontation with one's own existential fragility, where the previous modes of understanding and coherences of the own world collapse, are no longer reliable.

> [...] traumatic experiences will effect different responses in individuals, depending on the culture in which they live. Cultures differ in how they promote conscious and non-conscious ways of dealing with distress. Individuals experience and endure suffering in different ways and with different symptomatic outcomes: "Thus the effort in the PTSD literature to isolate a simple cause-and-effect relation between trauma events and specific symptoms ignores the social and cultural embedding of distress that ensures that trauma, loss, and restitution are inextricably intertwined" (Kirmayer 1996, p.150; Bracken, 2002, pp. 73-74).

There is no privileged or neutral starting point to reality; we are all hermeneutically situated, because we are constitutively hermeneutical as human beings. Therefore, it is necessary to appropriate our hermeneutical situation, that is, to take charge of our world and incorporate into it, in its particular significance, the events that come to us. This is very complex normally with those events that are disruptive to our way of *being-in-the-world*[26], since they entail vital risk or a possible damage to the personal integrity of someone close to us (Lorente Martínez, 2012; Cruz-Villalobos, 2014a).

Just as things only have meaning in a context that makes them intelligible, events are also not loaded with an inescapable intrinsic significance, but are interpreted in different ways by those who live them. In the same way, the traumatic event is subject to the permanent process of dynamic interpretation. The traumatic event cannot be seen as a "thing" that is "stored" within a "subject", in its "interior", in a static way, and that needs to be purged, evacuated, drained as if it were a liquid, or found as a lost archaeological remains, buried in some corner of the brain. The trauma is not "an interior thing", but a hermeneutic phenomenon that implies a disruption of the being-in-the-world, of the

---

[26] For a more specific application of this and other Heideggerian concepts to the subject of trauma, see: Bracken 2002; Cruz-Villalobos, 2014a, 2014b.

complete human being who faces and suffers an event that exposes them normally to their finitude, to their death.

> The way in which one's world is meaningful and ordered will determine the way in which one experiences and reacts to any particular event. [...] If posttraumatic anxiety involves the withdrawal of meaningfulness and order, and if these are given by the background practical way of life in which we live, then helping people who have been traumatized requires an effort to rebuild this way of life (Bracken, 2002, p. 149-150).

The trauma in psychology is usually associated immediately with the PTSD. However, available epidemiological data show that this type of disorder is stranger than normal, and it is not the response that most people give after exposure to a traumatic event (Helzer, Robins, McEvoy, 1987; Breslau, et al.,1991; Yehuda & McFarlane, 1995; Breslau, Davis, Peterson & Schultz, 1997; Perkonnig, Kessler, Storz & Wittchen, 2000; Kubany, Ralston, & Hill, 2010; Miller, et al., 2012; Mollica, 2012).

As we indicated above, the neurophysiological reconsolidation of memories gives rise to new consolidation processes, which are not subject to an invariant or rigid pattern. This allows us to understand memory as a highly dynamic and labile process, permanently subject to modifications. Therefore, it is inconsistent to see the traumatic event as a static reality in the mind of a subject, as an event decanted, stable in memory, but rather as an experience that can be reconsolidated in memory also in a positive way, since a traumatic event can have multiple interpretations by the sufferer; It is open to various reconsolidations that can be in fact healthy and adaptive for the victims. This is what has been confirmed by the research carried out in recent decades on the positive coping of trauma, especially in the concepts of hardines, resilience and posttraumatic growth (Kobasa, 1979, 1982; 1993; Du Plessis, 2001; Calhoun & Tedeschi, 1999, 2004a, 2004b, 2006; Zoellner & Maercker, 2006; Eschleman, Bowling & Alarcón, 2010; Fletcher & Sarkar, 2013; Maddi, 2005, 2013; Wu, et al., 2013; Kent, Davis, & Reich, 2014; Southwick, et al., 2014; Berger, 2015).

In the field of medical and psychosocial sciences, it was thought for a long time that people who lived from childhood subjected to situations of suffering or trauma (poverty, marginalization, abuse, significant losses, etc.) were "condemned" to be individuals with chronic limitations to achieve a full life, that is, the maintenance of the "biopsychosocial deformation" (following a physical metaphor) exerted on their internal structures by traumatic external pressure was predicted. In recent decades this issue has been raised in new ways, as it has been observed that adverse experiences in life do not necessarily hinder human development. International and intercultural studies that have been done over several years (longitudinal investigations) offer clear evidence that many people —even those who are and have been exposed to multiple and severe risks and experiences of great stress in life— can reach be confident, competent and charitable adults. Living traumatic events can become one of the situations that most contribute to the life of a person. Without removing an once of the severity, seriousness and horror of those experiences, we can not deny that it is in extreme situations when the human being has the opportunity to rebuild his way of understanding the world, his relationships and his system of values, of such a way that in this reconstruction can be a really significant learning and personal growth (Werner & Smith, 1992; Vera, et al., 2006; Cruz-Villalobos, 2007, 2012).

Next we will dwell more specifically on the contributions of Positive Psychology regarding the confrontation of traumatic events, as a perspective that we believe can significantly contribute to the field of practical theology and particularly to our approach from psychological criticism to Paulines texts of 2 Corinthians on the confrontation of the adverse.

Chapter 3
Resources for Positive Coping with Trauma

Why in the land of pain
do two possible roots take hold
the root of bitterness
and the root of hope?

Why does pain hammer
on the anvil that is man
and, in the process, forge his life?

Why does pain
have millions of lecture halls
where it holds its master class?

Why dear God are there tears that burn
and tears that water thirsty ground?

L. Cruz-Villalobos (2004, pp. 42-43)[27]

After World War II, psychology became a science almost exclusively dedicated to healing, primarily focusing on pathology, neglecting the idea of the individually and communally healthy individual. In this context, Positive Psychology emerges as an alternative proposal (Snyder & López, 2002).

The field of Positive Psychology can be subdivided into various areas: a) the subjective level covers ideas such as wellbeing and satisfaction, flow, joy, happiness, optimism, hope, and faith; b) the individual level deals with positive individual traits, such as the ability to love, vocation, courage, interpersonal skills, esthetic sensibility, perseverance, forgiveness, originality, life purpose, talents, and wisdom; c) the group level addresses civil virtues such as responsibility, affection, altruism, tolerance, and work, among others (Seligman & Csikszentmihalyi, 2000).

---

[27] Unpublished translation by Ryan Flanders. In original Spanish version: "¿Por qué en la tierra del dolor / Se hunden dos raíces posibles / La raíz de la amargura / Y la raíz de la esperanza? // ¿Por qué el dolor martillea / En el yunque que es el hombre / Y en el medio se forja su vida? // ¿Por qué el dolor / Tiene millones de aulas / Donde dicta su cátedra magistral? // ¿Por qué amado Dios hay llanto que quema / Y hay llanto que riega?"

Seligman (2002) informs us that psychology had three main missions before World War Two[28]: to cure mental illness, to enable individuals' productivity and satisfaction, and to identify and promote personal abilities. Immediately after the war, thousands of psychologists discovered that they could make a living by treating mental illnesses, and in the academic field they discovered that they could receive grants for their research if they focused on studying pathologies. This resulted in great advances in understanding and treating mental illnesses and disorders. However, the great disadvantage was that the other fundamental missions of psychology, with a more positive nature, were forgotten, in such a way that

> [...] Psychology came to see itself as a mere subfield of the health professions, and it became a victimology [...] Psychology's empirical focus then shifted to assessing and curing individual suffering. There has been an explosion in research on psychological disorders and the negative effects of environmental stressors such as parental divorce, death, and physical and sexual abuse. [...] The message of the positive psychology movement is to remind our field that it has been deformed. Psychology is not just the study of disease, weakness, and damage; it also is the study of strength and virtue. Treatment is not just fixing what is wrong; it also is building what is right. Psychology is not just about illness or health; it also is about work, education, insight, love, growth, and play (Seligman, 2002, p. 4).

The most common approach, marked by a victimological perspective, is based on two assumptions that are currently observed with criticism: a) that trauma always results in serious damage, and b) that damage always indicates the presence of trauma (Gillham & Seligman, 1999).

Perspectives of this type have come to assume that individuals have a one-dimensional and largely invariable response to adverse or traumatic events. For example, in the case of grief, specific stages have been presented as being universal (Kübler-Ross, 2006, 2008, 2010), ignoring individual differences in responding to and coping with stressful

---

[28] Fundamentally in the USA, which was and continues to be one of the main world leaders in the field of psychological research.

situations. On the contrary, it has been observed that responses of intense grief and suffering are not inevitable and their absence does not necessarily mean that a disorder exists or will develop (Wortman & Silver, 1989; Silver, Wortman & Crofton, 1990).

The approach that incorporates the comprehension and work of individuals that have experienced traumatic events turns out to be highly relevant. Here, perspectives such as those of positive psychology provide more promising models in the clinical field[29].

For Cyrulnik (2002), professionals that work with victims have the potential to be a support that can cause repair processes to begin much more quickly. In the same way, when people responsible for social decision making facilitate spaces for creativity, dialogue, and social learning, many individuals who have suffered trauma end up transforming their sufferings and increase their levels of achievement, despite everything. However, when a person's life has been disorgani-zed at an early stage due to growing up in a household with neglecting or abusive parents, and the culture encourages the silence of victims, thus adding to the aggression, or leaves them to their own fortune because they are considered "irreparable", such persons will then see themselves as having a future that lacks, or is far from, hope.

Some authors have proposed that there are three habitual psychological responses individuals have when dealing with a traumatic event: a) to succumb to stress (primarily expressed by PTSD); b) resilience or the ability to recover; and c) posttraumatic growth (Hefferon & Boniwell, 2011).

Rodríguez Marín (1995), for his part, talks about coping with highly stressful events by employing the concept of coping resources, classifying them as: physical, psychosocial, and sociocultural. In addressing positive psychology in this present study, we will use an approach focused on the resources, especially for their usefulness in later elaborating applicable conclusions. We will follow a seismic architecture metaphor and will address: resources for resistance to trauma (hardiness); resources for recovery from trauma (resilience); and resources for rebuilding after trauma (posttraumatic growth). But

---

[29] Although they are obviously enriched by the contributions of the various perspectives mentioned (as well as others) that contribute significantly to the areas in which they are focused.

before addressing these issues we will focus on the important concept of religious coping, which will also be very important in the discussion of our research.

As we have indicated, the impact of traumatic events is well documented in psychological literature, particularly in the clinical field, which recognizes that individuals who experience traumatic events can present serious problems such as posttraumatic stress disorder (PTSD). Nevertheless, through innumerable literary works written throughout human history, the idea has been passed down that there are certain personal and social benefits that can come from experiencing adversity and suffering. For example, at times it is assumed that experiencing stressful and traumatic events may provoke positive psychosocial changes. This is also suggested, for example, by the majority of religions. But it is only in the last two or three decades that the theme of overcoming adversity and the growth that can happen afterwards has become a subject of empirical research in the field of social sciences, particularly psychology (Joseph, 2009).

With respect to coping with traumatic events, various constructs have been developed from positive psychology related to overcoming adversity in a healthy manner, the result of increasingly abundant research on the topic. In the present study, through the use of seismic architecture metaphor, we will analyze three large groups of resources related to positive coping with trauma, specifically resources for resistance to trauma or hardiness (Kobasa, 1979, 1982; Eschleman, Bowling & Alarcón, 2010; Maddi, 2005, 2013); resources for recovery after trauma or resilience (Garmezy, 1993; Du Plessis, 2001; Fletcher & Sarkar, 2013; Wu, et al., 2013; Kent, Davis & Reich, 2014; Southwick, et al., 2014); and resources for rebuilding after trauma or posttraumatic growth (Calhoun & Tedeschi, 1999, 2004a, 2004b, 2006, Zoellner & Maercker, 2006; Berger, 2015). Although this distinction is theoretical, it will allow us to more clearly visualize the resources, particularly psychosocial resources, available for coping with adversity, especially with what we consider traumatic, in that it implies the real or potential risk of personal death or death of someone close.

In the sections that follow we will analyze each of these groups of psychosocial resources that enable healthy coping with traumatic events.

3.1. Resources for Resistance to Trauma (Hardiness)

> *Fear doesn't make*
> *the red copihue[30] petals tremble.*
> *The canelo tree[31] doesn't lower its cup,*
> *for the invader to take a drink.*
> Rayen Kvyeh (Mapuche poet)[32]

If we define the concept of resistance in its most basic sense in material science, we could say that it corresponds to the opposition to change that solid materials possess, which is to say, opposition to compression, cutting, and bending. Therefore, a diamond could come to mind, which is one of the most resistant materials. In this way, when we refer to human resistance to trauma, we understand it as the set of resources that enables an individual subjected to harm or trauma to remain in his/her psychosocial state prior to the adverse experience.

Starting from this classification we will refer to types of loss, types of resources and their meaning, and the different resources available.

3.1.1. Type of Traumatic Event

For some authors, there is a dose-dependent relationship between the stimulus' intensity and the degree of impact after a traumatic event. Closely related to this are the characteristics of the event itself, the following characteristics being associated with more complex resistance (Pérez Sales, et al., 2002, Pérez Sales, 2006): a) Unexpected: the more unexpected a traumatic experience is, the greater its destructive potential on the individual's life and ability to inflict psychological damage; b) Prolonged: the longer the period of time exposed to adverse stimuli or experiences, the more the ability to resist

---

[30] National flower of Chile.

[31] Sacred tree of the Mapuche people.

[32] Quoted by Moens (1999) unpublished translation by Ryan Flanders. In Spanish: "El miedo no hace / temblar los pétalos del rojo copihue. / El canelo no inclina su copa / para el beba el invasor."

without sequelae is diminished; c) Repetitive: the more one adverse event is experienced, the greater its traumatic potential; d) Intentional: events resulting from willful and deliberate human action are psychosocially more difficult to resist.

These characteristics that inhibit resistance to traumatic events are associated with a reduction in the individual's perception of control, strongly confronting the basic beliefs and assumptions of the majority of people regarding how their world is ordered.

An example of the above is observed in the case mentioned by Pérez Sales (2006, p. 148):

> Many studies on Euro-American culture agree that the violent event that most frequently and severely provokes posttraumatic sequelae is physically violent rape (of men as well as women). Additionally, the consequences of this seem to directly depend on the degree of relationship between victim and perpetrator. The closer the relationship, the worse the long-term effects of the abuse. This means that, in addition to the act of rape, what this implies for the individual and his/her system of reference has to be observed, as well as the event's significance for questioning his/her past, present, and future).[33]

3.1.3. Significance of the Traumatic Event

The way in which someone narrates traumatic events to themselves will be very important for coping with them. Here, following various authors, (Pérez Sales, 2006; Cyrulnik, 2006, Kenneson, 2004; Crittenden, 2002; Guidano & Liotti, 2006; Johnson, 2009; Arciero & Bondolfi, 2009; Arciero, Bondolfi, & Mazzola, 2018) we can say that the following factors greatly influence the type of meaning assigned to adverse experiences: a) Personality: particular characteristics of

---

[33] Translated by the author. In Spanish: "La mayoría de estudios en cultura euroamericana coinciden en que el hecho de violencia que provoca una mayor frecuencia y severidad de secuelas postraumáticas es la violación sexual con violencia física (tanto masculina como femenina). Las consecuencias de ésta parecen depender directamente además, del grado de filiación entre víctima y perpetrador. A mayor cercanía, peores consecuencias a largo término del abuso. Es decir, que además del hecho de la violación, hay que ver lo que ésta supone para la persona y su sistema de referentes, así como el significado cuestionador que el hecho tiene para el pasado, el presente y el futuro de esa persona."

personality that affect the way in which individuals affectively situate and assign meaning to events; b) Critical development periods: stages of biological, cognitive, and psychosocial development with greater or lesser vulnerability than others with respect to certain events; c) Prior loss: conditioning (classical and operant, direct or vicarious) as well as biology is very important for interpreting present and future events, especially traumatic ones; d) Cultural affiliation: without a doubt, participation in specific culture turns out to be central in influencing the way one experiences events and life experiences[34]; e) Spiritual or religious beliefs: Closely connected to the above, but spiritual and religious beliefs are distinguished as forming the nucleus of all cultural or subcultural worldviews[35] and have been observed to function as the predominant element for interpreting personal and social experience.

3.1.4. Contextual Resistance Resources

Individuals that show resistance to high intensity adverse experiences without suffering deep or clinically significant alterations require social support networks and specific interactions that enable them to avoid major damage from suffering. Various factors have been observed that are associated with resistance that can be considered external or social resources.

Sharing traumatic events with others:
Communicating the traumatic experience has been observed to be beneficial, given that it enables catharsis or abreaction; coherence and internal meaning to be given to the experience, facilitating its integration; validation and social recognition of the experience; and other experiences to be shared as well as possibly useful ways of coping.

---

[34] This makes a lot of sense if we adopt Kenneson's understanding of cultures as "complex webs of convictions, practices, institutions and narratives that give shape and meaning to the realities of people's everyday lives" (Kenneson, 1999, pp. 23).

[35] This is even the case for atheistic or materialistic worldviews, especially if we understand religious belief as Paul Tillich does in linking it to the concept of *ultimate concern.*

However, sharing about traumatic events is not a universal necessity nor is it universally beneficial. Therefore it is important to keep the following in mind: a) Denial of traumatic events can be a useful tool for their progressive assimilation and forcing the narration of events can be harmful in these cases (cf. the concept of "secondary victimization"); b) If the traumatic experience is full of highly painful images or memories and the person has already begun to integrate them with their own defensive resources or mechanisms (dissociation, rationalization, abstraction, etc.), sharing the events could be a harmful setback; c) There are cultural elements that influence the connotation of the adequacy of sharing traumatic events, taking for an example how the public display of negative emotions is looked down upon in some cultures; and d) There are studies that demonstrate that promoting the narration of events immediately after the trauma has not been observed to be beneficial in preventing the appearance of posttraumatic symptoms in the medium and long term.

Thus, talking is potentially beneficial when it is the right moment of the personal process of assimilating the traumatic event and when the context and the listeners are involved in the task of clarifying and reassigning the experience's meaning (Snyder & Ford, 1987; Pérez Sales, 2006; Schnyder & Cloitre, 2015).

Permanence of significant affective bonds:

The feeling of security is largely based on bonds established with reality and with emotionally significant people. The violent breaking of these bonds can later lead to symptoms of self-protection. Establishing intense emotional bonds after a traumatic experience is very important. People that maintain significant bonds possess better resources for resistance to the consequences of traumatic events or to the possibility of new loss or adverse events. Nevertheless, overcoming the fear of future loss mentioned in the previous quotation is required (Goldsmith, 2004; Pérez Sales, 2006; Gasparre, Bosco & Bellelli, 2010).

Social context:

It has been observed that the social context in which a traumatic event is experienced turns out to be highly relevant to resistance levels displayed by those affected. To this respect, certain factors are highlighted, such as a feeling of belonging to a group of peers that have had a similar experience, that is, for the person to feel part of a community that can identify itself according to the collective narrative of being "survivors" (not victims in a passive sense). This may involve a social climate that allows public expression by those affected, not remaining silent or hiding, together with social validation of the suffering experienced instead of stigmatization; being inserted in a social, political, and economic context that allows those affected to keep control and the sense of self-determination over their own lives; life conditions that include social, public (government) and/or private support and that guarantee personal dignity (Schlecker & Fleischer, 2013)

3.1.5. Personal Resistance Resources

Research carried out during the 1960s and 1970s demonstrated that "stressful life events precipitated somatic and mental illness" (Kobasa, 1979, p. 1). But the same author states that the presence of "individuals with high stress scores who are not sick" (p. 2) has been observed.

Kobasa (1979, 1982) proposed the concept of *hardiness* as a mediator between stress and pathological manifestations, reducing the harmful effects of high stress levels on individuals' health. As a concept, hardiness, is one of the oldest terms that developed in the study of positive coping with adverse situations. Although not one of the most widely used in research, it is still used today and is distinguished from resilience and posttraumatic growth[36] (Mazlom, et al., 2015; Maddi, 2005, 2013; Grover, 2015; Vealey & Perritt, 2015; Abdollahi, et al., 2016; Singh, 2016; Thakur & Chawla, 2016).

For Kobasa and his collaborators, hardiness would be composed of three sub-constructs (Kobasa, 1979, 1982; Kobasa, Maddi & Courington, 1981; Kobasa, Maddi & Kahn, 1982, Maddi, 2013):

Commitment (vs. alienation): Believing in the truth, importance, and value of who one is and what one does. The tendency to significantly be involved in all life activities, including work, interper-

---

[36] Though as we shall see these three concepts repeatedly, depending on the author, they may overlap in their uses and definitions.

sonal relationships, and social institutions. This has not only an individual dimension, but collective as well, which is to say that helping others in situations of need is possible;

Control (vs. impotence): The tendency to think and act with conviction of the relevance of personal influence and responsibility during potentially traumatic events. Situations are analyzed, become predictable, and coping strategies are developed;

Challenge (vs. threat): Believing that change, and not stability, is the normal characteristic of life. Situations are perceived as opportunities and incentives for personal growth and not as threats to one's security. This would be related to cognitive flexibility and tolerating ambiguity.

Previous traumatic experiences that have been adequately integrated in the individual's autobiography can be considered personal resistance resources. These resources can even include the absence of previous traumatic events that create greater vulnerability (such as a history of early separation from parents, childhood abuse, or others). Along with this, the absence of mental disorders or psychiatric symptoms prior to exposure to the adverse event will also provide a good prognosis for resistance (Murphy & Moriarty, 1976; Garmezy, 1987, 1993).

Individuals that are able to integrate events into a coherent whole can better resist adverse events and their consequences, in contrast to those that develop processes of recurring "rumination" of the memories, falling into circular thought patterns that do not allow for adequate integration. Many symptoms, especially intrusive ones (nightmares, flashbacks, etc.) can be interpreted as unconscious attempts to integrate events with previous experiences of the world and their respective assumptions. And when finding a logic of the events is not possible, dissociating incomprehensible traumatic events from the conscience turns out to be a protecting mode, in order to preserve some basic assumptions about oneself and the world (Pérez Sales, 2006).

Convictions and religious practices can become resources for the integration of experience, which deliver a particular "logic" to events, allowing in some cases an adequate coping and a better resistance to the adverse (Prati & Pietrantoni, 2009). This is the field of study of religious coping (Pargament, 1997; Ganzevoort, 1998a, 1998b), which we will see in another section in more detail.

Searching for blame has also been observed to be a cognitive process that attempts to make order in the middle of the chaos of painful events. However, experiencing blame in an integrating fashion and not as self-recrimination can be beneficial for increasing resistance (in many cases, especially in victims). In the same vein, anchoring in the past has been observed as a way of not thinking about the painful present, seeking refuge in scenes lived that become gratifying. Also, and very connected with religious-type coping, certain types of focusing on a better (even ideal) future have been observed to enable the present to be seen as a stage that will soon be overcome.

Various characteristics related to resistance capacity have been observed that are among cognitive and behavioral personal resistance resources, in which we can highlight several tendencies (Pérez Sales, 2006): a) Selectively remembering positive elements in autobiographical memory, with the tendency to lessen or obviate the negative; b) Accepting a certain level of uncertainty and unpredictability in life. Assume that life also includes factors that are out of personal control; c) Comparing what has occurred to oneself with the people around you, thus being able to see positive elements: there are people who have had it even worse; there were moments in which one failed, but others in which one responded well; things could be worse; and one accepts that discomfort is normal and will pass with time; d) Seeing oneself as survivors, as people that come out of a traumatic event stronger and that, as a result, have more resources for confronting new situations; e) Perceiving the stressful stimulus as less threatening, seeing it as positive and controllable; f) Utilizing more adaptive mechanisms if the stimulus is perceived as threatening, especially transformational coping (seeing it as an opportunity for growth) instead of regressive coping (fleeing or avoiding the potentially stressful stimulus); g) Numerous studies point to less physiological reactivity to stress in the most resistant individuals; h) The use of humor; and i) Positive emotions that counteract negative events during the trauma process.

Referring to the construct of hardiness and complementing what we have proposed until now, DuPressi (2001) suggests that resistance is not a unitary phenomenon, and that of its three subcomponents, only commitment and control have adequate psychometric properties and are significantly and systematically related with health in the results of primary investigations. The lack of control and commitment would have direct effects on health due to being psychologically stressful in a relevant way.

Finally, we can mention the results of the meta-analysis about hardiness done by Eschleman, Bowling & Alarcón (2010) who concluded the following, based on an analysis of numerous investigations on the topic during the last thirty years: a) there is a positive relationship between hardiness and personality traits having to do with resistance to tension; b) a negative relationship has been observed between hardiness and personality traits associated with exacerbating the effects of stress; c) a negative relationship has been found between hardiness and coping styles associated with tension and regressive strategies; and d) a positive relationship has been observed between hardiness, social support, and active coping.

3.1.6. Family Resistance

In the literature, characteristics of families with greater resistance to adverse events (hardiness) have been examined as well as strong or healthy families that would possess more and better resources for attending to and mediating effects of crises that produce high levels of stress (DuPlessis, 2001). Among these families' characteristics we can mention the following:

Cohesion: This corresponds to the emotional bond or closeness between family members, and is considered to be one of the clinically strong strengths of families. It can also be described as family unity, loyalty, and cooperation between members (Minuchin, 1974; Epstein & Bishop, 1981; Lee & Brage, 1989; Bobele, 1989; McCubbin & McCubbin, 1992).

Communication: This refers to families where spontaneous, clear, and direct dialogue is developed, where important matters are discussed and communication is valued as relevant not only for resolving problems but also as an end in itself, in such a way that family members simply enjoy each other's company (Gantman, 1980; Stinnett

& De Frain, 1989; Trivette, Dunst, Deal, Hamer & Propst, 1990; McCubbin & McCubbin, 1992).

Flexibility/adaptability: This is when families are not rigid in their patterns of transactions and boundaries, and seek various alternatives, in response to adversities that are natural to development, accidental, or traumatic. This can be classified in categories of adaptability: very high (chaotic), moderately high (flexible), moderately low (structured), and very low (rigid) (Minuchin, 1974; Gantman, 1980; McCubbin & McCubbin, 1992).

Problem-solving: This refers to the ability to commit to resolving problems through designing and evaluating options that can satisfy family needs according to available resources (Epstein & Bishop, 1981; Cederblad, Dahlin, Hagnell & Hansson, 1995; Tallman, Shaw, Schultz & Altmaier, 2010).

Spirituality and values: This corresponds to a worldview that incorporates perspectives of transcendence (in general with a religious or spiritual connotation), which implies a system of common ethical values, participation in a religious community, and activities that present symbolic content associated with the meaning and purpose of life (Stinnett & De Frain, 1989; Stinnett, 1979; McCubbin & McCubbin, 1992; Trivette, Dunst, Deal, Hamer & Propst, 1990; Lee & Brage, 1989).

Identity and family rituals: This is the aspect of family related to symbolic modes of significant familiar idiosyncratic communication (rituals) and traditions, understood as certain patterns, themes, and motivations for which unity in life is recognized as familiar and placed in the context of a relationship with the larger community in which the family belongs (McCubbin & McCubbin, 1992; Gunn, 1980; Wolin & Bennett, 1984).

Affective response capacity: This implies the basic family mood characterized by warmth, humor, concern for others, the ability to share honest feelings openly with others and respond to expressed feelings with empathy and acceptance (Lee & Brage, 1989; Epstein & Bishop, 1981; Will & Wrate, 1985).

Limits and roles: Clear limits between family members and between family generations, which means that the parents do not behave like children and the children do not fulfill the functions of spouse or parent (Lee & Brage, 1989; Minuchin, 1974; Gantman, 1980).

Social support: The use of contextual social resources that involve active participation in the community, both by offering services in accordance with resources and by seeking extra-familiar help with the problems that require it. There are three main levels of social support: 1) Emotional support, which brings the individual to believe that he or she is loved and cared for, 2) support for self-esteem, which brings the individual to believe that he or she is appreciated and valued, and 3) support network, which brings the individual to believe that he or she belongs to a communication network that includes reciprocal obligation and mutual understanding (Trivette et al., 1990; Cederblad et al., 1995; Schlecker & Fleischer, 2013).

Autonomy: Strong families would be capable of achieving a balance between intimacy and autonomy. Each family member is seen as a separate and unique individual, and individual differences are respected (McCubbin & McCubbin, 1992; Lee & Brage, 1989; Gantman, 1980).

Coherence (of life): The ability to be positive and see the positive in almost all aspects in life, including the ability to see crisis and problems as an opportunity to learn and grow. This also corresponds to the trust that the world is understandable (internal and external environments are structured, predictable, and explainable), manageable (resources are available to satisfy demands), and significant (life's demands are challenges worthy of investment) (Trivette et al., 1990; Bigbee, 1992).

3.2. Resources for Recovery from Trauma (Resilience)

A man is a man anywhere in the universe if he still breathes.
It doesn't matter if they've taken his legs so he doesn't walk.
It doesn't matter if they've taken his arms so he doesn't work.
It doesn't matter if they've taken his heart so doesn't sing.
None of this matters, because a man is a man anywhere in the world if he still breathes,
and if he still breathes he should invent some legs some arms, and a heart to fight for the world.
José María Memet[37]

---

[37] "La misión de un hombre que respira", in: Arteche, Massone & Scarpa (1984, p.315), translated by the author. In Spanish: "Un hombre es un hombre en cualquier parte del

92

3.2.1. Definitions

Resilience is a recent concept in the social sciences and psychology, and the variety of meanings assigned to it has been widely discussed (Cutuli & Masten, 2009; Driver, 2011; Hutcheon & Wolbring, 2013; Fletcher & Sarkar, 2013).

Originally, in the fields of physics and engineering, where the concept of resilience originated, it was generally used in studying the elasticity of solid materials. Basic electromagnetic force at the molecular level, which enables objects to keep their shape, is clearly demonstrated at the moment when two objects come into contact. Here elasticity or resilience is seen as one of the most important material properties. Therefore, in this field, resilience is understood as, "the property that enables an object deformed by a force to recover its original shape once the force stops" (Lucena, 2006, p. 105).[38]

If an object deformed by a force returns to its original size and shape after the force stops, it is said to be elastic or to have resilience. Elastic forces react against the deforming force to keep the solid object's molecular structure stable (UNNA, 2010).

Generally, in the fields of social and medical sciences, it has been thought that individuals who live under situations of suffering and trauma since childhood (poverty, societal exclusion, abuse, important losses, etc.) are "condemned" to have chronic limitations to achieving a full life. That is, it is predicted that "psychological deformation" (using a physical metaphor) will be maintained on their internal structures by exterior traumatic pressure. What is certain is that this topic is currently being re-examined, since it has been seen that adverse or traumatic experiences in life do not necessarily hinder one's personal development. International and intercultural studies carried out during many years (longitudinal research) offer scientific evidence that many

---

universo si todavía respira. / No importa que le hayan quitado las piernas para que no camine. / No importa que le hayan quitado los brazos para que no trabaje. / No importa que le hayan quitado el corazón para que no cante. / Nada de eso importa, por cuanto, un hombre es un hombre en cualquier parte del / universo si todavía respira y si todavía respira debe inventar unas piernas, unos / brazos, un corazón para luchar por el mundo."

[38] Translated by the author. In Spanish: "la propiedad que permite a un cuerpo ser deformado por una fuerza y recuperar su forma original una vez que esta deja de actuar."

people, even those who are or have been exposed to multiple and severe risks and highly stressful experiences, could become self-confident, competent, and caring adults (Werner & Smith, 1992).

Towards the end of the 1970s, conversations began in a new area related to developing the concept of resilience within the social sciences. Discussion around this concept began in the field of psychopathology (the study of mental problems), in which, surprisingly and with great interest, it was found that children raised in families where one or both parents were alcoholics during the children's development did not exhibit biological or psychosocial deficiencies. On the contrary, they reached an adequate quality of life (Werner & Smith, 1977, 1992, 2001).

If hardiness, as we have seen, mainly refers to the organism's condition or the modes of enabling the organism to not suffer, or to minimize major damage from the sudden presence of adversity, resilience refers to immediate recovery after a certain level of damage has been inflicted on the individual or group.

Resilience questions the chronicity of the negative or the damage. It allows us to see adverse circumstances from a perspective based on the possibility of serious hope for recovering from the trauma. Resilience makes us rediscover realistic hope in the midst of adversity (Vanistendael, 2003).

The concept of resilience is closely linked with extreme and traumatic adversity, as indicated by Gómez and Kotliarenco (2011). Resilience is understood as a strength at the personal, family, or community level, a strength that opposes potential devastation from adversity. One cannot talk about resilience without taking into consideration the adverse conditions that involve a high probability of negative results for a person or group. In this way, then, adversity is the seed, or necessary condition, for resilience (Cyrulnik, 2003).

Many definitions of this concept have been developed, among which we can highlight the following synthesis.

With respect to resilience, one can distinguish two components. (1) Rresistance to destruction, that is, the capacity to protect one's integrity under pressure and forge positive life behavior despite difficult circumstances. (2) On the other hand, we have a pragmatic definition of resilience being the capacity of a person or social system to develop and grow in the presence of great difficulties. This component speaks of a process that continues throughout life, in a permanent interaction between the person (or social system) and the surroundings (Vanistendael, 1994, 2003).[39]

Others see resilience as a dynamic and complex process that results in positive adaptation to maintain competent functioning in contexts of great adversity, stress, and risks (Kaplan, et al., 1996; Luthar & Cicchetti, 2000; Hartman & Winsler, 2005; Cutuli & Masten, 2009; Van Kessel, MacDougall & Gibb, 2015).

3.2.2. Review of the Construct and its Investigation

Although the experiences of resilience and similar concepts have existed during all human history, the academic study of resilience dates back to Norman Garmezy's pioneering research during the 1960s and 1907s.with children of schizophrenic parents. In these studies that sought to investigate the etiology and prognosis of a serious psycho-pathology, Garmezy (1974) found that among these children with a high risk for psycho-pathology there was a subgroup that had surprisingly healthy patterns of adaptation. Garmezy and his colleagues tried to identify the factors associated with their unusual and outstanding wellbeing, taking into special consideration the fact that these cases tended not to be considered exceptional in the majority of investigations until that point. This signified an important change in focus at the time, in giving attention to positive results and protecting factors, especially in the context of lives subjected to adversity.

Anthony (1974), in the same vein as Garmezy, describes a group of children that he calls "invulnerable", those who showed themselves to be resistant to being wrapped up in the psychopathology of their parents, even maintaining a compassionate attitude towards them. Rutter (1979) observes certain common characteristics in these

---

[39] Such definition, as in other cases (Grotberg, 1995) implies that resilience is taken as a concept that includes both hardiness and positive transformation. This is similar to Yates & Luthar's (2009) definition: Resilience is a dynamic developmental process wherein the individual is able to utilize resources in and outside of the self to negotiate current challenges adaptively and, by extension, to develop a foundation on which to rely when future challenges occur.

children, such as high creativity, effectiveness, and competency. Murphy and Moriarty (1976) observe that resilient youth also have common characterristics, such as social charisma and the ability to relate well with others, the capacity to experience a wide range of emotions, and the ability to regulate the expression of emotions.

One of the most relevant historic milestones in the study of resilience corresponds to investigations carried out by Emmy Werner, who studied children in high-risk situations on the Hawaiian island of Kauai. The longitudinal study began in 1954 with a cohort of all known pregnancies on the island, with various monitoring evaluations that continued for various decades (Werner & Smith, 1982, 1992, 2001). The first reports about this group emphasized that these children lived in conditions of extreme poverty, poor quality in their childcare, and notorious family instability and disorganization. The main protecting factors that distinguished the better adapted children from the more poorly adapted children included: affective bonds with the family, informal support systems outside the home, and personal attributes such as sociability.

In the 1980s, the academic contributions of Garmezy, Masten and Tellegen (1984) and Michael Rutter (1987) stand out. Their research provided methodological and conceptual guidelines for studying resistance.

Especially at the beginning of the 1990s, various changes occurred in the conceptual approach to studying this construct. In the first studies on this topic, efforts were made to identify the personal qualities of resilient children, such as autonomy or self-confidence. As the studies progressed, the researchers recognized that flexible adaptation could occasionally be related more directly with factors external to the child. Therefore, they presented three groups of factors involved in the development of resilience: a) attributes of the children themselves, b) aspects of their families, and c) characteristics of their widest social environments (Garmezy, 1987; Rutter, 1987; Werner & Smith, 1982, 1992). Another important change that affected future studies, approaches, and the broadening of the concept of resilience was the recognition that positive adaptation despite adversity is never permanent (as a stable condition of the individual), but rather that there exists a continuous dynamic in the development of new vulnerabilities and new strong points with the change of life circumstances (Garmezy & Masten, 1986; Werner & Smith, 1982). Also, there would be a certain specificity in resilience, since researchers warned that at-risk children could show notable strengths in some areas but, at the same time, notable deficiencies in others (Luthar, Doernberger & Zigler, 1993).

In the first decade of this century, a growing and massive interest in the topic of resilience has been observed, although the methodological conceptual rigor of its study and application is being questioned (Luthar, 2006).

3.2.3. Descriptions of Resilience

Edith Grotberg (1997) designed a framework that makes it possible to characterize a resilient person (especially children). Scales for measuring resilience have been developed (Saavedra & Villarta, 2008; Saavedra & Castro, 2009) using Grotberg's framework. The scales use expressions such as: "I have", "I am", and "I can" to describe the characteristics of individuals that display high levels of resilience, such as self-esteem, self-confidence, confidence in one's surroundings, autonomy, and social competence.

To summarize the personal and interpersonal conditions displayed by individuals who more easily overcome adversity, we present an adaptation of Grotberg's framework below (Munist, Santos, Kotliarenco, Suárez, Infante & Grotberg, 1998):

I have

- People around me I trust and who love me, no matter what
- People who set limits for me so I know when to stop before there is danger or trouble
- People who show me how to do things right by the way they do things
- People who want me to learn to do things on my own
- People who help me when I am sick, in danger or need to learn

I am

- A person people can like and love
- Glad to do nice things for others and show my concern

- Respectful of myself and others
- Able to learn what my teachers teach me
- Willing to be responsible for what I do
- Sure things will be all right
- Sad, I recognize it and express it, confident I will find help
- Surrounded by people that appreciate me.

I can

- Talk to others about things that frighten me or bother me
- Find ways to solve problems that I face
- Control myself when I feel like doing something not right or dangerous
- Figure out when it is a good time to talk to someone or to take action
- Find someone to help me when I need
- Make mistakes and mess up without losing my parent's affection
- Feel and express affection

Below we present a synthesis of the concept of resource that we have developed in an attempt to integrate a significant number of aspects present in individuals with high levels of resilience.

Table 1: Resilience Resources (Adapted from Cruz-Villalobos, 2009)

A. PERSONAL RESOURCES	B. CONTEXTUAL RESOURCES
A.1. Biological: - Satisfied physiological needs (food, shelter, sleep, health, etc.)	B.1. Basic: - Instances sufficient for satisfying physiological needs (food, shelter, sleep, health, etc.)
A.2. Affective: - Self-esteem - Good mood - Experiencing and coping with stress positively	B.2. From specific people: - Relationship of unconditional acceptance and support with at least one person (significant bond) - Expression of high and positive expectations towards them
A.3. Cognitive: - Creativity - Command of adaptation and conflict resolution strategies	B.3. From the social environment: - Informal network: family, friends, neighbors, church, etc. - Opportunity to significantly partici- pate and contribute to the social environment

A.4. Spiritual/Existential:	– Access to relationships with positive adult role-models in a variety of extra-familiar contexts
– Capacity to discover meaning and coherence for life.	
– Sense of transcendence	– An educational/work environment that is open, containing, and has clear limits.
– Sense of purpose and future	
– Flexible faith or believe system	
AB. Relational:	
- Autonomy	
- Social competencies and abilities	
- Sense of belonging	
- Initiative to establish significant bonds	

To more clearly convey the complex and multidimensional nature of resilience, we can refer to Polk (1997), who has synthesized four patterns present in the literature regarding individual resilience.

Disposition pattern: this corresponds to the individual's physical and psychosocial attributes that facilitate resilience. These include an individual's aspects that promote a positive attitude towards life's pressures, and could include a sense of autonomy and confidence in oneself, and based sense of self-esteem, good physical health, an average or superior level of intelligence, and a socially valued physical appearance.

Relational pattern: this refers to an individual's role in society and their relationships with others. These roles and their relationships can range from close and intimate relationships to relationships established with the wider social system.

Situational pattern: this corresponds to certain aspects related to the link between an individual and a particular stressful situation. This can include the individual's capacity to resolve problems, to evaluate situations and possible responses, and to take measures in response to a situation.

Philosophical/ideological/religious pattern: this refers to a person's worldview or their life paradigm. This can include different beliefs that promote resilience, such as believing in the positive aspect any experience could have, believing that self-development is important, and believing that life has a purpose.

Most researches haveconsidered resilience to be strictly an individual characteristic. However, it is a multi-layered construct that is not only seen through an individual's capacities but also at different relational levels, ranging from couples, families, and groups, to cities, civilizations, and even international alliances (Cacioppo, Reis & Zautra, 2011).

3.2.4. Family Resilience

Much has been written about resilience in its individual dimension, to the point that the concept is almost understood as a "quality" of special individuals. But the phenomenon is much more dynamic and complex. More recently, studies and theoretical development has begun on the concept of family and community resilience. This has involved a "renewed way of looking at resilience, no longer as personal protective armor but as a relational and ecosystemic gearbox that allows potentially deteriorating or stagnating situations to be identified" (Gómez & Kotliarenco, 2011, p.105).[40]

Although the notion of resilience itself arose in the study of particular individuals, researchers have begun to approach the family as a context for the individual's resilience, and even as a unit of analysis itself (Frankel, Snowden & Nelson, 1992). The importance given to the family in the make-up of resilience has been gradual. Initially, the family was attributed considerable importance but only as a resource for developing the individual's resilience, without strictly addressing family resilience, since the family was merely considered as a context for the individual (Caplan, 1982; Silliman, 1994; Hawley & DeHann, 1996). McCubbin and McCubbin (1988) have developed a set of typologies of resilient families, addressing family as part of the puzzle and not only as a contextual factor, in a way that, from this perspective, it is not individuals but rather the family that plays a central role[41].

---

[40] Translated by the author. In Spanish: "renovada forma de mirar la resiliencia, ya no como una coraza personal de protección, sino como un *engranaje relacional y eco-sistémico* que permite encontrar oportunidades donde podría darse el estancamiento o deterioro."

[41] One can also speak about marital resilience. It has been observed that the married couples who possess significantly more strategies for effectively resolving adversity are couples who have experienced moderate stress during the first months of marriage,

From this approach, family resilience can be defined as:

> Characteristics, dimensions and family properties that help families become resistant to shocks to change and allow them to adapt to crisis situations (McCubbin & McCubbin, 1988, p. 247).

Or, as follows,

> Key processes that allow families to cope more effectively and emerge stronger from the crisis and persistent tensions, either from within or outside the family (Walsh, 1996, p. 263).

Or possibly as,

> A set of processes for reorganizing meaning and behavior activated by a family subjected to stress, in order to recover and maintain optimal levels of functioning and wellbeing, balance resources and family needs, and take advantage of opportunities in their surroundings (Gómez & Kotliarenco, 2011, p. 124[42]).

Research on the strong points of families has been effective in identifying and describing the characteristics of healthy families. These findings have provided valuable guidelines for the development of family strengths, especially in the educational field (Lee & Brage, 1989). However, research in this field has primarily been descriptive and has not possessed a coherent and integrating theoretical framework.

Currently, it is Walsh (1996, 2003, 2004, 2007) who has developed the most comprehensive model of family resilience, around three main components: belief systems; organizational patterns; and communication and problem solving.

Shared belief system: According to Walsh's model, resilient families develop common belief systems that facilitate their growth and recovery after traumatic events through the process of normalizing and contextualizing stress and adversity. This enables a sense of coherence that redefines crisis as a challenge with which it is possible to cope positively on a family level. A belief system that promotes adaptive

---

showing less secondary effects of stress in the future compared to married couples who have had less early stress experiences (Neff & Broady, 2011).

[42] Translated by the autor. In Spanish: "Conjunto de procesos de reorganización de significados y comportamientos que activa una familia sometida a estrés, para recuperar y mantener niveles óptimos de funcionamiento y bienestar, equilibrar recursos y necesidades familiares, y aprovechar las oportunidades de su entorno."

coping with disruptive episodes on a family level requires a positive and realistic perspective of situations. This enables the search for and development of possible alternatives and acceptance of the inevitable. It has been observed that belief systems with these characteristics tend to be linked with family perspectives that integrate transcendence and spirituality as important factors at the moment of assigning meaning to events.

Organizational patterns: Families have organizational patterns that mediate responses to family crisis, adversity, or trauma. Such patterns can mark tendencies towards either mobility or stagnation. Due to the fact that high stress events demand internal restructuring of family systems, flexibility in response to the risk of family dismantlement is seen as a primary resource characteristic of resilient families that are able to reorganize their structure and dynamic to adapt to new challenges brought on by adversity. This capacity for family reorganization has been called connectedness (Walsh 2003, 2004), and involves mutual support and commitment in pursuit of common goals.

The capacity to regulate and balance external support with the use of autonomous resources within the family also plays a central role in a family's adaptive process, since any extreme tendency in this sense could hinder resilient coping.

Communication and problem solving: Lastly, according to Walsh, family resilience involves a series of communicative abilities, such as clarity, characterized by messages and behaviors that are clear, direct, and coherent, along with clarification of the critical situation. Other examples include sincere emotional expression between family members where emotional empathy is of prime importance, tolerance towards differences and negative emotions, communication and intimacy between the parents, and promotion of positive interactions. Finally, notable development of abilities related to cooperative problem solving is also important. This involves identification of problems and related stress factors, the exchange of creative ideas, shared decisions that involve negotiation and reciprocity, and conflict resolution that is achieved through reachable goals, recognizing success, learning from failure, and a proactive posture amongst family members.

3.2.5. Multidimensionality of Resilience

Community and Ecological Resilience:
Resilience has evolved as a construct and increasing attention has been given to the community and, in broad terms, to the environment or ecosystem as a source of protection mechanisms that may be linked to overcoming adversity (Ungar, 2012).

In particular, social support has been observed to be a resource closely linked with resilience, since it would potentially have a moderating effect on the consequences of stress in families, as well as a direct effect on individual and family adaptation. Social support would not be merely a resource for individuals, but also a characteristic of the community itself. A constitutive dimension of resilience has even been considered, since overcoming adversity requires resources beyond the limits of the individual and the immediate family, such as religious communities, the neighborhood, and the work or school environment (Du Pressis, 2001; Cortés & Cruz, 2011).

Community resilience has been defined as the degree of adjustment between individuals or families in relation to the community or environment, in contexts of adversity (Du Pressis, 2001).

The ecological perspective of resilience is the most recent (Ungar, 2012). Distancing itself from individualistic approaches, the complexity and multidimensional nature of this phenomenon and the resources that enable its development are being addressed.

Neurobiological resilience:
As is well known, "the brain is the primary organ for developing and implementing stress response, and therefore is responsible for initiating regulatory control of resilience mechanisms" (D'Alessio, 2010, p. 19, translated by the author[43]). Such mechanisms appear to activate in response to changes induced by stress. To conclude this review of the construct of resilience, it is therefore important that we refer to the neurobiological aspects that have been discovered recently as being involved in this phenomenon, in a general way.

---

[43] In Spanish: "el cerebro es el órgano central en la elaboración y la ejecución de la respuesta al estrés, y por lo tanto, el responsable de la puesta en marcha y del control regulatorio de los mecanismos de resiliencia."

Empirical evidence suggests that determinants of resilience are complex and include social, psychological, and biological (genetic and epigenetic) factors. In resilient individuals, constitutional, biological, and genetic variables interact with learned environmental and behavioral variables to resolve certain adverse situations, avoiding or preventing a psychiatric disorder. We can therefore consider resilience as a complex function or property of biological systems, which operates on different levels or organizational systems of living beings (from the molecular or cellular level to the social and environmental adaptation level). Resilience allows the organism to adapt to situations and permanent change, and makes it possible for the system to return to a prior state of physiological and adaptive functioning when a stress factor inflicts harm or provokes alteration (D'Alessio, 2010, p. 14).[44]

The brain is in charge of implementing all vital functions (cardiovascular, hormonal, metabolic, immunological, etc.) and self-regulates by inducing changes in neurobiological learning mechanisms. All of these responses controlled by the brain, which have been called *allostasis*[45], have the adaptive function of maintaining the organism's

---

[44] Translated by the author. In Spanish: "La evidencia empírica sugiere que los determinantes de la resiliencia son complejos e incluyen factores sociales, psicológicos y biológicos (genéticos y epigenéticos). En los individuos resilientes, las variables constitucionales, biológicas y genéticas interactúan con las variables ambientales y las conductas aprendidas para resolver determinadas situaciones adversas, evitando o previniendo un trastorno psiquiátrico. Podemos entonces considerar a la resiliencia como una función o propiedad compleja de los sistemas biológicos, que opera en los diferentes niveles o sistemas de organización de los seres vivos (desde el nivel molecular y celular hasta el nivel social y de adaptación ambiental). La resiliencia permite al organismo adaptarse a las situaciones y a los cambios permanentes; por un lado, mantiene la homeostasis de las funciones biológicas principales, y por el otro, hace posible que el sistema regrese a un estado previo de funcionamiento fisiológico y adaptativo, cuando un factor estresante provoca daño o alteración."

[45] This concept is closely related to *homeostasis*, which is governed by a series of values that enable a narrow range of variability to be regulated in the organism, and describes mechanisms that keep constant a series of controllable variables on which life depends. In contrast to homeostatic mechanisms, allostatic mechanisms possess much broader values. While the environment's continuity and adequacy are achieved in homeostasis through stability, in allostasis they are achieved through instability and change. Allostatic mechanisms are capable of change within certain instability, by way of biological buffers, so that homeostatic systems remain stable.

dynamic equilibrium. Nonetheless, in response to prolonged or chronic exposure to different stressors, systemic deregulation would take place in certain individuals (some considered more susceptible or less resilient) that would allow normal stress mediating processes to become hyper-activated. This would have maladaptive repercussions for the individual and his/her social environment by overcoming the limit of resilience[46] (though not necessarily definitively), to use the metaphor from the study of material resistance in physics (Toth, et al., 2007; McEwen, 2008).

From a neurobiological perspective, it is observed that early experiences condition the stress response such that genetic, constitutional, and environmental factors would be involved in resilience (D'Alessio, 2010). Examples of this have been observed in experimental models developed with laboratory animals. These have demonstrated that experiences in early postnatal development stages are significant positive conditioning factors for regulating behavioral, emotional, biological, and hormonal stress responses. A notable case of this demonstrates that maternal care favors the development of a higher excitability threshold in the adult animal's stress response, with lower levels of potentially harmful stress hormones such as cortisol and adrenaline.

Neurogenesis (particularly in some areas of the hippocampus) and brain plasticity in general are regulated by a complex system of mediators, neurochemicals that include different types of neurotrans-mitters, hormones and peptides (neurotrophins, opiates) that are affected by severe stress. While some of these mediators are involved in functions of adaptive plasticity and therefore are related to resilience, others may increase the risk of damage (vulnerability). Many of these chemical mediators have been involved in clinical conditions such as depression and anxiety (D'Alessio, 2010).

---

[46] "Elasticity (or resilience) limit: The maximum force that could be applied on an object for it to be able to recover its original shape once the force stops. If excessive force is applied on an object, surpassing the elasticity limit, it will lose its recovery capacity and, as a result, loose its elasticity and we remain deformed." (Lucena, 2006, p. 105, translated by the author). In Spanish: "Límite de elasticidad (o resiliencia): Valor máximo de la fuerza que puede aplicarse a un cuerpo para que este sea capaz de recuperar su forma original al cesar la fuerza. Si se aplica una fuerza excesiva a un cuerpo, sobrepasando el límite de elasticidad, éste perderá la capacidad de recuperación y, en consecuencia perderá su elasticidad y quedará deformado."

Brain tissue has the capacity to permanently change its structure and function. This is known as neuroplasticity[47]. Stress has been shown to affect the plasticity of the hippocampus and the amygdala, provoking changes that have been linked with damage protection functions on the one hand, and the development of psychological disorders (PTSD, depression) on the other. However, not all individuals have the same risk of maladaptive response to prolonged stress, since, as we have seen, some people are more resilient than others in response to the same adversity, due to a wide number and type of factors involved (McEwen, 2001, 2002; Karl & Werner, 2006).

Overlap between psychological and biological findings on resilience in the literature is most apparent for the topic of stress sensitivity, although recent results suggest a crucial role for reward experience in resilience. Today improving the understanding of the links between genetic endowment, environmental impact and gene-environment interactions with developmental psychology and biology is crucial for elucidating the neurobiological and psychological underpinnings of resilience (Rutten, et al., 2013).

Recent research has begun to identify the environmental, genetic, epigenetic and neural mechanisms that underlie resilience, and has shown that resilience is mediated by adaptive changes in several neural circuits involving numerous neurotransmitter and molecular pathways. These changes shape the functioning of the neural circuits that regulate reward, fear, emotion reactivity, and social behaviour, which together are thought to mediate successful coping with stress.

Some psychosocial factors and possible neurobiological underpinnings associated with resilience are as follows (Feder, Nestler & Charney, 2009, p. 447):

Facing fears and active coping: facing fears promotes active coping strategies such as planning and problem solving. The ability to face one's fears might be facilitated by stress inoculation (exposure to tolerable levels of stress) during development, and might be linked to the optimal functioning of fear extinction mechanisms. Active, or

---

[47] This is a term that is difficult to use in reference to resilience, due to being an opposite concept in physical terms. Resilience, as elasticity, refers to the capacity to return to prior form, whereas plasticity implies the maintenance of deformation caused by an external agent.

'fight–flight', responses in animals have been linked to more transient activation of the hypothalamus-pituitary-adrenal (HPA) axis, although the relationship between HPA axis activity and active or passive coping might not be straightforward, as positive associations have also been found. Physical exercise, which can be viewed as a form of active coping, has positive effects on mood, attenuates stress responses and is thought to promote neurogenesis.

Optimism and positive emotions: positive emotions might contribute to healthier cognitive responses and decreased autonomic arousal. Mesolimbic dopamine pathways might be more reward responsive and/or stress resistant in individuals who remain optimistic when faced with trauma. Accordingly, resilience in animals has been related to specific molecular adaptations in the mesolimbic dopamine system.

Cognitive reappraisal, positive reframing and acceptance: cognitive reappraisal involves reinterpreting the meaning of negative stimuli, with a resulting reduction in emotional responses. Resilient individuals might be better at reappraisal or might use reappraisal more frequently. Neurobiological mechanisms that underlie some of these processes include memory suppression, memory consolidation and cognitive control of emotion.

Social competence and social support: social competence and openness to social support promote resilience in children and adults. Mutual cooperation is associated with activation of brain reward circuits. Oxytocin enhances the reward value of social attachments and reduces fear responses. Future research might identify potential differences in these measures in resilient individuals.

Purpose in life, a moral compass, meaning and spirituality: a sense of purpose and an internal framework of beliefs about right and wrong are characteristic of resilient individuals. Religious and spiritual beliefs and practices might also facilitate recovery and finding meaning after trauma. Brain imaging studies are beginning to identify the neural correlates of human morality.

Along this line, recent research has begun to identify the environmental, genetic, epigenetic and neural mechanisms that underlie resilience and has shown that resilience is mediated by adaptive changes in several neural circuits involving numerous neurotransmitter and molecular pathways. These changes shape the functioning of the neural circuits that regulate reward, fear, emotion reactivity and social behavior that together are thought to mediate successful coping with stress (Feder, Nestler & Charney, 2009; Boivin & Giordani, 2013).

3.3. Resources for Rebuilding After Trauma (Posttraumatic Growth)

Not only so, but we also glory in our sufferings,
because we know that suffering produces perseverance;
perseverance, character; and character, hope.
Apostle Paul, *Romans 5:3-4*

3.3.1. Definition

The concept of posttraumatic growth is closely related to resilience. If we understand resilience as the capacity to move forward and recover the state prior to the adverse experience, posttraumatic growth particularly emphasizes the fact that many people subjected to traumatic events not only replenish themselves and are able to recover, but also learn much from traumatic experiences and are positively strengthened upon overcoming them, moving beyond previous levels of personal development (Calhoun & Tedeschi, 1999).

Tedeschi and Calhoun (2000, 2008) have identified some results of what would be posttraumatic growth itself, such as, for example: an increased appreciation of life's value; an increase in personal strength; strengthening of personal relationships, particularly the most significant ones; appreciation of new possibilities that life offers; and positive changes in the spiritual level.

Posttraumatic growth is seen from various models as a process of constructing and reconstructing the traumatic event's meaning. This can encompass specific situations or life experiences as a whole and involves developing capacity to positively cope with similar or different future adversity (Acero, 2011).

The potentially traumatizing events may become traumatic experiences. In that case they yield negative emotions and high stress aspart of the definition of traumatization. But impactful events are not always traumatizing (hardiness) and thus negative emotions and high stress may not occur. On the other hand, a state of intense suffering is not incompatible with posttraumatic growth. On the contrary, it has been found that in many cases posttraumatic growth does not happen without the presence of negative emotions (Calhoun & Tedeschi, 1999). As Acero declares (2008), posttraumatic growth does not eliminate suffering, but rather tends to coexist with it. But it is hopeful to confirm data that indicates that 60% of people who recognize some negative effect of the traumatic event are capable of recognizing a positive effect of the same experience on their lives. The posttraumatic growth perspective is an approach that does not seek to change the basic idea of traumatic situations' negative character, but rather to see if it is possible to find non-negative elements (Pérez Sales, 2006).

> Going through a traumatic experience is perhaps one of the situations that most contributes to a person's life. Without neglecting the severity, seriousness, and horror of these experiences, we cannot forget that it is in extreme situations when human beings have the opportunity to return to constructing their ways of understanding the world and their belief systems, in a way that this reconstruction can lead to learning and personal growth (Vera, Carbelo & Vecina, 2006, p. 47).[48]

3.3.2. Characteristics

In a review of the literature, various authors that study the positive effects of traumatic situations (rape, incest, grief, cancer, HIV, heart attacks, disasters, combat, etc.) group them in three categories (Calhoun & Tedeschi, 1999, 2001, 2004a, 2004b, 2008; Vera, et al., 2006; Pérez Sales, 2006; Acero, 2008, 2011):

---

[48] Translated by the author. In Spanish: "Vivir una experiencia traumática es quizá una de las situaciones que más aportan a la vida de una persona. Sin quitar un ápice de la severidad, gravedad y horror de estas vivencias, no podemos olvidar que es en situaciones extremas cuando el ser humano tiene la oportunidad de volver a construir su forma de entender el mundo y su sistema de valores, de manera que en esta reconstrucción puede darse un aprendizaje y un crecimiento personal."

Changes in the perception of oneself: This is the tendency to feel stronger, more reaffirmed in oneself, with more experience and more capacity to confront future difficulty.

Changes in interpersonal relationships: This is the tendency to describe that friends or family have grown closer after the event. The death of a family member, for example, can have an impact in increasing the amount of time dedicated to being together. Further, the need to share what happened, discuss it, and seek explanation can also cause other people to open up and share feelings, to accept the help of others, and to use social support more.

Changes in life philosophy and spirituality: The tendency to appreciate what one has and value details more. After a traumatic event, an important percent of people changes their scale of values, giving priority to other aspects, taking life more seriously, and enjoying the small things more. Although some people feel that their religious beliefs break down, for many it involves a rediscovery or strengthening of their faith, which in turn could result in increased personal security, feeling of control, and meaning of life.

With respect to the last type of change mentioned that is observed in people that exhibit posttraumatic growth (life philosophy and spirituality), Acero (2008, p.7) informs us from his clinical experience that:

> In working with parents whose children have died or with people that have experience kidnapping or have lost a limp from exploding landmines in Colombia, experience itself has particularly allowed us to see that spirituality is one of the areas individuals most report changes in overtime, despite the fact that spirituality is one of the areas they see as most challenged. This is because people tend to reconsider their initial value scale and learn to see life in a more transcendent way.

According to the results of meta-analysis of more than 100 investigations on posttraumatic growth carried out by Prati and Pietrantoni (2009), we can say that some of the factors most associated with posttraumatic growth are optimism, social support, spirituality, and coping modalities centered on acceptance, reconsideration, religious experience, and seeking support. Among these, positive reevaluation of the event and religious-type coping are observed as more statistically significant. However, the authors concluded that these coping strategies would promote posttraumatic growth to the extent that active efforts arise to confront the problem or resulting emotions.

Below we outline the primary factors and their respective correlations regarding posttraumatic growth, according to the discussion carried out by Linley and Joseph (2004) as well as Prati and Pietrantoni (2009):

Social support: A moderate relationship between social support and posttraumatic growth has been observed. Social support would promote a more favorable assessment of the event and more effective coping strategies. It would also contribute to the formation of alternative narratives of the events that facilitate change of schemas and integration of traumatic events. In this topic, active search for social support is related to an increase in quantity and quality of social support for the affected individual. Tedeschi and Calhoun (2004b) propose that the degree to which individuals are involved in revealing information concerning their emotions about the traumatic event, and how others respond, can play an important role in posttraumatic growth. In longitudinal studies, one of the best predictors of posttraumatic growth in longitudinal studies is emotional expression. Generally, regarding the importance of emotional expression, studies have found positive relationships between PTG and self-revelation (Tedeschi & Calhoun, 2004b; Schexnaildre, 2011), social support (Tedeschi & Calhoun, 1996; Prati & Pietrantoni, 2009) and social sharing (Páez, Martínez & Rimé, 2004; Páez, Basabe, Ubillos & Gonzalez, 2007; Gasparre, Bosco & Bellelli, 2010).

Optimism: This has been presented with a moderate relation to posttraumatic growth. According to Prati and Pietrantoni (2009) research on the topic provides diverse data. In some investigations a close relationship is seen, and in others a looser relationship. Optimism would promote growth through its effects on threat assessment and facilitating adaptive strategies (positive reevaluation, active coping, and seeking social support), as indicated by various authors (Schaefer & Moos, 1998; Wagner, Knaevelsrud & Maercker, 2007).

Spirituality: This has been shown to have a moderate relation with positive changes at the root of traumatic crisis. Spirituality can promote posttraumatic growth by providing a sense of community or community support and beliefs that favor the process of creating positive meaning to integrate adverse experiences. Cadell, Regehr, and Hemsworth (2003) affirm that spirituality and/or religiosity plays an important role in creating meaning and transformational coping. Pargament, et al. (2004), propose that factors explaining the beneficial effect of spirituality include health variables (for example, healthcare practices and immune response), psychological variables (for example, coherence and self-esteem), and social variables (for example, social support and sense of community). Changes in spirituality or religiosity can play a vital role in the individual's posttraumatic growth and understanding (O'Rourke, Tallman & Altmaier, 2008). Some clinical and neuroimaging results suggest that patients with PTSD experience difficulty in synthesizing traumatic experience in a complete and coherent narrative. Religiosity and spirituality correspond to an experience strongly based in the personal search of understanding in response to life's questions and meaning. Narrative constructions based on healthy perspectives facilitate the integration of traumatic sensorial fragments into a new affective and cognitive synthesis, thus reducing posttraumatic symptoms (Peres, et al., 2007).

Religious coping: This modality is closely related to the above, but has been highlighted in the meta-analysis of Ano and Vasconcelles (2005) and of Prati and Pietrantoni (2009) as being one of the strongest characteristics for predicting posttraumatic growth. Two types of religious coping have been distinguished. One is positive and reflects confidence in a relationship with a transcendent force (e.g., God), a sense of spiritual connection with others, and a vision of the world as good. In contrast, negative religious coping methods may reflect underlying spiritual tensions (e.g., demonic struggles) and important conflicts within oneself, with others, and with the divine (Pargament, 1997; Pargament, Feuille & Burdzy, 2011). However, religious experience and practice is not only a factor affecting the way in which adverse events are coped, but rather a bidirectional reciprocal influence would exist between coping and religion (Ganzevoort, 1998a, 1998b). Positive and negative forms of religious coping are respectively related with positive and negative psychological adjustment to stress. Nevertheless, religious coping, closely related to spirituality, refers to specific modes of religion as a resource for dealing with and overcoming adversity, as well as mediating the interpretation of different high or low stress events. Religious coping helps to provide meaning to the experience and a sense of control over life situations, provides psychological wellbeing in complex situations, gives intimacy and support between members of the faith community, and helps people make important life changes.

3.3.3. Resources for Posttraumatic Growth and its Factors

Following Vázquez, Castilla and Hervás (2009) in their outline of factors and resources involved in posttraumatic growth, we can highlight the following:

Characteristics of the traumatic event: As we have already mentioned, the personal interpretation or meaning a traumatic event possesses is fundamental for coping and recovery. However, as Tedeschi and Calhoun (2004a, 2004b) have proposed, posttraumatic growth would have the particular characteristic of arising after what these authors have called seismic situations (Calhoun & Tedeschi, 1998), which means their intensity is quantitatively and qualitatively so high that they involve collapse in various areas of life. This could trigger a process of recomposition or reconstruction played out in what has been called posttraumatic growth, which are states of personal development with significant qualitative changes in subjective well-being after experiencing a traumatic event. Along these lines, results of recent investigations could be interpreted as indicating a statistically significant relationship between PTSD diagnosis and high posttraumatic growth levels (Lindstrom, et al., 2011), and traumatic events that challenge an individual's fundamental beliefs have been seen to be among the main predictors of posttraumatic growth (Loiselle, et al., 2011).

Sociodemographic variables: Some researchers have considered this variable to be generally inconsistent (Linley & Joseph, 2004). Regarding the relationship between gender and posttraumatic growth, even though consistent results in research do not exist at the moment, a tendency to consider that women present higher rates has been observed in the literature (Tedeschi & Calhoun, 1996; Tallman, et al., 2010). Regarding age, some authors suggest younger people are more likely to exhibit posttraumatic growth, particularly due to cognitive flexibility in regards to themselves and the world (Powell, et al., 2003). There still have been no investigations carried out that provide significant data regarding other sociodemographic variables.

Personal traits: Different personal variables have been associated as predictors of growth experienced by people exposed to adverse situations, but no credible data exist. Among these personal variables is a certain tendency towards extroversion, openness to new experiences, proactive disposition, problem-focused coping strategies, prevalence of positive emotions, the capacity for emotional expression, and optimism (Tedeschi & Calhoun, 2004a; Vázquez, Hervás & Pérez; Tallman, et al., 2010; Loiselle, et al., 2011).

Expressing affection: Some studies have demonstrated that affective expression, particularly through writing, facilitates posttraumatic growth (Ullrich & Lutgendorf, 2002; Fernández Sedano & Pennebaker, 2011). This would be directly related with social support received, perceived, and sought by the individual exposed to trauma, as we indicated previously, according to the studies of Prati and Pietrantoni (2009). In cases where parents who have lost a child, having people to tell about an experience was found to be beneficial for their mood at 18 months, and was even positively associated with posttraumatic growth after this period (Nolen-Hoeksema & Davis, 1999; cf. Nolen-Hoeksema, Wisco & Lyubomirsky, 2008).

Cognitive factors: Reviews of various investigations regarding studies on possible positive posttraumatic consequences have indicated that cognitive variables would be most significant, such as: the capacity for threat assessment, problem-focused coping, and optimism (Linley and Joseph, 2004). Rumination, intrusive images and thoughts, and avoidance, at least in the initial trauma stage, have been observed to be significantly associated with high posttraumatic growth, despite involving unpleasant emotions (Ullrich & Lutgendorf, 2002; Hogan & Schmidt, 2002). Accordingly, some have affirmed that posttraumatic growth is a result of attempts to restore some useful cognitive guidelines for living (Tedeschi & Calhoun, 2004).

3.3.4. Theoretical Models of Posttraumatic Growth (PTG)

With reference to the phenomenon of PTG, we could highlight two main perspectives: its conceptualization as a result of struggle with a traumatic event, (Schaefer & Moos, 1992, 1998, Tedeschi & Calhoun, 1995, 2004a) and its form of coping understood as a process (Affleck & Tennen, 1996).

Models of PTG as a Result:

When PTG is understood as a result of coping with trauma, it denotes a beneficial and significant change on the individual's entire life, and could be considered as an "antithesis" to Posttraumatic Stress Disorder (PTSD). However, this is not the case, since the two concepts describe independent phenomena and cannot be considered as two extremes of one continuum, as adaptation/maladaptation to trauma would be. In this sense, it is important to understand that the domains of PTG are distinct from those that could be considered as general emotional adjustment. PTG is not the same as simple increased wellbeing or diminished anxiety (Tedeschi & Calhoun, 2004a). Growth and emotional distress can coexist.

PTG is seen as a type of sub-product of attempts to confront a traumatic event, and involves considering its result in greater terms than those present before the event, or not equal (resilience), or inferior (disorder such as depression, addiction, or PTSD). In this vein, O'Leary & Ickovics (1995) describe three possible results after coping with a traumatic event: a) returning to the historic functioning level (recuperation); b) an inferior level (survival); or c) a higher functioning level (prosperity).

Schaefer and Moos (1998) developed one of the most representative models of this approach to PTG.

It is the most general and classic model, and is formulated from a general approach to coping. It is quite complex since it includes environmental factors (personal relationships, social support, economic resources) as well as personal factors (sociodemographic characteristics, resilience, optimism, previous experience). According to this proposal, both groups of factors are affecting the way life crises are experimented, which is to say they would determine the processes of cognitive evaluation and the type of coping employed, which in turn would determine the crisis' repercussions, including possible PTG. In addition to environmental and personal factors, these authors also highlight the importance of factors related to the event (effects of the crisis' severity, duration, moment, and impact on the individual) (Vázquez, Castilla & Hervás, 2009, pp. 34-35).[49]

Perhaps the most representative model of this approach to PTG was developed by Tedeschi and Calhoun (1995, 2004a). These authors conceptualized the growth process as follows. A traumatic event, which is an event of "seismic" proportions, removes or destroys some key elements of an individual's important objectives and vision of the world. This represents a higher-order challenge to objectives, beliefs, and the emotional capacity for managing distress. Distress initiates a recurring and complex reflection process that seeks to develop behavior that allows the distress to diminish. At first, rumination is more automatic than deliberate; it is characterized by the frequent return to thinking and reliving related aspects of trauma. After the first success of the adaptive process, rumination transforms into a more deliberate reflection on trauma and its impact on personal life. Cognitive processes related to analyzing the new situation, searching for meaning, and reevaluating what occurred would play a key role in developing personal growth. In this way, PTG is conceptualized as a multidimensional construct that includes changes in beliefs, objectives, behaviors, and personal identity along with development of a new life story, increased wisdom, and maturity. Social support and a certain degree of permanent discomfort are central variables at the beginning of

---

[49] Translated by the author. In Spanish: "Es el modelo más general y clásico, y está elaborado desde una aproximación general de afrontamiento. Es bastante completo ya que incluye tanto *factores ambientales* (relaciones personales, apoyo social, recursos económicos) como *factores personales* (características socio-demográficas, resiliencia, optimismo, experiencias previas). Según esta propuesta, ambos grupos de factores estarían afectando la forma de experimentar las crisis vitales, es decir, determinarían los procesos de evaluación cognitiva y el tipo de afrontamiento empleados, los cuales a su vez estarían determinando las repercusiones de la crisis, incluyendo un posible CPT. Además de los factores ambientales y personales, estos autores también destacan la importancia de los *factores relacionados con el acontecimiento* (efectos de la gravedad, duración, el momento de la crisis y su alcance en el sujeto)"

the process enabling PTG, and they influence the achievement of PTG as a result. Factors related to personal characteristics before the trauma, beliefs, and personal objectives are also highlighted, such as deliberate rumination, changes in cognitive schemas, and the development of a new life narrative (Zoellner & Maercker, 2006).

Models of PTG as a Process:

> Authors that present posttraumatic growth as a process suggest that finding benefits or personal development experiences in a traumatic context can have positive effects on the process of overcoming the trauma. Therefore, perceiving benefit would in reality be one more element of the process, which along with others would enable the event be given meaning and thus be adaptively assimilated (Vázquez, Castilla & Hervás, 2009, p. 32).[50]

Within the approaches that address PTG as a process, that is, as a type of coping strategy for managing severe stress, we find Taylor's perspective (1983). Taylor proposed that positive assessment is a central element in cognitive adaptation to threatening events. From his perspective, PTG ends up being a type of positive illusion (Taylor & Armor, 1996) that includes self-aggrandizement, unrealistic optimism, and exaggerated perceptions of control, associated with successful adjustment to stressful events, including extremely adverse conditions.

Davis, Nolen-Hoeksema, and Larson (1998), for their part, have interpreted PTG as a particular conceptualization of meaning, recognizing that in the marked Western tendency to believe that major life events are controllable, intelligible, and nonrandom (Kelley, 1972), the role of constructing meaning after loss or traumatic events would be fundamental for coping. In this perspective, PTG would be a particular way of assigning meaning to extreme stress events. The authors (Davis, et al., 1998) propose that research has paid too much attention to causal attribution ("why did it happen?") as opposed to other important

---

[50] Translated by the author. In Spanish: "Los autores que plantean el crecimiento postraumático como un proceso sugieren que encontrar beneficios o experiencias de desarrollo personal en el contexto de una situación traumática puede tener efectos positivos sobre el proceso de superación de dicha experiencia. Por tanto, la percepción de beneficio sería en realidad un elemento más del proceso, que junto con otros, permitirían dotar de sentido al acontecimiento y así asimilarlo de forma adaptativa."

conceptualizations of meaning, such as benefit attribution ("what for?").

Park and Folkman (1997) propose another model in this vein, distinguishing between the situational and global meaning in the conception of meaning in contexts of stress and coping. According to them, global meaning encompasses an individual's hard beliefs and the objectives he/she values. Situational meaning, on the other hand, gives shape to the interaction between an individual's global meaning and the specific circumstances he/she must cope with. A traumatic event would threaten global meaning, which would initiate a meaning creation process that involves looking for the traumatic event's benefits, changing the situation's meaning to accommodate it to the global meaning, or modifying, for example, the philosophy of life in ways that would involve lasting changes in global meaning.

Filipp (1999) develops a conception of PTG as an interpretive process that would involve a specific way of processing information when coping with traumatic events. According to this author, people face loss and trauma by passing through three processes. First, during the first two weeks immediately after a traumatic experience, people talk and think openly about the event. After this would come an inhibition stage lasting approximately six weeks, where individuals stop talking about the event but continue thinking about it. After this, people normally enter an adaptation phase in which they do not talk or think about the event, assuming a more or less satisfactory interpret-tation of the event (Pennebaker & Haber, 1993). This model coincides with the stages of posttraumatic coping and PTSD treatment described by S. Noy (2004): Alert; Impact; and Posttrauma.

The process and factors present in the development of PTG are varied and differ in some measure depending on the model of interpreting this phenomenon. Nevertheless, there are some common assumptions, among which the following are highlighted (Zoeller & Maercker, 2006): a) The degree of exposure to a traumatic event is linked with PTG, which is to say, developing PTG would be in cases of severe trauma principally; b) In PTG, traumatic experience has a devastating effect on the individual's predominant belief system. The individual's worldview is challenged and invalidated by their traumatic experience; c) Because of the trauma, the individual exhibiting PTG begins to reconstruct meaning of the event, as well as his/her value systems, from the experience; d) PTG is a multidimensional construct that incorporates a set of changes in the individual's perceptions of his/herself, the world, and his/her social interactions with family and friends; and e) PTG is produced with time and can reflect different adjustment patterns at different moments.

3.3.5. Suffering, Coping, and Growth

It is important to clarify that discomfort and growth may coexist in the experience of posttraumatic growth. The experience of learning or growth does not necessarily override suffering, but rather can coexist with it. Negative emotions resulting from the traumatic experience can turn out to be important elements for the growth process when experienced simultaneously (Calhoun & Tedeschi, 1999, 2008; Fernández-Abascal, 2007).

In PTG we face the possibility of a radical disruption of the individual's experience, involving an equally radical reconstruction, since, upon considering the possibilities for development opened up from the trauma, one can downplay the high costs for the individual and his/her environment such that the profound suffering could be involved with, and coexist in, such learning.

Research on the matter has found results that concur with the coexistence mentioned between discomfort and growth. Studies have discovered a positive correlation between PTSD and PTG (McCaslin, et al., 2009; Hafstad, et al., 2010; Kilmer & Gil-Rivas, 2010); between subjective severity and PTG (García, et al., 2014); and between subjective severity and PTSD (Morris, et al., 2005; Boals & Schuettler, 2009).

In breaking down fundamental assumptions that have given coherence and meaning to life, trauma itself initiates processes that can lead to both PTSD and PTG (Calhoun & Tedeschi, 1998, 2004a).

Distinction between Resilience and PTG:
To make a distinction between these two important constructs, it is important to consider how they are defined. Defining resilience as the capacity to learn from an adverse experience and remake oneself or be

transformed (Grotberg 1995) coincides with the basic elements present in the concept of PTG. In contrast, defining resilience as positive adaptation in a context of risk and adversity (Cutuli & Masten 2009) or as the capacity to move forward in difficult times and lift oneself up and continue after a fall (Driver, 2011), important differences arise between the concepts, differences that are reflected in studies addressing the topic.

The study carried out by Levine et al. (2009) in Israel, with adolescents exposed to terrorism and members of the military, gives us evidence on the difference between resilience and PTG as independent concepts. Despite being two constructs that allude to a trauma's aftermath in a positive way, they represent different processes. In this investigation, resilience was conceptualized as the act of moving past an adverse experience without mental health problems and, therefore, significant changes. In contrast, PTG was described as the ability to change after the adversity or trauma, in such a way that an event that sufficiently disrupts the course of survival would involve reconfiguring life's meaning and coherence. According to this conceptualization, resilient individuals do not pass through a period of major dysfunction after a traumatic event, but rather remain at functional levels despite it, without experiencing significant psychopathological symptoms. On the other hand, PTG does not only refer to maintaining prior functionality, but to personal, social, and/or transcendent development beyond the previous state (Calhoun & Tedeschi, 2000).

The evidence concerning the effect of PTG on psychological adjustment in the medium and long terms indicates that PTG is associated in the majority of studies with greater emotional adjustment. This was observed in a review of Tennen and Afleck (2005) where this association is present in 14 studies out of 20. In the same vein, a meta-analysis carried out by Helgeson, Reynolds and Tomich (2006) found that a greater level of PTG was associated with lower levels of depression and a greater level of psychological wellbeing. These results coincide with a review of longitudinal studies carried out by Zoellner and Maercker (2006), where PTG was observed to predict lower levels of depression and PTSD in the long term.

Finally, we can mention that across studies the results show that the interrelationships between resilience (defined by a lack of posttraumatic stress disorder following trauma) and posttraumatic growth with high levels of resilience were associated with the lowest posttraumatic growth scores. Although growth and resilience are both salutogenic constructs they would be inversely related (Hobfoll, et al., 2007).

Having carried out a review of the principle contributions and perspectives from Psychology with respect to trauma, giving special attention to positive coping, in the next chapter we will concentrate on an exegetical study of four selected passages in 2 Corintians that deal with this topic.

3.4. Religious Coping

> *When pain is to be born,*
> *a little courage helps more than much knowledge,*
> *a little human sympathy more than much courage,*
> *and the least tincture of the love of God more than all.*
> C.S. Lewis

Although not necessarily considered as a positive coping resource for trauma, below, to conclude this chapter, we will briefly examine the topic of religious coping. This will be one of the most important concepts and research fields for our discussion in subsequent chapters, where we will seek to develop a practical-theological understanding of positive coping with trauma.

3.4.1. Religion, Faith, and Trauma

By nature, human beings constantly seek to position themselves in an environment that for them makes sense, has meaning, and is coherent. This stems from their superior cognitive abilities that respond to the complexity of their nervous systems. However, the difficulty of this continuous attempt to configure the surplus of meaning associated with a natural environment is augmented when the wealth of stimuli unique to a social and cultural environment that require interpretation is added to the mix.

Human experience, which is constitutively hermeneutical, is constantly put to the test, especially when one's life or integrity (or that of someone close) is at risk, or in other words, when faced with a traumatic event. Traumatic events, therefore, are an arduous test of the experiential continuity of people, both as individuals and as a group. And it is in this context that the study of the religious phenomenon has a significant connotation. The religious experience presents itself as a relevant factor in the search for life's narrative coherence and as a hermeneutical modality for assigning meaning to events, especially to those that are the most disruptive or traumatic (Cruz-Villalobos, 2014a).

In Rudolf Otto's classic treatise about the experience of the sacred entitled *The Idea of the Holy* (1917/1980), he addresses and defines the concept of the sacred as that which is *numinous*[51], or in other words, that which one experiences in a non-rational and non-sensory way. This involves feeling something that is overwhelmingly powerful, tremendous, terrifying, and/or fascinating, and whose primary and immediate object is outside the self of the one who experiences it.

The numinous would be manifested in the individual as an absolutely dependent conscience, not merely as a personal, self-referred condition, but rather as an upheaval that involves the whole person and re-directs him/her towards something or someone that transcends them, that is above their individual reality. Along these lines fits Tillich's (1976-1982) definition of the faith experience, which is understood as the state of experiencing an ultimate or fundamental preoccupation or concern.

Humans, like all living beings, concern themselves with many things, especially those that biologically condition their own existence. However, differently than other living beings, humans also experience more abstract concerns, of a cognitive, esthetic, social, political, and religious nature. The urgency of these needs can be varied, and can present different priorities. In life, a person will always tend to attach to one need as fundamental or ultimate. This demands complete and total commitment to fully fulfill that need, even if it requires submission to the need or rejection of all other concerns such that they are no longer considered preliminary (Tillich, 1976).

---

[51] Neologism used by R. Otto to refer to the experience of the sacred.

Whatever that fundamental concern may be, what is accepted in the act of faith is not only the unconditional demand of that which is experienced as a concern but also the promise of ultimate fulfillment. In this way, faith understood as such is a uniquely human experience that involves the whole person and every one of his/her circumstances, since faith, as the ultimate concern, is an act done at the center of personal life and includes all of its elements. In fact, we can say that faith, understood in this way, is an individual's most personal act, which always involves the way in which he/she seeks meaning in the midst of continuous disruption in the human experience, as notably occurs when coping with adverse or traumatic experiences. Such experiences are those that drastically disrupt the basic assumptions that enable understanding and integration of human life as an experience of coherent and significant continuity.

In light of the above, it is not strange to say that one of the most common ways that people confront adverse circumstances or traumatic events is through religious and/or spiritual practices. And it is in the field of the psychology of religion that the positive and negative effects of this coping style have begun to be widely studied (Pargament, 1997; Pargament, Koenig & Perez, 2000; Trevino & Pargament, 2007).

3.4.2. Research on Religious Coping Methods

Research on religious coping has examined cases related to extreme events involving violence and natural disasters where people witness or are directly exposed to a drastic risk to their personal integrity. Research also shows that people use religious coping to deal with stress factors present in daily life, and not necessarily in traumatic situations. Religion appears as a factor that expresses the way in which a person conceives of his or her life and articulates the meaning and coherence of their experience in connection to the sacred and their ultimate concern.

From the perspective of coping theory, religion can be understood as a dynamic transaction process between the individual and his/her life situations within a wider sociocultural context (Pargament, 1997). The majority of theories and researchers focused on coping in general have ignored the religious dimension, in response to which Kenneth I. Pargament (1990, 1996, 1997) has developed one of the most complete theories of religious coping. In his works, he has defined the aspects of religious coping as efforts undertaken by people in order to understand and deal with stressful factors in life in reference to the sacred.

> Pargament's theory stresses several points: 1) religious coping serves multiple functions, including the search for meaning, intimacy with others, identity, control, anxiety-reduction, transformation, as well as the search for the sacred or spirituality itself; 2) religious coping is multi-modal: it involves behaviors, emotions, relationships, and cognitions; 3) religious coping is a dynamic process that changes over time, context, and circumstances; 4) religious coping is multi-valent: it is a process leading to helpful or harmful outcomes, and thus, research on religious coping acknowledges both the "bitter and the sweet" of religious life; 5) religious coping may add a distinctive dimension to the coping process by virtue of its unique concern about sacred matters; and 6) because of its distinctive focus on the ways religion expresses itself in particular life situations, religious coping may add vital information to our understanding of religion and its links to health and well-being, especially among people facing critical problems in life (Pargament, Feuille & Burdzy, 2011, pp. 52-53).

3.4.3. Types of Religious Coping

Leading researchers tend to divide religious coping into two different outcomes: positive religious coping and negative religious coping. The first has been observed to be significantly correlated with greater levels of posttraumatic adaptation than the second. In general terms, it has been observed that people who employ positive religious coping methods are inclined to seek spiritual support and try to articulate meaning in traumatic situations. Conversely, people who employ negative religious coping methods tend to experience adverse events as times of conflict (or spiritual warfare), question themselves frequently in response to what occurred, and doubt about things related God and faith (Pargament, 1997).

In 1988, Pargament and his colleagues identified three basic styles of religious coping to stress: a) the collaborative religious coping style that involves active and interiorized personal interaction with God, where both the individual and God have a predominant role; b) the deferring religious coping style, in which individuals depend on God and delegate to him all personal responsibility for confronting the stressful situation; c) the self-directing religious coping style, where the person assumes that it is God's will that they be proactive and participate responsibly in the resolution of their problem.

In terms of the clinical effectiveness of these religious coping styles, it has been observed that the collaborative style presents greater advantages for people (Phillips III, et al., 2004).

Pargament developed a research tool (the RCOPE scale) for measuring religious coping, with which he has been able to precisely describe an important number of methods that he classifies as follows (Pargament, Feuille & Burdzy, 2011, p. 56):

1. Religious Methods of Coping to Find Meaning:

1.1. Benevolent Religious Reappraisal: Redefining the stressor through religion as benevolent and potentially beneficial.

1.2. Punishing God Reappraisal: Redefining the stressor as a punishment from God for the individual's sins.

1.3. Demonic Reappraisal: Redefining the stressor as an act of the devil.

1.4. Reappraisal of God's Powers: Redefining God's power to influence the stressful situation.

2. Religious Methods of Coping to Gain Control:

2.1. Collaborative Religious Coping: Seeking control through a problem solving partnership with God.

2.2. Active Religious Surrender: An active giving up of control to God in coping.

2.3. Passive Religious Deferral: Passive waiting for God to control the situation.

2.4. Pleading for Direct Intercession: Seeking control indirectly by pleading to God for a miracle or divine intercession.

2.5. Self-Directing Religious Coping: Seeking control directly through individual initiative rather than help from God.

3. *Religious Methods of Coping to Gain Comfort and Closeness to God:*

3.1. Seeking Spiritual Support: Searching for comfort and reassurance through God's love and care.

3.2. Religious Focus: Engaging in religious activities to shift focus from the stressor.

3.3. Religious Purification: Searching for spiritual cleansing through religious actions.

3.4. Spiritual Connection: Experiencing a sense of connectedness with forces that transcend the individual.

3.5. Spiritual Discontent: Expressing confusion and dissatisfaction with God's relationship to the individual in the stressful situation.

3.6. Marking Religious Boundaries: Clearly demarcating acceptable from unacceptable religious behavior and remaining within religious boundaries.

4. *Religious Methods of Coping to Gain Intimacy with Others and Closeness to God:*

4.1. Seeking Support from Clergy or Members: Searching for comfort and reassurance through the love and care of congregation members and clergy.

4.2. Religious Helping: Attempting to provide spiritual support and comfort to others.

4.3. Interpersonal Religious Discontent: Expressing confusion and dissatisfaction with the relationship of clergy or congregation members to the individual in the stressful situation.

5. *Religious Methods of Coping to Achieve a Life Transformation:*

5.1. Seeking Religious Direction: Looking to religion for assistance in finding a new direction for living when the old one may no longer be viable.

5.2. Religious Conversion: Looking to religion for a radical change in life.

5.3. Religious Forgiving: Looking to religion for help in shifting to a state of peace from the anger, hurt, and fear associated with an offense.

A meta-analysis of 49 studies on religion as a coping style (Ano & Vanzoncelles, 2005), identified which of the above listed coping methods could be considered to be significantly positive. Among them were Religious Purification (3.3); Spiritual Connection (3.4); Seeking Support from Clergy or Members (4.1); Religious Conversion (5.2); and Religious Forgiving (5.3).

The same study identified the religious coping strategies that are significantly negative, which were Punish God Reappraisal (1.2); Reappraisal of God's Powers (1.4); Pleading for Direct Intercession (2.4); Spiritual Discontent (3.5).

The study also identified forms of positive psychological adjustment that are strongly correlated with positive religious coping methods, including: acceptance, happiness, optimism, and having a purpose in life. Conversely, forms of negative psychological adjustment strongly correlated with negative religious coping methods were also identified, including: anxiety, burden, negative mood, and callousness.

More recently, Pargament and his collaborators (2011, p. 57) indicated that the two types of religious coping can be characterized, in synthesis, as follows:

Positive Religious Coping:

1. Looked for a stronger connection with God.
2. Sought God's love and care.
3. Sought help from God in letting go of my anger.
4. Tried to put my plans into action together with God.
5. Tried to see how God might be trying to strengthen me in this situation.
6. Asked forgiveness for my sins.
7. Focused on religion to stop worrying about my problems.

Negative Religious Coping:

8. Wondered whether God had abandoned me.
9. Felt punished by God for my lack of devotion.
10. Wondered what I did for God to punish me.
11. Questioned God's love for me.
12. Wondered whether my church had abandoned me.

13. Decided the devil made this happen.

14. Questioned the power of God.

Pargament (1990) identifies three possible interactions between religion and coping: a) religion can be a part of all elements of the coping process (appraisal, coping activities, outcomes, support, and motivation); b) religion can contribute to the coping process in terms of preventing certain subsequent events or consequences (through the lifestyle of the person participating in the religion), and influencing the way the events are interpreted or perceived. (attributing meaning; sense of control); c) religion can be significantly affected by the coping process (inverse of the two previous interactions).

3.4.4. Reformulations of Religious Coping

Religious coping, despite having been described so clearly by Pargament, has subsequently been reformulated as a more complex, multidimensional phenomenon. This is because up until recently, studies on the subject have placed their emphasis on the interaction between religion and coping in a unidirectional way, that is, how religion affects coping responses. Despite the fact that it has been theoretically recognized that religion could be affected by experiences of coping with adverse situations, in the research field this has been neglected.

R. Ruard Ganzevoort (1998a, 1998b) emphasized the multidimensional character of religious coping. In his reform-lation of this research field he indicates that dimensions related to the influence of traumatic events on religiosity, as well as the dimensions of personal identity and social context, are highly relevant and important for understanding this phenomenon. Additionally, the same author affirms that each of these dimensions should be conceptualized as a dynamic process, and the phenomenon should be understood in all its multifaceted complexity, where religion is also seen as a biological process that includes all aspects of human life. Such research that is limited to studying certain religious convictions, feelings or specific actions cannot do justice to the rich variety of religious experience.

Research in psychology of religion frequently reveals different outcomes between religion and spirituality. A person's religion is seen as a set of belief systems and moral values, often developed in an institutional context, under an assumed common tradition. Religion is generally more organized and formal than spirituality, and with more sociological elements. Spirituality, in contrast, is more private and intimate, and expresses one's own intrinsic relationship with the sacred. In the study of the psychology of coping, religion and spirituality can play very different roles (Paloutzian & Park, 2005).

Pargament (1997) makes a distinction between people that are: a) religious and spiritual; b) religious and not spiritual; c) spiritual and not religious; and d) not religious and not spiritual. According to Pargament, significantly better outcomes for adaptation in the face of adversity have been observed in people in the religious and spiritual group, and worse outcomes have been observed in the religious and not spiritual group. Non-significant effects have been seen in the spiritual and not religious group, and inconclusive outcomes have been observed in the not religious and not spiritual group. Along these lines, spirituality without a specific religious expression does not show to produce positive outcomes as a coping style, but religiosity without active spirituality produces negative consequences. Some research, however, suggests that spirituality itself is relevant as a help for dealing with high-stress situations (Vespa, etc al., 2011).

The effectiveness of religion and spirituality as coping mechanisms is still a subject for discussion. In fact, today there are divergent proposals that point towards the negative effects of religion itself (Fiala, 2009). However, a great body of research has been published that make evident a general positive effect that religion/spirituality (especially religious participation and practices regarding to positive religious coping) has on variables related to health, such as: minor depression, quicker recovery from depressive episodes, lower suicide rates, less substance use, abuse and dependence, lower rates of heart disease and hypertension, a better functioning immunological system, a better functioning endocrine system, lower cancer rates, better prognosis in cancer cases, lifespan, better self-reported wellbeing, and happiness (meaning of life, hope, optimism, and forgiveness). There is a great deal of evidence for the effectiveness of positive religious aspects for many people, both those who suffer from illness, disability, or disaster as well as their caretakers. Religion and spirituality have consistently been identified as factors that can aid in the recovery from adverse events (Koenig & Cohen, 2002; Pargament, et al., 2004; Oman & Thoresen, 2005; Moreira-Almeida, Neto & Koenig, 2006; Harris, et al., 2008; Hood, Hill & Spilka, 2009; Huguelet & Koenig, 2009; Yoffe, 2012, 2013; Koenig, 2012, 2015; Koenig et al, 2015; Lassi & Mugnaini, 2015; Mollica, et al., 2016).

Chapter 4
Suffering and Coping in the Bible

No one said a word to him,

because they saw how great his suffering was.

Job 2:13b

Suffering is understood as the perception or interpretation of pain, whose polysemy is affected by many different personal and contextual factors (Morris, 1996, 2015; Cruz-Villalobos, 2014a, 2014b). Some of the most relevant contextual factors in coping with adversity are religious. The various religious and wisdom traditions make known the great number of different ways suffering can possibly be interpreted. These interpretations make up an important part of coping mechanisms employed when a traumatic event is experienced (Riggs, 2006; Villega Besora, 2006; Eisen & Laderman, 2007).

Religions have always been linked with the themes of pain, suffering, the attribution of meaning to suffering, and attempts to manage them. For example, this is observed in religions such as Buddhism, where suffering is central to its way of understanding the world and its practices of liberation[52].

Suffering also plays an important role in Christianity, beginning with the central Christian icon of the cross and the violent death of its primary figure, Jesus Christ, as well as the importance of the resurrection as victory over death and as a fundamental event in the Christian faith (1 Cor 1:17-18; 15).

Human suffering, whether experienced as physical pain, or as intense mental or emotional discomfort, is addressed throughout the Bible. The Old Testament (OT), the intertiestamental literature, and the New Testament (NT) do not share a unified position on the matter, but instead present multiple and varied perspectives that we will briefly and in a general way summarize below (written in such a way

---

[52] In fact, the Four Truths focus primarily on the theme of suffering and overcoming suffering, as the base for understanding existence. The Four Noble Truths are: 1) The Truth of Suffering: existence is suffering; 2) The Truth of the Cause of Suffering: desire, attachment, and ignorance are the causes of suffering; 3) The Truth of the End of Suffering: humans can experience a state of consciousness that is free of suffering (nirvana); 4) The Truth of the Path that Leads to the End of Suffering: this path is called the Noble Eightfold Path (Rueda & Zabaleta, 2006).

that it serves as an introduction for readers more familiar with psychology than with Christian theology), referencing various authors specialized in the topic (Brueggemann, 1985, 1986; Wallace, 1991; Smith, 1996; 2002; Inbody, 1997; Laato & de Moor, 2003; Crenshaw, 2005; Ehrman, 2009; Brueggemann & Linafelt, 2012).

4.1. Old Testament Perspectives

In accounts of Genesis (3-4), human suffering is shown as a reality that arises in the context of the defective condition in which creation ends up as a result of human disobedience. In this sense, suffering is an intruder in the created world, which initially "was very good" (Gen 1:31). Along these lines, Old Testament prophets speak of a future time when suffering in creation will be eliminated. Often they describe a future reality of new international wellbeing (Is 11:6-9; 25:6-9; 65:17-25; Hosea 2:21; Amos 9:11-15; cf. Rom 8:18-25; Rev 22:1-5; cf. Smith, 1996).

Personal and national suffering being caused by sin is an explanation that is present throughout the OT. It is observed in the judgement of God on entire peoples for not respecting his plan for morality, with retributive justice being a predominant factor (Deut 27-28; Prov 2:21-22; 3:33-34; 11:27-28; 24:19-20; Jonah; Ez 25: 8-17; Is 21; Jer 50-51). Books such as Esther, Lamentations, and Judges can be read as key examples of the principle of retribution. However, the situation of Israel is shown to be unique, because God, in his faithfulness, had promised to the patriarchs that he would never destroy the nation, despite its sin, although he would discipline it for its disobedience (Lev 26:42; Psalm 106:40-46; cf. Brueggemann, 2007; Routledge, 2013).

Standing in contrast to the idea of retribution is the problem of the suffering of the righteous and the innocent. This gives rise to theodicy which seeks to "justify God" and attempt to find meaning in misfortune and suffering that is compatible with the goodness and omnipotence of God[53].

---

[53] The topic of theodicy is vast, and to this day continues to be a matter of great debate. Here we will not delve deeply into this discussion, which has taken place primarily within the philosophy of religion, ethics, and systematic theology. We will only make general reference to the ways Scripture addresses the topic. For more on contemporary philosophical and theological reflection on theodicy, see: Howard-Snyder, 1996; Laato &

Although in a way that is neither explanatory nor abstract, the OT addresses suffering in situations where retribution is complex and problematic, and offers at least three types of justification for the suffering of the righteous and/or innocent. As laid out by Smith (1996), these include the following.

Eschatological justification: God's retributive justice is postponed and suffering is seen as a stage specifically established according to the divine calendar that plays a purifying role in the life of the righteous who will be vindicated at the end of times as martyrs that suffered and/or lost their life for their holy testimony (Dan 11:35; 12).

Corrective justification: The suffering of the righteous is reparative or corrective, in that God disciplines the righteous person for the purpose of keeping their hearts steadfast and in line with his will (Prov 3:11-12; Ps 94:12; Dan 11:35).

Justification of atonement: Suffering is a vicarious and redemptive experience, no matter if it is experienced collectively or individually[54] (Is 42; 44; 49; 50; 52; 53).

In a special way, the book of Job questions the usual ways that retributive justice is interpreted, where suffering and bad things in life are seen as the result of moral evil on the personal and/or communal level. The suffering of the righteous for no apparent reason is the primary topic central to the book of Job. Job suffers in extreme ways, but nevertheless is presented as righteous. His friends appear on the scene (in the middle poetic section that occupies most of the book), defending the principle of retributive justice and concluding that Job cannot be innocent, as he insists, if he is suffering in such a way. From the narrative introduction, the reader knows that Job's friends are wrong and, therefore, Job does not lie about his moral condition that God finally confirms in the final narrative section. However, the

---

de Moor, 2003; Berthold, 2004; Cristaudo, 2008; Matustik, 2008; Neuhouser, 2008; Theide, 2008; Bergmann, Murray & Rea, 2011; Ellens, 2011; Poma, 2013. There is also psychology of religion literature on theodicy, which links it directly to for example the fundamental assumptions theory of Janoff-Bulman (1992). And in the practical theological field there have also been stydies in this line, such as: Van der Ven & Vossen (1995); Vossen (1993); Vermeer, Van der Ven & Vossen (1996, 1997); Hutchison, Greer & Ciarrocchi (1999).

[54] This form of justification is mostly applied in the NT interpretation of the death of Jesus as Messiah (e.g. Mt 1:21; Rom 3:19ss; John 3:16-17)

motives and reasoning behind Job's suffering and ruin are never explained to him, although the narrative section at the beginning of the book notes the influence and power granted to an angelic adversary (*Satan*) to cause the disasters. God appears to Job without offering explanations, only asking him a series of rhetorical questions designed to make it clear that there are many things that exist beyond human understanding. Suffering is presented as a mystery. Job accepts his suffering without questioning God's wisdom, righteousness, or justice, and God ends up "restoring" everything he had lost (Job 42; cf. Alonso Schökel, 1971; Léveque, 1987; Gutiérrez, 1995; Dell & Kynes, 2012; Balentine, 2015).

The book of Ecclesiastes also questions the causal relationship between justice and wellbeing in life. The text proposes that the destinies of the righteous and the ungodly are the opposite of what they should be, and that this part of life's absurdity and lack of sense is one more example that everything is vanity (*hebel*). Here, human suffering can be thought of as a meaningless experience, that it is only a vanity of vanities[55], along with being an inherent reality of the human condition (7:15; 8:14; 12:13-14; cf. Alonso Schökel, 1996; Vilchez-Lindez, 1995; Seow, 1997; Rudman, 2001; Christianson, 2005, 2007).

4.2. Intertestamental Perspectives

In the intertestamental literature, personal and collective suffering is also addressed from various perspectives that we will discuss below, referencing various authors (Paul, 1978; Diez-Macho, 1984; Aranda-Pérez, García-Martínez & Pérez-Fernández, 1996; Smith, 1996; Neusner & Avery-Peck, 2003).

Intertestamental texts present suffering as the inherent quality of a fallen world, and describe a future where Israel will be restored to a state of total prosperity through the intervention of a messianic figure who will establish the kingdom of God, which is characterized by the absence of suffering under the government of the righteous and just.

---

[55] As Alonso Schökel (1996) points out, the phrase "*vanity of vanities*" (Ecc 1:2; 12:8, KJV) that frames the book is a superlative. The term *hebel* means breath, or something without substance, emptiness, space, nothing. It can be translated as a light breath, a whisper, or more, complete emptiness, total meaninglessness, nothingness.

There are also several texts that show the image of a personified agent of evil who is seen as one of the causes contributing to the condition of human life. The final defeat of this source of evil also involves the end of suffering. (Pss Sol 17; 1 En 10:13-16;; T Dan 5:10-11).

The notion that national calamity originates from sin is also prominent in intertestamental literature (2 Macc 6:13-16; 7:32-38; Jub 23; T Mos 8; 2 Bar 78:3-4). However, eschatological hope is observed in intertestamental texts that speak of a final vindication of the people of Israel, in some cases, at the hands of a Messiah (1 En 90,; T Mos 8-10).

Regarding alternative ways of understanding the suffering of the righteous, intertestamental literature mainly assumes the same postures as the OT, with the eschatological argument being observed in various texts. With God's retributive justice towards the ungodly being postponed, the righteous momentarily suffer unjustly in this life. They are called on to be patient and to persevere in their suffering, while placing hope in God's eschatological justice and salvation that will be manifest in the end. The advent of the final salvation and blessing of the righteous will come after suffering increases to the most drastic levels. In turn, the ungodly will be punished and destroyed (2 Macc 6-7; 1 En 100:1-3; 107; 2 En 50:1-6; 51:3-5; 65:6-11; 4 Ezra 9:1-6;; 2 Bar 15:7-8; 44:13-14; 70-71; Jub 23).

The corrective function of the suffering of the righteous is also observed in intertestamental literature. Perseverance and purity are stimulated by adversity, because the righteous desire to maintain the benefits of righteousness, whether in this life or the next, through their faithfulness. Along these lines, the righteous that suffer penalties should have an attitude of acceptance, patience, and even joy in response to God's treatment of them as a father that rigorously disciplines and forms his sons and daughters (Pss Sol 10:1-2; 13:9-10; 16:1-11; Jud 8:27).

Finally, the atoning interpretation of the suffering of the righteous is also found in the intertestamental literature, but not with messianic allusions as clear as those found in the OT (4 Macc 1:11; 6:29; 17:21; T Mos 9:6-10:1).

4.3. New Testament Perspectives

In briefly reviewing the ways in which the NT addresses the topic of suffering, we can acknowledge that they follow similar lines to those that we find in intertestamental texts and the OT, as we will see below.

In his letter to the Romans, Paul suggests that all of creation is subject to degradation or progressive ruin (*phthora*), groaning as in the pains of childbirth, awaiting its final liberation (Rom 8:19-22). He also attributes the current dominion of death ("the last enemy", 1 Cor 15:26) to the effects of Adam's sin, that impacts all humanity. Christ's death and resurrection came to intervene in this human condition by making possible its definitive transformation at the end of times (Rom 5:12-17; 1 Cor 15:20-22).

An eschatological vision is seen in the NT similar to that which is found in OT prophetic texts that speak of a new heaven and a new earth (2 Pet 3:13; Rev 21:1). The NT also presents a perspective that personifies evil and attributes to it an important role in causing human suffering (Mark 9:14-27; Luke 9:37-43; Eph 6:11-12; 1 Pet 5:8-9).

In contrast to the OT and the intertestamental texts, the NT places strong emphasis on Jesus' victory over adversity, even death, recognizing him as the Messiah. He is seen as the one who brings the kingdom of God to the world, as well as the progressive abolition of death's dominion that culminates in complete, eternal, and final good in his second coming. In this way, stories of healings and exorcisms told in the gospels can be read as signs of a spiritual assault on the prevailing evil (Mat 12:25-29; Mark 3:23-27; Luke 10:18-20; 11:17-22; John 12:31; 16:11). Along these lines, the authors of Ephesians and Colossians write about the exaltation of Christ over all the powers of the present age (Eph 1:19-22; Col 2:15), and they describe believers as those who can resist and overcome those powers, since they have been rescued from the dominion of darkness and brought into the kingdom of the Son (Col 1:13).

The notion that national suffering is a consequence of disobedience to God seems to continue in the NT. Jesus warns that Israel's rejection of the kingdom of God will bring the wrath of God on the Nation (Mark 12:1-12; Mat 12:38-45; 21:33-46; 23:33-38; Luke 11:29-32; 19:41-44; 20:9-19). Cities are also in danger of judgement for rejecting Jesus or his emissaries (Mat 11:20-24; Luke 10:13-15). Similarly, Paul believes that the nation of Israel is temporarily rejected by God until the Gentiles are fully included (Rom 11).

The OT, the intertestamental texts, and the NT share an understanding of the suffering of the righteous. The perspective of suffering as a corrective experience is addressed in various passages of the NT such as in Hebrews 12:3-13, where the author cites Proverbs 3:11-12. For its part, the book of James identifies trials and temptations as means to develop perseverance (*hupomone* in believers (Jam 1:2-3), a perspective also proposed in 1 Peter 1:3-9. In the Pauline texts, we also see the idea that God uses suffering and adversity as a means of disciplining or sanctifying believers in order to enact change for good (*metanoia*) in their lives (1 Cor 5:1-8; 2 Cor 11:17-33), just as can be observed in latter writings such as 1 Timothy 1:20.

On the other hand, and mainly in Paul's letters, an interpretation of Jesus' passion and death is emphasized from a perspective of atonement[56] (Rom 3:19-26; Gal 2:16-21; 1 Cor 15:3-22). For their part, the Synoptic Gospels also show a Jesus that interprets his death as atoning and vicarious. At the Last Supper, Jesus is identified as the Passover lamb (Mat 26:26-28; Mark 14:22-24; Luke 22:19-20), and also as the suffering savior of Deutero-Isaiah (Mat 20:28; Mark 10:45; Luke 22:37; Is 53). In line with some passages in Acts and 1 Peter, we can also see that the first generation of Christians interpreted Jesus' suffering and death as an atoning sacrifice (Acts 8:32-33; 1 Pet 2:21-25).

One of the most prominent perspectives on suffering in the NT alludes to its eschatological character. For example, in the Beatitudes, both Matthew and Luke write that the arrival of God's kingdom will bring about an eschatological inversion[57], where the righteous who presently suffer will not suffer in the end, and those that enjoy the present times will be punished (Mat 5:3-12; Lc 6:20-26).

---

[56] Here we will not delve into the extensive discussion about the concept of "justification" as it relates to the death of Jesus Christ, which Pauline experts often focus on (Sanders, 1974; Dunn, 1990, 1998, 2008; Crossan & Reed, 2004; Borg & Crossan, 2009; Wright, 2002, 2005, 2009, 2013a, 2013b), since we are only interested in briefly referencing interpretations of suffering.

[57] Very much in line with the motif of *anyata*, as a classic literary topic.

Among the teachings of Jesus, we can also highlight the warnings given to his disciples about suffering as a constant element of following Him, until the kingdom of God is fully established. Those that follow Christ, particularly those that proclaim the Good News, will face resistance, hostility, and persecution by those who are opposed to God's kingdom, especially when the end is near. In this way, suffering is presented as being inevitable for the sons and daughters of God's kingdom (Mat 10:19-23; Luke 12:11; Mat 20:22-23; Mark 10:38-39; Mat 24:9-10; Mark 13:9-11 Luke 21:12-18; John 7:6-11; 15:18-25; 17:14). This eschatological understanding of suffering is also found in other parts of the NT (Rom 8:16-18; al 3:3-4; Phil 1:27-30; 1 Thes 1-3; 2 Thes 1:4-10; Heb 10:32-34; Jam 5:11; 1 Pet 2:18-20; 3:13-4:19; Rev 2:10; 4.22).

Another way of interpreting suffering is found in Pauline writings related to God's discipline of God's people. As an Apostle of Jesus Christ, Paul interprets his suffering in part as a way of ensuring awareness of his own weakness and dependence on God, since only in the midst of weakness and powerlessness can the power of the Lord be seen more clearly (2 Cor 1:8-10; 4:7-12). Paul states that God sent him a "thorn in [his] flesh, a messenger of Satan" so that he wouldn't become conceited because of his great revelations (2 Cor 12:7)[58].

Suffering can also take on new meaning for members of the body of Christ, the community of Christian faith. This is because it offers believers an opportunity to share in the sufferings of their Lord (2 Cor 1:5ss; Rom 8:17; Mar 10:39). Thus believers consider themselves bound in a certain way to the suffering produced by sin, knowing that they will participate in the coming glory (Phil 1:29, 3:10; Rom 8:29; 1 Pet 4:1-2).

4.4. Synthesis of Perspectives

The interpretive perspectives on suffering that we can identify in Scripture, following Vossen and Van der Ven (1995, pp. 18-19) include:

The retaliation model. This model is concerned with the view that God sends suffering as a punishment for sin. God is represented as

---

[58] Here we only briefly refer to 2 Corinthians, as this and other paragraphs will be the focus of study later in this work.

absolute-transcendent, as a distant supreme judge, sitting on high well above the weal and woe of humankind. The emphasis is placed on his omnipotence, which enables him to guide human reality and to cause suffering where people have deserved it.

The plan model, containing an absolute transcendent view of God, in which God determines world and human events to realize his intentions. It can be seen as an answer to the problem of innocent suffering, which the retaliation model raises. A God who regulates everything according to a certain (hidden) plan also has more distance than proximity to the tragedy of human suffering. Only later or at the end of time, or in a broader perspective, it will appear that all happened for the good.

The therapy model, which holds a midway position between the absolute and immanent-transcendent models. Suffering is seen as an instrument for the personal growth and development of man: suffering teaches and chastens. God is less distant than in the first two models, because the suffering finally has an experienced positive effect on the sufferer. Yet, God's proximity is restricted, because the positive experience is one 'after the event'; during the suffering God is at a great distance.

The compassion model, here all traces of a causative relation between absolute-trascendent and God and suffering have disappeared. The image of God is no longer absolute-transcendent and God's omnipotence is pushed into the margin to make room for his love. In this model suffering is a mystery, senseless in itself, and God is only close to the sufferer in pity.

The vicarious suffering model, here too God is immanent-transcendent. Rooted in the image of the suffering servant of deutero-Isaiah, God is the close inspirer to self-sacrifice for the benefit of others. God's love is broadened here from the 'dyadic' love between the suffering individual and God to the solidarity bond of with suffering humanity.

The mystical model portrays suffering as a way to intensify the intimate relation between God and man. God does not 'use' suffering in this: there is not a bit of absolute-transcendent manipulation by God of human reality. But within the mystery of suffering, humans may experience a longing for complete and intimate unity with God.[59]

In the next section, we will describe our hermeneutic methodological framework and introduce the study, life and work of Paul, to later focus on Pauline writings that address suffering and coping more broadly and directly, such as 2 Corinthians.

---

[59] Other attempts at synthesis can also be seen in these authors: Smith, 2002; Laato & de Moor, 2003; Crenshaw, 2005; Villegas Besora, 2006; Ehrman, 2009

Chapter 5
Approaching the Study of Paul

I will show him [Paul]
how much he must suffer for my name.
Acts 9:16

In this chapter we will make an introduction to the study of Paul and his letters that allows us to locate ourselves in the broader context of his second letter to the Christians of Corinth, thus initiating our explanatory or exegetical approach that will soon be deepened by addressing the selected paragraphs.

5.1. Approaching Paul

Our study now turns to the Bible, the ancient text of Christian wisdom. We will study select writings by one of the most relevant and noteworthy authors of this book. Without a doubt, Paul is one of the most relevant figures in Christian history. For many, he is second only to Jesus, given that his life and work have drawn so much interest since very early on. With detractors and followers, the Apostle Paul is one of the most outstanding characters in the New Testament, in addition to being one of its primary authors (Küng, 1995; Brown, Fitzmyer & Murphy, 2004).

The study of Paul, his life, and his ideas has been extensive throughout the history of Christianity, and particularly in the last quarter century, as we will see later. It is also worth mentioning the notable interest in Paul found in the works by authors fundamentally connected to the field of philosophy. This is seen in both contemporary authors and those from the last century, who have seen Paul's ideas as a rich source of discussion about various topics: from the ontological and epistemological to matters of politics and current public events (Deleuze, 1993; Badiou, 1999; Žižek, 2001, 2005; Heidegger, 2005; Agamben, 2006; Taubes, 2007; Caputo & Alcoff, 2009; Hinkelammert, 2013).

Our interest in Paul is not related to his life, work, or theology in general terms. Rather, we will focus on finding and understanding hermeneutical keys present in the mechanisms for coping with difficult

145

situations and traumatic events found in certain passages of 2 Corinthians.

Coping with adversity is a recurring theme in Scripture, as we saw in Chapter 4. While the example of Paul is one of many, it nevertheless is of great importance to us since his writings are among the few in the Bible that can be considered autobiographical, with a reasonable degree of certainty. These writings also make specific reference to personal suffering and coping. We are also dealing with a person of flesh and bones, full of conflict and struggles, who is vulnerable and tenacious at the same time. In this way, Paul presents himself to us as a close reference, not as a superior and idealized Messiah who is perfect in the fulfilment of his work and defeats death itself, but rather as just one more follower of Jesus, who was able to recover from serious difficulty and become stronger.

How did Paul do it? What does he tell us in his letters about the real possibility of moving on from extreme adversity? How did he theologically guide and pastor the communities he oversaw through such relevant and often urgent topics such as facing life threatening challenges? These questions arise when considering the facts that we have about the Apostle's life and work.

The book of Acts has been quite heavily questioned as to whether it is a trustworthy source about the events of Paul's life, given that it is eminently more theological than historical in nature. In this way, experts tend to methodologically place less value on texts written after the authentic Pauline letters when referring to facts about Paul's life, and even his original thinking (Fitzmyer, 1972; Munphy-O'Connor, 1991, 2004; Sánchez Bosch, 1998; Agamben, 2006). In our case, these letters will be the base reference. However, it is appropriate for our line of research to notice how in Acts the Lord said to Ananias about Saul, "Go! This man is my chosen instrument to proclaim my name to the Gentiles and their kings and to the people of Israel. I will show him how much he must suffer for my name" (Acts 9:15-16). As we will see in detail when we review the list of ailments Paul describes, particularly in 2 Corinthians, his life as a Christian was marked by suffering, which on many occasions involved grave danger to his physical safety and imminent risk to his life.

It is easy to fall into idealizing Paul as a tireless minister of the Gospel, with brilliant intelligence and courageous initiative, leaving in

146

the background the severity of his sufferings (as we will see in detail in the specific chapters on 2 Corinthians). But the Apostle himself mentioned in his letters how difficult it was to serve the Lord, as we observe in the lists of his sufferings laid out in his letters (1 Cor 4:9-11; 2 Cor 4:8-10; 6:4-10; 11:23-33; 12:10; Rom 8:35-36). Understanding these confessions allows us to enter into Paul's experience just as he wanted, as he himself said to the Corinthians, "We do not want you to be uninformed, brothers and sisters, about the troubles we experienced" (2 Cor 1:8).

In different aspects, Paul's life and ministry was marked by suffering: suffering from failure and betrayal; from illness and physical exhaustion; and from persecution, punishment, and hardship experienced for preaching the Gospel, in various places and circumstances. Events that are today categorized as traumatic were abundant in the Apostle's life. One cannot say that Paul liked to dwell on the critical situations that he went through. This painful aspect of his life was not of central or excessive interest to him. However, as we have mentioned, various passages in his letters inform us about the specific nature of the difficult situations he had to suffer and deal with (Debergé, 2005).

In line with what we have discussed in previous chapters regarding traumatic events and the different processes involved in coping with them, Paul's case is of great interest to us, since the autobiographical accounts found in his letters present us with explicit testimony of how this Apostle faced adverse experience and how he guided early Christian communities in how they could cope with such circumstances.

Our exploration of parts of 2 Corinthians, chosen for various important reasons as we explained in the introduction of this work, will be conducted in a progressive manner, first establishing the writings in their broadest context, to then approach them with an informed perspective and delve carefully into their message.

In the following chapter, we will introduce some aspects of Paul and his work. We will mention various perspectives for study that exist, and we will perform a general overview of his letters, placing special emphasis on his correspondence with the Corinthians.

There are two main sources of information about Paul as a historical figure: his own letters, and the Acts of the Apostles. As we mentioned before, the latter has been questioned as a reliable historic source, considering that it is fundamentally theological in nature more than it is historical. To reconstruct his story, most Pauline specialists have relied on information derived from his own letters,[60] and not later texts (Bornkamm, 1978; Murphy-O'Connor, 1996, 2004; Porter, 1999, 2004, 2009).

In general terms, Paul's body of work is a small collection of letters. NT specialists agree that at least seven of these letters are authentic, which together are often referred to as the Undisputed Letters, or "authentic Pauline letters". These letters can be classified in three chronological subgroups in the following way. The First Letter (50-51 AD): 1 Thessalonians; The Intermediary Letters (in the mid-50s AD): 1 Corinthians, 2 Corinthians, Philippians, Philemon, and Gala-tians; and The Last Letter (57-58 AD): Romans. There are also six "Disputed Letters", also called the "Deutero-Pauline Letters", about which experts are divided regarding their authenticity. These are: 2 Thessalo-nians, Ephesians, and Colossians (whose authenticity is the most debated), and Titus, 1 Timothy, and 2 Timothy. These last four letters are widely considered to be not authentic (pseudepi-graphical), probably written by some of his disciples at the end of the first century, or by a "Pauline school" that sought to adapt Paul's message to new contexts (Bornkamm, 1978; Porter, 2002, 2004; Brown, 2004; Harding, 2004; Brown, Fitzmyer & Murphy, 2004; Vanni, 2006; Stamps, 2007).

One of the primary sources about Paul's life is the autobiographical paragraph of Philippians 3:5-6. There the Apostle reveals numerous facts about his life, including that he: a) was circumcised on the eighth day according to the Law (Lev 12:3); b) was of the people of Israel, meaning he was ethnically an Israelite by birth; c) was from the tribe of Benjamin, which means he knew that his tribe descended from a son of Jacob born in Palestine; d) was a Hebrew of Hebrews, which for some specialists could be a linguistic distinction for a Jew that knew Hebrew (or Aramaic), or rather, a designation for a

---

[60] For a more in-depth comparison, see the table presented by Brown (2004, pp. 560-1), where he draws a parallel between two undisputed letters and Acts in regards to Paul's life from his "conversion" until his (planned) visit to Rome. It is noteworthy, as Bornkamm notes (1979), that Luke never mentions Paul's letters in his account, which might indicate that at the time Acts was written there still was not a collection of authorized letters that would have been disseminated throughout most of the church.

descendent of Jews that spoke the language; e) was a Pharisee by training and attention to the Law, being a member of one of the most rigorous and fundamentalist Jewish sects of the time; f) persecuted the church, showing that he went above and beyond what was normally required, to the point of zealously fighting to protect his faith from those who threatened it; g) a follower of the laws of the Torah, who perceived himself as extremely rigorous and publicly unimpeachable (Murphy-O'Connor, 2004; Heil, 2010).

As highlighted by Porter (2009), Paul mentions some of these facts elsewhere in his letters, and adds new details. For example, in Romans 11:1, the Apostle mentions that he is an Israelite, a descendant of Abraham, from the tribe of Benjamin (just as he affirms that he is a Jew in Galatians 2:15). In 1 Corinthians 15:9, he recognizes that he persecuted the church. In 2 Corinthians 11:2, he affirms that he is Hebrew, an Israelite, and a descendent of Abraham. In Galatians 1:13-14, he notes that he was a persecutor of the church, zealous for the traditions of his fathers. And in Galatians 1:23, he mentions that there were people in the church who were suspicious of him for having been a persecutor.

Although Paul was a Jew, which today is not questioned but instead has even been emphasized in new currents of research about the Apostle and his thinking (which we will address shortly), he was undoubtedly also a man of Greek culture. He lived within and under the influence of the Greco-Roman world, at various levels. His letters are written in Greek, he quoted the Greek Old Testament frequently in his letters, and he used the classic structure of Greco-Roman letters (Sampley, 2008).

The detail given to us by Acts that he was born in the city of Tarsus in Cilicia (Acts 22:3), which unfortunately is not corroborated in Paul's letters, gives us a plausible panoramic understanding about the type of culture that the Apostle could have had. Tarsus was known as one of the most important academic centers of the era, along with Athens and Alexandria, especially for its traditions in philosophy and education (particularly stoical). If Paul was educated there, before going to Jerusalem for his training as a Pharisee, this could explain his sophisticated use of Greek (Murphy-O'Connor, 2004; Porter, 2006b).

Paul, as a Jew of the diaspora, was a person marked by multi-culturalism and multilingualism. Acts, though not confirmed in the

Pauline letters, states that Paul was a Roman citizen in addition to being a citizen of Tarsus (Acts 16:37; 22:25-28). Although several scholars have doubted the Apostle's Roman citizenship, none doubt his belonging to Roman society and culture, which is evident in his writings and facilitated his work as a missionary. Especially in the last thirty years of his life, Paul was a tireless traveler of the Mediterranean, which was possible thanks to the political context governed by the Empire (*Pax Romana*). The Empire's transport modes and routes allowed for the virtual unification of the territory and expedited connectivity between its main regions. It also leant a certain level of religious tolerance that helped enable a Jew of the diaspora like Paul to travel freely through maritime and overland routes available throughout the imperial territory (Den Heyer, 2000; Schnelle, 2003; Sampley, 2008; Porter, 2009).

Various worlds collide in Paul. Studying him is a great challenge that evokes all the complexity of a personality and body of work that is so loved and so critiqued as his. As we have shown, the Apostle of the Gentiles belonged to two civilizations, the Jewish and the Greco-Roman. In the NT, he is presented as a man of intense character, who is not easy to live with when the mission is at stake: Mark, Barnabas, the Corinthians, the Galatians, and many others knew it from personal experience (Cothenet, 1985).

There is a great body of research that attempts to give account of Paul's life, though many authors have not come to a consensus on specific dates and facts. Comparative chronological tables exist, but we will not focus our attention on them in this dissertation (Fitzmyer, 1972; Bornkamm, 1978; Holzner, 1989; Murphy-O'Connor, 1996; Brown, 2002; Brown, Fitzmyer & Murphy, 2004; Freed, 2005). Here we will only highlight some relevant facts and events found in his letters:

Paul talks about his life as a Jew: "For you have heard of my previous way of life in Judaism [...] I was advancing in Judaism beyond many of my own age among my people and was extremely zealous for the traditions of my fathers (Gal 1:13-14; cf. 2 Cor 11:22; Rom 11:1; Phil 3:4-6).

Paul persecuted the followers of the Jesus movement: "For you have heard of my previous way of life in Judaism, how intensely I persecuted the church of God and tried to destroy it (Gal 1:13; cf. Gal 1:23; 1 Cor 15:9; Phil 3:6).

Paul had a special religious experience, typically called a "conversion". He describes this experience as "a revelation from Jesus Christ" and says that God "was pleased to reveal his Son in me" (Gal 1:12, 15-16; cf. 1 Cor. 9,1; 15.8).

Paul believed that God had called him to preach his Son "among the Gentiles" (Gal 1:15-16; 2:2, 8-10), a mission clearly emphasized by Paul (1 Thes 2:16; Rom 1:5, 13; 2:24; 11:11-25; 15:7-27; 16:26).

Paul intended to arrive in Rome on his way to Spain (Rom 15:22-33; cf. 1:8-15).

5.2. Interpretations of Paul

There are twenty-seven books in the New Testament, thirteen of which are attributed to Paul. If we include the book of Acts, where Paul is one of the main characters throughout most of the text, it turns out that half of the NT books are associated directly with the life and thought of this man. Notwithstanding Paul's prominence in Christian canon and history, the interpretation of his words, both in his authentic letters and in dispute, has been the source of many important discussions. His words have been and continue to be complicated to understand, resulting in varied interpretations, just as the author of 2 Peter says:

> Bear in mind that our Lord's patience means salvation, just as our dear brother Paul also wrote you with the wisdom that God gave him. He writes the same way in all his letters, speaking in them of these matters. His letters contain some things that are hard to understand, which ignorant and unstable people distort, as they do the other Scriptures, to their own destruction (2 Pet 3:15-16).

At the time 2 Peter was written, it appears that there was already a collection of Pauline epistles with an accepted level of relevance "like the rest of the Scriptures". Additionally, it seems they were interpreted in diverse ways (in "distorted" (gr. *streblousin*) ways in some cases) and were difficult to understand. Here we cannot conduct a detailed review of the history of the ways that Pauline texts have been interpreted, but we will briefly focus on some of the most relevant points on the topic that are presently being discussed.

Studies about Paul have been abundant and have generated great discussion, especially in recent decades. Old points of consensus have been questioned, and new perspectives on central aspects of Pauline thinking have emerged, together with new methodological approaches in research. Problematic issues have been raised regarding the nature of Paul's theology, the rhetoric of his writings, and the social analysis of his churches. Specific criticisms have also been developed from, for example, feminist and postcolonial perspectives of his messages (Bassler, 2010).

One of the most important theological questions that makes it possible to even talk about a Pauline theology as such, was raised by the Pauline Theology Group (1986-1995) of the Society of Biblical Literature, which questioned the application of systematic theology to Paul's theological thought. This was because, when talking about a Pauline theology in a systematic sense, an artificial harmonization came about that produced a theological viewpoint that was coherent, but based on arbitrary selections of Paul's ideas (Bassler, 1991; Hay, 1993; Bassler, Hay & Johnson, 1995; Hay & Johnson, 1997).

Paul was a fervent and intelligent writer, but he did not develop a theological system in line with the dogma of recent centuries. In theological terms, Paul developed a highly contextual discourse, responding to the needs of the communities he pastored. In different contingencies, he gives specific responses, that could even be seen as contradicting each other, much to the dismay of many who study his theology today. In this way, since the only information available in his letters are contingent expressions, the possibility of an internally coherent theological core should be considered very carefully, and for some authors, should be newly reconstructed from its own context (Sanders, 1983; Borg & Crossan, 2009; Bassler, 2010).

As Bassler (2010) observes, discussion about what constitutes the core of Pauline theology has been arduous, regarding whether it is an integrated set of beliefs and convictions, or a theology that emerges in specific given circumstances, and since contingencies change, it was always a work in progress, a theology in continuous development without a set nucleus.

Beyond these questions about Paul's theology as a conceptual whole, some specific aspects of his thinking have also been vigorously debated to the present day. Perhaps the most emblematic example, one that resulted in the formation of a new and later well-developed perspective, came out of the publication of *Paul and Palestinian Judaism* by Sanders (1977), a work that opened the debate about the Apostle's Jewish character, with an emphasis not seen in the work of specialists until then[61].

Discussions about Paul and his writings have not only addressed content, but have also focused on more formal dimensions, taking an interest that goes beyond what the Apostle said and looking at *how* he said it, or the ways he laid out his reasoning. The first studies along these lines sought to make relevant connections between Pauline writings and Greco-Roman rhetorical conventions. They descriptively classified the letters by their formal structure and predominant kind of rhetoric used, managing to clearly situate Paul in the primarily oral culture to which he belonged (Betz, 1979; Watson, 2010).

Later works have been increasingly more complex in their analysis and conclusions. There, rhetorical criticism has illustrated the richness of the authentic Pauline texts and the thematic and compositional unity or diversity of some letters (e.g., 1 Cor and 2 Cor), and has also attempted to reconstruct some of their intended readers. They have examined the Apostle's strategies to persuade and the use of certain power dynamics (which for some are questionable), among many other aspects, through studying specific rhetorical devices in the Pauline texts (Martin, 1990; Mitchell, 1993; Kittredge, 1998; Polaski, 1999; Given, 2001; Forbes, 2008; Schellenberg, 2013).

However, this type of research presupposes that what Paul said could be perfectly separated from the way in which he said it. This is questionable, in the sense that many of Paul's statements could have much more complicated, theological, and pastoral roots than what is generally assumed (Heil, 2005; Bassler, 2010; Malcolm, 2013).

Another research focus has been the political criticism present in Paul's writings. For some scholars, the Roman Empire was not only the political background of the Apostle's work, but also the foundation of his message, in the sense that his gospel was also a message against the Empire. This had concrete implications, such as being the reason for his execution in Rome (Georgi 1991; Elliott 1994; Horsley, 1997, 2000,

---

[61] Sanders' work opens a very rich discussion that has been developed under the name of a "New Perspective on Paul", which we will not address here given our research focus.

2004; Crossan, 2007; Crossan & Reed, 2004; Crossan & Borg, 2009; Wright, 2002, 2009, 2013a, 2013b).

According to Paul himself, he was a Jew, a "Hebrew of Hebrews" (Phil 3:5). However, if we follow the descriptions found in Acts, he was a citizen of Tarsus, a prominent urban center of the time that was thoroughly Hellenistic. His letters show that he was immersed in Hebrew scriptures and thought, but nevertheless wrote and spoke Greek, and primarily used the Septuagint when quoting scripture. On the other hand, he saw his apostolic calling as a ministry to specifically preach the Jewish Messiah to the Gentiles of the Roman Empire (Porter, 2004, 2006b; Schweitzer, 2006; Becker, 2007; Eisenhaum, 2014).

It is understandable that this topic has been investigated by Pauline specialists, but it is not easy to find a unique and precise approach. This is especially true because the concepts of "Judaism" and "Hellenism" have had important and different variations and connotations in history. Recently, it has been shown that the understanding of Judaism and Hellenism as being clearly separate realities with well-defined limits should be discarded. Judaism in Paul's days was not only characterized by its diversity, but also all forms of Judaism where already Hellenized, to greater or lesser degrees, due to the strong influence of Greco-Roman culture (Porter, 2009; Bassler, 2010).

As we can see, current interpretations of Paul and his writings are many, with various approaches. However, the most general perspectives can be summarized into at least four (Bird, 2008, 2012):

The traditional Protestant View in which Paul is seen as a preacher of the grace that stands in contrast to the Jewish legalism of the second temple, which in some cases took a supersessionist perspective that implicitly or explicitly viewed the church as a substitution for Israel.

The so-called New Perspective on Paul, which in great measure proposes that the problem Paul faced with Judaism was not legalism, but rather ethnocentrism. Seen in this way, Paul would argue that the Jews should accept that God has acted historically through Jesus, as the Messiah, to bring them and the Gentiles to the eschatological consummation of God's kingdom.

A perspective that emphasizes Paul's apocalyptic vision and suggests that the Apostle proclaimed the invasive and cosmic act of God's

154

salvation over the powers of this world, to rectify and renew all creation, making the old order and its religion obsolete.

The so-called Radical Perspective on Paul, a viewpoint that is among the most recently developed. This understands the Apostle as being first and foremost a Jew that observes the Torah, who tried to unite the Gentiles with the Jews, with salvation for the Gentiles being through Christ, but for the Jews by remaining under the auspices of the Mosaic covenant.

The panorama is extensive. Understanding Pauline thought is arduous. Here we only conduct a brief review to establish a framework for studying him and immerse ourselves in his life's work, his writings, and especially 2 Corinthians.

5.3. Paul's Letters

When looking at the thirteen books attributed to Paul as a whole, it is apparent that they were written to attend to pastoral needs. This means that they were written to specific local congregations for well-defined reasons, with some being written to individuals. These letters would have been read publicly in the churches, probably in the context of communal worship (1 Thes 5:27; Col 4:16). Some would have been meant to circulate among various local or regional communities (2 Cor 1:1; Col 4:16; Gal 1:1). Additionally, there are letters that Paul wrote that have not been preserved (1 Cor 5:9; 2 Cor 2:4; Col 4:16).

Factors considered when doubting their authorship include differences in style, tone, vocabulary, and content between these last six letters and the seven that are considered authentic. The letters carrying Paul's name but whose authorship is attributed to another person are called pseudepigraphical, meaning they were deliberately written under Paul's name by someone else. They are also considered to be post-Pauline, which means they are a continuation of the Pauline tradition after his death by supposed disciples of the Apostle[62]

---

[62] Some experts have proposed that the pseudepigraphical letters could be considered *anti-Pauline* regarding certain topics, such as slavery and patriarchy. Along these lines, one could speak of at least "three Pauls": a radical Paul, from the seven undisputed letters; a conservative Paul, from the probably inauthentic letters; and a reactionary Paul, from the certainly inauthentic letters (Crossan & Reed, 2004; Borg & Crossan, 2009).

(Bornkamm, 1978; Porter, 2002, 2004; Brown, 2004; Brown, Fitzmyer & Murphy, 2004; Stamps, 2007).

The Greek word *epistole* (letter) originally referred to an oral communication sent through a messenger. This term was widely used for different types of documents in the ancient world, and could include a wide variety of commercial, government, and legal documents, as well as political and military reports, along with other types of correspondence, especially personal. Paul's letters follow the framework of the Greco-Roman model, but he adapted them freely for his purposes, often combining Hellenistic and Helleno-Judaic customs (O'Brien, 1993).

At the end of the first century, some of Paul's letters had already been distributed among various churches. The circulation and collection of Paul's letters indicate that they were valued early on for their importance for the universal church, and not only as a response to local circumstances. There would have been an important editorial task, both with regard to collecting the letters as well as to the texts themselves. For those that accept the Deutero-Pauline hypothesis, the edited publication of these letters would have been a deliberate attempt by an individual or group within a Pauline school to consolidate Paul's apostolic authority and his theology for future generations[63] (Patzia,1993).

The Pauline letters are of central importance to Christian history and theology, since they are the first testimonies of the life and faith of the first Christians, and date earlier than the composition of the canonic Gospels. As such, they present a firsthand perspective on the

---

[63] This brings up a complex topic that continues to be discussed, since "pseudepigraphy was not received without question in the ancient world. Establishing the authorial authenticity was important for many kinds of literature. Within the New Testament canon, it appears that pseudepigraphy was the basis for rejecting some post-New Testament writings like 3 Corinthians and the Gospel of Peter. This means that any pseudonymous writing in the New Testament canon must have been included because the deception was undetected or overlooked. But the matter of deception is more than authorship with the post-Pauline letters. The so-called inauthentic letters are personal and situational, meaning that the details about Paul's life in these letters and the situation which frames these letters is fictional, making them more forgeries than a continuation of Pauline thought. The burden of proof, therefore, is on those who dispute the authenticity of the named sender in the Pauline letters. The matter of Pauline pseudepigraphy is still an important interpretative issue" (Stamps, 2007, p. 266).

expansion of Christianity beyond Palestine's borders. These letters also provide a base for many core declarations of Christian faith and life in history, reason why from early times Paul has been considered one of the greatest Christian theologians. It is for this reason that interpreting and understanding Paul's letters has occupied an important place in the life and theology of the church since the end of the first century until today.

In the next chapter, we will stop at Paul's correspondence to the Corinthian Christians, thus initiating our exegetical approach to the Pauline texts of 2 Corinthians, which we will review later in more detail.

5.4. Paul's Correspondence with the Corinthians

The city of Corinth was located on the far west side of the isthmus between central Greece and the Peloponnese, controlling important trade routes[64]. It was a Roman colony (*Colonia Laus Iulia Corinthiensis*), populated mostly by *libertini* (freed or escaped slaves) along with some Roman war veterans, Greek slaves, and free men drawn by opportunities for business and trade in the area. It was also the host of the Isthmus Games (between AD 7 and AD 3, which attracted a great

---

[64] This route was especially important because many traders preferred to transport goods across the isthmus instead of going around through the dangerous waters south of the Peloponnese. There were two ports nearby: Lachaeum, located 2.5 km to the east on the Corinthian Gulf and connected to the city by long walls; and Cenchreae, 14 km to the east on the Saronic Gulf. Because of these important characteristics, Corinth became a vibrant hub of trade, as well as industry (primarily ceramic). Overlooking the city was the Acrocorinth, a steep, flat-top rock adorned by the acropolis, which in ancient times contained a famous temple to Aphrodite, among other things. From the end of the 4th century BC until AD 196, Corinth was primarily ruled by the Macedonians, but in that year, it was liberated with the rest of Greece by Quinictius Flamininus and joined the Achaean league. After a period of opposition to Rome, and a social revolution under the dictator Critolaus, the city was conquered by Mummius in AD 146 and its inhabitants were sold as slaves. Later, Corinth was rebuilt in AD 46 by Caesar, and began to recover its earlier prosperity. Augustus made it the capital of the new province of Achaia, separating it from Macedonia. From then on, it was ruled by a proconsular Roman governor, continuing its prestige as being a cosmopolitan city and religious center, with temples for old and new cults (Murphy-O'Connor, 1983; Harrop, 1991; Coutsoumpos, 2008).

number of people and generated important business exchanges of various types (Légasse, 2005).

To obtain an overall view of Paul's relationship with the Corinthians, below we share Guthrie's chronological synthesis from his recent commentary on 2 Corinthians (2015):

A Chronology of Paul's Interaction with the Corinthians
(Guthrie, 2015, p. 18).

Spring 50 (March?): Paul arrives in Corinth for the first time.

Summer 51 (July?): Paul is brought before Gallio.

Autumn 51 (September?): Paul leaves Corinth, sailing for Syria, arriving by mid-October.

Late spring 52 (May?): Paul arrives in Ephesus for a period of extensive ministry.

Summer or autumn 52: Paul receives news of the Corinthians and writes the "Previous Letter" (1 Cor. 5:9).

Autumn 52: Apollos joins Paul in Ephesus.

Summer/autumn 53: Paul writes 1 Corinthians and sends it to Corinth (Timothy sent to Macedonia).

Early spring 54: Timothy arrives in Corinth, finding the church in disarray.

Late spring 54 (May?): When shipping opens, Paul travels to Corinth for the "sorrowful visit" (2 Cor. 2:1), then returns to Ephesus.

Summer 54: In Ephesus, Titus reports to Paul, who writes the "sorrowful letter" (2 Cor. 2:3–4).

Late summer 54 (Aug.?): The riot in Ephesus precipitates Paul's leaving the city after teaching for two years and three months (Acts 19:8–10).

Autumn–winter 54/55: Paul ministers in Troas, then Macedonia, where he writes 2 Corinthians.

Winter–autumn 55: Paul evangelizes in Macedonia and Illyricum (Rom. 15:19).

Autumn/winter 55: Paul makes his way back through Macedonia to Greece.

January–March 56: The apostle stays for three months in Corinth and writes Romans.

Spring 56 (end of March?): A plot causes Paul to abort a trip back to Syria by sea and reroute travel through Macedonia.

April 56: Paul sails, leaving Philippi after the Feast of Unleavened Bread (Acts 20:6) on a trip that takes him back to Jerusalem, where he is taken into Roman custody.

The letter of 2 Corinthians contains passages that, in the opinion of most scholars, reflect very different circumstances. It specifically references the state of Paul's relationship with the church in Corinth. Different parts of the letter allude to his hopes to visit the community soon. The letter also has distinguishable breaks in its emotional tone and its content. These and other discrepancies have brought many scholars to see 2 Corinthians as a composite text. But perspectives vary on its literary and chronological reconstruction (Taylor, 1991).

The integrity of 2 Corinthians is a difficult topic. Some even propose that a solution will never be reached (Barrett, 1982). This is due to the immense variety of conclusions that have been reached about the letter's composition. The debate continues, started more than two hundred years ago by J.S. Semler, and papers on the topic are still being produced (Betz, 1985; Taylor, 1991).

The many theories[65] about this letter's composition have been categorized by the number of letters/fragments of which it is composed. Aside from the quantitative matter regarding the number of parts, the place occupied by some fragments is debated regarding their respective significance in Pauline chronology. An emblematic example of this is the location of 2 Corinthians 8 and 9. Specialists generally tend to see

---

[65] For a more detailed study of this topic, we recommend the following: Bornkamm, 1978; Bultmann, 1985; Carrez, 1986; Cothenet, 1985; Gilchrist, 1988; Taylor, 1991; Kurz, 1996; Sánchez Bosch, 1998; Brown, 2002; *Chang,* 2002; Murphy-O'Connor, 2003; Porter, 2004; Freed, 2005; Becker, 2007; Roetzel, 2012; Vidal, 2007, 2012; Guthrie, 2015.

chapters 1-9 as a unit. However, for those that view 2 Corinthians as essentially two letters, 2 Corinthians 1-9 and 2 Corinthians 10-13, the debate has been whether chapters 10-13 were written before chapters 1-9 (and therefore could be considered "the tearful letter") or after (Chang, 2002).

Details of the academic debate on the composition and chronology of 2 Corinthians is beyond the scope of our work. Here, we focus on one of the plausible hypotheses recently proposed by some specialists (Roeztel, 2012; Vidal, 2007, 2012[66]). This will enable us to analyze our selected paragraphs of 2 Corinthians, in a critical and orderly way.

According to Vidal (2007, 2012; cf. Becker, 2007), Paul's correspondence with the Corinthians (1 Cor and 2 Cor) is made up of six letters/parts, which could be reconstructed and reordered as follows:

Table 2: Reconstructing Paul's letters to the Corinthians

(cf. Becker, 2007; Vidal, 2007, 2012)

Canonic Text	Reconstruction	Paragraphs
1 Corinthians	First letter to the Corinthians (Cor A)	1 Cor 6:1-11; 10:1-22; 11:2-34; 15:1-58; 16:13-18
	Second letter to the Corinthians (Cor B)	1 Cor 1:1-5:13; 6:12-9,27; 10:23-11,1; 12:1-14,40; 16:1-12, 19-24
2 Corinthians	Third letter to the Corinthians (Cor C)	2 Cor 2:14-7:4
	Fourth letter to the Corinthians (Cor D)	2 Cor 10:1-13:13
	Fifth letter to the Corinthians (Cor E)	2 Cor 1:1-2:13; 7:5-8:24
	Letter to the communities of Achaia (Cor F)	2 Cor 9:1-15

---

[66] Especially this last author, from whose work we will borrow the structure for analyzing our selected passages from 2 Corinthians.

This reconstruction of the Corinthian letters, as interpreted by Vidal (Ibid.), involves the following considerations regarding their general context and content. For us, this seems to help us understand the breaks in theme, style, and affective tone seen in 2 Corinthians[67]:

1 Corinthians:

Cor A: 1 Cor 6:1-11; 10:1-22; 11:2-34; 15:1-58; 16:13-18. This would correspond to a letter probably written in the fall of AD 52 in Ephesus (1 Cor 15:32; 16:15-18). In this letter, Paul attempts to solve the problems of the Corinthian community, which was split in regards to its leadership. Additionally, they were unable to fully distinguish themselves from the practices and worldviews of Corinthian civil society, falling into a type of Hellenistic syncretism. The letter also alludes to a pronounced lack of intra-communal integration, as found in a social stratification of the ecclesial community that responded to the social and urban reality of Roman Corinth at the time. It is a letter that seriously warns the community, especially the wealthier minority, about various problems. The variety of themes it addresses had to have affected its structure, which does not seem to have been very rigid. Only some fragments were preserved, and were included in the final edition (within Cor B), which would have been the base letter for composing 1 Corinthians in its present form. They can be seen as small glosses (11:2; 11:19 and 15:56) as well as longer additions (15:9-10 and 15:39-41).

Cor B: 1 Cor 1:1-5:13; 6:12-9:27; 10:23-11:1; 12:1-14:40; 16:1-12,19-24. This letter was surely written in the spring of AD 53 in Ephesus (1 Cor 16:8,19), and was a response to a letter sent by the Corinthian community. It would have been delivered by Titus, who was also charged with organizing a collection of funds in Corinth and Achaia for the poor in Jerusalem (1 Cor 16:1-4; 2 Cor 8:6,10; 9:2; 12:17-18). The letter reveals that the earlier problems in Corinth had worsened. The warnings in Cor A seem to have been misinterpreted, or outright rejected (1 Cor 5:9-11). As a warning letter, its structure is not very coherent. This is because at the beginning of the letter it attempts to respond to multiple pastoral problems about which Paul would have

---

[67] This is important for the study we are conducting, which focuses on the psychological dynamic of Paul coping with his adversities lived.

been informed orally by "Chloe's household", and answers different questions asked in a letter from the Corinthians to Paul, in the second part. We can say that it has been preserved in its entirety, since it served as a base for composing 1 Corinthians in its present form. They can be seen as small glosses (1:2b; 1:16 and 7:21b) as well as longer additions (2:6-16; 12:31b-14:1b and 14:33b-36).

2 Corinthians:

2 Corinthians, has a much more complex structure due to being made up of multiple texts, yet it could be reconstructed as follows:

Information about an earlier letter written by Paul "with many tears" (2 Cor 2:3-4 and 7:8,12), probably does not refer to Cor A, Cor B, or a lost letter, but rather to one that must be discovered within 2 Corinthians in its present form. For many authors, this letter corresponds to 2 Cor 10:1-13:13)[68]. As an antecedent to the literary structure of this letter (composite), we see that the account of Paul's journey from Troy to Macedonia in search of Titus continues perfectly in 7:5ss (his arrival to Macedonia and meeting with Titus). Therefore, these texts must belong to the same letter. The text found in 2:14-7:4, which interrupt the sequence between 2:13 and 7:5, has a single apologetic theme, indicating that it may have been originally an independent letter. For its part, chapter 9, in which Paul addresses generosity in giving, is a duplicate of chapter 8, which deals with the same topic. For this reason, it is unlikely that these chapters are from the same letter. The radical shift in content and tone, albeit back to an apologetic theme, found in 10:1-13:13 is done in a distinct way that is inconsistent with the tone of Chapters 8 and 9 about generosity, and even prior chapters. It is a section marked by unease, tension, sarcasm, and irony, that make one think that it could be the letter written "with many tears" (2:3-4; 7:8,12). On the other hand, according to 12:14 and 13:1-2 that letter was written after a second visit to Corinth by Paul, and before a third planned visit.

---

[68] See the comparative charts of Chang (2002) and Roetzel (2010), presented earlier, which note the main authors that endorse this posture.

From the above, we can derive that 2 Corinthians is plausibly composed of four letters, possibly written in the following chronological order:

Cor C: 2 Cor 2:14-7:4. This letter was written in the summer of AD 53 in Ephesus. It refers to a new stage in the Corinthian community's development. Christian missionaries in Corinth take advantage of the community's situation and aggravate their problems. Their praxis and conceptual understanding of mission, which differ from the Pauline approach, bring about harsh and generalized criticism on the part of Paul. The only part of Cor C that is preserved is the body of the letter, which is primarily Paul's defense of his ministry in the face of these accusations. Information about these accusations would have been delivered by Timothy upon returning from the journey mentioned in Cor B (1 Cor 4:17; 16:10-11). As we said before, 7:2-4 fits immediately before 7:5ss, paragraphs that refer directly to the tribulation and the comfort and joy that follow. The passage of 6:14-7:1 could be considered a posterior addition.

Cor D: 2 Cor 10:1-13:13. This letter must have been written in the fall of AD 53 in Ephesus, after Paul's failed visit to the Corinthian community (2 Cor 12:14; 13:1-2). It addresses a situation of the community that is more critical and complex than that referred to in Cor C. It seems that the opposing missionaries have been successful in their work, and the disparagement of Paul has grown. Because of this, the Apostle had a painful and direct experience in his meeting with the Corinthians (12:14; 13:1-2). Cor E referred to it as a letter written "out of great distress and anguish of heart" and "with many tears" (2 Cor 2:3-4; 7:8,12, NIV). Its tense and hard tone resembles the Letter to the Galatians. Paul skillfully uses many Hellenistic rhetorical devices that are typically used in texts of confrontation and forewarning, such as irony, comparisons, parody, or direct invective. The beginning of this letter has not been preserved, but its body and conclusion are intact.

Cor E: 2 Cor 1:1-2:13; 7:5-8:24. This letter was written in the summer of AD 54, most certainly in Macedonia (2 Cor 2:12-13; 7:5-16; 8:1-2). It is eminently a letter of reconciliation with the Corinthian community, after Paul was freed from prison in Ephesus and he met up with Titus upon his return from Corinth. Titus himself, along with other delegates, delivered the letter to wrap up the matter of the collection of funds in Corinth (2 Cor 8:6, 16-24). The first part (1:12-

2:13; 7:5-16) contains Paul's recollections of his relationship with the community, with a tone that was still apologetic to a degree. The second part (8:1-24) is an official letter of credence for the collection of funds for Jerusalem, and uses a terminology and style that is similar to that found in Hellenistic letters of credence of the time that were used to send official delegations. This letter was completely preserved, except for the end (although it is feasible that the end corresponds to 13:11-13). It only appears to have a small gloss at the beginning (1:1c).

Cor F: 9:1-15. This letter was surely written at the same time as Cor E, in the summer of AD 54 in Macedonia, as a circular letter written to all the communities in the region of Acaia (2 Cor 9:2) for the purposes of laying out the final steps for the collection (2 Cor 9:2, 4). The same individuals delivered this letter as Cor E, since they would have also been the official delegates for the collection in the communities of Acaia. Only the body of this brief letter is preserved.

Regarding this or other possible reconstructions of Corinthian correspondence, we can concur with Becker (2007) that the editor probably did not omit much material when composing 2 Corinthians, except for some beginnings and endings that he considered expendable, since important gaps are not noticed . It is possible that the editor used Cor E as a framework for Cor C; that way the conciliatory tone could prevail and could finally place the recommendation on the collection. Probably later Cor D was added, because the warning against errors, divisions and dangers of the communities used to be included at the end of this type of documents. The editor did not have to worry about the success of the collection (which could be discouraged by the strong tenor of Cor D), because surely the facts mentioned in the letters that were integrated into 2 Corinthians were no longer of immediate interest, since this the wording could most likely be an update of the message to new contexts that had nothing to do with the specific problems that Paul was trying to solve in Corinth.

Chapter 6
Hermeneutic Methodological Framework

In this chapter we will make a brief introduction to the methodology used in this research. We will dwell on the hermeneutical framework that we have chosen and we will also make a description of the exegetical approach that we will make to the selected Pauline texts.

6.1. Psychological Biblical Criticism

> People will read the gospel again and again and I myself read it again and again. But they will read it with much more profit if they have some insight into their own psyches. Blind are the eyes of anyone who does not know his own heart, and I always recommend the application of a little psychology so that he can understand things like the gospel still better (Jung, 1973, p. 463).

The Bible can be seen as a text immersed in historical, political, social and literary processes. However, it can also be seen as emerging from psychological processes of various types. The Psychological Biblical Criticism argues that the text emerges as part of a particular psychological context, of an individual and / or community, so deeply moved by the content he wishes to convey that he feels compelled to do so. The resulting text is a historical material that tells us about the past, but it is also a document that expresses the nature and psychological processes of human beings, through a wide variety of related experiences and using a vast number of literary genres. Along with this, the Bible, is also a text that has historically shown to have a great transformative power of its readers, who interpreting its contents (through psychological processes), have given it various senses, meanings and applications that have come to have marked influence on human history, affecting political, economic, social and cultural processes (Rollins, 2002; Kille, 2009).

Often biblical scholars remained skeptical of accepting that the Bible was a richly psychological document. Contrary to these, normally specialists in practical theology, preachers and pastoral counselors have paid attention to the psychological aspects of Scripture. Since pastors and counselors have not often considered specialized Bible study as a primary focus in their work (but rather a means for the purposes of fostering growth, change and fulfillment in the lives of those with whom they work), many authors in this line they have written about the Bible from a psychological perspective, but with weak methodological rigor and few references to field research (Kille, 2002).

In the field of psychological studies, although classical authors such as James, Freud or Jung, address Biblical subjects, they did not develop a formal biblical hermeneutic. Rather, given their particular perspectives, they managed to provide concepts and tools, making contributions for a critical psychological approach of Scriptures, which allow exploring and exposing psychological factors present in the process of producing the text, in the text itself and in its recipients. The fact that there is no psychological exegesis that can replace the critical methods of biblical scholars, does not imply that critical psychological approaches should be underestimated (Rollins, 2002).

The contemporary world has been immersed in a culture marked by psychological concepts and perspectives. That is why in order to enter into meaningful communication with today's society, some basic understanding of psychological theories and categories is important. Although the Bible cannot be characterized as "a psychological text" proper in a contemporary sense, since its authors and editors did not know anything about modern psychological theories, today one of the tasks of hermeneutics is to shorten this distance so that the ancient texts will be intelligible to an audience that has incorporated psychological perspectives in much of their discourse and understanding. This is why Psychological Biblical Criticism has emerged as a significant perspective in contemporary biblical studies. Although implicitly it has been present through the adoption of theories and assumptions based on psychology on human cognition, emotion and interaction (in approaches, for example, such as feminist, deconstructionist, structuralist and response to the reader), it is the growing work of biblical scholars, theologians and psychologists who have tried to apply psychology explicitly to the interpretation of the Bible, who have brought a new level of coherence and methodological self-awareness to this field of study (Kille, 2009).

The dual objective of Psychological Biblical Criticism is to improve the repertoire of critical perspectives on the Bible, adding a vision of the text as a psychic product and as a source of comments on the nature of human psychological life, its understanding of health and health mental dysfunction, as well as the study of prescriptions given for pastoral care. Along these lines, a psychological hermeneutic will examine the writings for signs of psychic factors that might be working on the choice of material, subjects, images and modes of expression of the author / editor. From a critical psychological perspective, a review of the nature of the power of influence of the texts on the mental life and behavior of the readers can also be made, together with evaluating the dynamics of biblical interpretation (formal and informal, scholarly or spontaneous) of the reader and the analysis of the structures, processes and psychosocial dynamics present there. A psychocritical hermeneutic can also be dedicated to understanding the catalytic effect that the biblical text has exerted and / or exerts on individual readers or entire communities, activating consciousness, will and imagination for new courses of creative, critical, moral or creative action and certain specific moments of the story. Also from this approach, an explanatory chronicle can be made of the therapeutic and psychopathogenic effects caused by the text and provide information on the psychodynamics of the processes that produce them. Likewise, following the Augustinian saying: *salus animarum suprema lex* ("the health of the soul is the supreme law"), we can state that the Psychological Biblical Criticism considers its fundamentally therapeutic function as the original purpose of a canonical text, that is, the concern for the nature and destiny of the human "soul" and the strategies for its healing or transformation (Rollins, 2002).

For Ellens (2012), the perspective of Psychological Biblical Criticism today can be raised from four basic convictions: a) Although the Bible is part of a historical, social and literary process, it is also part of a psychological process in which unconscious and conscious factors converge; b) these psychological factors are present in each participant of the process that constitutes the text, that is, in the biblical authors, in the communities they represent, in the stories and materials they retain, in the copyists, translators and biblical editors, as well as in the interpreters and preachers, in the scholars and in the effects that the Bible has generated and continues to generate in individuals and in entire cultures, for better and for worse; c) an essential function of the Bible is to serve as a manual on the perennial experience of the "human soul", its trials, problems, successes and victories, using a wide range of literary forms: "The Bible is a book of the soul, written to the soul, over the soul, for the care and healing of the soul" (Rollins, 1999, p. vii); d) finally, as important as the historical, social, political, economic and cultural factors that are present in the production of a text and its interpretations, the conscious and unconscious psychic factors can become very determinant of what is recorded in a text, how it is said, why it is said, how it is read, how it is interpreted and how it is received, translated and applied that interpretation.

6.2. Psychological and Hermeneutic Perspectives

Given the complexity of the Bible text in its writing, transmitssion, editing, compiling, canonization, translation, proclamation and understanding on the one hand, and the plurality of often contradictory psychological theories on the other, how can we find an appropriate fit between text and theory? And, further, how can we evaluate the effectiveness of psychological approaches to the Bible? (Kille, 2002, p. 128).

Much of the skepticism about psychological approaches is based on the tendency to apply psychological categories and ideas in artificial and improper ways to the biblical text. Typical have been cases where it is sought to give a psychological profile to biblical characters, in most cases in search of psychopathologies. The classic work of Albert Schweitzer (1948), published in 1913, now presents a critical stance on the matter, questioning those who presented psychopathological portraits of Jesus, indicating that they were usually works that ignored the historical development and context of the writings of the gospel

This is why the main authors who have developed Psychological Biblical Criticism have paid close attention to the historical and contextual aspects of the text (Rollins, 1999, 2002; Kille, 2001, 2003, 2009, 2015), in order to avoid an inappropriate approach to the text, superimposing psychological models over the Scriptures. For this they usually talk about the three worlds of the text: the world behind the text, the world of the text itself and the world in front of the text. Where the world behind the text includes the context in which a text arose, historical situations, the world of authors and their communities; the world of text considers its narrative structures and its semantic and linguistic characteristics; and the world in front of the text becomes the dialogue in which the reader interacts with the text in an effort to understand it in a meaningful and relevant way. These three worlds are intimately interconnected, but are raised in this way to facilitate the rigorous search for an approach to the text respecting each of its dimensions.

To achieve a rigorous analysis of the text, which allows us a relevant understanding, we have to avoid hermeneutical fallacies, such as: a) the intentional fallacy, which corresponds to the claim of an exegete to reach out to discern one's mental mentality and intentionality of an author; b) the evolutionary fallacy, which refers to the exegetical claim that a description of the origins of a textual tradition would imply a definition of the fundamental meaning of the text; c) the fallacy of the effect, which occurs when the meaning of a text is considered equivalent to the subjective experience of value given by a specific recipient; and d) the fallacy of misplaced concretion, which is related to an anachronically inappropriate sympathy between a reader and a text (Van Aarde, 2015).

Psychological Biblical Criticism when speaking of the three worlds of the text seeks to get rid of these fallacies and stick to the text itself, but without letting its wealth in psychological terms be lost. To do this, through his attention in the world behind the text and the text itself, he seeks to let the documents of the past speak in his own language and contextual historical, grammatical, linguistic, literary reality. Always being cautious about the real capacity we have to recover a world and its background. Well, although biblical characters and their behaviors and relationships can realistically reflect human beings, we should not assume that these characterizations are necessarily historical, nor should we go beyond the text by assuming details not described, which speaks more about the interpreter than about the text itself. This is very important when using a psychological hermeneutical perspective, since we can tend to apply theoretical models (clinical, psychopathlogical or personality) in an arbitrary way (Kille, 2002).

For the psycho-critical approach, the world in front of the text is one of the facets of analysis more proper and where it can offer a greater contribution. There the focus is on those who read or listen to the text and how they are affected by it. It is here that, as Ricoeur (1976, 2002, 2016) put it, the reader understands himself in front of the text. Here there is a generative dynamic between the historical document and the contemporary reader.

The effect of a text on a reader is a part of what Rollins has called the *Nachleben*, the "afterlife" of the text, in contrast to the historical-critical concern for the original "setting in [past] life." The fact that more psychological biblical interpretations have come from psychologists and pastoral counselors than from biblical scholars reflects this difference in the focus of attention. Such people work with individuals who have been, and continue to be, affected by their encounters with the sacred text and stories. Both the therapeutic and pathological potentials of the Bible are worked out in the lives of contemporary readers (Kille, 2002, p. 132).

Science and psychology models can be used as a lens by which a text can be seen in a novel way with productive results in new dimensions of knowledge. Given the nature of the human mind and personality, it is imperative to recognize that the reciprocal contribution of all scientific disciplines is essential for a more complete approach to human reality. Particularly, when looking for a collaborative reciprocity between psychology and biblical sciences and theology, we must take care not to try to make our psychological interpretations or conceptualizations fit our worldview or theological perspective or that our theology fits our particular psychology, but rather to do statements discernible from each other, in such a way that it requires modifications of both disciplines or that allows a more complete and clear understanding of each of them.

Psychological data, with their respective perspectives, models, paradigms, and worldviews can be useful to illuminate a biblical text by broadening the perception of the internal coherence of the text, solving problems in it or deconstructing a supposed coherence of the text, thus expanding the path that leads us to a critical understanding and a more finished application of the text message. On the other hand, theological data, with their respective perceptives, models, paradigms, or worldviews may be useful to illuminate the internal coherence or lack thereof in the "living human document" (Gerkin, 1984), with a view to fostering the progress in the development or transformation of the person who requires psychological, pastoral or ecclesial assistance. In this way, biblical studies, theology and psychology can be seen as different perspectives and fields of discourse, which deal with the same subject, that is, the nature and functions of the human being that are sometimes expressed in the documents of the Bible. The illumination that psychology can bring to biblical studies, on the other hand, is the light it offers on the nature and function of the human being as author, context, initial audience, interpreter, later audience and modified object of the text. The light granted by biblical and theological studies to psychology can be found regarding the clarification it offers about the nature and function of the text of Scripture as a modifier, context, audience and interpreter and, in that sense, author of the human being as "Living document" (Ellens, 1997).

One of the most complete definitions made regarding the perspective of Psychological Biblical Criticism is that of Rollins:

> The goal of a psychological-critical approach is to examine texts, their origination, authorship, modes of expression, their construction, transmission, translation, reading, interpretation into kindred and alien art forms, and the history of their personal and cultural effect, as expressions of the structure, processes, and habits of the human psyche, both in individual and collective manifestations, past and present (1999, pp. 77-78).

Twenty years have passed since the elaboration of this definition and even the field of this approach shows a weak coherence, since it covers many different methods and approaches, which make a more abundant bibliographic corpus of representative works more necessary, along with a more critical reflection finished methods and approaches in the biblical field. This weakness of the perspective may be due to the fact that psychology as a discipline is extremely broad and under its name includes innumerable subdisciplines, approaches, methods and often contradictory models. This has an impact on what is and can be the critical psychological perspective of Scripture. However, the challenge of developing methodologically rigorous research papers, which allow new access to biblical texts and themes, thus opening up its significant wealth for the contemporary world, is relevant enough to work creatively and seriously in this regard.

Then, after having made this brief review of our psychological-critical perspective, we will refer to the particular methodology that we will use in the present investigation, which implies an approach from the model of the Hermeneutical Arc of Paul Ricoeur to Pauline texts in the perspective of the Psychological Biblical Criticism.

6.3. Hermeneutical Arc and Psychological Biblical Criticism

To begin, we will understand by hermeneutics the theory, or theoretical practice, that seeks to explain and understand historical texts. In this way, the field of action and the object of study of hermeneutics is defined. As a discipline, it tries to answer questions such as: What should we do to really understand what a text says? How to understand the world of the text if we have never been there? What should we do to access what the text wants to say without ending up simply reading what we want to hear? (De Wit, 2001).

According to Gadamer (1993; De Wit, 2001; Cruz-Villalobos, 2012), the historical distance between the text and the current reader is not necessarily an obstacle. For him the deep meaning of a text goes beyond the momentary and contingent, since a text would not depend only on the historical moment of the author and his original audience, because the current reader's situation would be constitutive of the message, since understanding would not be to "re-produce", but rather a productive (or constructive) process. In this process, each person who reads a historical text does so from their own context, from their own experience, which as historically situated and distanced pre-comprehension, can obstruct or facilitate the meaning of a text. In this line, to understand a text would be to discover the question that it wants to answer, the question that the text problematizes directly or indirectly.

For J. L. Segundo (1975, 1985), the continuous change in our interpretation of the Bible as a function of the permanent variations of our present reality, both individual and social, implies being attentive to the circular character of the interpretative or hermeneutic act, since each new reality obliges us to interpret the Scriptures anew, to change reality with it and, therefore, to return later to interpret. The hermeneutic circularity, in the perspective of Segundo, demands new

174

questions and new answers: questions that arise from the present and that are relevant and pertinent, in such a way that they force us to change our previous conceptions. On the other hand, if the interpretation of the Scripture does not change together with the present problems, the latter will remain unanswered, and thus the hermeneutical circularity stops, which implies giving answers that may be obsolete.

Paul Ricoeur[69] (1995, 2016), for his part, considers that the task of hermeneutics is to reconstruct the set of operations by which a work rises on the background of living, acting and suffering to be given by a author to a reader who receives it and changes its action in that process, that is, its life is affected in a particular way. As he puts it when dealing with the distinction between "explain" and "understand" (Ricoeur, 2002), these do not constitute the poles of a relation of exclusion, but rather the relative moments of a complex process that for him constitutes the interpretation. These two moments make up, for Ricoeur, the structure of hermeneutic work by means of what he called "hermeneutical arch". This form of description of the process of understanding is what we will use in our current work from the perspective of Psychological Biblical Criticism.

As De Wit (2001) puts it, both an analytical, methodical and explanatory attitude and an existential attitude have an appropriate place in Ricoeur's hermeneutic model. Exegesis, like naive reading are only phases or moments of the process of understanding. The process culminates when the old text is re-contextualized in the situation of

---

[69] As one of the main exponents of hermeneutics, Ricoeur has made enormous contributions to interpretive theory and has offered numerous ideas on the nature and use of language. Based on various elements of phenomenology, post-structuralism and the theory of speech acts, among others, his hermeneutical conception has had great influence in fields such as biblical and theological interpretation. The work of this author on topics such as metaphor, symbol, narration and time, including the hermeneutical themes of tradition, authority and criticism have proved to be of great interest to many scholars of various areas of knowledge. For Ricoeur the central hermeneutical problem is the conflict, merely apparent according to him, between explanation and understanding. For the articulation between these two processes formulates a theory of the text in terms of autonomy, distancing and appropriation. This author argues in favor of the autonomy of the text with respect to its original author. It also maintains the conception of distancing between the text and the reader, providing the text with a state of objectification, which is addressed through exegetical mediation, and proposes overcoming this alienation by means of the appropriation of the text by the reader (Porter & Robinson, 2011).

the current reader and his community. For Ricoeur, it is the very nature of the text that demands a process of dialectical interpretation. Well, each historical text has a certain internal objectivity, but it also has a referential potential that can be updated in a new context.

To describe what is involved in the act of interpreting texts, Ricoeur proposes the model of the hermeneutical arc, which is a process that goes from naive understanding to academic understanding, through explanation. To understand an ancient literary text, this author emphasizes that it requires two attitudes on the part of the interpreter: one that wants to update the referential potential of the text, that is, the connection with the extralinguistic world, and also a more analytical and methodological attitude, which he wants to take the text as a literary and linguistic system that has its own world to discover. Following the synthesis made by De Wit (2001), we will present the three moments of the comprehensive process according to Ricoeur:

Naive (naïve) reading or pre-comprehension: corresponds to the first disposition before the text, marked by the personal conjecture, since the reader, using his intuition, performs a pre-comprehension or anticipation of the meaning or message of the text. It is therefore the preliminary process, an approach that must be validated by other instruments, beyond the intuition or immediate appropriation of the content of the text, which lacks scientific rigor, and is marked fundamentally by the experience and context of the reader's world, far from the author and his original community. This is a stage of analysis that is carried out without a dictionary, without Hebrew or Greek grammar, without concordance, without knowledge or historical perspective, but which, nevertheless, is necessary as a first approximation to the text, as an opening to the comprehension process.

Explanatory or exegetical reading: given that the first reading of a text, is marked by our being located, by our pre-under-standing or prejudgments, can facilitate but also block our understanding of the text, it is essential to make an explanatory round that let us take charge of the distance that separates us from the world of the text. The text itself contains elements of its own in which fundamental aspects of its identity and character were inscribed. In his grammar, in his semantics and in the development of his plot the text shows elementary aspects of his message. This stage is what has been called exegesis, which corresponds to the theoretical practice that tries to reconstruct controllably the meaning or the historical meanings of the text. It is a work that seeks to explain the spectrum of meanings that the text possibly had in its time of origin, in its original literary context. The deployment of the text, of its own world, is therefore sought. While the naive reading is a first phase, tending to the incorporation, the appropriation, the assimilation of the text, the exegesis tries to respect the peculiarity of the text to the maximum, through the use of own instruments. As a exegetical second stage of the comprehensive process can not and should not eradicate the naive readings, with which maintains a dialectical relationship, which seeks to indicate the limits of legitimacy of the first asystematic approach to the text. Exegetical reading helps to find the elements of the text that allow a respectful appropriation and rereading, which accounts for the wealth of historical material and aspects not easily seen from a naive reading.

Application, appropriation or comprehensive knowledge (compréhension savante): this is the final stage of the comprehensive process that went through a validation phase (exegesis) and culminates in the updating of the text in the historical world of the interpreter and his community. It is the moment of a productive reading that leads to a new perception of the world and a new praxis of the interpreter. It is the stage where the text is re-contextualized, where it is provided with a new reference, in such a way that it manages to illuminate a historical moment different from that of the author and encourages a praxis that may not have been foreseen by the author and his original readers. It is, therefore, a communitarian and pragmatic phase where the referential potential or the reserve of meaning of the text unfolds in a new reality, its message is incarnated in the social, political and / or religious life of the one who interprets it. Like the exegetical stage, it also requires its own instruments, because when looking for the re-contextualization of the old text to a psycho-socio-political reality not known by its author, a socio-analytical mediation is needed that allows it to contribute with a "exegesis" of contemporary reality in one or several of its dimensions.

In consideration of this proposed model, we can indicate that for Ricoeur (1977, 2002), understanding does not consist in the immediate capture of the psychic life of others or in the emotional identification with a specific mental intention that the author had. Understanding must be mediated by the set of explanatory procedures that methodically complement it. Explanation and understanding are, for Ricoeur, two stages of a unique hermeneutical process, where the comprehension precedes, accompanies, closes and involves the explanation. On the other hand, the explanation analytically develops understanding.

> [...] if it is true that there is always more than one way of constructing a text, it is not true that all interpretations are equal [...]. The text is a limited field of possible constructions. The logic of validation allows us to move between the two limits of dogmatism and skepticism. It is always possible to argue for an interpretation, to confront interpretations, to arbitrate between them, and to seek for an agreement, even if this agreement remains beyond our reach (Ricoeur, 1973, p. 108).

The comprehensive work for Ricoeur (2002, 2016) implies, therefore, a rigorous work that aims to put the text in our world, seeks to unveil the world of the text. In this way, what is to be understood is not in the first place to the speaker behind the text, but rather to that of the spoken, "the thing" or "the world" of the text. In other words, it is not about the search of the author and his intentions that are hidden behind the text, but about explaining the being-in-the-world displayed by the text. For this, Ricoeur proposes the explanatory or exegetical distancing that finally allows a legitimate appropriation of the meaning of the text, which does not assume a naive direct application of the contents as if there was a contemporaneity with the author and his original readers. This appropriation or comprehensive knowledge must involve the reader deeply, in such a way that he understands himself (in a new way) before the text insofar as it is not closed on himself, but open to the world that redescribes and remakes. For this reason, Ricoeur, states that the comprehensive process involves in a certain way a self-understanding process.

In the present work we will apply this methodology of the hermeneutical arc, beginning with a naive psychological reading of the texts, which pays attention to the posttraumatic coping theme that Paul describes in autobiographical writings of 2 Corinthians and allows us to select those that are more explicitly related to this topic. Then we carry out a methodical exegetical reading, that seeks to unfold the world of chosen texts, that of what they speak in their own historical and cultural context, also attending to the semantic richness they possess as writings. Finally, a rereading is proposed in which the "reserve of meaning" (Croatto, 1994) of the texts is updated by having our findings discussed, referring to the Pauline praxis front adversities, with the current praxis and constructs on positive coping of traumatic events.

> Each praxis constitutes a horizon of compression from which a message (text) is read, in this case the Bible. [...] what really generates and guides the rereading of the Bible are successive practices. These make the sense of the texts grow, a sense that is later expressed in new texts, which in turn condition new practices, and so on in a hermeneutic rotation that is both pregressive and enriching (Croatto, 1994, p.101).

Within this hermeneutical methodological framework, as we said, we will work from the perspective of Psychological Biblical Criticism, articulating three fields: psychology (in our case psychology of positive coping with trauma), the Bible (specifically a few paragraphs from 2 Corinthians), and the rigorous tradition of critically reading the biblical text (Rollins, 1999; Kille, 2000; Ellens, 2012).

Regarding our decision to choose Psychological Biblical Criticism as our methodological perspective, it is worth mentioning that we have considered it in particular because of the types of themes that we will address, which correspond to a psychological phenomenon (positive coping with traumatic events) that is associated with the sacred in the case of the Apostle Paul. When exegetically analyzing the biblical text, we have also chosen to use resources in a critical historical way, instead of taking more current approaches such as, for example, the Narrative or Canonical Criticism. We especially did this for reasons related to the nature of 2 Corinthians and the selected paragraphs. Second Corinthians is an epistolary text, notably written in the style of a diatribe and not as a continuous literary narrative. Breaks in its discourse are also evident, which require passages to be reordered in order to achieve minimal psychological coherence, and to leave the selected paragraphs in their precise chronological context within Paul's relational dynamic with the Corinthians, and thus allow for better comprehension of the document. On the other hand, the selected texts contain autobiographical testimony that refers explicitly to coping with highly stressful events. We will study these events for the significance of their specific details, and then examine the psychological dynamic they reveal (particularly in relation to the factors associated with psychological resistance), which is to say, as examples of positive coping with trauma. In all of this, we will search for how these writings can shed light on the adverse circumstances of contemporary readers, on both the personal and communal/ecclesial levels. If we understand "practical theology as hermeneutics of lived religion" (Ganzevoort, 2009a, p.1), it seems us that Psychological Biblical Criticism, when used as a heuristic perspective within the methodological use of the hermeneutic arc, allows us to adequately address the Apostle Paul's coping with traumatic events as our study object.

We began with a review of current research and models in the field of psychology on trauma and positive coping, along with a few important points of connection with religiosity and spirituality as coping mechanisms. In this way, when approaching the Bible, 2 Corinthians presents us with very interesting material, since in various places it explicitly alludes to coping with extreme adversity.

In this line, therefore, we have begun the present work with a naive reading of the Pauline texts of 2 Corinthians, selecting those that have been most significant in psychological terms, since they describe the particular ways in which the Apostle faces extreme adversities, which he himself mentions in detail. After this, we began an exegetical detour by investigating general aspects of Paul, his writings and, particularly, his correspondence with the Corinthians. As part of our explanatory approach, which allows us to open the world of the text, we will stop next in the selected paragraphs of 2 Corinthians, assigning a chapter to each one, to explore them exegetically. At the end of each of these chapters we will arrive at a synthesis of the Pauline hermeneutical keys found in the texts regarding the confrontation of traumatic events, that is, about the ways in which the Apostle interprets the adverse events that he has to suffer.

We will thus go through the hermeneutical arc in the perspective of Psychological Biblical Criticism, going from our initial naive reading of psychological type to an exegetical approach, which will allow us to discover the interpretative keys that Paul uses to face the traumatic events experienced. Finally, we arrive at a comprehensive reading, in our case from the psychology of positive coping of trauma (and its main concepts: hardiness, resilience and posttraumatic growth) that will allow us to integrate the Pauline hermeneutical keys found in a practical theological vision of posttraumatic coping.

Diagram 1: Hermeneutic Arc in the Perspective of Psychological Biblical Criticism

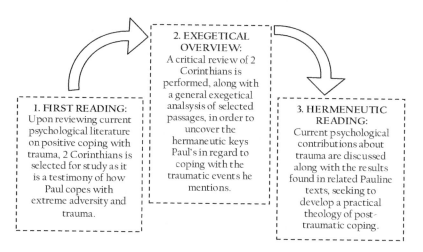

It is important to keep in mind that in our study we will use Ricoeur's hermeneutical arc as a methodological matrix, which we will access from the perspective of Psychological Biblical Criticism.

We will use in a specific way the model of the three worlds of the text proposed by psychological hermeneutics. Our first approach to the text (initial reading) incorporates "the world in front of the text", since we approach 2 Corinthians with a perspective drawn from our prior review of positive psychology of posttraumatic coping. From here the paragraphs that refer to the coping of traumatic events as Paul describes them catch our attention and move us to wonder how the Apostle faces, interprets, and overcomes these events.

In the second step of the Ricoeur arc (explanatory or exegetical reading), we will incorporate the study of what psychological criticism calls "the world behind the text" and "the text itself." Here we approach the Pauline texts from an exegetical perspective.

Thirdly, we reach the last stage of the arc (hermeneutic reading), which is where we seek to update the text, connecting it with what the psychological hermeneutic calls "the world in front of the text." At this point, we discuss our findings on the coping of the adverse in Paul, in conversation with the recent research on positive coping with trauma, seeking to articulate a practical theological understanding of coping.

6.4. Introduction to our Exegetical Analysis

We have chosen to make an exegetical description of the selected section using some historico-critical contributions that, in our opinion, are appropriate to the text due to its strong heterogeneous character, because the Pauline discourse in 2 Corinthians is psychologically incongruent if we accept the canonical order, given that, for example, after making a friendly and cordial request for financial contributions (in Chapters 8 and 9), the letter continues with a tough section characterized by the apologetic use of irony, sarcasm, and exhortation.

We will address the four main paragraphs that deal with our general topic of investigation, coping with adversity. We will seek to allow the texts to reveal their reserve of meaning about this important topic.

In 2 Corinthians Paul presents the greatest number of references to his personal sufferings. Here we find the three primary and most complete lists of adversities suffered by the Apostle (2 Cor 4:8-10; 6:4-10; 11:23-33). With respect to these catalogues of adverse circumstances, which were common in ancient times, in recent research some authors have concluded that "[...] although Paul may have been familiar with the literary tradition of peristalsis catalogues in his surrounding cultures, his unique argumentation and stylistic diversity reflect concrete epistolary and historical circumstances. Scholars also acknowledge marked differences in Paul's use of the tribulation tradition" (Joseph, 2012, p. 11).

In the Apostle's lists, along with observing important enumerations and descriptions of specific circumstances, we find descriptions of Paul's implicit and explicit ways of coping with the adversities. In other words, interpretations of the meaning of the adverse events, their origin, and their purpose. We also find implicit descriptions of specific attitudes and behaviors, in response to the events of adversity (Volf, 1990; Smith, 2002; Lim, 2009).

Second Corinthians also presents itself as a text written with special characteristics appropriate to dealing with trauma and positive coping, as it is an eminently pastoral letter where theological reflection on the life of the church and associated Christian praxis is frequent (Quesnel, 1980; Carrez, 1986, Thompson, 2006). The paragraphs of 2 Corinthians that we will soon address will be examined in two parts: a general exegetical review of the content, and later, a critical analysis from a psychological perspective. In this, we will identify the key concepts, categories, and modes of interpretation that Paul utilized when coping positively with the traumatic situations. The first step will allow us to delve into the Apostle's message and its historical and linguistic context, examining his discourse for meanings, values, and attitudes related to coping with adversity in the selected texts.

The second part of our analysis will be directly guided by our research question: What insights regarding coping with adversity can we find in the writings of the Apostle Paul (particularly in 2 Corinthians) and in recent research on positive coping with trauma for the purposes of building a practical theology of posttraumatic coping[70]?

We will search for answers to this question that may allow us to form a well-founded theoretical understanding based on systematic-cally compiled and analyzed information. In the process to make a critical psychological analysis of the Pauline texts we will be dividing data into similar groupings and defining concepts or preliminary definitions of the information about the phenomenon to be studied, which in our case are examples of coping with adversity found in 2 Corinthians. After initially recording this information, we will compile the primary concepts into categories, a process that will provide us with new ways of understanding the phenomenon studied. Finally, the categories will be organized and integrated in order to articulate a clear and coherent theological understanding of the examples of Paul's

---

[70] The last part of this question will be addressed in the discussion section of this thesis, where we will highlight possible connections between the Pauline writings and current research on positive coping with trauma, with the end-goal of developing a theology of posttraumatic coping and its related concepts.

positive coping with traumatic events (Strauss & Corbin, 1994; Bernard & Ryan, 2010; Oktay, 2012).

The selected texts of 2 Corinthians (4:7-5:10; 6:3-10; 11:21b-12:10; 1:3-11) will be analyzed in the order of the reconstruction that we have assumed (Vidal 2007, 2012), following the division of the main passages as found in the Greek New Testament (Aland, et al., 1994), except when indicated otherwise.

Chapter 7

Exegetical Analysis of 2 Corinthians 4:7-5:10

7.1. Paragraph A (2 Cor 4:7-5:10)[71]

4:(7) But we have this treasure in jars of clay to show that this all-surpassing power is from God and not from us. (8) We are hard pressed on every side, but not crushed; perplexed, but not in despair; (9) persecuted, but not abandoned; struck down, but not destroyed. (10) We always carry around in our body the death of Jesus, so that the life of Jesus may also be revealed in our body. (11) For we who are alive are always being given over to death for Jesus' sake, so that his life may also be revealed in our mortal body. (12) So then, death is at work in us, but life is at work in you. (13) It is written: "I believed; therefore I have spoken." Since we have that same spirit of faith, we also believe and therefore speak, (14) because we know that the one who raised the Lord Jesus from the dead will also raise us with Jesus and present us with you to himself. (15) All this is for your benefit, so that the grace that is reaching more and more people may cause thanksgiving to overflow to the glory of God.

(16) Therefore we do not lose heart. Though outwardly we are wasting away, yet inwardly we are being renewed day by day. (17) For our light and momentary troubles are achieving for us an eternal glory that far outweighs them all. (18) So we fix our eyes not on what is seen, but on what is unseen, since what is seen is temporary, but what is unseen is eternal.

5:(1) For we know that if the earthly tent we live in is destroyed, we have a building from God, an eternal house in heaven, not built by human hands. (2) Meanwhile we groan,

---

[71] From now on we will list the four selected paragraphs of 2 Corinthians as follows: 4: 7-5: 10 (Paragraph A); 6: 3-10 (Paragraph B); 11: 21b-12: 10 (Paragraph C); and 1: 3-11 (Paragraph D). This should not be confused with the enumeration of the Corinthians letters made by Vidal (2007, 2012).

longing to be clothed instead with our heavenly dwelling, (3) because when we are clothed, we will not be found naked. (4) For while we are in this tent, we groan and are burdened, because we do not wish to be unclothed but to be clothed instead with our heavenly dwelling, so that what is mortal may be swallowed up by life. (5) Now the one who has fashioned us for this very purpose is God, who has given us the Spirit as a deposit, guaranteeing what is to come.

(6) Therefore we are always confident and know that as long as we are at home in the body we are away from the Lord. (7) For we live by faith, not by sight. (8) We are confident, I say, and would prefer to be away from the body and at home with the Lord. (9) So we make it our goal to please him, whether we are at home in the body or away from it. (10) For we must all appear before the judgment seat of Christ, so that each of us may receive what is due us for the things done while in the body, whether good or bad.

7.2. Exegetical Commentary

As we mentioned before, this passage probably makes up part of the third letter to the Corinthians (Cor C: 2 Cor 2:14-7:4), written in the summer of 53 AD in Ephesus, in the context of the start of an important crisis in the church of Corinth resulting from the arrival of Christian missionaries that aggravated existing problems to the detriment of the community and its relationship with Paul. It seems the Apostle's praxis and approach to ministry was quite different than that of these missionaries, who strongly criticized Paul's work and way of carrying out the mission. When he wrote this letter, Paul seems to not yet have a clear image of those opposing him, though he did later when writing Cor D (2 Cor 10:1-13:13) after a visit to Corinth that ended up being a failure. This letter is eminently apologetic in nature, as we will see upon analyzing the selected passage below (Vidal, 2007, 2012).

Second Corinthians 4:7-5:10 is a part of Cor C that introduces themes different from the previous context, characterized by the style of paradoxical discourse[72]. Paul addersses the topic of human mortality and contrasts it with the sufficiency of God. He also highlights the living power of Jesus' resurrection, pointing out what is in store at the end of times for those who follow him.

The entire passage of 2 Corinthians 4:8-5:10 is structured in a very particular way. We can observe a dynamic of dialectical argumentation in this text[73]. Paul makes a series of paradoxical assertions between negative experiences and positive responses to them; between the temporary and the eternal; between the irrelevant and the transcendent. These contrasts are introduced in verse 7, where the Apostle sets up the theme of the power of God (of Christ and his message) in contrast with the brokenness of his messengers. We can visualize this dialectic in Box 1.

2 Corinthians 4:7-9

4:(7) But we have this treasure in jars of clay to show that this all-surpassing power is from God and not from us. (8) We are hard pressed on every side, but not crushed;

---

[72] Most of the passages we have selected from 2 Corinthians can be classified as diatribe, since they are written in defense of Paul's ministry against those opposing him in Corinth. A heavy use of paradox is found in these passages as a mode of argument, though we can also consider this style to be an expression of the antithetical parallelism that is characteristic of Hebrew poetry. Paul's use of paradox is multi-layered and to analyze it requires different approaches. For example, we could take a rhetorical approach and a theological approach, with neither being incompatible with the other. A notable characteristic of the authentic Pauline writings is the predominant use of paradox in his letters to the Corinthians (particularly 2 Cor) and the Philippians. In contrast, it is notably absent in the main theological letters (Rom and Gal). This can be explained by the purpose of the letters: while in Corinthians and Philippians Paul must strongly deal with personal enemies, defend his ministry, and resolve pastoral problems, in Romans and Galatians he lays out a basic overview of his theology (Hotze, 1997; Sainsbury, 1988; Sorensens, 2005).

[73] One common type of Pauline paradox, which we will observe in various instances in our analysis of the selected texts, is what we can call a "dialectic between life and death". In large part, these paradoxes fundamentally stress that life is superior to death (as well as concepts associated with death), special examples of which can be found in three paragraphs: 2 Corinthians 4:7-12; 6:8-10; and 1:3-11. The other main type of paradox is related to the theme of "strength in weakness found in 1 Corinthians 4:9-13; 2 Corinthian 11:21b-12:10, and Philippians 3:7-11. Although the transitions between these two generic types of basic paradoxes found in the work of Paul are not so clear, important sub-types can emerge through close analysis (Hotze, 1997).

perplexed, but not in despair; (9) persecuted, but not abandoned; struck down, but not destroyed [...]

2 Cor 4:7. The first verse in this section shows a double contrast: first, between the treasure (*thesauros*[74]) of the light of the gospel, or Christ himself (cf. 2 Cor 4:4-6), and the jars of clay (*ostrakinois skeuesin*[75]), which have minimal value; and second, between the supernatural power of God and human weakness. Paul does not only refer to himself in feeling like a jar of clay, but rather to anyone that has stored up the good news of salvation. We can understand that the treasure is the presence of God in Christ, who "made his light shine in our hearts" (2 Cor 4:6). We can also see it as the "gospel that displays the glory of Christ, who is the image of God" (2 Cor 4:4). This message is Jesus himself, recognized as Christ and Lord. Paul notes that this proclamation and presence is invaluable, a treasure that we carry as if we were jars of clay.

The foundational characteristic of the image Paul paints here seems to be the contrast between the incomparable value of Christ and the gospel, and how fragile and vain the followers of Chris are in comparison. In this way, Paul points out a paradoxical element of the messenger of the gospel, and Christians in general, who know themselves to be fragile and poor, but nevertheless possess and contain an ultimate good. He also identifies himself as a vessel that can show

---

[74] For the meaning of greek terms, we will use the following from here on out: Kittel, Bromiley & Friedrich (1964); Brown (1985); Coenen, Beyreuther & Bietenhard (1990); Freedman (1992); Newman (1993); Friberg, Friberg & Miller (2000); Thayer (2006). Other references will be cited in specific instances. In this work all the words in Greek (and Hebrew) are presented in transliterations to English (without use of tildes), since they are used as a general reference, especially thinking of readers of fields not involved with the biblical languages.

[75] In that time, this type of container (*ostrakinois skeuesin*) was used for various purposes, from holding valuable items like jewels or coins, to everyday consumables such as liquids or food. Because of the material they were made of, these containers were very fragile. They were therefore low-cost and easy to replace. It is possible that Paul could also be referring to clay or earthenware lamps that were lit with oil to provide light. This could be connected with the previous verse (2 Cor 4:6) and its allusions to the light of creation (Gen 1:3). In this way, describing the human condition of being made out of clay can refer both to original human fragility as well as to holding the light of Christ (Bishop, 1971; Mason & Robinson, 2004; Beale & Carson, 2007).

others "the light of the knowledge of God's glory displayed in the face of Christ" (2 Cor 4:6; cf. Mat 5:14-16). This means that he has a transcendent perspective of his self-worth, not based in aspects of his own self, but rather the gift he received, the sublime and unconditional divine presence. For Christians, the metaphor of the clay jar allows us to understand that Christ's servant or messenger should never exalt himself or project an image of personal power, but instead should be a faithful vessel and dispenser of God's message and powerful presence[76].

Paul was living proof of this fragility and vulnerability, having continually faced suffering, mistreatment, and extreme adversity, which on many occasions involved traumatic events where his physical integrity was gravely damaged and threatened by the imminent possibility of violent death[77].

Box 1: Argumentation Through Contrasts (2 Cor 4:7-5:10)

Negative	Positive
4: in jars of clay	(7) But we have this treasure to show that this all-surpassing power is from God
and not from us. (8) We are hard pressed on every side,	
perplexed,	but not crushed;
(9) persecuted,	but not in despair;
struck down,	but not abandoned;

---

[76] It is interesting that the author of Acts also connects this image of the vessel with the Apostle, where the risen Jesus describes Paul as a "chosen vessel (*skeuos*, cf. 2 Cor 4:6a, where the same term is used) of Mine to bear My name before Gentiles" (Acts 9:15, NKJV). When bearing Jesus' name, the messenger should remain a jar of clay, to show the power of God, or the extraordinary quality of *his* power (2 Cor 4:7b) in a way that the whole world can see that God is the source of true goodness and to him alone be all the glory. This is most evident in the midst of the adversity and suffering that Christians face. As Acts mentions next: "For I will show him how many things he must suffer for My name's sake" (Acts 9:16, NKJV).

[77] We will examine this in more detail later on in our analysis of 2 Corinthians.

(10) We always carry around in our body the death of Jesus,	but not destroyed.
Are always being given over to death for Jesus' sake,	so that the life of Jesus may also be revealed in our body.
in our mortal body.	(11) For we who are alive so that his life may also be revealed
(12) So then, death is at work in us,	but life is at work in you. (13) It is written: "I believed; therefore I have spoken." Since we have that same spirit of faith, we also believe and therefore speak, (14) because we know that the one who raised the Lord Jesus from the dead will also raise us with Jesus and present us with you to himself. (15) All this is for your benefit, so that the grace that is reaching more and more people may cause thanksgiving to overflow to the glory of God (16) Therefore we do not lose heart.
Though outwardly we are wasting away,	yet inwardly we are being renewed day by day.
(17) For our light and momentary troubles	Are achieving for us an eternal glory that far outweighs them all;
(18) So we fix our eyes not on what is seen,	but on what is unseen;
since what is seen is temporary,	but what is unseen is eternal.
5: (1) For we know that if the early tent we live in is destroyed,	we have a building from God, an eternal house in heaven, not built by human hands.
(2) Meanwhile we groan,	

	longing to be clothed instead with our heavenly dwelling,
(3) because when we are clothed,	
	we will not be found naked.
(4) For while we are in this tent, we groaned and are burdened, because we do not wish to be unclothed,	
	but to be clothed instead with our heavenly dwelling, so that what is mortal may be swallowed up by life. (5) Now the one who has fashioned us for this very purpose is God, who has given us the Spirit as a deposit, guaranteeing what is to come.
that as long as we are at home in the body we are away from the Lord.	
	(6) Therefore we are always confident and know
	(7) For we live by faith, not by sight (8) We are confident, I say, and would prefer to be away from the body and at home with the Lord.
	(9) So we make it our goal to please him
whether we are at home in the body,	or away from it.
	(10) For we must all appear before the judgment seat of Christ, so that each of us may receive what is due us for the things done while in the body, whether good
or bad.	

The condition of weakness and vulnerability is seen as an opportunity for good to be manifest, as a carrier of the higher power that transcends one's own capacity. Paul considers himself to be the person that is least qualified to be an Apostle, given that he persecuted the church (1 Cor 15:8-9). There may have been others more qualified according to the criteria of this world, but God chooses his servants among those that are impaired in some way, who are despised (1 Cor 1:25-31).

The first two verses (2 Cor 4:8-9) echo 1 Corinthians 4:11-13: "To this very hour we go hungry and thirsty, we are in rags, we are brutally treated, we are homeless. We work hard with our own hands. When we are cursed, we bless; when we are persecuted, we endure it; when we are slandered, we answer kindly. We have become the scum of the earth, the garbage of the world-right up to this moment." As we will see, this is very much in line with the other lists of tribulations that Paul makes later on (2 Cor 1:8-10; 6:4-10; 11:23-27; 12:10).

Here Paul makes a contrast between four different sets of experiences that illustrate the thesis of the verse before (2 Cor 4:7): the first of each pair is related to adversity and suffering (which corroborate the "jars of clay"), while the second ("but...") signal the action of God as a source of power that allows one to overcome the calamity, as a demonstration of the "treasure" and "enormous power" of God that are available to those that serve him.

2 Cor 4:8a. It is important to note that the Apostle is writing in the first person plural, thus involving his brothers and sisters in the experiences he describes. There are four types of tribulation that Paul describes with negative phrases, each of which is followed by a verb. They have faced difficulty "on every side" (*en panti*), which speaks to the multidimensionality of their afflictions (physical, psychological, social, spiritual), and can also indicate a variety of types of affliction, which he lists with detail here and elsewhere. The phrase "hard pressed" (*thlibo*) alludes primarily to the acts of squeezing or pressing (like grapes when making when), referring to the pressures and stresses of the world. When faced with this, Paul says he does not feel "crushed" (*stenochoros*), a term alluding to anxiety and anguish[78]. Paul indicates that in the midst of the adversity he does not feel anguished, or suffocated, is not

---

[78] It is interesting that these concepts in Latin (*anxietas* and *angustus*) come from the ancient indo-european term *angh*, which means to strangle, squeeze, press (Gómez de Silva, 1998). These uses are connected to suffocation, which is consistent with the fact that in the majority of ancient cultures life was associated with breathing and death with the cesation of breathing, as indicated by the terms *ruaj* from Hebrew and *pneuma* from Greek (Wolff, 1973; Bultmann, 1981).

afraid of dying, and does not feel trapped when faced with death, not even it is imminent (cf. 2 Cor 1:8-11).

2 Cor 4:8b. Here we see a play on words: *a-poroumenoi* (to be disoriented, perplexed), but not *ex-a-poroumenoi* (to be in despair). Paul's team has at various occasions felt lost or perplexed, but nevertheless, they have not been completely disheartened and hopeless, and have always been able to find a way through adversity (cf. 1 Cor 10:13).

2 Cor 4:9a. "Persecuted, but not abandoned". Here Paul describes their experience as those that feel (*diokomenoi*) the pursuit of their enemies (cf. Mt 5:10-12), but that never feel left behind (*enkataleipo*) and abandoned in the middle of the conflict, helpless (Robertson, 2003). Here one can hear the echo of the promises of the God of Israel "[...] for the Lord your God goes with you; he will never leave you nor forsake you" (Dt 31:6); "[...] the valley of the shadow of death [...] you are with me" (Psalm 23:4a); "Do not be afraid; do not be discouraged, for the Lord your God will be with you wherever you go." (Jos 1:9b).

2 Cor 4:9b. "Struck down, but not destroyed", being thrown or knocked down (*katabalo*), as the Roman wrestlers would do, lifting their opponent up before throwing them to the ground. However, for Paul, these continual falls did not result in destruction, death or total loss (*apolumi*). Here, Barrett (1977) observes a dialectic framed theologically in the crucifixion-resurrection duality, which Paul makes explicit in the next verse.

2 Corinthians 4:10-12

4:(10) We always carry around in our body the death of Jesus, so that the life of Jesus may also be revealed in our body. (11) For we who are alive are always being given over to death for Jesus' sake, so that his life may also be revealed in our mortal body. (12) So then, death is at work in us, but life is at work in you.

2 Cor 4:10a. Here, Paul alludes to the itinerant lifestyle of never-ending pilgrimage (*peripherontes*, lit. "to carry about") as a missionary. He describes this condition as a continuous experience where he physically experiences both the death and the resurrection of Jesus.

When he says "We always carry around in our body the death (*nekrosin*) of Jesus," Paul does not use the most common word for death (*thanatos*), but instead a word that describes death as a process, the mortification of the body which is the process of its final weakening, agony, and decomposition (*nekrosis*). However, Paul could have been referring to both the agony and death of Jesus (Fitzgerald, 1988).

Just as Jesus suffered and died, the work of Paul and his co-workers was also marked by extreme adversities, the dangers of death and suffering. The Apostle's proclamation is defined by the message of a suffering Christ who died, and not just any death, but death on the cross (Phil 4:8; Gal 3:1). As did his Lord, Paul shows a disposition to physically suffer for him, carrying his death and agony in his body. The scars on his skin were certainly proof of his sufferings for Jesus (Gal 6:17). They are therefore not the markings of just any suffering, they are not the wounds or scars of just any adversity: for Paul, he and his co-workers physically carry the agony of the Lord Jesus Christ himself on their bodies. There are one with him in suffering, even in death if necessary, for their cause (cf. Phil 4:7-11).

2 Cor 4:10b. "So that the life of Jesus may also be revealed in our body". Based on the detailed lists of adversities that Paul described, he could have easily died on various occasions. However, he and his co-workers hold on the hope of being freed from death (although there were times when he almost lost home, cf 2 Cor 1:8-18). And given that they could face inevitable death at any moment, the Apostle says that they remain confident that they would arrive in the presence of the Lord Jesus and be resurrected as he was (cf. Phil 1:21-26; Rom 8:11; 1 Cor 15). The hope of the resurrection is what allows him to face his own death as an event that does not hinder him in a disruptive way. When death is foreseen, it ceases to be deeply distressing.

In verses 10 and 11, Jesus' name is mentioned three times. It seems to be grammatically unnecessary, but it is possible that Paul used this reiteration to show how inspiring his Lord was to him, as an perfect example of perseverance, especially in moments of intense suffering, but also in how he defeated death through his own resurrection.

2 Cor 4:11. Paul sees his life as a continuous exposure to death (cf. 2 Cor 6:9) for the cause of the gospel, just as Jesus himself had predicted for his followers (Mt 5:11-13; 10:16; Mr 13:9; Jn 16:2). "We who are alive," those who have experienced life through Jesus, or those Christians that have not yet died, before the *parousia* (Barrett, 1973)[79].

It seems that the Apostle had in mind the idea of a suffering people: "For your sake we face death all day long; we are considered as sheep to be slaughtered" (Rom 8:36, cf. Psalm 44:22). For Paul, this surrender to death links him to his Lord, since in the same way that Jesus gave himself up for Paul (Gal 2:20), so Paul wants to follow his example and become like him in everything, even in death (Phil 3:10).

For Paul, "carry around [...] the death of Jesus" is directly connected with its counterpart: that "the life of Jesus may also be revealed in our (mortal, *thnete*) body (*sarki*)" (v.10b). This last way of referring to one's body can be translated as "flesh condemned to death", and evokes a condition of fragility and decomposition of the human constitution, but also the condition of those that physically suffer for the cause of the gospel and redefine it from a place of hope in Jesus, who is seen as a real presence that can infuse his own transcendent life into those who are "condemned to death" (2 Cor 4:14; 1 Thes 4:14; Rom 8:11).

For Paul, apostleship becomes the earthly manifestation of the gospel, and apostolic suffering can be understood as the physical epiphany of the crucified Christ that he himself announces. The Apostle identifies himself with Jesus, and this allows him to understand himself as a follower of someone who experienced extreme suffering and agony (which he had experienced himself in his ministry). When Paul suffers while preaching the gospel, it is a concrete, physical representation of the passion of Jesus Christ himself. He becomes a tangible conveyor of the message, since the sufferings of an apostle, and of any follower of Jesus, are a manifestation of Christ's suffering and death, and therefore a form of proclaiming the gospel (cf. Furnish, 2007; Plummer, 2013).

2 Cor 4:12. Paul mentions that Jesus' death is a work in him and his co-workers, and that Jesus's life is at work in the Corinthians. For the Apostle, the wellbeing of his brothers and sisters in the faith is

---

[79] Here, the verb *paradidomi*, can be translated in a passive voice: "we are being given over", or in the middle: "we give ourselves over to death", in the sense of surrendering voluntarily, or not resisting, when death for the cause of Jesus presents itself (Fitzgerald, 1988).

fundamentally important when he faces adversity, as he mentions here and elsewhere (1Thes 3:37-8; 2 Cor 4:13, 15; 2 Cor 7:4-7).

On numerous occasions, Paul and his partners experienced suffering and calamitous events, seeking a greater good for the benefit of other disciples and/or communities. This did not necessarily imply that those communities did not suffer themselves for following Jesus. Nevertheless, Paul was certain that the life of Jesus was already working in his readers. "The "life" at work in the Corinthians speaks of spiritual life afforded the Corinthians by the proclamation of the gospel under the power of the Spirit" (Guthrie, 2015, p. 261). A life that not only is manifested at the final resurrection, but in the day-to-day life of a community that resists adversity and comes out on the other side even stronger than before.

In synthesis, we can say that the life of the Apostle and his co-workers, just like Jesus, was marked by continuous suffering, but also perseverance and overcoming the adversity they experienced. All of the work, wear and tear, and suffering Paul and his partners went through in carrying out their mission acquires meaning for the fact that it was all done to benefit the churches, in this case the church in Corinth. They were commissioned by God to make the spiritual life that Christ obtained for them become a concrete reality and firm hope in those communities (O'Rourke, 1972).

2 Corinthians 4:13-15

4: (13) It is written: "I believed; therefore I have spoken." Since we have that same spirit of faith, we also believe and therefore speak, (14) because we know that the one who raised the Lord Jesus from the dead will also raise us with Jesus and present us with you to himself. (15) All this is for your benefit, so that the grace that is reaching more and more people may cause thanksgiving to overflow to the glory of God.

2 Cor 4:13-14. This section opens with a phrase taken from Psalm 116:10 (Psalm 115:10, LXX). The psalmist is presented as someone who is conscious of his vulnerability and total dependence on God for survival in the midst of affliction. Faced with death, he prays to God for deliverance. It is possible that Paul is identifying himself with the psalmist, since when faced with affliction it is common to meditate on the meaning of life and death, as expressed in the psalm. "We also (*kai hemeis*) believe (*pisteos*) and therefore speak (*elalesa*) [...]". What do they believe in, and what are they speaking about? Verse 14 gives us the answer: in Jesus as risen Lord (*egeiras*), and in the resurrection of his followers to be together in his presence. The resurrection is a central truth in Paul's preaching (cf. Rom 6:4-5; 8:11; 1 Cor 6:14; 15:15, 20; Phil 3:10-11).

> Mostly Paul speaks of faith in terms of trust in Christ or in God. It is the basic attitude that brings people out of their sinfulness into a right relationship with the Deity. So fundamental is faith that the term may be used to categorize the whole Christian way, and the expression "the faith" comes into being, not simply as a way of referring to the trust in Christ that is so basic, but as a means of drawing attention to the whole body of teaching and practice that characterizes the Christian group. (Morris, 1992, p. 229)

For Paul, faith in God is vitally important. It is significant that Christian conversion could be summed up by the simple act of believing (cf. Rom 1:16; 1 Cor 1:21). But the Apostle does not refer to a rational acceptance of specific ideas, or a superficial or emotional experience. Rather, he speaks of a deeply intimate experience (Rom 10:9) that is primarily focused on the fact that God raised Jesus from the dead, and that Jesus is the Messiah and Lord.

The recognition of Jesus as Messiah and Lord is intrinsic to the Christian faith, along with recognizing the miracle of his resurrection (Bultmann, 1962). In this way, faithfulness (*pisteos*) is understood as trust in Jesus as the Christ, and also takes on an eschatological dimension. What is believed and preached (*elalesa*) is the resurrection of Jesus, as well as hope in the resurrection itself and the communal (*parastesei*) encounter with the risen Lord. This eschatological faith stands in radical contrast with the brevity and fragility of the present life and its sufferings, which Paul has mentioned.

2 Cor 4:15. According to this verse, the act of thanksgiving invites a more abundant grace, which we can also find in the Old Testament (2 Cron 20:19-22; Psalm 18:3; Psalm 50:23). The Greek verb *pleonazein* (multiply) indicates that God multiplies his grace as more people receive it, and in this way is glorified. In the case of Paul, his mission seeks the immediate good of those that come to faith in Jesus

Christ in a way that ultimately and fundamentally seeks the glory of God (cf. Rom 11:36, 15:6; 1 Cor 1:31, 10:31; Phil 1:11; 2:11). In Paul, this focus is also relevant when facing his tribulations.

Considering himself the spiritual father of the Corinthians, the Apostle is truly interested in their lives and is fully disposed to serve them and seek their benefit. For them, he was willing to suffer great penalty, including being exposed to death. And this he connects to grace, the undeserved gift of God through Christ, which he received as a calling and a mandate that redefined his life, and was to be shared with everyone. In this way, grace is multiplied, expands, and generates gratitude in many.

2 Corinthians 4:16-5:5

4:(16) Therefore we do not lose heart. Though outwardly we are wasting away, yet inwardly we are being renewed day by day. (17) For our light and momentary troubles are achieving for us an eternal glory that far outweighs them all. (18) So we fix our eyes not on what is seen, but on what is unseen, since what is seen is temporary, but what is unseen is eternal.

2 Cor 4:16. This verse is similar to the one that starts the chapter: "Therefore, since through God's mercy we have this ministry, we do not lose heart" (2 Cor 4:1). The ministry of Paul and his co-workers, as he has been saying, has been very costly. However, despite the suffering that this has brought them, they are not dismayed or discouraged (*egkakoumen*). They are even looking to encourage others in the midst of their own sufferings.[80]

Here Paul continues with the positive/negative dialectic that we have observed throughout this section, referring to facets of the human condition: the exterior self (*exo anthropos*)/interior self (*eso anthropos*); and destruction (*diapftheiretai*)/renovation (*avakainoutai*).

As proposed and developed by Bultmann in his *Theology of the New Testament* (1958), where he examines the anthropological concepts

---

[80] A good example of this is found in Paul's letter to the Philippians, where he writes with gratitude and in good spirits in the midst of such an adverse context as the conditions in prison were at that time.

found in Pauline theology, Paul's perspective is framed within a holistic Hebrew perspective of human beings and not a Greek perspective, even in this passage of 2 Corinthians it could appear that this is not the case[81].

Paul shares his life, giving an account of the adversities and afflictions experienced over the years, and the physical and psychological toll of his missionary pilgrimage with his partners. He sees that he is progressively wasting away, as a result of his arduous service but also as the natural result of his humanity. His "exterior human face", as one could literally translate the term *exo anthro-pos* (Friberg, Friberg & Miller, 2000), his visible self and appearance, is completely disintegrating (*thiaphdseiro*). This is not happening on the inside, which for Paul relates to his perspective on life as a container holding the treasure of God in Christ, his existence seen from the eternal reality to which he has been called, but has already begun to experience.

Paul does not believe in the transmigration of souls, but in the resurrection, an idea rejected by the Greek philosophers (cf. Acts 17:32). Therefore, here he is not adapting himself to an audience with a dualistic understanding. To assume that Paul has an understanding of humanity founded in the Old Testament[82] has various implications.

---

[81] Here we have chosen to take this perspective that sees continuity between Paul's thinking and Hebrew anthropological concepts. But we understand that it is a topic of discussion, since some others see a marked Platonic or Hellenistic influence on Paul's anthropology. Others propose that, although we cannot recognize a purely Hellenistic perspective in Paul's writings, his approach would be a creative synthesis of both Hebrew and Greek sources (Jewett, 1971; Gundry, 2005; Van Kooten, 2008; Engberg-Pedersen, 2010; Tasmuth, 2014; Wasserman, 2014). Here we cannot enter into this discussion in-depth, since it goes beyond our primary topic of study, but we will briefly address some of what has been proposed in line with what we are focused on, which seem relevant for our research.

[82] The language of the Semitic culture was very concrete, and even abstract concepts where described by the Hebrews by using words or categories that were predominantly material. Such is the case of the understanding of human beings, which does not separate the body from the *psuche* (Pidoux, 1969). In the NT, the Greek translation of *nephesh* is used, which even though it has been interpreted under Platonic or Aristotelian influence in different theological traditions, according to various authors we can suggest that *psuche*, in its New Testament usage, corresponds to the Hebrew term *nephesh*, and not to the concept of "soul" in neither the dualistic Greek, Stoic, or Epicurean sense. (Ferrater Mora, 1955; Bultmann, 1958; Eichrodt, 1975; Wolff, 1975; Aguilera, 1988; Ruiz de la Peña, 1988;

In the Corinthians' way of the thinking, common wisdom about human destiny was derived from widely held Platonic philosophy of the day that taught that the soul was immortal and imprisoned in the body which was conceived as its prison. As Socrates says according to the Platonic dialogue:

> Every wisdom seeker knows that until the moment when philosophy takes hold of his soul, this is a defenseless prisoner, chained feet and hands to the body, forced to look at reality not directly, but only through the bars of his prison and wallowing in complete ignorance (Phaedo, 82e).

Considering this, we might ask: What would the Platonic sages of Corinth think of Paul's proclaiming the bodily resurrection of Jesus, announcing not the liberation of the body in death, like the brave Socrates, but the reintegration of his body and soul into eternal life? All this would have been considered foolish, since a bodily resurrection, in Platonic logic, was like taking on the most vile bonds that imprison us here and now until eternity (Crossan & Reed, 2006).

Commonly translated as *psuche*, the Hebrew term *nephesh* carries a complex range of meaning, in such a way that we do not have a directly equivalent term in our modern languages. In the Hebrew worldview, human beings are from the beginning solely made as living *nephesh*, where sensory experiences are always understood as a whole, not making major distinctions between different feelings, since sensations act together when encountered in the world. It is the self as *nephesh* that perceives reality. The *nephesh* is holistically made up of all

Pedersen, 1991; Pannenberg, 1985, 2004; Thorsteinsson, 2010; Boeri & Salles, 2014; Løkke, 2015). For most scholars, in the NT we do not find texts where the *soma-psuche* scheme unequivocally appears as distinct components of the human person. In the many places that use the two terms at the same time, they take a different meaning than the Greek (or modern Cartesian) dichotomous understanding. When *psuche* is used by itself, we recognize the Hebrew term *nephesh*. Particularly, the Pauline concept of the human person is founded in the OT, which certain specific nuances, which we will not explore with the depth it deserves given how much time this would take. Paul does not seem to ever utilize the concept of soul (*psuche*) in the Hellenistic way of understanding it as an immortal substance that can be separated from the body. Paul does not talk about a liberation of the body, and neither does he seek redemption through immaterial fusion with divinity nor an eternal existence as a bodiless spirit, but rather, he speaks of permanent bodily resurrection (Bultmann, 1958; León-Dufour, 1974; Ruiz de la Peña, 1988; Wright, 2008; Lehtipuu, 2015).

the aspects and dimensions of the human being, including its appearance, voice, smell, color, and hairy skin, for example. But, in a special way, a fundamental aspect of the *nephesh* is the way it acts, and relates to the world and with others (Wolff, 1975; Pedersen, 1991; Cruz-Villalobos, 2014b).

On the other hand, within this understanding, everything that a person possesses and that belongs to his environment is penetrated and made up by his *nephesh*: his body, clothes, tools, house, animals, the totality of his possessions: his world. Along these lines, the *nephesh* is more than the body, but the body is a concrete manifestation of the *nephesh*. In the Hebrew mentality, *nephesh* and the body are so intimately united that one cannot distinguish between them. We could even say that they are more than "united", saying that the body is the *nephesh* in its visible, exterior form (Pedersen, 1991)[83].

In the Pauline dialectic, as his outer existence evidently weakens and is destined to slow destruction, his inner reality is renewed, because he is strengthened by God, even in the middle of the most arduous of adversity. And this is not just for Paul, as an exceptional man, but it is a reality that he continues to describe in the plural thus including his co-workers. He is also encouraging the church in this understanding, disposition, and implied conduct.

In this way, the disciple of Christ can experience the progress of his new life day after day, gaining strength to trust in God, proclaim the good news, and face any adversity and suffering. Although he outwardly wastes away, being naturally subject to deterioration, this does not happen in his innermost being, where he knows that he is sustained by an eschatological hope in the resurrection that inspires him to continue, and allows him to be renewed and overcome adverse circumstances (cf. Rom 8:35-39).

Paul continues his argumentation by contrasts in verses 17 and 18, where he juxtaposes "our light and momentary troubles" (4:17) with the fact that they achieve "[...] for us an eternal glory that far outweighs

---

[83] The contrast presented by Paul, where he speaks of "the outer self that wastes away" and "the inner self that is renewed," is also similarly seen in texts where Paul's authorship is debated, such as "your old self, which is being corrupted by its deceitful desires" (Eph 4:22) and "the new self, which is being renewed" (Col 3:10). The anthropological concepts implied her also include the complete human person.

them all", which requires a perspective where "we fix our eyes not on what is seen, but on what is unseen, since what is seen is temporary, but what is unseen is eternal" (4:18).

2 Cor 4:17. By describing the afflictions (*thlipseos*)[84] that he experiences as light (*elaphron*) and momentary (*parautika*), Paul sets up a contrast between that which is ephemeral, instantaneous, and vain (cf. *hebel*), and that which is permanent/eternal (*baros*) and splendid/"far outweighs them all" (*doxes*) (cf. *kabod*). Their adversities, which are subject to this ephemeral time and place, are light and momentary in the light of that which is glorious and permanent. And these tribulations are impactful in that they bring about (*katergazomai*) the ability to understand more deeply the greatness of the good that is to come (Martin, 1986)[85].

Thus, the Apostle juxtaposes that which is momentary and insignificant (the present affliction), with that which is eternal and transcendent (the coming glory). By doing this, he relativizes what he has suffered, but not in himself. In this way, he is not trivializing suffering, or a nullifying the body and its distress, to the point where it no longer is relevant. Clearly, Paul is talking about great adversities, which almost cost him his life on various occasions and should not be forgotten. He thematizes them at various points, but always in reference to the greatness of the supreme good God has given, and how God makes it possible to overcome the suffering and experience, in the present moment, a taste of the glorious power of the resurrection that is near. I consider that our present sufferings are not worth comparing with the glory that will be revealed in us (Rom 8:18).

2 Cor 4:18. How is it possible to come to such an understanding of suffering? In this verse, Paul gives indications of how to arrive at this particular way of seeing and facing adversity. Here the Apostle sets up a dialectic on the focus of attention, the perspective between what is seen (*ta bletomena*) and what is unseen (*ta me bletomena*). Paul writes

---

[84] The words for "tribulation" or "affliction" (*thlipsis, thlibo*) and "suffering" (*pathoma*) occur more frequently in 2 Corinthians than anywhere else in the NT (Orr, 2016).

[85] We can connect this idea with Paul's use of the concept *sunergei* (to work togther) in Romans 8:28-29, where he proposes that from experiencing divine affection, everything can be understood as an opportunity to carry out God's work, which is described as formation of a large family of sons and daughters in the likeness of Jesus.

that, when one centers their meticulous attention (*skopounton*) on invisible things, their afflictions are put in their rightful place, as well as the coming eternal glory that has already begun to manifest itself in the new life received from God by the believer.

Paul invites the disciples of Christ to not focus on things that can be seen, which coincide with the negative side of what he has been showing in his dialectic argument: adversity and suffering, which for Paul are in the category of the temporary, the fleeting, and the momentary. His invitation is to focus on what is not being seen, which is not temporary but rather eternal, and carries an enormous weight of glory (2 Cor 4:17), and in the future resurrection (2 Cor 4:14) as a concrete participation in the coming transcendent reality. This eschatological goodness, however, has already begun to be manifest as a present treasure[86], but in "jars of clay" (2 Cor 4:6-7).

Paul does not juxtapose or differentiate between the physical and the spiritual, but between the earthly and the heavenly, and between the temporary and the eternal. He does not seem to take a dualistic view, as we have said in reference to his Hebrew anthropological conception. Additionally, he does not approach the topic of suffering in a speculative or apologetic way (along the lines of a theodicy), but rather from a pastoral perspective, placing emphasis on coping with these afflictions positively. In this way, he encourages a confident eschatology, that is not alienating, since the Apostle takes charge of his sufferings, does not forget them, and interprets them in a constructive way that is connected with his hope for the future.

By emphasizing eternity and that which is perpetual (*aionios*), Paul relativizes all that he experiences in the present times, reduces its significance, and removes its connotation of definite finality (ultimate). The "inner" and "invisible" reality, the treasure of lasting glory that the believer has received and enjoys in part already by having the Spirit as a guaranty, allows him to overcome adversity and move forward with the hope of eternity.

---

[86] Knowing "the power of the resurrection" (Phil 3:10) could connote a foretaste of the coming glory in the present life, which is to say, seeing the resurrection not just in from an eschatological perspective, but also as being imminent, although also transcendent, since its full manifestation is expected at the end times.

5:(1) For we know that if the earthly tent we live in is destroyed, we have a building from God, an eternal house in heaven, not built by human hands. (2) Meanwhile we groan, longing to be clothed instead with our heavenly dwelling, (3) because when we are clothed, we will not be found naked. (4) For while we are in this tent, we groan and are burdened, because we do not wish to be unclothed but to be clothed instead with our heavenly dwelling, so that what is mortal may be swallowed up by life. (5) Now the one who has fashioned us for this very purpose is God, who has given us the Spirit as a deposit, guaranteeing what is to come.

This paragraph is a prime example of Paul's use of the modality of contrasts, which has been used surrounding the theme of suffering since verse 8 of chapter 4. It presents some exegetical difficulties, as some authors have noted (Cassidy, 1971; Harris, 1970, 1971, 1985; Duff, 1991; Hanhart, 1997; Lambrecht, 2003; Furnish, 2007; Seifrid, 2015), especially in regards to Paul's anthropology found here. In our commentary, however, we will focus on the text from the assumption that Paul is fundamentally writing with pastoral intention, which seeks to care for and impart hope on the communities receiving his letter, as well as his apologetic intentions regarding his ministry, which we will also see in this paragraph.

In light of the previous verses (2 Cor 4:16-18), which speak of the inner and outer self, and encourage the readers to not focus on what is seen but rather on what is unseen, Paul returns here to the theme of the resurrection to refer to the future destiny of the present human condition: the anticipation of what we believe, and the hope that what has been promised will be fulfilled, that affects the way in which Christians live in the present time (Bultmann, 1985).

2 Cor 5:1. In this verse, Paul uses a metaphor that continues with the play of contrasts that he has been using to this point. He talks about the current existence as being our present (*epigeios*) home (*oikia*), which is temporary (*skenos*, in the sense of a hut or a camping tent). If this present reality that we are collapses, disintegrates, or is destroyed (*kataluo*), the Apostle says that we already have (*echomen*) a building (house or home, *oikodome*) from God, which is not built (*acheipopointon*) by humans, but is eternal in heaven (*aionion en toiis ouranoiis*).

Paul already developed the theme of the resurrection in certain detail in previous letters (1 Thes 4 and 1 Cor 15), and here he does not appear to contradict what he had said, although he does provide a more applied perspective, placing emphasis on the *hic et nunc* dimensions of the resurrection, along the lines of what he says in Philippians 3:10 about knowing "the power of the resurrection". The Apostle can say "For we know" (2 Cor 5:1a, cf. Rom 8:28) because he has a certain knowledge reinforced by experience[87], and in this way he has also though the Corinthians about this topic. As he shows in 1 Thessalonians 4:14, his intention is not to embark on abstract speculation about immortality, but respond to a concrete reality of suffering, and seek to provide comfort and hope. In this way, trust in the resurrection enables one to face death in different way than normal. It allows for an interpretation that helps those who believe to overcome the instinctual fear of death (O'Rourke, 1972).

The allusion to the tent easily connects to the idea of the tabernacle in the desert (Num 4), which is described as a wood frame covered by curtains that wore out with time when Israel lived in Canaan, and was replaced by the temple of Solomon. The temple and the tabernacle were similar in their core function, since they were the space destined to guard the symbol of God's presence, the Arc of the Covenant, and where his presence was manifested. Similarly, Paul probably wants his readers to compare and contrast the temporary existence with the eternal existence after the resurrection. God's presence, now understood as the Holy Spirit, inhabits believers as if they were the new temple, which is already definitive, but fully developed only after the resurrection (cf. 1 Cor 2:12; 3:16; 2 Cor 6:16; Rom 8:9-11).

Therefore, Paul again presents a contrast, this time between present existence, which is temporary, limited, and life in the future, which is eternal, glorious, and should be awaited with total certainty (2 Cor 4:17; Rom 8:18).

---

[87] In fact, as mentioned by Barnett (1988), Paul speaks the language of experience. He does not speculate in an abstract way, and does not develop explanatory theories. When he refers to the knowledge of faith, he does not tend to theorize, but instead speaks from facts, from life experience (cf. Boff, 2002).

2 Cor 5:2-3. The temporary life of today is presented in verse 2 as a continuous anxious groaning (*stenazomen*, from *stenos*, narrow), as a constant expression of the incomplete self that, just like all of creation according to Paul, longs for the full adoption and redemption of their body (Rom 8:23). The desire is to be clothed (*endusamenoi*), not in a platonic sense where the body is the prison of the *psuche*, but in the sense of becoming alive. Clothed when Christ comes again, and thus avoiding the total and complete deterioration of death, or complete nakedness (*gumnoi*) (2 Cor 5:4), being remade into a new way of being that is heavenly (*ouranos*), lifted up, permanent, in physical yet "heavenly bodies" (*somata epouranion*) or "spiritual bodies" (*somata pneumatikon*) (1 Cor 15:40-44) [88].

The verb *endusamenoi* means to put on clothes over what one is wearing, as in putting on a coat or cape (Hughes, 1962). Therefore, the longing that Paul writes about is not directly related to the resurrection of the dead, but rather to the transformation to a glorious body, before experiencing death, when Christ returns (cf. 1 Cor 15:51). Paul says that the heavenly body is put on over the earthly body. Obviously, upon death bodies decompose and are not clothed by immortality immediately, and because of this Paul applies the image of new clothes for the believers that are present when Christ returns, but not on those who died before, about which he instead talks about the resurrection. Paul himself longs to be with the Lord (2 Cor 5:8; Phil 1:23), but he would prefer to meet up in his return and be transformed, before dying and having to "wait for" the resurrection (1 Thes 4:13-17; 1 Cor 15:51; Phil 3:21) (Harris, 1985).

2 Cor 5:4. The Apostle has said "hard pressed on every side, but not crushed" (2 Cor 4:8). However, in this verse he says that the groaning of being in this temporary hut, the precarious existence of the present, is agonizing, or more specifically, devastating, and heavy (*bareo*). In verse 4 (which evidently parallels verse 2a), Paul declares his longing to not have to experience death, and instead be covered with

---

[88] In speaking about the temporary existence of the "physical body", Paul suggests that whether through death and resurrection when Jesus comes, or through meeting Jesus at his arrival, the body is transformed (1 Cor 15:42, 51; Phil 3:20-21; 1 Thes 4:15-17). In both cases, a body is awaited which is qualitatively distinct, glorified, but a body nonetheless. The dualist notion of a "disembodied" existence does not fit in here.

immortality in such a way that his mortality is "devoured" or "swallowed whole" (*katapote*) by life (cf. Murray, 2005; Furnish, 2007; Guthrie, 2015).

The resurrection, the glorious transformation, and the dissolution of death in life are described as being the complete works (*katergazamenos*) that God will perform in his people. For Paul, because of this, believers should be confident that it does not matter how severe their sufferings may be in this life, the promise of the resurrection or final transformation is there for them. If Jesus was raised from the dead, then those who follow Christ can with total certainty hope for full and permanent existence. Here lies the idea of a type of exchange process between modes of being: from temporary to eternal; from mortal to eternal; from vain to glorious (Moule, 1965; Simundson, 1992).

2 Cor 5:5. Paul closes this paragraph indicating that God has given his own Spirit as a guaranty of the things that will be revealed in the future. In this way the present life and its imperfect temporality becomes an indication of the future and its fullness (Bultmann, 1985).

But it is not a hope which is disconnected from the experience of the present, since the Spirit, as a guaranty and reality in the moment, encourages believers as they wait. The Apostle also speaks about this in 2 Corinthians 1:22, where he mentions that the Spirit functions as a seal (*sfragizo*), just like the markings that indicated the ownership of property at the time; or as a down-payment or earnest-money (*arrabon*) deposit, which is the term used in this verse, the portion of the purchase that is given at the beginning to guarantee final and complete acquisition of the good that was purchased (cf. Rom 8:23 & Gen 38:17,18, 20). It is a guaranty of what has been promised, an anticipation of what is to come, in such a way that the present life is organized around the promise, which in all certainty will be soon be fulfilled (Behm, 1962; Thayer, 2006).

2 Corinthians 5:6-10

6) Therefore we are always confident and know that as long as we are at home in the body we are away from the Lord. (7) For we live by faith, not by sight. (8) We are confident, I say, and would prefer to be away from the body and at home with the Lord. (9) So we make it our goal to please him, whether we are at home in the body or away from it. (10) For we must all appear before the judgment seat of Christ, so that each of us may receive what is due us for the things done while in the body, whether good or bad.

2 Cor 5:6. Certainly, Paul indicates that one can have bravery and courage because of the guaranty that the Spirit gives to Christians (2 Cor 5:5), which assures them that they will receive final fulfillment. The use of the word "confident" (*tharrheo* or *tharseo*, possibly deriving from *thrasos* (bold, daring, cf. 2 Cor 5:8; Mt 9:2, 22; 14:27; Mr 6:50, 10:49) here seems to connote a fear that fades with the security of knowing that God is in control of what is happening in a given moment, in the perspective of the work he has done already and the promises he has made, as we observe in the majority of Biblical references in this regard (cf. Acts 23:11; John 16:33; 2 Cor 10:2; Heb 13:6) (Thayer, 2006).

Continuing with his dialectic argumentation, here Paul presents a contrast between someone who lives in his own homeland, and a foreigner. We can be confident and have courage in the face of adversity (which is the theme of the context), when we assume the fact that our present bodily reality, which is our home/homeland (*endemeo*), simultaneously implies that we are "away from our homeland" (*ekdemeo*) as foreigners or pilgrims (*paroikos*, cf. 1 Pet 2:11; John 17:14-16) in this world. We are exiled from the full presence of God and the enjoyment of his glory, which will become our reality through the transformation or resurrection of our bodies.

2 Cor 5:7. This is to walk as pilgrims, like permanent migrants. This long-suffered walk in life, before meeting Christ returned and being transformed/resurrection, is a pilgrimage of faith, with trust (*pistis*) in what God has promised, which in the present is seen in glimpses, and held as a deposit.

The Apostle again sets up the visible/invisible dialectic (cf. 2 Cor 4:18), indicating that the walk of faith does not stop and focus on what can be physically seen (*eidos*), and which definitely relates to the negative sides already mentioned, such as:

  – affliction and perplexity (2 Cor 4:8);
  – persecution and abandonment (2 Cor 4:9);
  – carrying around the death of Jesus in the body (2 Cor 4:10);

- living exposed to death for the cause of Jesus, in our mortal body (2 Cor 4:11);
- the work of death in us (2 Cor 4:12);
- our outer-self (2 Cor 4:16);
- our light and momentary troubles (2 Cor 4:17);
- things that are seen, temporary (2 Cor 4:18);
- our earthly tent that is destroyed and from which we groan, because of the undesired possibility of being unclothed in death (2 Cor 5:1-4);
- our concrete separation from God (2 Cor 5:6).

Accordingly, Paul's perspective on the Christian walk is based in eschatological confidence, in the hope of a glorious reality that is near, which we cannot yet see, but that is guaranteed by the Spirit (2 Cor 5:5) and can be enjoyed in hope and anticipation, and thus staying courageous (*tharrheo*) when faced with difficulties. This is said by Paul elsewhere (such as 1 Cor 13:12-13 and Rom 8:23-25), as well as in letters whose authorship is questioned, such as the letter to the Colossians:

> Since, then, you have been raised with Christ, set your hearts on things above, where Christ is, seated at the right hand of God. Set your minds on things above, not on earthly things. For you died, and your life is now hidden with Christ in God. When Christ, who is your life, appears, then you also will appear with him in glory (Col 3:1-4).

2 Cor 5:8. In this verse, Paul again uses the verb *tharreo* (v. 6), emphasizing that we can face this life with courage, even to the point of considering it good (*eudokeo*) that one can be a foreigner in their own body (the agonizing death that he speaks of un v. 4) to be at home with the Lord. This is very much in line with what he proposes in his letter to the Philippians, where he talks about the complex dilemma he experiences between the life of serving Christ and his communities on one hand, and his longing to be fully with Christ (Phil 1:20-25)[89].

---

[89] There are authors who propose that here there are three alternatives for this existence: a) be alive when Christ comes, and receive a transformed and glorified body; b) die, abandon the body, and live at home with the Lord, with a "discovered" soul; c) remain in the body due to one's obligation to serve the church. And there is a broad topic of discussion concerning the "intermediate state", however, it seems to us that, for Paul, this possibility does not exist, especially if we adhere to his underlying Hebrew anthropology

2 Cor 5:9. Here, Paul describes how his ambition, or fundamental desire (*filotiempoomai*), is to completely please (*euarestos*) his lord, just as Jesus himself was described, defining his life as a continuous pursuit of pleasing the Father and only doing his will (Mark 14:34-39; Mat 26:38-42; Luke 22:41-42; Jon 5:36, 8:28-29), regardless of his condition: in life or in death (Phil 1:20).

2 Cor 5:10. The Apostle finishes this section by alluding to the final judgement to cap off this argumentative unit, where the way in which one sought to please Christ through this bodily life, or not, will be evaluated. No one will remain free from being called to appear before the judgement seat, since it is necessary, obligatory (*dei*). Each one's work will be held as evidence by God himself, who "will bring to light what is hidden in darkness and will expose the motives of the heart. At that time each will receive their praise from God" (1 Cor 4:5).

The importance of the present time is emphasized here, since all conduct will be evaluated in the court of Christ. This helps to avoid placing too much emphasis on the future, since each moment in the here and now is relevant. Paul presents an eschatological perspective that, instead of alienating the individual or the community from the world, energetically places them in the present with hope and courage. The Christian experience is seen as a walk with sights set on the horizon that has been promised, of which a deposit is undeniably experienced already through the Holy Spirit, who enables Christ's followers to live a life in the present that is marked by a positive perspective in the middle of tribulations.

By discussing the topic of final judgement to cap of this argumentative unit (2 Cor 4:7-5:10), Paul strongly reinforces the idea that the perspective and behavior that Christ's followers maintain in the midst of adversity will be presented as evidence in front of the Lord. For this, Paul's testimony of courage and perseverance through his

---

that has a preeminently monistic character. As we have mentioned, this is a topic that we cannot address here in detail, for the complexity and depth to which it has already been explored (cf. Bultmann, 1958; Ellis, 1961; Moule, 1966; Pidoux, 1969; Jewett, 1971; Eichrodt, 1975; Wolff, 1975; Ruiz de la Peña, 1988; Pedersen,1991; Murphy-O'Connor, 1994; Pannenberg, 2004; Gundry, 2005; Van Kooten, 2008; Engberg-Pedersen, 2010; Tasmuth, 2014; Wasserman, 2014).

afflictions is seen as an example of service to God and others, worthy of seriously taking into account.

In accordance with what he have considered until now, we can observe that, for Paul, the resurrection (and final transformation) is not simply about life after death, but rather participating in the resurrection and glory of Jesus Christ. The Apostle seems to understand that participating in the life of his Lord, also implies participating, at least in part, in his suffering. For Paul, just as Jesus himself went to glory through a journey of shame and suffering, his followers should been ready to do the same if necessary, since they will participate in the final goal, which is eternal life with him (cf. 2 Cor 5:15).

7.3. Hermeneutical Keys Analysis about Coping from Paragraph A

After completing our general exegetical commentary, we will now focus on the keys for interpreting adversity that can be observed in the text, as we will do with each selected passage. First, they will be presented in a table, organized by categories and specific concepts, and noting the corresponding verses of 2 Corinthians from which they were pulled. After the table, we will give a brief explanation from a theological perspective, of the Pauline hermeneutical keys about coping with adversity, in accordance with the general categories that have been found. Later, in chapter 11, we will discuss all our findings from the perspective of the Psychological Biblical Criticism, when we finish the study of the chosen passages of 2 Corinthians.

Table 3: Hermeneutical Keys about Coping from Paragraph A

(2 Cor 4:7-5:10)

CODE	CATEGORIES	CONCEPTS	2 Cor
A1	Paradoxical Identity	Fragile container of glory, and significant contribution to others	4:7, 16
		Personal identity as a medium of grace, carrier of good for many	4:7
		Non-victimized transcendent identity	4:9
		Suffering Christian identity	4:10

A2	Experience of faith as faithfulness and perseverance	Theologically originated resistance (faith/faithfulness, hope, and love)	4:8-9; 5:6-10
		Confidence in the power of the resurrection	4:9, 13
		Ethical coping that is more than just speculative (theodicy), focused on the kingdom of God in this live, and glorifying God being the ultimate concern	5:1-4, 9
A3	Resignification of death and/or traumatic events	Positive resignification of death	4:8-9; 5:1-2
		Positive resignification of traumatic events	4:10-12
		Appropriating and relativizing what has been suffered	4:10-12; 16-18
		Shifting one's focus away from suffering	4:16-18
A4	Eschatological coping	Coping based on theological promises	4:9; 5:1-5
		Hope in the resurrection as a coping mechanism	4:10-12
		The resurrection as communal hope	4:14
		Eschatological resignification of the present adversity	5:1-4
A6	Identification with Jesus as a model for coping	Identification with Jesus Christ in his death and resurrection	4:10-11
A7	Altruistic coping	Focusing on the good of others before one's personal adversity	4:12,15
A8	Thanksgiving	Thankfulness for the positive action of God in adverse situations	4:15
A9	Detachment from the material and the visible	Focusing on the ultimate good and detaching from what is fleeting and preliminary	4:16-5:8
A10	Expression of traumatic events	Appropriation, remembering, and communicating traumatic events to others	4:8-10

Explanation of the table: The table summarizes the hermeneutical keys about coping found in the passage. The first column lists the code (the capital letter indicates the passage and the number indicates the specific key); the second column lists the category of the key; the third column presents the concepts within each category; and finally, the fourth column indicates the specific biblical references.

A1. Paradoxical identity:

The first key about coping that we observe in this passage is the particular way in which Paul views himself. His identity is described in a paradoxical way: as a fragile container of glory, that is weak and vulnerable, but at the same time has the potential to significantly contribute to the lives of others (2 Cor 4:7, 16). The Apostle sees himself as a medium of grace, who does not deserve his condition as a carrier of superior good for others (2 Cor 4:7).

In the midst of the adversities that he faces, Paul shows a transcendent identify, which enables him to understand himself not in a victimized way as someone that only passively endures adversity, but as someone that can continually overcome (2 Cor 4:9) constant suffering in this life, which reminds him about, and makes him long for, his future resurrection and glory in Christ (2 Cor 4:10).

A2. Experience of faith as faithfulness and perseverance:

Another category of coping that we find in the Pauline text refers to an understanding of faith as faithfulness and perseverance in all circumstances. One discovers a perspective on adverse events that is based in a resistance around the so-called theological virtues: faith, hope, and love. This means that it is a coping mechanism where faithfulness to the Lord (especially manifest in the midst of suffering), hope in him (as a fundamental resource for resistance united with a future vision of fullness), and the conditional bond of affection that God has established for him through Christ, are essential for being able to overcome any kind of difficulty. Therefore, faith is described as an operational way of persevering through present adversity, as faithfulness in situations of opposition, on a foundation of a eschatological vision of victory and glorious final transformation (2 Cor 4:8-9; 5:6-10).

Also in this category, we see in Paul, as a coping mechanism, a profound confidence in the power manifested in the resurrection of

Jesus, which he applies to his own experiences of suffering and "death" (2 Cor 4:9, 13). Paul knows he is a living witness of the power of the resurrection in his own body, having survived so many severe events. This confidence allows him to hopefully cope with whatever comes.

When reflecting on his sufferings and the threats of death that he has had to experience, the Apostle does not speculate for the purpose of justifying God (theodicy) as to why he allowed what happened to Paul and his coworkers to happen. Instead, he assumes an ethical perspective, centered on the hope for the future that brings him to focus on God's reign over his own life, which in turn pushes him to constantly seek to please him, his Lord, and persevere in all circumstances (2 Cor 5:1-4, 9).

A3. Resignification of death and traumatic events:

In this passage we also observe a category of coping with adversity that refers to the resignification of death and, therefore, events where one's life is at risk or personal integrity is threatened. Paul assigns a positive meaning to death (2 Cor 4:8-9; 5:1-2), which is way of facing life-threatening situations. In the same way, he positively re-signifies traumatic events (2 Cor 4:10-12).

Along these same lines, while taking charge of his multiple experiences of suffering he has had (not denying them, but rather thematizing them at various points to generally legitimize or defend his ministry), Paul assigns them a connotation that is different from normal, by relativizing and interpreting his sufferings as events that did not end up being necessarily negative (2 Cor 4:10-12).

Despite addressing the topic of his sufferings multiple times, the Apostle does not present himself as a passive victim mired in adversity, but instead we observe him placing his focus on an eternal and permanent reality that allows him to transcend the bad that he currently suffers, by neither focusing on it nor assigning it permanent meaning (2 Cor 4:16-18).

A4. Eschatological coping:

This category is closely related to the previous one. Among the primary coping resources that Paul presents in this passage are those that are related to the future, which a continual anticipation of a final and positive event.

The Apostle bases his perseverance and resistance in theological-eschatological promises (2 Cor 5:1-5). One sees an example of coping based on a certainty in the resurrection of Jesus Christ, which Paul directly connects with the hope in his own resurrection or glorious transformation (2 Cor 4:10-12). This hope is also communal (2 Cor 4:14).

Paul permanently re-signifies adverse situations in an eschatological way, reading the present from a perspective of hope in the glorious future transformation or resurrection that has been promised (2 Cor 5:1-4).

A5. Identification with Jesus as a coping mechanism:
Another category of coping refers to the Paul's identification with Jesus, his sufferings, and his resurrection. This identification enables him to understand himself as a follower of his Lord, who experiences extreme suffering and agony, just as he himself had experienced in his apostleship. Paul sees this identification as a fundamental part of his mission to proclaim the gospel, to the point where he could be considered a manifestation (epiphany) of the message of the cross in his suffering body. When the Apostle suffers while preaching the gospel to potential converts, he is a concrete, bodily representation of the passion of Jesus Christ. He becomes a tangible carrier of the message, since his sufferings are a manifestation of the suffering and death of Christ and, therefore, are a way of proclaiming the gospel (cf. Gal 3:1; 4:13; 5:11; 6:17).

The Apostle also identifies with the resurrection, which is the victory over death itself, and therefore all adversity and suffering. In the same way that Jesus victoriously emerged from death, by identifying himself with his Lord, Paul sees himself as being victorious over his many afflictions, and even death itself. Thus, the Apostle also sees Jesus as a model to follow which encourages him in the midst of tribulation (2 Cor 4:10-11).

A6. Altruistic coping:
Paul describes himself and his coworkers as people who remain focused on the good of others, particularly Christian communities, in the midst

of suffering. He shows himself as satisfied that his suffering leads to the good of others, even though it comes at a high cost for himself (2 Cor 4:12,15).

A7. Thanksgiving:

Here, and frequently in other Pauline writings (1 Th 5:18; Phl 4:6; 1 Cor 15:57; Rom 1:8; 1:21; 6:17; 7:25; 14:6; 16:4), we see the act of thanksgiving. Giving thanks for the positive intervention of God in adversity is also observed as a characteristic of Paul's coping with tribulation. It is observed, therefore, an approach centered on the positive aspects present in the context of adversity, which are made explicit as thanksgiving to God and shared as a community witness (2 Cor 4:15).

A8. Detachment from the material and the visible:

In an extensive section of the analyzed passage, we observe that Paul focuses on the ultimate good, understood as the resurrection or glorious final transformation, in contrast with the experience of precariousness and bad events in the present time. He detaches from all of the good and bad he experiences in the present, which for him are fleeting, and totally preliminary (2 Cor 4:16-5:8).

A10. Expression of traumatic events:

The final way of coping with adversity we can highlight is the Apostle's practice of remembering and communicating in his letters the adverse events he has experienced, assuming them and integrating them in his biographical narrative, and not denying them. We observe this in various writings of his, particularly in his lists of sufferings (2 Cor 4:8-10; cf. 1 Cor 4:9-11; 2 Cor 6:4-10; 11:23-33; 12:10; Phil 4:11-12; Rom 8:35-36).

Chapter 8
Exegetical Analysis of 2 Corinthians 6:3-10

8.1. Paragraph B (2 Cor 6:3-10)

(3) We put no stumbling block in anyone's path, so that our ministry will not be discredited. (4) Rather, as servants of God we commend ourselves in every way: in great endurance; in troubles, hardships, and distresses; (5) in beatings, imprisonments, and riots; in hard work, sleepless nights, and hunger; (6) in purity, understanding, patience and kindness; in the Holy Spirit and in sincere love; (7) in truthful speech and in the power of God; with weapons of righteousness in the right hand and in the left; (8) through glory and dishonor, bad report and good report; genuine, yet regarded as impostors; (9) known, yet regarded as unknown; dying, and yet we live on; beaten, and yet not killed; (10) sorrowful, yet always rejoicing; poor, yet making many rich; having nothing, and yet possessing everything.

8.2. Exegetical Commentary

This passage, just like the previous one, very likely forms part of Paul's third letter to the Corinthians (*Cor C: 2:14-7:4*) and, therefore, the context is the same. Paul continues to develop an apologetic discourse in response to the missionaries that oppose his ministry that have arrived in Corinth.

All throughout this passage, Paul seeks to defend his ministry, making it clear that he has been a minister who is perseverant, useful, and sincere about Jesus Christ. For this, he presents another one of his lists or catalogues of the difficulties that he had to endure for Christ. The previous that we looked and anticipates these adversities (4:8-11),

221

and later on he makes another quite detailed description (11:23-33) along the same lines, which we will also review. [90]

Here we observe that Paul defends his ministry with his integrity and strength of character in the face of crisis and suffering. His apologetic is based in experience more than just being a theoretical argumentative discourse. It is based in his way of life, in how he concretely faced extreme adversity which he had to overcome. If his opponents talked about their works and talents, Paul, for his part, refutes them through his character and perseverance amidst crisis and suffering. We see the use of coping with adversity as an apologetic tool, since the Apostle's opponents could not seem to appeal to it.

2 Corinthians 6:3-10, as a part of Cor C, very closely follows in the same line as 2 Corinthians 4:7-5:10, also being a paradoxical diatribe responding to the same general category of life/death contrast proposed by Hotze (1997), which in this case exhibits a degree of outstanding poetic eloquence.

The structure of this passage exhibits very particular characteristics, as we will see below (Bultmann, 1985; Vidal, 2012):

> (3) We put no stumbling block in anyone's path, so that our ministry will not be discredited. (4) Rather, as servants of God we commend ourselves in every way:

[*a heading that does not describe adversities, but rather Paul's attitude, and introduces the list of 18 propositions that belong in Greek with "en"*]

> in great endurance;

[*list of nine plural prepositions beginning using the work particle "en", translated as "in"*]

> in troubles,
> hardships,
> and distresses,
> (5) in beatings,
> imprisonments
> and riots;

---

[90] Although the topic has been up for discussion, it is very probably that these lists correspond to genuine experiences of suffering and real calamities that Paul suffered, and not simply just a rhetorical use of list of adversity typically used in those times (Hodgdon, 1983; Fitzgerarld, 1988; Sampley, 2008; Plummer, 2013).

in hard work,

sleepless nights

and hunger;

[*list of four pairs of single nouns preceded by "en", which can be translated as "in"*]

(6) in purity, understanding,

patience and kindness;

in the Holy Spirit and in sincere love;

(7) in truthful speech and in the power of God;

[*a noun in the genitive case, followed by two pairs of opposing nouns preceded by the particle "dia", which can be translated as "through"*]

with weapons of righteousness in the right hand and in the left;

(8) through glory and dishonor,

bad report and good report;

[*seven contrasts, all starting with the particle "hos", which can be translated "as" or "like"*]

genuine, yet regarded as impostors;

(9) known, yet regarded as unknown;

dying, and yet we live on;

beaten, and yet not killed;

(10) sorrowful, yet always rejoicing;

poor, yet making many rich;

having nothing, and yet possessing everything.

Also, as we will see below in Box 2, the structure of the text is set up through an argumentation by contrasts, where Paul uses paradoxical language and juxtaposition[91], just as we observed in the previous passage (2 Cor 4:8-5:10).

---

[91] It is very possible that Paul's paradox style lies within Hebrew poetic tradition, which he surely knew well, which is very much characterized by parallelism. Parallelism is to Hebrew poetry what rhyming is to Western poetry. Instead of phonetic harmony, Hebrew poetic parallelism involves grammatical harmony or (when two lines of poetry have the same internal structure) or semantic harmony (when the meaning of both lines is complementary or opposite). Parallelism can be basically classified as: a) synonymous (when the second line contains an idea that is identical or similar to the previous line); b)

Box 2: Argumentation Through Contrasts (2 Cor 6:4-10)

Negative	Positive
	(3) We put no stumbling block in anyone's path, so that our ministry will not be discredited. (4) Rather, as servants of God we commend ourselves in every way: in great endurance;
in troubles, hardships and distresses;	
5) in beatings, imprisonments and riots; in hard work, sleepless nights and hunger;	(6) in purity, understanding, patience and kindness; in the Holy Spirit and in sincere love; (7) in truthful speech and in the power of God; with weapons of righteousness in the right hand and in the left;
	(8) through glory
and dishonor,	
bad report	and good report; genuine,
yet regarded as impostors;	
yet regarded as unknown;	(9) known;
dying,	and yet we live on;
beaten,	and not yet killed;
(10) sorrowful,	yet always rejoicing;
poor,	yet making many rich;
having nothing,	and yet possessing everything.

antithetical (where the second line expresses a thought that contrasts with the previous line); c) synthetic or constructive (where the first line serves as a bases for the following line, which in turn adds new content). Among the Hebrew literary figures related to paradox that are employed by Paul is the oxymoron, which is the union of two semantically incompatible expressions, which when combined cannot have any conceivable literal reference in reality (as we will see in a special way in our analysis of 2 Cor 6:3-10). Another common Hebrew literary figure found in Paul is irony, which, if not recognized as such, could lead to misunderstanding, since the literal meaning tends to be exactly the opposite of what should be understood. The context is thus fundamentally important for understanding it (as we observe in 2 Cor 10-13) (Martínez, 1984; Follis, 1987; Zogbo & Wendland, 1989; Watson, 1996; Orton, 2000).

Although Paul could have been familiar with the literary tradition of the peristasis catalogue, which was commonly used at the time, his argumentation has unique and stylistically distinct characteristics. Experts also recognize marked differences in Paul's use of this tradition, which is evident in this passage (2 Cor 6:4b-10), which is not merely a simple list of difficulties, but is combined with a list of virtues and antithesis, with the primary objective of defending the legitimacy and character of his ministry to the Corinthians. Paul seeks to be accepted by the church in Corinth, on the basis of how he presents himself, his faithfulness and perseverance amidst drastic adversity, his secureness, and his apostolic generosity (Fitzgerarld, 1988; Sampley, 2008; Joseph, 2012).

Below we will offer a general exegetical commentary of this second selected passage, primarily addressing its aspects that are related to our central theme.

2 Corinthians 6:3-4a.

(3) We put no stumbling block in anyone's path, so that our ministry will not be discredited. (4a) Rather, as servants of God we commend ourselves in every way: in great endurance; [...]

Paul previously had been referring to the characteristics of the ministry or service (*diakonia*) that he had been assigned, which he calls a ministry of reconciliation (*diakonian tes katallages*, 2 Cor 5:18). He now will describe the himself and his coworkers as servants[92], emphasizing their irreproachable character, as he does in other parts of 2 Corinthianss (1:12; 2:17; 4:1-2; 12:19).

2 Cor 6:3. The Apostle tries to not be a stumbling block for the believers[93]. However, what seems to primarily worry him is putting the

---

[92] The term *diakonos* is generally used by Paul in its Greco-Roman meaning, which is connected to the tasks of servants or slaves in the home (Bouttier, et al., 1996). On the other hand, as we see in 1 Corinthians 12:5, Paul talks about a diversity of service (*diaconatos*), and in 2 Corinthians 9:10-15 we find the diaconate firmly established in the work and life of the church, to the point that it became an essential element in the lives of all the disciples of Jesus.

[93] The weight that Paul gives to causing others to fall or bringing them scandal can be illustrated in the synoptic Gospel's exhortation to not cause others to stumble, and the

honor of the ministry he has been called to at risk, more than people in particular, including himself. The emphasis he places on this is demonstrated by the clause in this verse, which in the Greek includes an emphatic negation: "We put no stumbling block in anyone's path (*medemian en medeni didontes proskopen*)".

2 Cor 6:4a. Paul desires to please the one who sent him, to not let him down or dishonor the transcendent ministry that he has been charged with (2 Cor 5:9; Gal 1:10). Because of this, with a clean conscience he can present himself together with his co-workers, as upright servants of God who are well-suited for the task they have been given, exemplary in everything, without any shame[94] (1 Cor 4:16; 11:1; Fil 3:17).

It is worth mentioning that Paul's emphasis on defending his ministry is not centered on himself, since that would be fully contradictory to his own statements to the matter (2 Cor 3:1-3; 5:12), and his self-recommendations are formulated in a way that differs from ancient styles of defense and Greco-Roman defense letters that the opposing missionaries in Corinth surely brought (Murphy-O'Connor, 2004).

The recommendation that Paul makes for himself and his co-workers fundamentally points to a virtue that can only be revealed in adversity: perseverance (*hupomone*). For Paul, this character quality seems to be a central characteristic in the life of every worthy servant of God. It is an attitude that involves a test of character by fire (cf. Jam 1:2-4; 1 Pet 1:7.), and makes evident the power of God's resources in the fragile and limited reality of the person that serves him, just as he indicated in the previous section (2 Cor 11:21-12:10), and as we will see later in the other passage we have selected (2 Cor 11:21-12:10).

In stylistic terms, in the Greek text we can see that *hupomone* is at the top of the list that the Apostle presents in this section, which helps us understand the structure and meaning of the text. The

---

hyperbolical threat that it would be better to tie a large millstone around one's neck and be thrown into the sea, than to cause a child to stumble (Mark 9:42; Mat 18:6-7; Luke 17:1-4).

[94] In ancient times, particularly in biblical contexts, the topic of honor and shame has been studied with certain detail, and here we will only mention a few relevant references: Gilmore, 1987; Matthews & Benjamin, 1996; Crook, 2009.

enumeration of experiences and qualities is made in reference to this cardinal virtue that Paul says he possesses in the face of the adversities, particularly the ones he names (Bultmann, 1984).

From the verb *hupomeneno* (to stay/remain in place), is derived the noun *hupomone*, which implies the capacity to endure or withstand, the moral strength to resist adverse situations with courage, which goes beyond passive resignation or patience, especially refers to human relationships (*makrothumia*) (Hoad, 1991; Dupont-Roc, 1996).

For Paul, *hupomone* does not derive from fearlessness or personal strength, nor from insensitivity or apathy towards misfortune or adversity, but in faith and hope placed in God, in the middle of a world marked by misfortune which will disappear as such in the end (Rom 8:18-25). In contrast to Greek ethics (particularly Stoic[95] and Epicurean), which considered passive suffering to be bad and shameful[96], Paul thought that affliction could produce perseverance

---

[95] It is worth mentioning that the city of Tarsus was recognized as an important center of Stoic philosophy, having among its residents a recognized master of this school, Atenodoro, friend of Cicerone, who became the tutor of Augustus, as indicated by Seneca in his letters to Lucilius (I, X 5) (Cothenet, 1985). It is possible that Paul would therefore have been influenced by this philosophy in his upbringing, if Tarsus was truly his native city. However, as we will see, important differences can be observed in his understanding of suffering and adversity, and ways of coping, compared to this and other contemporary Greek schools of philosophy.

[96] For the Stoics, the virtue of perseverance or resistance was one of their fundamental ethical concepts, around which the other virtues were structured. However, in the Stoic mentality, individuals should disconnect from all that disturbed them in their pursuit of impassivity or apathy, which was the prime Stoic ideal. Their only concern was to not cause disturbances for others or themselves: *kathaper oi arroostoi* (Ferrater Mora, 1955). Perseverance was therefore basically understood to be apathetic resignation. If the Stoic ethic notably differs from Paul's ethic, it is in regards to the question of *pathos*, since for the Stoics suffering had absolutely no value, as it involved not going along with the general economy of the universe, which for them had perfectly come about purely for the conservation and benefit of living beings (through instinct for the animals, and reason for humans). The Stoics distinguished between four fundamental emotions or sufferings (*pathos*): two related to the supposed goods (the desire for future goodness and the enjoyment of current goodness), and two related to the presumed badness (the fear of future badness and affliction for present badness). The first three can be experienced in moderation by the wise, however, suffering or affliction by present badness belonged to the fools, and should be rigorously avoided, since for the wise Stoic there were no bad things that one had to suffer for, since the wise man was aligned with perfection in the order or meaning of the universe (*logos*) without disturbance. The condition of the wise

and, in turn, develop a trustworthy and approved personal character (*dokime*) (Rom 5:3-4; cf. Jam 1:2-4), far from an attitude of complaining or hopelessness in affliction. On the contrary, Paul describes a disposition to glorify God regardless of the circumstance, knowing that this perseverance comes only as a gift from God (Rom 15:5-6) (Hauck, 2002).

For Paul, the term *hupomone* denotes the steadfastness and faithfulness of Christians in the middle of trials, sustained by their eschatological hope. This is even more emphasized when understanding that, for the Apostle, adversity and suffering are an unavoidable part of following Christ (1 Thes 2:14-16; 3:3-4; Gal 6:12; Phil 1:29-30; Rom 8:16-17). Thus, this attitude should be developed and be evident in the lives of the servants or ministers of Christ that have roles of caring for communities of faith. Situations of adversity are the best opportunities to grow in *hupomone*, since it is there that faithfulness and hope is put to the test (1 Thes 1:3; Rom 8:25; 12:12; 15:4-5; 2 Cor 1:6-7; 6:4).

2 Corinthians 6:4b-5

[...] in troubles, hardships, and distresses; (5) in beatings, imprisonments, and riots; in hard work, sleepless nights, and hunger; [...]

Here, Paul lists some of the adversities that he has had to endure, in thematically coherent groups. As we said before, he begins with a list of nine plural prepositions beginning with the particle *en*, which can be thematically put into three groups (Barrett, 1973; Martin, 1986; Seifrid, 2015):

The first group names the adversities in general terms: *thlipsesin* (pressure, straits, affliction), *anagkais* (restriction, malaise, calamity),

---

man is, therefore, fundamentally one of apathy (*apathos*). In this way, this notion is incompatible with the idea of a wise or worthy man being one who at the same time is suffering, sick, or weak (terms often used by Paul), since within the ideal of the Stoic man were the notions of being healthy (*hugieia*) and resistant or strong (*ischus*) (Aguilera, 1988; Thorsteinsson, 2010; Boeri & Salles, 2014; Løkke, 2015).

and *stenojoriais* (narrowness, distress, trouble)[97]. These words are synonyms, and are used here by Paul to allude to external dangers, both natural in origin (e.g., storms, shipwrecks), as well as human (e.g., persecution, punishment), which imply a desperate or oppressive situation from which there was no viable (or at least not providential) escape.

The second set of terms that has to do with adversity or affliction imposed by the authorities that Paul had to encounter (especially in contexts of civil and/or religious persecution): *plegais* (beatings, flogging), *phylakais* (imprisonments), *akatastasiais* (riots, uprisings, revolts). Paul refers to these types of afflictions in certain detail in 2 Corinthians 11:24-25[98]. We do not have much direct information directly from Paul about the riots or uprisings that Paul was linked too. However, this type of suffering, which was intentionally inflicted upon him by opponents to his cause or by the largely indifferent Roman authorities, was probably among the hardest on Paul, since it could have cost him his life on multiple occasions (2 Cor 1:8-11). This category also carried the wait of being a tribulation intentionally directed by others, where Paul experienced the inverse role of the one he played before he became a follower of Christ, since he went from being a persecutor to being persecuted, from a victimizer to a victim of political and religious oppression (1 Cor 15:9; Fil 3:6).

In *the last group*, Paul presents a list of adversities associated with the exercise of his ministry itself, the direct personal cost that this involved many times: *kopois* (effort, hard word, laborious toil), *agrupniais* (insomnia, sleepless nights), *nesteiais* (fasting, hunger).

As a travelling missionary, Paul had several options available to him for survival, based on the customs of the philosophers, teachers, and professors of the era. Some travelling teachers set a price for their

---

[97] The book of Acts makes evident that tribulations were a constant part of Paul's ministry, since he suffered significant adversities in practically every place where he preached the gospel and founded communities.

[98] Events like these are narratively illustrated in Acts, such as the story where Paul and Silas were beaten with rods in front of the Roman magistrates in Philippi (Acts 16:22). This same narration gives certain details of the possible imprisonment of Paul and Silas (Acts 16:23-40), showing the typical conditions of detention in those times, which according to Paul he experienced frequently (2 Cor 11:23).

teaching; others lived on voluntary contributions or donations; but the majority took up residence in the house of a wealthy family as private tutors for their children, receiving room and board. There were also the cases of slaves that fulfilled the function of teachers in the houses of wealthy families, especially in the Greco-Roman context (Bradley, 1994; Ciccotti, 2005).

Paul, for his part, persistently seemed to not have accepted any of these options. He did not want to receive any kind of payment, and voluntarily chose to offer his services of preaching and teaching for free (1 Cor 9:17-18), although he recognized that the servants of Christ that preached the good news had the right to receive a salary (1 Cor 9:14-15). Paul did not receive payment for his apostolic works, since it seems that he did not want to depend on the communities or some of its wealthiest members[99], and neither did he want to be a burden for the churches (1 Tes 2:9; 2 Cor 12:13-14). This way of assuming his ministry also seems to have apologetic intentions, so that he could not be accused of having selfish and material interests in carrying out his apostolic labor, and also not set himself up to be a stumbling block for anyone (2 Cor 6:3). An exception to the rule were the sporadic donations that he received, especially from the church in Phillipi, which were always given to him when he was far from that community (2 Cor 11:8-9; Phil 4:15).

Paul chose to work with his own hands to support himself (1 Cor 4:12)[100], which entailed its own complications. As Mesters (1993)

---

[99] According to Murphy-O'Connor (2004), in the East there was a custom of a complex connection between parties regarding the acceptance of a gift, which involved obligatory reciprocation through giving a similar or better gift in return. Rejecting a gift was also complicated, to the point that it could be very offensive.

[100] Various proposals have been made as to the origin of Paul's profession. For some, it is probable that he belonged to a family of textile merchants in Tarsus, where he would have learned the profession of tent-making. This would also explain the fact that he had a large network of contacts around the Mediterranean of people connected to this industry, such as those described in Acts: a purple cloth dealer, tentmakers in Corinth, and dyers in Ephesus (Reynier, 2009). But if we follow Murphy-O'Connor (2004), it is coherent with the Apostle's character that, beyond simply following a family profession, Paul learned it because it was useful for the traveling ministry that he was called to develop. What better to be a tentmaker, which were necessary in almost all urban contexts in that time, especially in big cities, with their ports and markets, like those that he selected in which to preach and establish communities. Beyond that, a profession of this type did not demand more than a small set of tools that were easy to transport.

points out, for a free man like Paul it was not easy to find employment, and manual labor was also demeaning in Greco-Roman culture, as it was seen as being for the slaves or free poor. Paul himself writes with certain irony: "Was it a sin for me to lower myself in order to elevate you by preaching the gospel of God to you free of charge?" (2 Cor 11:7). He also likely referred to the same thing when he wrote this line: "Though I am free and belong to no one, I have made myself a slave to everyone" (1 Cor 9:19).

The adversities association with the conditions of his apostolic mission involved "hard work, sleepless nights and hunger" (2 Cor 6:5b), since Paul must have had low income, for which he had to work "night and day" (1 Thes 2:9), going "without sleep" (2 Cor 11:27) and experiencing exhaustion and physical wear (1 Cor 4:12). And on many occasions this income was not sufficient to cover his basic expenses, and he had to go through times of needs, including times of scarce food and insufficient clothing (1 Cor 4:11; 2 Cor 11:9, 27; Phil 4:12)[101].

Although this type of adversities where not abrupt and instead maintained over time, they were afflictions that the Apostle also faced in a notable way, and give us the socio-economic contexts of the other experiences he mentions.

2 Corinthians 6:6-8a.

(6) in purity, understanding, patience, and kindness; in the Holy Spirit and in sincere love; (7) in truthful speech and in the power of God; with weapons of righteousness in the right hand and in the left; (8) through glory and dishonor, bad report and good report; [...]

---

[101] It is possible that Paul's difficulties along this line were due to the fact that he had to dedicate a great part of his day to his apostolic work, which prevented him from working during normal hours, therefore requiring him to work at night (in addition to the time dedicated to prayer, surely following the example of his Lord: Mark 1:35; Luke 6:12). Additionally, given that his ministry was constantly on the road, he could not have a fixed residence for very long (cf. 1 Cor 4:11), which would have enabled him to have his own place of business, and a stable client base. In most places where Paul founded communities, he was surely underemployed in a workshop of some kind near the market of the city (Mesters, 1993).

This section is a list of singular nouns preceded by the particle *en* (in), where Paul continues his defense, now laying out a positive list of virtues that have characterized his ministry in the midst of the adversities through which he has had to persevere (*hupomone*). Based on the structure of the paragraph, we can consider that *hupomone* is the head of this positive list, which is to say, the Apostle has also persevered in these virtues in the middle of affliction. Paul continues with a list of eight divine gifts that can be organized into two groups.

2 Cor 6:6. The first group of terms begins with *hagnoteti* (purity), which appears as a noun only here in the NT, since it is most frequently used as an adjective, and normally refers to purity in the sense of sexual relations and morality, as well as with personal conscience. Paul has a calm and clean conscience regarding his behavior as a servant of Christ (1 Cor 4:1-4) (Murray, 2005; Guthrie, 2015).

This list continues with the work *gnosei* (understanding/knowledge), which the Apostle knows he possesses (11:6), but not in its Greek sense, but rather aligned with what he has already proposed on the topic: a spiritual understanding, which has been revealed and is glorious (1 Cor 4:6), that cannot be separated from experiencing and having a relationship with the Spirit of God (1 Cor 2:9-16), since that which is contrary is futile and fleeting (1 Cor 3:18-20; 8:1). It is an understanding that is more relational and experiential, always connected with love, instead of being discursive and abstract (1 Cor 13:2, 9-13) (Martin, 1986).

The third word in this group is *makrotumia* (patience, long-suffering). This term is very closely related to *hupomone*[102], however it has its own particular connotation. In the Greek usage, it tends to refer to interpersonal relations in particular, meaning the patience one has for another more than for events or circumstances. Paul uses this word primarily to refer to the patience of God himself towards humans (Rom 2:4; 9:22; cf. Ex 34:6; Nm 14:18; Psalm 103:8) who delay the manifestation of his righteous judgement. It also implies a stable attitude towards another person that does not get dragged down in

---

[102] "While *hupomone* is the courageous fortitude which endures adversity without murmuring or losing heart, *makrotumia* is the forbearance which endures injuries and evil deeds without being" (Plummer, 1975, p.196).

emotional distress. God's own patience commits Christians to have a similar patience with their neighbor (1 Thes 5:14) (Hoad, 1991; Dupont-Roc, 1996).

At the end of this list, Paul mentions *chrestoteti* (kindness, usefulness, benignity), emphasizing his permanent disposition to actively seek the good of others, being useful to those he serves, to the point that his existence is defined as such (Phil 1:21-26). Both this term as well as the previous one (*makrotumia*), are fruits of the Spirit for Paul, and one of the primary expressions of *agape* (Gal 5:22; 1 Cor 13:4) (Murray, 2005; Guthrie, 2015).

2 Cor 6:7a. The second group of terms, which in this case are pairs, begins with *en pneuma hago* (in holy spirit/in the the Holy Spirit). Paul probably is not placing the Holy Spirit in a list of virtues, but instead is assigning it the predominant place that it is always assigned in the Christian life. Therefore, this list is more coherently understood by recognizing that Paul is referring to the holiness of spirit, a (human) spirit that is holy (Plummer, 1975; Bultmann, 1984; Keener, 2005).

This holiness, purity, or honesty of spirit is also expressed in the sincerity or lack of hypocrisy of love (*agape anupokritos*, cf. Rom 12:9), as he next will mention. This theme is very relevant for the Apostle, as a seal of his apostleship, which he addresses in the context of his defense against false ministers in this same letter[103].

For Paul, all of these virtues are intimately connected: the holiness of spirit, love without hypocrisy and, as he continues saying, the word of truth (*logo aletheias*). In this list the adjectives are interchangeable, since the Paul's spirit, love, and word are holy, sincere, and true. These are characteristics that he wants to highlight as being central to and constant in his ministry, marks of his service in adversity,

---

[103] Just as he says to the Corinthians themselves: "Unlike so many, we do not peddle the word of God for profit. On the contrary, in Christ we speak before God with sincerity (*eilikrineia*), as those sent from God (2 Cor 2:17); "Now this is our boast: Our conscience testifies that we have conducted ourselves in the world, and especially in our relations with you, with integrity (*haplotes*) and godly sincerity (*eilikrineia*). We have done so, relying not on worldly wisdom but on God's grace" (2 Cor 1:12); and "we have renounced secret and shameful ways; we do not use deception, nor do we distort the word of God. On the contrary, by setting forth the truth plainly we commend ourselves to everyone's conscience in the sight of God (2 Cor 4:2).

which are always the manifestation of God's power (*dunamei theou*) in his life, as he points out when mentioning this last pair of words in the list. In this way, he once again states the origin of his *hupomone* in his sincere ministry through affliction: God himself, and not human power (1 Cor 1:18-31; 2 Cor 4:7-18; 12:5-10).

2 Cor 6:7b. The next phrase (*"with weapons of righteousness in the right hand and in the left"*) cannot be disconnected from what immediately precedes it: Paul is defending his ministry, which is founded in preaching and teaching the good news (*logo aletheias*), is his weapon (*hoplon*) of attack (*dexion*, lit. right [hand]) and of defense (*aristeron*, lit. left [hand])[104]. In this way, verse 7b can be considered as the end of the previous list, joining it with the last four phrases, which we can paraphrase as follows: in sincerity and in knowledge, in patience and in goodness, in the holy spirit and in sincere love, in the word of truth and in the power of God, through offensive and defensive weapons of righteousness.

2 Cor 6:8a. The next two clauses, which are composed of antonimical adjectives, begin a section (6:9-10) where Paul uses contrast as a primary resource, through paradox, and develops a antithetical parallels. The first contrast, *dia doxes* (through glory, honor) *kai atimias* (and dishonor, infamy), exhibits the general connotation of the antithetical phrases that follow, although in an inverse way: first the positive, and then the negative. Moving forward it will be the reverse, such as the pair that immediately follow: *dia disfemias* (through defamation, bad report) *kai eufemias* (and praise, good report). This contrast seems to point to a level that is distinct from the previous contrast, since it indicates one's condition in the eyes of others, and their opinion of it. This is not the case for glory and dishonor, which could refer to a personal condition in itself, of greater magnitude, in line with the paradox of the jar of clay that contains the glorious message (2 Cor 4:7, 16-5:9).

Paul's ministry was recognized by many of the Corinthians (1 Cor 16:15-18), and thus he had good report. However, others spoke

---

[104] In the Greco-Roman use, the sword or the lance are for attacking with the right hand, and the shield is for defense in the left hand, which is where the use of these terms may come from (Robertson, 2003).

badly of him behind his back, defaming him (1 Cor 4:10-13, 19; 2 Cor 10:10; 11:17). The directly proportional relationship between the virtues described above and a good reputation is contradicted in Paul's case, and to his many adversities and afflictions is added the defamation from both his beloved brothers and his adversaries.

2 Corinthians 6:8b-10.

(8b) [...] genuine, yet regarded as impostors; (9) known, yet regarded as unknown; dying, and yet we live on; beaten, and yet not killed; (10) sorrowful, yet always rejoicing; poor, yet making many rich; having nothing, and yet possessing everything.

In the final section of this list of difficulties, we find seven contrasts, each preceded by the particle *hos*. This section is presented in a very similar way to 4:8-9, as a type of antithetical parallelism. One also notices the same type of contrast between the visible and the invisible, between the fragile and the powerful, between death and life, between the vain and the eternal, found in the previously studied passage (2 Cor 4:7-5:10). However, here we find a new element, since the nature of misfortune as an apparent reality is highlighted, especially by the use of the adverb of comparison *hos* (as).

In this set of contrasts (see Box 2), Paul leaves the negative column under the connotation of simple appearance or irrelevance. The negative and adverse aspects are not definitive for the Apostle and his co-workers, since they experience a solid and definitive live sustained by the power of God, which allows them to transcend the pain that they suffer. Additionally, if they effectively have to withstand these negative aspects that are mentioned, these at their core are redefined as being irrelevant, but exclusively in comparison with the "glory that far outweighs them all" (4:17) that accumulates and is anticipated through the presence of the Spirit (5:5), which allows them to know that they already possess everything, in Christ (6:10).

2 Cor 6:8b-9a. This list of adversities falls in line with Paul's defense of his ministry, arguing in favor of his apostleship in service to the message, in other words, he makes evident his faithfulness as a preacher and teacher of the gospel. For this reason he begins the contrasts by proposing that he and his co-workers, though they are accused of being impostors (*planoi*, lit. vagabonds, with the connotation of a wrongdoer), are really truthful (*aletheis*, very much in line with: *hagnoteti*, *agape anupokritos*, and *logo aletheias*, fom 6:6-7). Regarding those that those who dishonor, speak poorly of, and consider him and his co-workers to be frauds, it is possible that Paul thinks that they do it basically because they do not know them, because they are unknown (*agnooumenoi*). Although he could also be alluding to the fact that his adversaries wanted to ignore them as a form of disdain. Nevertheless, they know that they are blessed and have good report with those that know them well, though they know that it is only God who knows them fully, and who will judge them (1 Cor 4:4; 13:12; 2 Cor 5:11;).

2 Cor 6:9b. The next contrast echoes Psalm 118:18, emphasizing how that which could have been life-threatening did not result in their death (2 Cor 1:8-11; 4:9-12). The scene narrated in Acts 14:19-20 (and which Paul confirms in 2 Cor 11:25, at least in the fact of having been stoned) is an eloquent illustration of the contrast that is described here: dying (*apothneskontes*) and yet (*idou*) we live on (*zomen*); beaten (*paideuomenoi*), and yet not killed (*thanatoumenoi*).

2 Cor 6:10. The paragraph ends with a series of contrasts that brings the antinomy to its climax, much in the style of the paradoxes of the beatitudes in Matthew (5:3-12) and Luke (6:20-26). They address the central themes of Paul's experience, since extreme adversity normally involves sadness, depression, and a fallen spirit, as well as instability and need, being vulnerable and weak, and event being existentially irrelevant and fleeting (cf. Psalms 39:4-7). These experiences are those that Paul assumes, relativizes, and confronts, redefining them from their opposites: sorrowful (*lupoumenoi*), yet always (*aei*) rejoicing (*chairontes*)[105]; poor (*ptochoi*, but not just simply poor, rather it is the same term used in the beatitudes, as someone who lacks what is necessary to live), yet making many (*pollous*) rich (*ploutizontesa*); having (*echontes*) nothing (*meden*), and yet possessing (*katechontesno*) everything (*panta*).

---

[105] The topic of joy is found frequently in 2 Corinthians, only surpassed by the topic of sorrow. The verb *chairein* occurs eight times in 2 Cor 2:3; 6:10; 7:7, 9, 13, 16; 13:9, 11; and the noun *chara* occurs 5 times: 2 Cor 1:24; 2:3; 7:4, 13; 8:2. For its part, as a verb and a particple, *lupein* occurs nine times in 2 Cor 2:2 (twic), 4, 5; 6:10; 7:8 (twice), 9, 11; the noun *lupe*, seven times: 2 Cor 2:1, 3, 7; 7:10 (tsice); 9:7 (Freedman, 1992; Barnett, 1993).

Paul knows that he possesses joy and wealth, particularly in the middle of adversities that are physical, psychological, social, and even ecclesial (from his adversaries within the faith communities.

Through grave difficulties, the Apostle interprets his bad condition as a situation of limited relevance, as a momentary and fleeting affliction (cf. *parautica alfron tes thlipseos*, 2 Cor 4:17). But he does not disregard what he experiences and does not deny it at any point, and instead he reinterprets it in light of what he considers to be foundational and truly transcendent: the coming glory offered in Christ, of which he is a herald. For this, and from his precarious condition of poverty and fragility, Paul speaks of a wealth given by his Lord (2:8-9), which allows him to know that he possesses everything, as he himself knows to possess him (1 Cor 3:21-23; 6:19; Rom 14:7-8).

Paul knows how to overcome concrete problems, the insufficient satisfaction of his basic needs of food, clothing, and shelter (2 Cor 11:27; Phil 4:11-13). He knows how to live in poverty, in material precariousness, since it is clear for him that all he possesses (which seemingly was never much during his ministry), he holds as if he did not have it, similar to being a servant or renter that could be removed at the will of the owner at any moment. The Apostle does not feel that he truly owns anything, including himself, since everything that can be seen he understands as being temporary, fleeting (1 Cor 7:30-31).

For its part, the expression "possesing everything" (*katechontesno panta*) gives the understanding of firm possession (Robertson, 2003). The important things from both the present and the future are, in the truest sense, in the possession of the believer, because he possesses everything in Christ, although the fullness of this possession is eschatological. Therefore, one should live in this paradox of persevering in taking joy that, in the midst of the sorrow of these days, in having Christ we will have neither too much nor too little, even under the pressure of the most arduous adversities.

Here resonate the words of the synoptic gospels: "Blessed are the poor" (*makarioi ho/oi ptochoi* in Matt 5:3 and Luke 6:20, respectively), where Matthew adds "in spirit" (*to pneumati*). Paul is a "blessed poor man" that follows the way of his Lord who voluntarily made himself poor in order to enrich many (2 Cor 8:9).

We know that Paul worked with his own hands to pay for his material necessities and not be a burden to anyone (1 Thes 2:9), and because of the type of job he performed, he most certainly belonged to the poor class of society, at least during his apostolic ministry. The Apostle speaks of enrichment in a sense that transcends others, despite his poverty, since, as we will see soon, upon analyzing the passage of 2 Corinthians 11:21b-12:10, the power of God is made manifest in weakness, in the poverty of those who persevere in serving him in the midst of their afflictions and placing their hope in him.

Paul knows that he undeservedly possesses these eternal gifts, and knows that he is called to share them. He defines his mission as the work of enriching others and promoting their lives, despite the high physical cost that this could have on him, since his focus is placed on that which is foundational and transcendent. However, this perspective does not at all diminish the Apostle's permanent disposition to concern himself for the material wellbeing of his brothers and sisters in the faith and ensure that their needs are met, as we observe in his initiative regarding the collection for the church in Jerusalem (2 Cor 8-9).

Paul wants to freely share the grace he received (Matt 10:8), with the intention that his communities in turn do the same thing, for the glory of God, even in the middle of great affliction. For this he says: "You will be enriched in every way so that you can be generous on every occasion, and through us your generosity will result in thanksgiving to God" (2 Cor 9:11).

8.3. Hermeneutical Keys Analysis about Coping from Paragraph B

In this section, as we did previously, we will take a look at the hermeneutical keys about coping with adversity that can be observed in the paragraph. We will organize the information into specific categories and concepts, in the same way as before, which have been taken from the respective verses and paragraphs in the analyzed section. Then, we will conduct a comprehensive synthesis, from a theological perspective, of the keys we have found.

Table 4: Hermeneutical Keys about Coping from Paragraph B (2 Cor 6:3-10)

CODE	CATEGORIES	CONCEPTS	2 Cor
B1 (A1)	Paradoxical identity	Paradoxical perseverance, powerful-weakness. Paradoxical experience of victorious impotence	6:8-10
		Confidence in what one inalienably and intrinsically possesses, in the midst of adversity. Perception of fullness is fundamental.	6:10
B2 (A2)	Experience of faith as faithfulness and perseverance	Coping based on the desire to be a persevering servant of God.	6:3-4
		Pursuit of an irreproachable character: being grateful to God, with a clean conscience in all circumstances.	6:3-4a
		Perseverance as a central virtue of the Christian experience.	6:3-10
		Perseverance as a virtue based in the power of God, through faith and hope, not as an attribute of personal merit.	6:3-4a
		Cardinal and *theological* virtues as coping mechanisms.	6:6-7
B3 (A3)	Resignification of death and traumatic events	Suffering and adversity as a necessary secondary cost that is assumed for the fulfillment of one's mission.	6:4b-5
		Adversity as a corroboration of the purity, sincerity, and character of one's mission.	6:6-7a
B4 (A7)	Altruistic coping	Focus is not put on one's self, but on not being a stumbling block or defaming the ministry.	6:3
		Attention placed on relational qualities that seek the good of others.	6:6,10
B5 (A9)	Detachment from the material or visible	Detachment from what is material and preliminary. Christ as one's everything. Focus placed on the eternal and the invisible.	6:8b-10

B6 (A10)	Expression of adverse events	Appropriation of every adversity suffered, and telling others about it (not denying it).	6:8-10

Explanation of the table: The table summarizes the hermeneutical keys about coping found in the passage. The first column lists the code (the capital letter indicates the passage and the number indicates the specific key); the second column lists the category of the key; the third column presents the concepts within each category; and finally, the fourth column indicates the specific biblical references.

B1. Paradoxical identity:

Just as we saw in the previous passage, where various indicators appeared about this type of key for interpreting adversity (2 Cor 4:7, 9, 16), in the dynamic of coping, for the Apostle the way that he perceives himself, his personal identity, is fundamental.

In this section, we also find in Paul a paradoxical way of understanding oneself, which on one hand involves his awareness of his own fragility and personal impotence, and on the other hand, his strength and power in the face of adversity, founded in God, and which allows him to see himself as presently possessing an incommensurable and eternal good, which is he is called to share with others (2 Cor 4:8-10).

B2. Experience of faith as faithfulness and perseverance:

We also find this category on various occasions in this text, just like in the previous one (2 Cor 4:8-9, 13; 5:1-4, 6-10). Paul understands faith as faithfulness and perseverance in his service to the Lord, especially in the face of all adverse events.

The Apostle shows a marked desire to be a servant of God that fulfills the mission given to him with perseverance (2 Cor 6:3-4). With an irreproachable character that seeks to be grateful to God, and keeping a clean conscience in his actions (2 Cor 6:3-4a; cf. 2 Cor 1:12; 2:17; 4:1-2; 12:19).

Perseverance is seen as an integral part of the life of a follower of Jesus Christ. From here one can see positive coping with tribulation as a virtue, a set of qualities relating to the a maturity of Christian character that are developed by the power of god, through faith and hope placed in him, not as an attribute of personal merit (2 Cor 6:3-4, 8-10).

These qualities can themselves be understood as resources for coping with adversity. It is in this way that Paul perseveres through extreme difficulties "in purity, understanding, patience and kindness; in the Holy Spirit and in sincere love; in truthful speech and in the power of God; with weapons of righteousness in the right hand and in the left" (2 Cor 6:6-7).

B3. Resignification of death and traumatic events:

Just as we mentioned in the analysis of the first passage, Paul assigns a positive meaning to his death (2 Cor 4:8-9; 5:1-2), and this deeply affects the way in which he faces circumstances that put his life and/or that of his co-workers at risk (2 Cor 4:10-12, 16-18).

The suffering that resulted from the multiple adversities experienced is interpreted by the Apostle as a necessary secondary cost, which he assumes, of the fulfillment of his mission (2 Cor 6:4b-5), and also as an opportunity to corroborate his clean conscience, sincerity and purity of spirit, work, and love in serving Jesus Christ, through hard opposition (2 Cor 6:6-7a).

B4. Altruistic coping:

Just as in parts of the first passage analyzed (2 Cor 4:12, 15), here we also find that Paul faces circumstances of suffering with his attention placed on the good of others, particularly those that he serves in his work as an apostle of Jesus. He focuses on not being a stumbling block, and on not defaming his ministry for the good of those that will be blessed by it. The Apostle faces evil, persecution, and torment in his life as a servant of the church, with continuous disposition to seek the good of others even though this does not produce a direct benefit for himself in the short or medium term. In other words, he does this altruistically, for love (2 Cor 6:3, 6, 10).

B5. Detachment from the material:

Just as in a significant part of the first passage (2 Cor 4:16-5:8), here we also find a relativization of that which is not definitive. Paul shows a marked detachment from the material and a disregard for what is shown to be negative: dishonor, sadness, poverty, or extreme lack of resources. This is because he has his attention placed on the supreme and transcendent good that is found in Christ, which for him is *his everything*, sufficient for future and eternal fullness, but also for the present time, the anticipation of glory (2 Cor 6:10).

B6. Expression of adverse events:

Finally, we also find in this passage another example of Paul's practice of remembering and communicating in his letters the traumatic events he experienced, in a way that those events are not denied nor forgotten. Instead, the Apostle appropriates them, integrates them into his personal story; they are a part of him, and they do not permanently disrupt the continuity of his life (2 Cor 6:8-10).

Chapter 9
Exegetical Analysis of 2 Corinthians 11:21b-12:10

9.1. Paragraph C (2 Cor11:21b-12:10)

(21b) Whatever anyone else dares to boast about —I am speaking as a fool— I also dare to boast about. (22) Are they Hebrews? So am I. Are they Israelites? So am I. Are they Abraham's descendants? So am I. (23) Are they servants of Christ? (I am out of my mind to talk like this.) I am more. I have worked much harder, been in prison more frequently, been flogged more severely, and been exposed to death again and again. (24) Five times I received from the Jews the forty lashes minus one. (25) Three times I was beaten with rods, once I was pelted with stones, three times I was shipwrecked, I spent a night and a day in the open sea, (26) I have been constantly on the move. I have been in danger from rivers, in danger from bandits, in danger from my fellow Jews, in danger from Gentiles; in danger in the city, in danger in the country, in danger at sea; and in danger from false believers. (27) I have labored and toiled and have often gone without sleep; I have known hunger and thirst and have often gone without food; I have been cold and naked. (28) Besides everything else, I face daily the pressure of my concern for all the churches. (29) Who is weak, and I do not feel weak? Who is led into sin, and I do not inwardly burn? (30) If I must boast, I will boast of the things that show my weakness. (31) The God and Father of the Lord Jesus, who is to be praised forever, knows that I am not lying. (32) In Damascus the governor under King Aretas had the city of the Damascenes guarded in order to arrest me. (33) But I was lowered in a basket from a window in the wall and slipped through his hands. 12:(1) I must go on boasting. Although there is nothing to be gained, I will go on to visions and revelations from the Lord. (2) I know a man in Christ who fourteen years ago was caught up to the third heaven. Whether it was in the body or out of the body I do not know—God knows. (3) And I know that this man—whether in the body or apart from the body I do not know, but God knows— (4) was caught up to paradise and heard inexpressible things, things that no one is permitted to tell. (5) I will boast about a man like that, but I will not boast about myself, except about my weaknesses. (6) Even if I should choose to boast, I would not be a fool, because I would be speaking the truth. But I refrain, so no one will think more of me than is warranted by what I do or say, (7) or because of these surpassingly great revelations. Therefore, in order to keep me from becoming conceited, I was given a thorn in my flesh, a messenger of Satan, to torment me. (8) Three times I pleaded with the Lord to take it away from me. (9) But he said to me, "My grace is sufficient for you, for my power is made perfect in weakness." Therefore I will boast all the more gladly about my weaknesses, so that Christ's power may rest on me. (10) That is why, for Christ's sake, I delight in weaknesses, in insults, in hardships, in persecutions, in difficulties. For when I am weak, then I am strong.

9.2. Exegetical Commentary

One of the primary reasons that discussion about the unity of 2 Corinthians as a Pauline letter has been wide and ongoing has been the marked break in style and content in Paul's discourse starting in chapter 10. However, scholars of 2 Corinthians agree that these chapters form a unit, where the Apostle makes a strong call of attention to the believers of Corinth, threatens the church with discipline, defends himself against criticism from his rivals, and reproaches and accuses the critics from among the Corinthian believers themselves (Barrett, 1982; Betz, 1985; Taylor, 1991; Kurz, 1996; Roetzel, 2010).

There are different positions among specialists regarding the place occupied by chapters 10-13, as we indicated in the introductory section of this chapter. Here, based on the psychological coherence of the discourse, we assume that 2 Corinthians is an edited compilation of different letters, with chapters 10-13 most likely being the "letter of tears" (2 Cor 2:3-4; 7:8,12).[106]

According to Vidal's (2007, 2012) recent description of the plausible composition of Paul's correspondence to Corinthians, this passage is part of Cor D (2 Cor 10:1-13:13). Under this assumption, as we indicated previously, this letter must have been written in the fall of the year 53 in Ephesus, after an unsuccessful visit of Paul to the Corinthians (2 Cor 12:14; 13:1-2). It reflects a situation of the church that is more critical and complex than that of Cor C, since the opposing missionaries had succeeded in effectively discrediting Paul.

This letter highlights Paul's great ability for using rhetorical devices typically used in Greco-Roman culture for apologias, arguments, and diatribes, such as irony, comparison, parody, and direct invective. In this line, chapters 10-13 are among Paul's toughest discursive critique of his opponents.

The problems addressed in 1 Corinthians had been created by members of the same church. Those mentioned in 2 Corinthians most likely refer to outsiders, i.e., Hebrew missionaries (2 Cor 11:22) who became hard opponents of Paul, both in his message and in his methods of carrying out his apostolate. It could even be their intention to take control of the congregation by attacking Paul's authority as an apostle.

According to Paul's opponents, he was not sincere in his intentions and wanted to dominate his fellow servants by restricting their spiritual development (2 Cor 1:17-18, 24; 6:12; 7:2; 10:2-4). The fact that Paul's only recommendations came from himself, and that he did not carry letters of recommendation when he arrived in Corinth (which was the custom of delegates of the Sanhedrin at the time), was questioned (2 Cor 3;1; 4:2, 5; 5:12; 6:4; 10:12-13, 18; 12:11). They also criticized that his preaching and letters were confusing (2 Cor 1:13; 4:3; 6:2-3) and even claimed that he had harmful and selfish intentions (2 Cor 2:2, 4-5; 7:2-3, 8; 10:8; 12:16-18; 13:10). They also mocked his

---

[106] For a deeper dive into the debate of the unity of 2 Corinthians and the place of chapters10-13 in this letter, see: Bornkamm, 1978; Carrez, 1986; Gilchrist, 1988; Akin, 1989; Danker, 1989; Murphy-O'Connor, 1991; Welborn, 1995; Kurz, 1996; Sanchez-Bosch, 1998; Brown, 2002; Chang, 2002; Long, 2004; Murray, 2005; Furnish, 2007; Vidal, 2007, 2012; Seifrid, 2015.

insignificant and feeble physical appearence, in comparison to his bold writings (2 Cor 10:1-2, 9-11; 11:6; 13:3-4, 9).

Paul defends himself from these critiques, as we have observed in the previous passages, but here will see it in an especially intense way. He defends the authenticity of his ministry, his pure intentions, and his ceaseless perseverance. But in this section we can observe that he specifically addresses the accusations about his insignificant physical appearance and his weakness.

The first section (11:21b-29) of this paragraph (11:21b-12:13), can be divided into three general parts, in which the idea of self-exaltation is found starting each paragraph: v. 21b (*tolma*); v. 30 (*kauchesomai*); v. 12:1 (*kauchasthai*); and v. 12:11 (*kauchomevos*). The list of conditions, circumstances, and experiences related with suffering that Paul writes here is presented in segments that consist of short sentences, which can be grouped in five sets of statements, of which one is a parenthetical commentary, two are conclusions, and one is an introduction[107].

2 Corinthians 11:21b-23a.

(21b) Whatever anyone else dares to boast about —I am speaking as a fool— I also dare to boast about. (22) Are they Hebrews? So am I. Are they Israelites? So am I. Are they Abraham's descendants? So am I. (23a) Are they servants of Christ? (I am out of my mind to talk like this.) I am more.

2 Cor 11:21b. This verse starts a new apologetic list, which in this case takes on a markedly ironic style. Paul says that he is speaking as a

---

[107] In stylistic terms the first group of affirmations has four questions with brief answers and a parenthetical commentary (vv. 22-23a), which describe physical descent and spiritual mission. The next one presents three statements regarding suffering, listed in ascending order of severity and followed by a conclusion (v. 23b). The third continues with a series of four statements regarding suffering and ends in a commentary (vv. 24-25). The fourth is a sequence of eight descriptions of danger, introduced by a description of his travels (v. 26). The last group has five lines, three of which highlight two experiences, and two highlight the sufferings (v. 27). These five groups are followed by comments regarding Paul's concern for the churches, his personal weakness and sin (vv. 28-29) (Murray, 2005; Guthrie, 2015).

fool/crazy person, and paradoxically uses his sufferings and assumed weakness as his standard of validation, glory, and strength.

"Whatever anyone else (his opposers) dares to boast about (*tolma*, intrepidness, courageousness), –I am speaking as a fool (*in aphrosune lego*)– I also dare to boast about (*tolmo hago*)". Here the apostle uses a term for foolishness or madness that is less severe than what he used in 1 Corinthians 3:19 (*moria*). It can include the idea of wickedness and evil, but here it mainly refers to recklessness (Furnish, 2007).

Paul begins a delicate rhetorical game in this section, because, although "imprudently", he openly boasts and is proud of himself, apparently contradicting his own words to the Corinthians and the fundamental biblical principle of not falling into vain glory. (1 Cor 1:31; 2 Cor 10:17-18, cf. Jer 9:23-24)[108].

The use of irony and paradox saves Paul from "sinning through arrogance". Because, as we will see later, Paul glorifies himself in his weakness and his sufferings, not in his abilities or achievements, which he always attributes to God (1 Cor 15:10).

2 Cor 11:22. This verse is an opening that seems to head towards a typical apologia that seeks to establish Paul's dignity based on on his lineage, as was typical among aristocrats who used to boast of their lineage, or among Jews who were proud of their descendence from Abraham (Keener, 2003). Paul asks: Are they Hebrews? Are they Israelites? Are they descendents of Abraham? And he he responds to all three questions in the same way: "So am I" (*kago*).

The epithet of "Hebrew" (*Ebraioi*) to describe Abraham first occurs in Genesis 14:13. Egyptians used to referr to descendants of Jacob as Hebrews (cf. Gn 39:14, 17; 40:15; 41:12; 43:32; Ex 1:15, 16; 2:6, 7, 1). Paul describes himself as a Hebrew of Hebrews (Fil 3:5). Both terms, Hebrew and Israelite (*Israelitai*), frequently overlap, and both of them

---

[108] Regarding the boasting, Akin (1989) has observed eight principles found in 2 Corinthians: 1) *kauchesis* apologetics is innaproriate (12:19); 2) boasting is not *kata kurion* but *kata sarka* and, therefore, it is done in *aphrosune* (11:17); 3) boasting should not be *ametra* (10:13,15); 4) *sugkrisis* is prohibited (10:12); 5) boasting is appropriate if one boasts *en kurio* (1 Cor 1:31; 2 Cor 12:5, 9,10); 6) boasting is appropriate if one is boasting about *ta tes astheneias* (11:30; 12:5, 9, 10); 7) one can boast but from the role of a *aprhon* (11:1, 10, 16, 17, 21, 23; 12:11); 8) boasting is sometimes necessary (*dei*, 11:30; 12:1a), but it is useless (*ou sumpheron*, 12:1b).

were used to refer to the Jews in Paul's time. But being used together, as they are here, must be because one adds a kind of connotation to the other. As opposed to "Israelite", the term "Hebrew" is often used in the New Testament to designate the language of the Jews in Palestine.[109]

The expression "seed of Abraham" (*sperma Abraam*) it is pretty common in Paul's letters. Even thoug his enemies could have used this term, Paul always relates this expression with Christ and with all the communities of believers (Rom 4:13, 16, 18; 9:7; 11:1; Gal 3:29).

The opponents of Paul, at least in Corinth during this time, were Jews. There is a temptation to read 2 Corinthians similarly to Galatians, where the opponents were Judaizers, who sought to impose the rules of *shabbat*, circumcision, and food laws on the converted pagans. However, Paul does not address these types of issues in 2 Corinthians. The opponents of Paul in Corinth may simply have exacerbated the tendencies that already existed in Corinth towards pride, sectarianism, and fascination with sophistic rhetoric, spiritual gifts, and charismatic experiences, as well as a critical view of Paul (Witherington, 1995).

A key to identify the character of Paul's opponents in Corinth can be found in the immediate context of our passage: 2 Corinthians 11:13-15. The adversaries of Paul presented themselves as "apostles of Christ", "workers", "servants", in other words, in the same way as Paul did (2 Cor 11:12). However, their "deceit" and "masquerading" was them inauthentically pretending to be "servants of righteousness" (*diakonoi dikaiosunes*).[110]

---

[109] Hebrew, however, was rarely spoken and Aramaic was the dominant language of Palestine during the first century. Therefore, "Hebrew" was often used to designate Aramaic, a language closely related to the other. Paul, therefore, could be boasting of being an Aramaic-speaking Jew, who has inherited the language from his parents, who were surely of Palestinian origin, since the Jews who lived elswhere had no need to know Aramaic (Murphy-O 'Connor, 2004). Also, Paul may be referring to the fact that he was a Jew both by father and mother line, since mixed marriages were frequent in the diaspora (Reynier, 2009).

[110] Previously Paul contrasted two ministries, those of Moses and of Christ (2 Cor 3:4-18). The first, a "written code", that "kills" and is "a ministry which condemns", and the second as a "new pact", "a ministry of righteousness", written "in the Spirit", that "brings life" (2 Corinthians 3: 6, 9). Paul's ministry or service (*diakonia*), therefore, the ministry of righteousness in Christ (2 Cor 5:21), is the ministry of reconciliation (2 Cor 5:18-19, 6:3). Paul sees himself as a servant of righteousness through the cross of Christ, while his

2 Cor 11:23a. Here Paul begins a discourse which appeals to his condition of *suffering servant.* "Are they servants of Christ?" (*diakonoi Christou*). If the previous questions were related to his origin and descendence, this one is related to divine calling. If his opponents believe they are servants of Christ, here Paul appeals to the calling that Jesus gave him to be a suffering herald (cf. Hch 9:15-16).

Again, as parenthetical commentary, Paul repeats the idea of being a foolish/reckless/crazy person by saying that he is (*en aphrosune lego*), but using the term *paraphronon*, thus emphasizing an indirect statement outside of himself, because he considers himself to be superior (*huper ego*) to his opponents as a servant of Christ. But his superiority is paradoxical, as he will indicate in the list presented below which, it is worth mentioning, is one of the most detailed lists of his sufferings as an apostle.

2 Corinthians 11:23b-29

(23b) I have worked much harder, been in prison more frequently, been flogged more severely, and been exposed to death again and again. (24) Five times I received from the Jews the forty lashes minus one. (25) Three times I was beaten with rods, once I was pelted with stones, three times I was shipwrecked, I spent a night and a day in the open sea, (26) I have been constantly on the move. I have been in danger from rivers, in danger from bandits, in danger from my fellow Jews, in danger from Gentiles; in danger in the city, in danger in the country, in danger at sea; and in danger from false believers. (27) I have labored and toiled and have often gone without sleep; I have known hunger and thirst and have often gone without food; I have been cold and naked. (28) Besides everything else, I face daily the pressure of my concern for all the churches. (29) Who is weak, and I do not feel weak? Who is led into sin, and I do not inwardly burn?

---

opponents were servants of Moses, of righteousness through the "written code", which, however, do not bring "justice" itself, but "damnation" (2 Cor 3:7) (Barnett, 1993). Regarding the very message of the opponents of the Apostle, we can only speculate. Even its specific identity has been widely discussed and still continues to be, but here we can not go into this very specific topic in more detail. For a review of the subject, we recommend: Barrett, 1971; Gunther, 1973; Ellis, 1975; Kee, 1980; Forbes, 1983; Barnett, 1984; Georgi, 1986; Martin, 1987; Agnew, 1988; Kruse, 1989; Sumney, 1990; Murray, 2005; Furnish, 2007.

2 Cor 11:23b. Here Paul makes three statements about suffering, in order of increasing severity and followed by a conclusive phrase: "I have worked much harder, been in prison more frequently, been flogged more severely, and been exposed to death again and again". The superlative tone used by the Apostle in these phrases indicates the intensity of physical and psychological toll of his experience, fruit of: his arduous work to sustain himself and support the churches; the difficulty of the sufferings that he had to face as a result of the violent opposition to his mission; and the abundant circumstances in which his life was at imminent risk (cf. 1 Cor: 15:10; 2 Cor 4:8-11; 6:4-5).

2 Cor 11:24-25. This third group of affirmations continues with a series of four statements referring to Paul's specific sufferings and ends in a commentary. Among Paul's list of afflictions this is the one that give the most details, many of which are only found here. The book of Acts only mentions some of these events, leaving out most of them[111].

Up until Paul wrote this letter, Paul was beaten eight times: five times by Jews and three by Romans. He also survived to tell the experience of having been stoned by the Jews. More specifically, Paul mentions he received the punishment of lashings from the Jews, which was officialy forty strikes they stopped at thirty nine in case they may have been mistaken in their count and did not want to break the Law (Deut 25:3).[112] Although Paul does not indicate any specific circumstance in which he had suffered this penalty, having received it

---

[111] It is clear in these descriptions that Paul was exposed to innumerable experiences that today are called traumatic, that is, where the person is exposed to imminent damage to their personal integrity, or their life is put at risk (or witnesses such an event happen to someone else) (cf. Diagnosis of PTSD, APA, 2013).

[112] The detailed regulation of the lashings is found in the Mishnah, where it was stipulated that the convict should have his two hands bound to a pillar on each side, and the judge of the synagogue should take the convict's clothes, and tear it to pieces in order to expose his chest. A stone was put behind the prisoner, like a small platform, on which the judge stood with a strip of calf leather in his hand, from which hung two other strips. The piece that was held in the hand was a the length of the palm of one's hand, and a palm's width wide, and the end of the strip had to reach the navel (that is, when the convict was hit on the shoulder, the end of the strap should reach the navel). A third of the lashes should be given from the front, and two thirds from behind. He could not be whipped while standing or sitting but only when he was crouching down. Whoever hit him had to do it with one hand and with all his strength. If the prisoner died on the spot, the judge was not found guilty. But if he gave him one lashing too many and the prisoner died, the judge had to be exiled (Barclay, 1995).

five times attests to the frequency and severity of his conflicts with Jewish synagogues (Robertson, 2003).

Regarding the three beatings with rods (*tris herrab-disthen*), surely he is referring to a kind of punishment given by Romans. This consisted in a type of torture given by assistants to the magistrate (*lictores*) with birchwood sticks or rods, which was used to punish criminal guilty of serious crimes. This cruel punishment occasionally resulted in death, either during or afterwards, because of the severity of the wounds (Barclay, 1995; Deberge, 2005).

Paul's reference to the times he was stoned (*helithasten*) may refer to the one narrated in Acts 14:19. This scene is strange, because stoning was used as capital punishment, so that the chance of survival was normally zero. In this way, this could be seen as the narration of a miraculous event, or it could have been an incomplete execution, a spontaneous outburst of collective antagonism that did not seek his corroborated death as an application of capital punishment, which the Jews were not allowed to exercise autonomously[113] (cf. Jn 18:30-31). The list of extreme adversities continues by mentioning of three shipwrecks (*henauagesa*), included one full day and night (*nychthemeron*, a full day) in the high seas (*butho*, lit. above the depths).[114]

If Paul was adrift a whole day and night, the ship must have sunk far from land. Surviving three shipwrecks before he wrote this letter[115] is remarkable, since it seems that rescuing people was not commonn, because they did not have enough control of the ship to be able to change course and get close enough to a person to pick them up,

---

[113] The way in which Acts concludes the scene makes us think that it intends to indicate the occurrence of a miraculous event, because it describes Paul immediately getting up and entering the city of Lystra again (Acts 14:20), which It would have been physically very unlikely, given the serious damage that an execution of this type entailed, such as multiple fractures in the limbs, severe brain trauma, and/or damage to vital organs.

[114] Since passengers were not the primary source of revenue for the owners of the boats (who mainly transported goods) one could not obtain food, drink and safe shelter on the ship. The passengers had to gather their own provisions for a trip whose duration was unpredictable. Nobody cooked for the passengers, but they could use the galley stove after the crew had eaten. The fire could be extinguished or, even worse, accidentally spread to the deck and catch the boat on fire (Hughes, 1962).

[115] The shipwreck reported by Acts 27:13-44 would be a fourth shipwreck, if we accept its historical veracity.

or simply for not considering the life of an anonymous person as something worth the effort and risk of saving. It was also common for castaways who managed to reach land to be killed or taken as prisoners or slaves by the native inhabitants of certain areas. (Murphy-O'Connor, 2004).

2 Cor 11:26. The forth set of adversities that Paul lists here, is a sequence of eight descriptions of dangers (*kindunois*), that are introduced by a reference to his numerous trips (*hodoiporaiais pollakis*), in such a way that the list can be considered as a enumeration of the danger those trips involved for him, especially those made by land.

Murphy-O'Connor (2004) tell us that the conditions of travelling by land in Paul's time are well documented and allow us to clearly understand the Apostle's adversities in their original magnitude. The word *kindunois* keenly describes Paul's experience and makes evident the reality of the great risk that travelers ran in those times. Despite the fact that the Roman Empire made land travel expeditious on several main roads, which had solid bridges in most cases, the secondary roads were a very different reality. During the spring, higher water levels made river crossngs very dangerous. These natural hazards were significant, but sporadic compared to the threat posed by thieves, who were endemic. Travelers also faced the additional danger of being kidnapped and forced to work as slaves for landowners in nearby settlements. The Roman legions, which were based in Syria, Asia and Macedonia, did not protect the safety of the travelers, and only in exceptional situations were special detachments sent to confront a gang of thieves that were generating major problems. Only rich people or influential citizens had guards who protected them on their trips. Hence, travelers preferred to join caravans of merchants who hired mercenary soldiers for their protection. Even the smaller cities were exposed to bands of thieves or others that caused havoc, since the Roman military was dedicated only to sites of strategic importance. In the face of constant threats from runaway thieves or slaves, or even dangerous gangs of idle youth, villagers were suspicious of any foreigner or stranger who approached. There was also the threat of wild animals that could attack mortally without warning.[116]

---

[116] Lucius Apuleius (124-180 d.C.) in his book "The Golden Ass" or "Metamorphoses", graphically describes the Harsh realities of that time for travellers: "[...] by reason of the

Additionally, to understand the risks involved in Paul's journeys, it is worth mentioning that in those times in Asia Minor there were only inns on the main Roman roads, which were normally a day's journey apart (approximately 35 kilometers). The rooms of the inns were grouped around the three or four sides of the inner courtyard. There were public rooms on the ground floor and the private rooms were upstairs. Only those who had enough money could rent a private room, but most had to share the room with one or more strangers. The ease with which a robbery could be committed was enormous, especially at night or when travelers left their luggage alone to go to the bathroom or the dining room (Murphy-O'Connor, 2004; Ciccotti, 2005).

Paul was a tireless traveler during his apostolic ministry. The amount of kilometers traveled was immense, almost as many as a merchant of those years (Herranz, 2008). He made many trips (*hodoiporiais pollakis*). And as we have mentioned, his journeys were full of danger (*kindunois*), both by land and by sea, and in both cities (*polei*) and the countryside (*heremia*, lit. wilderness). But in the case of Paul, he also experienced dangers related to adversaries who opposed his ministry such: compatriots (*genous*), pagans (*hethnon*) and even, false brothers (*pseudadelphois*) in the faith (Gal 2:4). In sum, we are reading the testimony of a person who has been exposed to events that are quanitatively and qualitatively significant: great in number, variety and intensity.

2 Cor 11:27. This verse graphically describes the physical adversities that the Apostle already mentioned in general terms to the Corinthians (2 Cor 4:8-10; 6:4-5, 10). Here Paul describes his sufferings more specifically than anywhere else in his letters (cf. 2 Cor 2:13; 6:5; 7:5; 11:23; 1 Cor 4:11; Fil 4:11-13; Rom 8:35). [117] He does this over 5

---

great number of terrible Wolves which were in the Country about, so fierce and cruell that they put every man in feare, in such sort that they would invade and set upon such which passed by like theeves, and devoure both them and their beasts. Moreover, we were advertised that there lay in the way where we should passe, many dead bodies eaten and torne with wolves. Wherefore we were willed to stay there all night, and on the next morning, to goe close and round together, whereby we might passe and escape all dangers." (Apuleius, 2006, Book 8, Chap. 33).

[117] Regarding this type of afflictions, the Apostle mentions being trained in his letter to Philippians 4:11-13: 'I have learned to be content whatever the circumstances. I know

sentences, three of which mention two experiences and two of which describe only one. The second line goes with the first, and the third with the fourth:

I have labored and toiled

and have often gone without sleep;

I have known hunger and thirst

and have often gone without food;

I have been cold and naked.

The Apostle's afflictions have affected him in very elemental ways, such as having difficult in adequately satisfying his physical and basic needs. These types of needs are the physical requirements for human survival. We often see Paul postpone these needs, which shows that for him there are needs or motivations that come first, which allow him to transcend this level in a significant way.

2 Cor 11:28-29. Here Paul stops talking about the sufferings that affected him externally (*parektos*), in his hypostasis (2 Cor 4:16), and mentions his constant affliction from his responsibility to take care of the churches he founded.

The phrase: *he epistasis moi he kath hemeran,* can be translated as: what surrounds me crowds in every day (Robertson, 2003). Crowding (*epistasis*), like a multitude that crowds together, that piles in (cf. Acts 24:12). This is how much concern Paul has for the churches (*he merimna pason ton ekklesion*). He assumed his apostolic mission as a task of wide-reaching responsibility. Not only did he feel he was in charge of a specific congregation, but of all the churches (1 Cor 4:17; 7:17; 14:33; 2 Cor 8:18). They are added, therefore, to the extreme adversities that he had to suffer for the wellbeing of the people he served.

This concern or anxiety (*merimna*) was manifested in the Apostle, particularly as an intense empathy towards the weak (*asthenei,* lit. without bodily vigor, sick) and towards those who were made to stumble (*skandalizethai*). A concern for the desadvantaged similar to what he describes God as having (1 Cor 1:25-29). This type of care for

---

what it is to be in need, and I know what it is to have plenty. I have learned the secret of being content in any and every situation, whether well fed or hungry, whether living in plenty or in want. I can do all this through him who gives me strength.'

256

the churches makes Paul feel week himself[118] (*astheno*, cf. 1 Cor 9:22), especially when the little ones are scandalized or cause to stumble (cf. Mr 9:42; Mt 18:6; Lc 17:2), the Apostle burns (*pupoumai*) and is deeply irritated.

2 Corinthians 11:30-33

(30) If I must boast, I will boast of the things that show my weakness. (31) The God and Father of the Lord Jesus, who is to be praised forever, knows that I am not lying. (32) In Damascus the governor under King Aretas had the city of the Damascenes guarded in order to arrest me. (33) But I was lowered in a basket from a window in the wall and slipped through his hands.

This passage seems to connect two argumentative blocks that emphasize different aspects. Preceding it is the list of concrete adversities that simultaneously shows the Apostle's vulnerability and strength (11:16-29), and following it is an allusion to the special revelations given to him by the Lord, that Paul also connects with his weakness, but in a very specific way (2 Cor 12:1-13). Here we observe: a statement regarding the act of boasting (11:30); then a doxology to back up his honesty which can only give glory to God (11:31); and, finally, a brief account of his particular flight from Damascus (11:32-33).

2 Cor 11:30. Paul's paradoxical argument in this passage becomes more explicit. In this verse the Apostle declares what he has been doing at various moments of his defense, but also opens up a new paradoxical discourse that eloquently addresses the issue of his own weakness in the exercise of his ministry (2 Cor 12:1-13).

---

[118] Paul's apologetic discourse is paradoxical, as we have indicated. He addresses his weakness, with a hint of irony, because it was the bases of accusations made by his opponents (2 Cor 10:10). Paul empathizes with everyone's weakness and assumes it as his own. However, his resistance (hupomoné) is outstanding, considering the lists of extreme adversities he has overcome. He is only rescued from incoherence (from an explicit weakness and an evident strength in the face of so much adversity) by the fact that he attributes the cause of his resistance and the power behind his arduous and tenacious efforts to the grace of God: 'But by the grace of God I am what I am, and his grace to me was not without effect. No, I worked harder than all of them—yet not I, but the grace of God that was with me'(1 Cor 15:10). As we will see, the theme of his own weakness unfolds in a special way starting in verse 30 of this chapter.

Paul, poses in this argumentative bridge: "If I must (*dei*) boast (*kauchasthai*), I will boast (*kaujesomai*) of the things that show my weakness (*astheneias*)". This is a conditional sentence. The Apostle thus far has presented a detailed list of his afflictions, which reveal both the eminently suffering nature of his ministry and his resistance to a number of dramatic events. It could easily be thought that Paul is implicitly boasting about his capacity for resistance, his tenacity, and power in the face of tribulations. However, the Apostle wants to make it very clear that if he can be proud or boast about anything, it is not his strength and his resistance to adversity, but, paradoxically and ironically (given the accusation that was made against him, as we indicated), it is his lack of vigor, his weakness.

2 Cor 11:31. Paul introduces the shameful episode of Damascus in a solemn way, corroborating before God, through a doxology (cf. 2 Cor 1:3 and Rom 1:25; 9:5) that tells the truth about what happened. Perhaps he does this so that his readers do not believe that he is talking nonsense or simply making fun of himself, because he will take glory in an event that reveals his weakness and humiliation, something that is absolutely opposed to typical apologetic resources of that time (Sampley, 2008).

2 Cor 11:32. Paul's flight from Damascus[119], could have been left off the list of afflictions, for being a specific adversity. However, the

---

[119] We can place this event indicated by Paul within the first phase of his life as a Christian, after his encounter with Jesus on the road to Damascus. The Apostle indicates that his first decision as a Christian was to go to 'Arabia' (Gal 1:17), which geographically by then corresponded to the territory between the Red Sea and the Persian Gulf (Saudi Arabia). However, a Jew from Jerusalem in the first century would use the name Arabia to refer to a more specific area: Jordan and the two coasts of the Gulf of Aqaba, that is, the territory of Nabatea, whose king, Aretas IV, reigned from the City of Petra (Murphy-O'Connor, 1996; Reynier, 2009). Relations between the Jews and the inhabitants of Nabatea had always been tense. King Herod Antipas (or the tetrarch) was married to Faseilis, daughter of Aretas IV.
When he discovered that Herod wanted to divorce her to marry his brother's wife, Herodias, he fled to his father. In retaliation, Aretas IV invaded the territories of Herod and defeated his army, partly because the soldiers of Philip, husband of Herodias, changed sides. Antipas then appealed to Emperor Tiberius, who ordered Vitellius, governor of Syria, to attack Aretas. Vitellius gathered his legions and moved south, stopping in Jerusalem for the Passover of 37 AD, when news of the emperor's death arrived, and the invasion of Nabatea was never completed (Taylor, 2001). After the war between Antipas and Aretas IV, their relations reached a maximum tension, because they blamed Herod,

Apostle surely wants to illustrate his condition of fragility and weakness in a very graphic, and at the same time humiliating, way[120].

If Paul had a notable virtue, as the same sufferings that he mentions show, it was courage. Escaping from his adversaries, running away in an unworthy manner, without "cleaning the dust off his sandals" and with his head held high, was not normally an option for him. However, here the Apostle makes mention of an emblematic event in terms of his vulnerability (and even failure). It is perhaps one of the most humiliating events he experienced (though obviously not the most risky or painful), where he had to flee, and not in just any way, but as a child, such as Moses, in a basket.

2 Corinthians 12:1-6

(1) I must go on boasting. Although there is nothing to be gained, I will go on to visions and revelations from the Lord. (2) I know a man in Christ who fourteen years ago was caught up to the third heaven. Whether it was in the body or out of the body I do not know—God knows. (3) And I know that this man—whether in the body or apart from the body I do not know, but God knows— (4) was caught up to paradise and heard inexpressible things, things that no one is permitted to tell. (5) I will boast about a man like that, but I will not boast about myself, except about my weaknesses. (6) Even if I should choose to boast, I would not be a fool, because I would be

---

'their king', for the war and the imminent Roman intervention. When Paul arrived in Nabatea, probably around 34 AD, the conflict had already been growing for several years. It is in this context that the newly converted Saul of Tarsus performs his "mission to Arabia". Clearly, it was not the most conducive time to start spreading a message linked to Judaism to the inhabitants of Nabatea. It was quite possible that the message had been taken as an instigation to betrayal, which put Paul in serious danger. But he managed to escape. Even so, he was remembered as a dangerous person. That is why, three years later, the Nabatean authorities set out to ask him to account for their actions. Paul tells us that he spent three years in Damascus (Gal 1:18). When this city passed into Nabatean hands, Paul was cornered by a danger he had not foreseen, from which he had to escape (Sánchez Bosh, 1998; Murphy-O'Connor, 2004).

[120] In addition we could add to this the fact that the "mission in Arabia" seems to have been a resounding failure (Barrett, 1977; Martin, 1986; Furnish, 2007; Reynier, 2009; Guthrie, 2015).

speaking the truth. But I refrain, so no one will think more of me than is warranted by what I do or say [...][121]

2 Cor 12:1. Paul continues his defense by assuming a role of "foolish/reckless/insane" person (2 Cor 11:21b, 23a) and "glorifying" himself. He goes from one humiliating scene to another that is his greatest experience of contact with the glory of God. This verse is parallel to 11:30, but in this case it makes explicit the denial of this method's effectiveness. It does not have any benefit (*ou sumpheron men*) to do this, although apparently, in some way, it is necessary (*kauchasthai dei*).

2 Cor 12:2-4. Paul goes from boasting in his weakness, to put before his readers the highest defense of his ministry as a true apostle of the Lord, that is, the visions (*optasias*) and revelations (*apokalupseis*) that God gave him. Paul had been forced to defend himself from the contempt and aversion that his opponents in Corinth had generated towards him. He now defends himself not in a way that he could have (directly and presumptuously), but in an indirect, dissociated way. He speaks of himself in the third person (2 Cor 12:2-5), since he is probably afraid to fall into pride, just as the Lord himself, according to him, had foreseen (2 Cor 12:7).

Paul's defense in 2 Corinthians 10-13, as in Galatians 1-2, seeks to highlight the fact that his apostolic commission comes directly from God and Christ, and not through any human mediation (2 Cor 10:8; 13:10; Gal 1:1; 1:12; 2:7; Rom 1:1-7).

---

[121] In our commentary we will not be able to enter into all the complexity and richness of this passage (12:1-13). Research on several aspects that are addressed here by Paul is extensive. Many scholars, for exampled have studied aspects related to Paul's revelations and his experience of the 'third heaven', as well as his 'thorn in the flesh'. Likewise, the issue of weakness and its theological relevance is also widely studied, which in this passage is tackled in an emblematic way, as a perfect conclusion to what has already been raised in the passaged. For a deeper understanding of this and other topics present in 2 Corinthians 12, we recommend: Mullins, 1957; Andriessen, 1959; Smith, 1959; Bowker, 1971; O'Collins, 1971; Thornton, 1972; Giallanza, 1978; Crownfield, 1979; Barre, 1980; Black, 1984; Goulder, 1994; Kennedy, 1984; Akin, 1989; Garland, 1989; Morray-Jones, 1993a, 1993b; 1994; Thomas, 1996; Thrall, 1996; Hotze, 1997; Brown, 1998; Dunn, 1998; Walton, 1998; Johnson, 1999; Lambrecht, 2000; Abernathy, 2001; Goulder, 2003; Paillard, 2003; Barrier, 2005; Gooder, 2006; Vegge, 2008; Kowalski, 2013.

In 1 Corinthians 1:9, Paul defends his apostolate on the basis of his vision from the Lord. It is unlikely that the ascension to the third heaven (*tritou ouranou*[122], v. 2) refers to his vision of Jesus on the road to Damascus. Paul's own account of this event (Gal 1:15-16) does not indicate that it was a celestial ascent or prolonged mystical vision[123].

In verses 2 and 3 of this chapter we find a very typical Hebrew parallelism:

V. 2	*V. 3*
I know a man in Christ who fourteen years ago	And I know that this man
(whether it was in the body or out of the body I do not know, but God knows)	(whether it was in the body or out of the body I do not know, but God knows)
was caught up to the third heaven.	was caught up to paradise and heard inexpressible things, things that no one is permitted to tell.

The dissociated way that Paul describes his experience[124] is interesting, since, as he says in his parenthetical comments, only God knows how the revelation was given, whether it was an intimate, out-

---

[122] It can refer metaphorically to the highest heavenly dimension, following the use of the number three as a symbol of perfection, that is, the highest heaven where God dwells (Calvin, 1964).

[123] Even the three versions in Acts speak of a blinding light and a voice from heaven (9:1-9; 22:6-11; 26:12-18).

[124] This split or dissociated way of referring to oneself in the third person can also have a deeper mystical meaning. As indicated by Morray-Jones (1993b), in apocalyptic rabbinical traditions (such as Merkaba) the ascent to the heavens and the vision of the glory (*kabod*) of God (or of Christ, for Paul) involes a transformation of the visionary into another (hence, possibly, the third person singular). The "man in Christ" can be a kind of Paul's heavenly self or apostolic identity, which is connected in conformity with the image of the glorified Christ, who shares in his glory (Rom 8:29, 2 Cor 3:18). This contrasts with the earthly Paul, who is characterized by weakness, which in turn is the means through which the glorious eschatological reality is manifested, as he will indicate in the climax of the passage (2 Cor 12: 9-10).

of-body spiritual experience (*ektos tou somatos*) or if it occurred in a different place where he was brought physically, in his body (*in somati*).[125]

Although Paul feels compelled to cite his heavenly visions in defense of his apostolic authority, he is not willing to claim it as a personal achievement. The fact that he refers to himself as a "man in Christ [I know]" (*oida anthropon en Christo*, v. 2) shows that he is uncomfortable glorifying himslef (2 Cor 10:12), since he only sees it appropriate to glorify himself in the Lord (1 Cor 1:31; 2 Cor 10:17).

The use of the third person singular can also be connected to the language seen in Romans 7:15-25. Paul speaks of himself in a way that is so strange and disturbing to him that he describes it as something alien to himself. Here, however, the experience of his visions allows him to distinguish himself as a *weak man, victim of the thorn in the flesh* (2 Cor 12:7) instead of as an *ecstatic and glorified person* (2 Cor 12:2, 4) of him. He takes ownership of his weakness, and distances his identity from the ineffable glory that was revealed to him (Akin, 1989; Morray-Jones, 1993b).

2 Cor.12:5. Here, Paul makes a clear distinction between the "that [man] (*tou toioutau*) that had the visions and had been in the third heaven or paradise, from himself (*emautou*), who is identified by his weakness (*astheneiais*). The paradox of feeling proud of his weakness saves him from being prideful in the glorious revelations. Regarding the content of the revelation, it is described in an enigmatic way. It is not discursive or abstract, but rather can not be articulated by human beings (*anthropo lalesai*), or rather, is not permitted (*ouk exon*) to be articulated.

2 Cor 12:6. This text may seem to contradict verses 1 and 16 of chapter 11, if Paul's disassociation of himself is not taken into account. For he would be foolish to boast about himself, and thus not boast about the revealed revelation. He sees himself as "caught up" (*harpage*, v. 4), as a mere bearer of the glorious revelation (cf. 2 Cor 4:7). And

---

[125] These verses coul be seen as references to a dualistic anthropological perspective on Paul 's part, but this view is inadequate for several authors, as we indicated when analyzing the first paragraph (cf. Bultmann, 1955; Ruiz de la Peña, 1988; Pannenberg, 2004).

although this would be true (*aletheian*), the Apostle wants to be recognized by his fruits, by what he does and says, by what is seen and heard in him (*huper ho blepei me e akouei ti ex emou*), and not by what what he says about himself.

2 Corinthians 12:7-8

(7) *Therefore, in order to keep me from becoming conceited, I was given a thorn in my flesh, a messenger of Satan, to torment me. (8) Three times I pleaded with the Lord to take it away from me.*

Paul is clear that he should not end up glorifying himself in light of such extraordinary revelations (*huperbole ton apokaupseon*). Therefore, he believes that God takes care of this for him, through using a "thorn in the flesh" (*skolops to sarki*) of the Apostle, an angel of Satan or adversarial messenger (*aggelos satana*) that hits him with his fist (*kolaphize*), so that he does not become arrogant (*hina me huperairomai*, lit. to not over-elevate himself).

Paul's *skolops* has given rise to many different conjectures and discussions amongst scholars. In antiquity, this Greek term was used to refer to a pointy stake that was used as a means of torture, known as "impaling". The Greek words for "impale" and "crucify" were almost interchangeable. The term *skolops*, when used in a figurative sense, brings with it the sense of some acute and unbearable form of suffering, which could be both physical and mental (Ellicott, 2015).

Paul seems to be referring to a chronic ailment, and as M. Herranz (2008) observes, apart from minor passages which could only be understood as imprecise allusions to such an ailment, modern scholars have focused on two main texts in reference to this: Galatians 4:11-15 and our current passage of 2 Corinthians 12:1-10.

In a strict sense, it is impossible to accurately diagnose Paul's supposed suffering that he seems to alude to here, since details are very scarce and use metaphorical instead of technical language. However, when reading the texts we get the general impression that it was a very painful ailment, which probably manifested itself in violent and debilitating ways[126].

The Apostle is very likely indicating the physical weakness that led him to stop and preach to the Galatians (Gal 4:13-15). *Skolops to sarki* seems to allude to the same experience described as *astheneian tos sapkos*, which he mentions in the letter to the Galatians. Thus the context points to the condition when emphatically addressing the theme of weakness.

However, some scholars such as Murphy-O'Connor (2004) assert that careful analysis of the drastic adversities and the important achievements of Paul in the course of his ministerial life rule out any serious physical or psychological illness. Their reasoning is that nobody with a physical illness could have walked the thousands of kilometers that he traveled, through all kinds of terrains and under all possible climatic conditions that he endured. When considering these aspects, it is reasonable to think that Paul was generally physically strong and healthy, and had good mental health. In view of this, it is plausible that the thorn in his flesh could symbolically refer to the animosity that developed within the Christian movement against his ministry. When he speaks of a "Messenger of Satan" or an "adversarial messenger", he could be referring to the opposing missionaries that he calls "servants of Satan" (2 Cor 11:14-15). In all the communities Paul belonged to, including those he founded, there was always a group of believers who caused him pain and hampered his ministry, sadly frustrating his expectations. It is, however, difficult to assume this hypothesis, since it would be strange for Paul to refer again to the same sufferings he dealt with in the previous paragraph, where he speaks of the deep pain

---

[126] Although it exceeds the scope of our research for not being relevant within the perspective we want to address and discuss in the texts, it is worth mentioning that despite the nonspecific phrases that Paul uses to refer to his illness, there have been numerous attempts to more accurately diagnose his ailment. Among the most plausible hypothesis raised by scholars, three stand out: an eye disease, epilepsy or some type of nervous disorder, or an infectious disease (especially malaria). A wide variety of hypotheses have been made about what Paul's 'thorn' is including interpretations such as: guilt for the persecution of Christians, doubts about his own salvation, pagan enemies, conflicts about sensual passions, and others. All of the hypotheses could be classified into: physical afflictions, psychological problems, spiritual torments (e.g. a *demon*), and human opponents (Schweitzer, 1931; Mullins, 1957; Hisey & Beck, 1961; Price, 1980; Leary, 1992; Russell, 1996; Abernathy, 2001).

caused in him by the false brothers and the church leadership by his opponents who made others stumble (2 Cor 11:26, 28-29).

Although there are several hypotheses about Paul's medical condition, when considering the city where he was born, Tarsus, we note that, due to its geography, swamps, mosquitoes, and malaria were abundant there. Along these lines, for some recent authors Paul probably suffered from this disease, which, moreover, could have precipitated or accompanied his ecstatic experiences (Borg & Crossan, 2009).

For these authors, and following Ramsey (1898), Galations 4:13 and 2 Corinthians 12:7 point to a recurrent disease such as chronic malaria[127], which tends to manifest itself with very distressing paroxysms, where the patient is frequently bedridden for long stretches of time, unable to care for himself and experiencing very intense discomforts, such as acute headaches that can be compared to Paul's "thorns in the flesh".

Following this hypothesis, Paul could have contracted malaria during his youth in Tarsus, which had a very favorable climate for this parasitic disease. In this way, his recurrent crises may derive from this debilitating condition, which leaves him weak, vulnerable, and dependent on others. This hypothesis supports the fact that malaria can manifest itself chronically, causing relapses triggered by insufficient treatment, changes in weather or exposure to the cold, and alteration of individual resistance due to various causes such as malnutrition, immunosuppression and debilitating diseases. These conditions are all

---

[127] Malaria is a parasitic disease that involves high fevers, chills, flu-like symptoms and anemia, caused by a parasite that is transmitted to humans through the bite of infected anopheles mosquitoes. After infection, parasites (called sporozoites) travel through the bloodstream to the liver, where they mature and produce another form, called merozoites. Parasites enter the bloodstream and infect red blood cells. Health problems that can occur as a result of malaria include: brain infection (encephalitis), destruction of blood cells (hemolytic anemia), renal insufficiency, liver failure, meningitis, respiratory failure due to fluid in the lungs (pulmonary edema), and rupture of the spleen which leads to internal massive hemorrhage. In chronic forms, the signs and symptoms occur with the initial acute attack common to the condition, which includes symptoms such as: anemia, stools with blood, chills, fever and sweating, convulsions, intense headaches, jaundice, muscle pains, nausea, and vomiting. Chronic malaria is generally considered benign, although it can lead to debilitation and progressive anemia (Fairhurst & Wellems, 2015).

very much in line with those experienced by the Apostle Paul, as we have observed in his lists of afflictions (Fairhurst & Wellems, 2015).

Despite the likelihood of these commentaries, the nature of Paul's "thorn in the flesh" is always a hypothesis. We could even say that it is possible that Paul was intentionally ambiguous about this affliction, in order to extend its application to the lives of a greater number of people and circumstances. What we can say is that independent of the large number of hypotheses regarding the malaise that the Apostle suffered, he persevered in his ministry despite it, and without it ever disappearing completely (Carrez, 1986).

Finally, regarding thes verses, we can mention that here Paul seems to follow one of the traditions of the Old Testament, as is observed especially in Job, where Satan is seen as an instrument of suffering in the hands of God, who ultimately works for good according to his purpose (cf. Rom 8:28-30). This does not prevent him, however, from asking the Lord "three times" (either literally or symbolically, as a whole) to have that affliction taken away from him (Akin, 1989).

2 Corinthians 12:9-10

(9) But he said to me, "My grace is sufficient for you, for my power is made perfect in weakness." Therefore I will boast all the more gladly about my weaknesses, so that Christ's power may rest on me. (10) That is why, for Christ's sake, I delight in weaknesses, in insults, in hardships, in persecutions, in difficulties. For when I am weak, then I am strong.

After the allusion that Paul makes to his visions and revelations (2 Cor 12:1-6), he offers an antithesis that records a second revelation experience, but of a totally different character (2 Cor 12:7-10) that is marked by humiliation. For the Apostle, the true sign of a genuine apostolate lies in weakness and total dependence on the grace of God (Barrier, 2005).

Verses 9 and 10 could be seen as the conclusion of this whole section (2 Cor 11:21b-12:10). Here we see Paul's most beautiful and clear expression of the *power-in-weakness* paradox. This paradox has been present in of the passages where the Apostle has referred to his sufferings through lists, just as we have seen so far.

Here we observe the paradox of the Lord's negative-positive response, who refuses to respond to Paul's petition about "thorn in the flesh" in order to do a greater good by revealing his true power in the midst of weakness.

Along with the sublime glorious revelation, which could cause the Apostle to fall into pride, the Lord also reveals a complementary truth, saying to him (*kai eireken moi*): "My grace/undeserved kindness is sufficient for you, for my power is made perfect/fulfilled in weakness" (*apkei soi he charis mou, he gar dunamis en astheneia teleitai*). The *charis* is enough. The gift of God, which for Paul is undeserved, is sufficient for him to live and face any circumstance, even the most adverse and those that leave him in the complete nullity of his vulnerable, fragile human condition, since it is there, especially there, where God reveals his power that completely transcends human power. The Lord's power is revealed in Paul's powerlessness.

In the face of this revelation, the Apostle says: "Therefore I will boast (*kauchesomai*) all the more (*kauchesomai*) gladly (*hedista*, lit. with great pleasure; from *hedeos*, sweetly; and from *handano*, sensorial pleasure) about my weaknesses (*en tais astheneiais*).

This paradox breaks with usual apologetics, and allows one to brilliantly articulate two realities: on the one hand, the evident power of resistance that Paul seems to have through persevering through the great number of adversities and sufferings that he described in this letter and which are a seal of his apostolate (2 Cor 12:12); and on the other, his constant view of himself as weak/fragile (*asthenia*), impotent, and entirely dependent on God's grace.

In this apparent contradiction, Paul sees the possibility of full communication with the power of Christ himself. Because in the midst of his weakness, his precarious existence in this temporary, world as a simple and fragile jar of clay (2 Cor 5:1a, 7), he can experience a foretaste of the renewed existence powerfully given by God himself (cf. 2 Cor 4:15-5:4).

In verse 10, Paul concludes by saying that, in consideration of this revelation of God who manifests his power in weakness, he delights in/is pleased by (*gave eudoko*): weaknesses/illnesses/ frailties (*astheneiais*); insults (*hubresin*); needs/hardships (*anag-kais*); persecutions, and difficulties (*diogmois kai stenochorais*), for Christ (*huper Christou*). Summing up, again, in a short list the adversities suffered by their Lord.

He concludes with a corollary: for when I am weak/sick/ fragile, I am strong (*hotan gar astheno, tote dunatos eimi*). "This verse shows that in essence this paradoxical *kauchasthai* does not occur in a boasting with words toward others, but in the joyful shouldering of suffering" (Bultmann, 1984, p. 228).

9.3. Hermeneutical Keys Analysis about Coping from Paragraph C

As with the two previous passages, next, we will summarize the keys for intepreting the adversities observed in the text.

Table 5: Hermeneutical Keys about Coping in Paragraph C

(2 Cor 11:21b-12:10)

CODE	CATEGORIES	CONCEPTS	2 Cor
C1(A1, B1)	Paradoxical identity	Positive self-image, with paradoxical elements associated with fulfilling his call in the midst of suffering	11:21b-29
		Using irony to refer to himself paradoxically, describing himself as "superior" to others but in his suffering	11: 21b, 23
		Dissociation between being a container of glorious and ineffable revelation, and being personally weak and impotent	12:1-6
		Definition of himself in reference to the free and empowering gift of God.	12:9-10
C2 (A2, B2)	Experience of faith as faithfulness and perseverance	Self-evaluation of his ministry in function of his perseverance through adversity	11:23-29

C3 (A3, B3)	Resignification of death and/or traumatic events/suffering	Suffering redefined as a positive self-care experience and an experience of deepening one's knowledge of the empowering grace of God.	12:7-10
C4 (A4, B7)	Altruistic coping	Empathy and focus on the well-being of others in the midst of adversity.	11:28-29
C5 (A9, B5)	Detachment from the material	Focus on higher order needs not on the basic ones.	11:27
C6 (A10, B6)	Expression of adverse events	Appropriating all the adverse events suffered and communicating them to others (not denying them).	11:23b-29, 12:10

Explanation of the table: The table summarizes the hermeneutical keys about coping found in the four passages. The first column lists the code (the capital letter indicates the passage and the number indicates the specific key); the second column lists the category of the key; the third column presents the concepts within each category; and finally, the fourth column indicates the specific biblical references

C1. Paradoxical identity:

We have already observed this category in the two previous passages. In Paul's coping dynamic, the way in which he perceives himself, as his personal identity, is fundamental.

In this section, as in the others, we have found concepts that allude to Paul's perception of himself as being paradoxical, as well as positive and connected to perseverance in suffering (2 Cor 11:21b-29).

Especially in this passage, we observe the use of irony as an apologetic rhetorical device, which Paul uses to refer to himself paradoxically, particularly in the midst of adverse circumstances or conditions. He does this in such a way that he ironically describes himself as "superior" to his opponents, but specifically because of the sufferings he has had to experience and of his personal weakness (2 Cor 21b, 23).

Also, in relation to this category, we find a particular way that Paul refers to itself which indicates a certain personal dissociation between being a container of glorious and ineffable revelation, and being personally weak and impotent, who faces his sufferings. (2 Cor 12:1-6).

Finally, we also observe an understanding of himself exclusively in reference to the free gift of God (grace), which is manifested in response to his condition and awareness of his impotence, empowering him in the midst of suffering (2 Cor 12:9-10).

C2. Experience of faith as faithfulness and perseverance:

As in the two texts of 2 Corinthians studied previously, here we also find an understanding of faith by Paul, as being a particular type of praxis that is directly related to faithfulness and perseverance.

Here the Apostle performs a self-evaluation of his ministry based on his perseverance in the midst of adversity as a fundamental criterion (2 Cor 11:23-29).

C3. Resignification of death and/or traumatic events/suffering:

We also observed the resignification of traumatic events or sufferings in the previous passages. Here, we particularly find a redefinition of a particular type of suffering experienced as a positive experience of God caring for him in his spiritual condition (especially regarding staying humble and avoiding pride) that also enables him to deepen in his knowledge of God's empowering grace (2 Cor 12:7-10).

C4. Altruistic coping:

This particular way of dealing with adversity, which is also found in the previous passages, is observed here as an expression of empathy or affective resonance towards the suffering or adversity experienced by others. In this case, the "others" here are the church and its various local expressions, as communities of faith that Paul had founded or gotten to know (2 Cor 11:28-29).

C5. Detachment from the material or visible:

The relativization of evil, found in the previous sections analyzed, is observed here from Paul's notable focus on the highest human needs, in evident detriment of the basic needs that are associated with the satisfaction of what is fundamentally required for survival. (2 Cor 11:27).

C6. Expression of adverse events:

Finally, in this paragraph we also find another example of Paul's practice of remembering and sharing with others the adverse events he experienced. The Apostle takes charge of his sufferings and does not deny them, incorporating them into his biographical narrative in an explicit and intentional way (2 Cor 11:23b-29, 12:10).

Chapter 10
Exegetical Analysis of 2 Corinthians 1:3-11

If we are comforted, it is for your comfort.

2 Cor 1:6

10.1. Paragraph D (2 Cor 1:3-11)

(3) Praise be to the God and Father of our Lord Jesus Christ, the Father of compassion and the God of all comfort, (4) who comforts us in all our troubles, so that we can comfort those in any trouble with the comfort we ourselves receive from God. (5) For just as we share abundantly in the sufferings of Christ, so also our comfort abounds through Christ. (6) If we are distressed, it is for your comfort and salvation; if we are comforted, it is for your comfort, which produces in you patient endurance of the same sufferings we suffer. (7) And our hope for you is firm, because we know that just as you share in our sufferings, so also you share in our comfort. (8) We do not want you to be uninformed, brothers and sisters, about the troubles we experienced in the province of Asia. We were under great pressure, far beyond our ability to endure, so that we despaired of life itself. (9) Indeed, we felt we had received the sentence of death. But this happened that we might not rely on ourselves but on God, who raises the dead. (10) He has delivered us from such a deadly peril, and he will deliver us again. On him we have set our hope that he will continue to deliver us, (11) as you help us by your prayers. Then many will give thanks on our behalf for the gracious favor granted us in answer to the prayers of many.

10.2. Exegetical Commentary

Until now, we have looked at three emblematic passages that list Paul's afflictions, lists that have shown us how the Apostle faces adversity and at the same time provides direct or implicit orientation to the faith communities so they can overcome these types of events, and even be strengthened through them. Now, we will focus on the final passage selected, which deals in a special way with the theme of comfort, among others, in the context of difficulty and affliction.

As we mentioned previously, a possible reconstruction of 2 Corinthians as a set of multiple letters (Vidal, 2007, 2012), would place this passage in the letter *Cor E* (2 Cor 1:1-2:13; 7:5-8:24), written in the summer of the year 54, certainly while Paul was in Macedonia (2 Cor 2:12-13; 7:5-16; 8:1-2). Differing from the previous letters, this one is characterized by eminently being about reconciliation with the Corinthian community. The first part (1:12-2:13; 7:5-16) contains Paul's memories about his relationship with the community, with a certain tone that could even be apologetic; and the second part (8:1-24) is an official letter of credentials about the collection for Jerusalem, which uses terminology and a style similar to those of Hellenistic letters of credentials of that time, which were used to send an official delegation, in this case for the collection for the church of Jerusalem (Vidal, 2012).

2 Corinthians 1:3-4

(3) Praise be to the God and Father of our Lord Jesus Christ, the Father of compassion and the God of all comfort, (4) who comforts us in all our troubles, so that we can comfort those in any trouble with the comfort we ourselves receive from God. 2 Cor 1:3.

After the initial salutation, Paul normally includes a statement of gratitude at the beginning of his letters (1 Thes 1:2ss; 1 Cor 1:4ss; Phil 1:3ss; Phm 4ss; Rom 1:8ss). However, in this case we observe a type of doxology or benediction. Here Paul expresses a notable joy that goes beyond simple thanksgiving. The style of this opening show of gratitude is in line with Jewish liturgical benedictions (Ps 41:13; 72:19; 89:52; 106:48; 150:6; cf. Rom 1:25; 9:5; 2 Cor 11:31). It is a familiar Hebrew benediction that has been Christianized by the incorporation of Jesus as Lord and Christ *(tou kyriou hemon Iesou Christou)* (Quesnel, 1980; Carrez, 1986).

The doxology uses the names in one way, and later inverts than and turns them into an adjective:

Blessed be (*eulogetos*):

a) the God   b) and the God of all comfort

(*ho theos*)   (*kai theos pases parakleseos*)

b) and Father   a) and the Father of compassion

(*kai pater*)   (*ho pater ton oiktipmon*)

The first adjectivization can be translated as: the father from which all compassion comes (Meyer, 1884). Compassion is a very relevant term in Paul's writings, since given the fallen human condition (Rom 6:23; 7:14-25), reconciliation with God is always fruit of his compassion. God's compassion underlies all of the Pauline message. That God is a the father from which all compassion comes is much more than him having a sporadic attitude and behavior, since for Paul God is fundamentally compassionate and a source of compassion (*oiktirmos*).[128]

In saying that the Father of Jesus is the God of all comfort (*theos pases parakleseos*), Paul describes his compassionate character more deeply and specifically. The word *parakletos*, which has a passive form, literally means "called to one's side/aid". But, although this is in a passive form, it is active in its meaning, since it indicates a call to do something, to provide a service for the good of another.[129]

---

[128] The noun compassion is used to express the meaning of three Greek nouns: *eleos*, *splanchna* and *oiktirmos*. According to their original meaning, *eleos* refers to the act of relating to or being moved by feeling; *splanchna* to the place in the body where this feeling is experienced (heart, gut); and *oiktirmos* implies the externalization of compassion towards the misfortune of another. All of the corresponding verbs, in active voice, express the aspect of helping in this attitude: to take pity, to empathize with someone and, in passive voice, having compassion with regard to personal experience. The adjectives derived from the first two nouns characterize the corresponding behavior as a good quality (*oiktirmon*), or as a heartbreaking, piteous situation (*eleeinos*) (Esser, 1994, 1995).

[129] The verb *parakalein*, in its most general use, means "call", "summon", "convoke". It was particularly used to refer to the calling of an ally; of an advisor to counsel; or of a lawyer to defend someone in court. It always had the connotation of a calling to collaborate, serve, and help. In Greece, the *parakletos* was the friend of the accused, *called* to defend him, and was the one who should try to convince the judges to rule in favor of the defendant. It has also be found that *parakalein* refers to the calling to meet and regain strength, especially in battle. It is the word related to the harangues given by military leaders to their soldiers,

Paul is the one who most uses the words *parakaleo* and *parakletesis* in the NT, and more than half of those are in 2 Corinthians. The use of these terms, in the semantic line of comfort, is notably concentrated in these passages that we are reviewing in 2 Corinthians 1:3-7 (also seen in 2 Cor 7:4-13). Although these use of these terms is not exclusive to 2 Corinthians, Paul nevertheless uses God as the subject of the verb *parakaleo* only on this occasion (Orr, 2016).

2 Cor 1:4. For Paul, the Father of compassion and God of all comfort is the one that "who comforts us in all our troubles" (*ho parakalon hemas epi pase to thlipsei*[130] *hemon*), phrase that could refer to his own recent experience alongside his co-workers (2 Cor 1:8-9), but it could also be indicating a principle that derives from the compassionate and comforting character of the Father for all who are in adverse situations, and who could always expect compassion and comfort from him.

Verse 4 continues by indicating a purpose in the comfort that is received: "so that we can comfort those in any trouble with the comfort we ourselves receive from God" (*eis to duvasthai hemäs parachalein tous en pase thlipsei dia tes parakleseos hes parakaloumeths autoi hupo tou theou*). Here Paul connects the comfort of God as an agent, to the comfort that the one being comforted can extend to others that need comfort. One could even draw from this that the purpose of God's comfort is for the one receiving it to fulfill the role of comforter (*parakletos*) for those that need it, based on their experience of comfort.

Those who have received God's comfort are enabled to pass it on to those who need it "in any trouble" (*en pase thlipsei*). These words cover a wide range of possible afflictions that the readers could live

---

encouraging them to continue with the fight, beating back fear. In ordinary secular Greek, the word *parakalein* rarely meant "to comfort", in the sense of consoling, but in the LXX it was habitually given this meaning (Psalm 71:21; Is 40:1, 2; Job 16:2) (Brown, 1985; Barclay, 2002).

[130] The term *thlipsei* comes from *thlibo*, which literally means "to press", "to squeeze", "to envelop", and also "to be constricted"; *thlipsis* means "pressure", primarily in physical terms. In a figurative sense, *thlibo* means "afflict", "harass", with the nuances that could be involved: confuse oppress, or slander. In Greece, in philosophical contexts, this semantic group was used to refer to life's afflictions in general (Stählin, 2003).

through, just as he himself has experienced and escribed in his lists of sufferings.

2 Corinthians 1:5-7

(5) For just as we share abundantly in the sufferings of Christ, so also our comfort abounds through Christ. (6) If we are distressed, it is for your comfort and salvation; if we are comforted, it is for your comfort, which produces in you patient endurance of the same sufferings we suffer. (7) And our hope for you is firm, because we know that just as you share in our sufferings, so also you share in our comfort.

2 Cor 1:5. This verse presents a parallel comparison that correlates the suffering experienced with the comfort that is received, emphasizing what was said before:

a) For just as	a) so
b) we share	b) also our
c) abundantly	d) comfort
d) in the sufferings	c) abounds
e) of Christ	e) through Christ
(*hoti kathos eis hemäs*	(*ohutos dia toü Christoü*
perisseuei ta parhemata	*perisseuei kai he paraklesis*
toü Christoü)	*hemon*)

The phrase "the sufferings of Christ" (*ta parhemata tou Christou*), may refer to the pain and agony that Jesus suffered in *his passion and death*. But it could also refer to the sufferings that Christ's followers endure in the fulfillment of the mission given to them by Christ in favor of the church and God's kingdom. Both possibilities are not incompatible with each other, since according to Paul the followers of Jesus participate in the sufferings of their Lord (2 Cor 4:10; Gal 6:17; Phil 3:10).

2 Cor 1:6. In verse 6, Paul continues to highlight the vicarious nature of suffering as a function of the potential for comfort that one could give to others when the affliction has been overcome "If we are distressed" (*eite de thlbometha*), the underlying cause, the motive, or purpose, "is for your comfort and salvation" (*huper tes humon parakleseos kai soterias*).

Paul links his and his co-workers' tribulations and the comfort received from God, with the comfort and salvation/liberation of his readers, who are his brothers and sisters in the faith. In doing this, he amplifies the impact of the tribulation-comfort pairing to the general salvation process that transcends the specific comfort given from particular afflications.

The term *soterias* has broad meaning in the NT, denoting various types of liberation. It is used to refer to being healed from a disease, safety in a trip, or for perseveration in times of danger. Paul uses the term predominately to refer to the liberation from sin, and alluding to eschatological liberation (Morris, 1993).

For Paul, the comfort received after tribulation can have a multiplying impact that transcends the lives of the individuals and the community. This is because it can add to the work of liberation/salvation that Christ does in the lives of those who make up his body, so that they grow in his likeness (cf. Rom 8:28-29).

Paul seems to consider that the development of perseverance (*hupomone*) in suffering is a fundamental component of this salvation/liberation process. As he says in verse 6: "if we are comforted, it is for your comfort, which produces in you (*energoumenes*) patient endurance (*hupomone*) of the same sufferings we suffer (*hemeis paschomen*)." Therefore, the effect of adversity can produce in Christ's followers a life characterized by *hupomone*, just as Paul eloquently describes in the passage we reviewed previously in 2 Corinthians 6:3-10 (Jam 1:2-4).

As mentioned by Calvin (1964), Paul understands that his life and ministry are always linked to others, particularly those belonging to his communities of faith. This is such that all of the instances of compassion he experiences from God (among them, especially comfort in tribulations), he considers to be given not only for him, but as a blessing given so that he (and all Christians) can have greater capacity to help, care for, and comfort others (cf. Phil 1:21-26).

2 Cor 1:7. This verse, for its part, brings to light the consequences of what has been said until this point. Paul is interested in motivating the hope of the Corinthians, especially now that he has been freed from prison, has met with Titus, and has received good news about the church in Corinth after so many woes that they had given him. This letter (*Cor E* [131]) is marked by reconciliation and confort, but here the Apostle no longer doubts nor solicits the Corinthians' complicity and communion, since he now knows that they share in his pain, and take joy in his joy and comfort, as he would later teach to the Christians in Rome (Rom 12:15).

Paul says that he has a hope (*elpis*) that is firm/solid (*bebaia*) regarding his Corinthian brothers and sisters, having known that (*eidotes hoti*) just as they have shown themselves to be in solidarity/communion/participation (*koinonoi*) with him and his co-workers in their sufferings (*patematon*), and thus also (*ohutos kai*) share in their comfort (*parakleseos*). The hope is solid that the Corinthians will feel comforted with the comfort that Paul receives, since they have already taken part or shared in his sufferings, since they are newly connected with an attitude of help in solidarity and reciprocal comfort in tribulations.

Paul highlights this last aspect in verse 7, Christian *koinonia* [132], in relation to Christ and his church, especially in adversity, since the Apostle has an experience of love as a communal link that "always protects [...] always hopes, always perseveres" (1 Cor 13:7).

In general terms, what we observe in Paul about comfort in these last verses (2 Cor 1:4-7) are: comfort responds to all types of affliction (v.4); although it comes through a particular person (such as Paul), it always ultimately comes from God himself (v.4) and Christ

---

[131] Following, as we have already indicated, the plausible reconstruction proposed by S. Vidal (2007, 2012): *Cor E: 2 Cor 1:1-2:13; 7:5-8:24.*

[132] Among the associated terms we can mention: *koinonosi*, which means "partner", "participant"; *koinoneo* which manes "to take part in, to participate" (and occasionally "to impart"); and *koinonia* which means "partipcipation", "impartation", or "companionship, communion". Paul tends to give a theological connotation to the semantic group associated with *koinonoi*: communion with Christ, and with the gospel (1 Cor 1:9; 9:23; Phil 1:5) is a present reality and future consummation (1 Thes 4:17) which involves living, suffering, dying, inheriting, and reigning together with him (2 Cor 7:3; Rom 6:8; 8:17; 6:6). The Christian is called to feel (s)he is taking part in the sufferings of Christ (Phil 3:10), and at the same time hope and trust in the participation in his glory and resurrection (Phil 3:10; Rom 8:17; 2 Cor 4:13-18). Participation in Christ includes communion with the Spirit given by him (1 Cor 2:11-12; 2 Cor 13:13), and also involves communion with other Christians as co-participants in the faith (Phm 17), service (2 Cor 8:23), and grace and comfort in the midst of suffering (Phil 1:7; 4:14) (Hauck, 2003).

(v.5); comfort can be transmitted to others (v.4); one can suffer to facilitate the comfort of others (v.6); the experience of comfort can be connected to the salvation of the individual and the faith community, and their future perseverance (v.6), as well as to their profound affective solidarity (v.7), which in summary is also with Christ himself, since the community is his body (Orr, 2016).

2 Corinthians 1:8-11

(8) We do not want you to be uninformed, brothers and sisters, about the troubles we experienced in the province of Asia. We were under great pressure, far beyond our ability to endure, so that we despaired of life itself. (9) Indeed, we felt we had received the sentence of death. But this happened that we might not rely on ourselves but on God, who raises the dead. (10) He has delivered us from such a deadly peril, and he will deliver us again. On him we have set our hope that he will continue to deliver us, (11) as you help us by your prayers. Then many will give thanks on our behalf for the gracious favor granted us in answer to the prayers of many.

2 Cor 1:8. It seems that this final section plays an illustrative and narrative role, through a personal example from Paul's life that is related to what he proposed before. The Apostle alludes to troubles/tribulation (*thlipseos*)[133] suffered in Asia, which he does not want to be ignored or unknown (*agnoeis*), since it was an experience that overwhelmed the strength of Paul and his companions (*huperbolen huper dunamin*), extremely overpowering (*ebarethemen*), to the point that they ended up drastically losing hope for survival (*oste exaporethenai hemas kai tou zen*).

We cannot be sure of the exact event that Paul refers to, since the information provided is insufficient. Various hypotheses have been developed, most of which associated that event to certain incidents that occurred in Ephesus, capital of the province of Asia[134].

---

[133] As we indicated previously, the words for "tribulation" or "affliction" (*thiipsis, thlibo*) and "suffering" (*pathoma*) occur most frequently in 2 Corinthians than in any other part of the NT. But it is also worth highlighting that it appears most frequently in 1:3-11 than anywhere else in this letter (Orr, 2016).

[134] The riot instigated by Demetrius in Acts (19:23-41) is not coherent with the intensity of the adversity described here by Paul, since in that narrative the Apostle does not seem to

Paul's description of this adversity once again frames his discourse in the theme of personal, human, and Christian weakness, since with the phrase *kath huperbolen huper dunamin ebarethemen*, he makes it clear that what happened was way beyond his own capacity for resistance, such that he felt his death was imminent.

2 Cor 1:9. What was the purpose of this experience? What meaning does it have? Paul answers these questions in this text, saying that the "sentence of death" (*apokrima tou thanatou*) that he personally received along with his companions (*autoi en eautois*) happened so that they would not trust in or rely on (*pepoithotes*, lit. to be convinced by arguments) themselves, but rather on God, who could raise them up even in humanly insurmountable situations, including death itself, through the resurrection. This is because the God he trusts in is the one who raises the dead (*theo to egeironti tous nekrous*).

2 Cor 1:10. This verse expresses the conclusion of what happened, and synthesizes what Paul has arrived at regarding his experiences of mortal danger and rescue by God. The text has a parallelistic structure of temporal pairs:

---

be exposed to major risk. We do not know if Paul was imprisoned by the Roman authorities in Ephesus, although it is very likely that he spent part of his time in that city as a prisoner, in line with what he indicates in 2 Corinthians 11:23, and with all of the highly risky implications this had on his life. Murphy-O'Connor (2004) explains that in those times each city had its own magistrates, which were responsible for public order. Only the rich could be elected for municipal roles. In this way, positions were normally passed between the dominant families of the cities, who governed the city according to their own interests. Popular opinion could force the magistrates to take action in matters related to crimes of notorious public implication. But those who held the office of magistrate, instead of seeking to identify the true culprit, they tended to take the shortest route by accusing some foreigner who did not know anyone in the area. Additionally, regarding prisoners of low status or without relevant contacts, they usually expected to be paid bribes. If they were not paid, they could imprison them indefinitely or simply execute them through unjust and abbreviated procedures. Paul was surely exposed to these prevailing power dynamics on countless occasions, with the high risk that this always involved his safety and even survival. Another possibility that presents itself to us is that here he is alluded to physical ailments, a sickness, the "thorn in his flesh (2 Cor 12:7-10, see the previous textual analysis), but the text is written in plural which complicates an interpretation along this line. For our purposes, the specific historical circumstance is not very relevant, but what is important is its connotation of being a life-threatening and severely adverse experience.

Past:	Future:
a) He has delivered us from such a deadly peril, again,	b) and he will deliver us
(os ek telikoutou thanatou errusato hemas)	(kai hrusetai)

Present:	Future:
a) On him we have set our hope, that	b) he will continue to deliver us
(eis hon elpikamen)	(kai eti hrusetai)

The term used by Paul here for "to deliver" or "to rescue" is derived from *hreuo*, which means "to flow", and there is the idea of to take something out making it flow. The Apostle feels that God has rescued them, as if making them flow through a current, from mortal danger (cf. Guthrie, 2015; Seifrid, 2015).

Regarding what exactly was that danger of death, as we have said, there could be many possibilities. The text literally says that they have been rescued from "such a deadly peril". He does not talk about mere danger. According to the three lists of afflictions that we reviewed previously, we could say that many of the Apostle's experiences fit in the category alluded to here, which is to say, events of extreme adversity that have concretely placed his life at risk, where his chance for survival was very remote. These experiences have made him aware (by revelation, in the instance he alludes to in 2 Cor 12:6-10) of his vulnerability and personal weaknesses, leading him to totally depend on God's power, which effectively is manifest in such circumstances, saving his life.

The experiences of being rescued and delivered from situations of imminent death are for Paul the foundation of his hope. He anticipates that he will be delivered just as he was in similar circumstances before. According to the parallelistic structure of temporal pairs that we laid out, the argument would be: in the past we were delivered from imminent death, so therefore, we can expect that in the future God will also deliver us; today we can put our hope in him, since he will deliver us when it is necessary. But we cannot sustain ourselves, since we have encountered our weakness with total clarity upon experiencing such severe circumstances.

2 Cor 1:11. Finally, this verse closes the passage, and the forward, by returning to the theme of participation (*koinonia*) in fraternal suffering, which was addressed in verses 4 to 7.

Paul connects prayer/petition (*deesei*) with participation, the experience that is involved by being part of an other's life, both in their suffering and in their comfort. For the Apostle, petitions to God allow the community in prayer to be part of the experience of those for whom they intercede. Paul sees it as a concrete help (*sunupourgounton*, cf. *parakletos*), a work in favor of others which has results. It is not mere positive intentionality, but rather an action.

This work is communal petition, which when attended to by God, generates positive feedback, in line with what Paul laid out in verse 10. In this case it is associated with the gratitude (*eucharistethe*) of the communities that have seen God's work of deliverance in the lives of those who were in (especially extreme) affliction.

The sense of community in this verse is emphasized by the use of redundancy: one group suffers, another group prays/supplicates on their behalf many people (*pollon prosopon*) see and express their gratitude for the positive results of these supplications made to God upon the gift (*charisma*) being bestowed upon the afflicted that have been rescued from their tribulations. This is Paul's conviction, and for this reason he can also proclaim: "All this is for your benefit, so that the grace that is reaching more and more people may cause thanksgiving to overflow to the glory of God" (2 Cor 4:15).

10.3. Hermeneutical Keys Analysis about Coping from Paragrah D

Just as we have been doing with the previous passages, we will now take a look at the hermeneutical keys about coping with adversity that can be observed in the passage. We will organize the information into specific categories and concepts, and synthesize them.

Table 6: Hermeneutical Keys about Coping in Paragraph D

(2 Cor 1:3-11)

CODE	CATEGORIES	CONCEPTS	2 Cor
D1	God's comforting presence	Joyful awareness of God's active, positive, and permanent presence in the midst of adversity	1:3-5
D2 (A1, B1, C1)	Paradoxical identity	Understanding oneself as vulnerable and powerless, where God's power is manifest in his deliverance	1:8-9
D3 (A2, B2, C2)	Experience of faith as faithfulness and experience	Confidence in God's comfort and intervention in the middle of tribulation	1:3-11
D4 (A4)	Eschatological coping	Confidence in God's faithful act of deliverance in our adverse events	1:9-10
D5 (A6)	Identification with Jesus as a model for coping	Identification with Christ in his suffering	1:5
D6 (A3, B3, C3)	Resignification of death and/or traumatic events/suffering	Interpretation of adversities as experiences that facilitate the development of perseverance	1:6
D7 (A4, B7, C4)	Altruistic coping	God's comfort as a training experience for comforting others	1:4, 6
		Communion and solidarity in suffering as a communal, not individual experience	1:6, 7, 11
D8 (A9, B6, C6)	Expression of adverse events	Appropriating, remembering, and communicating about traumatic events to others	1:8-10
D9 (A8)	Thanksgiving	Thankfulness for the positive action of God in adverse situations	1:11
D10	Prayer	Prayer as a model for coping in solidarity	1:11

Explanation of the table: The table summarizes the hermeneutical keys about coping found in the passage. The first column lists the code (the capital letter indicates the passage and the number indicates the specific key); the second column lists the category of the key; the third column presents the concepts within each category; and finally, the fourth column indicates the specific biblical references.

D1. God's comforting presence:

At the beginning of this passage Paul expresses (in this case as a liturgical benediction) a joyful awareness of the active, positive, and constant presence of God in the midst of adversity for the benefit of his people, which guarantees his comfort in tribulation and his compassionate response to their suffering of (2 Cor 1:3-5)

D2. Paradoxical identity:

Just as we observed in the previous passages, here we also see the Apostle's coping dynamic as being directly related to the his self-perception during tribulation.

In this case, Paul and his companions' self-understanding is presented, having an awareness of their total vulnerability and powerlessness in the severe adversities they experienced, along with an explicit confidence in God's power that enables them to overcome the risk of imminent death (2 Cor 1:8-9).

D4. Experience of faith as faithfulness and experience:

Just like in the previous passages, faith is understood throughout as a dynamic that involves perseverance and faithfulness, particularly in situations of suffering and opposition, shown as a confidence in God's comfort and effective intervention in tribulation that allows one to continue ahead (2 Cor 1:3-11).

D5. Eschatological coping:

Just like the first passage we analyzed, here we also see a coping mechanism in Paul related to the foreseen positive future. In this case, it is expressed as full confidence in God's faithful act of deliverance in our adverse events, just has he had experienced in various similar circumstances (2 Cor 1:9-10).

D6. Identification with Jesus as a model for coping:

Here we also find elements that refer to Paul's identification with Jesus, particularly with his sufferings, just like in the first passage we analyzed.

The Apostle identifies the abundant sufferings that he and his co-workers endured with those of Christ himself, giving a sense of transcendence to his sufferings for the cause of the ministry to which he was called (2 Cor 1:5).

D7. Resignification of death and/or traumatic events/suffering:

This category is also present in this last passage, as in all of the previous passages, regarding the resignification of severe afflictions.

Here Paul reinterprets his sufferings from the comfort he received previously, as an experience that develops perseverance for future adverse events. He assigns them a positive connotation for himself and for others, as an event that, when overcome, can edify the community (cf. category of altruistic coping) (2 Cor 1:6).

D8. Altruistic coping:

This coping mechanism is ever-present in Paul, where the wellbeing of others is placed as the priority focus of attention, just as we say in sections of all the passages analyzed previously.

The Apostle understands God's comfort of a person in function of the good of others. The one who receives divine comfort is, through that comfort, enabled to play the role of comforter (*parakletos*) for those that need it (2 Cor 1:4, 6).

Paul also always understands coping with adversity in terms of communion and solidarity with the suffering of others, as a communal experience and not as an isolated individual. Solidarity is shown as a mechanism for coping in tribulation (2 Cor 1:6, 7, 11).

D9. Expression of adverse events:

This category is found in all of the selected passages. Here Paul explicitly emphasizes that he does not want the sufferings of he and his co-workers to be ignored, and specifically alludes to an event where he was exposed to imminent death, to the point of losing all hope in the possibility of surviving. Several of his afflictions found in the lists we have analyzed could fall within this category, where his life or integrity was in grave danger. The Apostle does not forget nor deny what happened, rather he remembers it and makes it known. In this way, he incorporates it into his life as well as his personal and communal identity (2 Cor 1:8-10).

D10. Thanksgiving:

As we saw in part of the first passage, here we again observe that gratitude is constantly present in the way that Paul faces adversities. Communal thanksgiving, and even foreseen and anticipated thanksgiving. The Apostle always pays attention to God's positive actions in adverse situations, and wants to make them known to many so that God can be glorified (2 Cor 1:11).

D11. Prayer:

Finally, here we can see prayer, and asking others for prepare as a coping mechanism. It is presented as spiritual solidarity in one's suffering or the suffering of others, as a type of fraternal communion, that hopes for effective results and is considered a real action which is more than simple positive intentions for the good of others (2 Cor 1:11).

Chapter 11
Towards a Pauline Practical Theology of Coping

Having completed our exegetical analysis of Paul's writings in 2 Corinthians related to traumatic events, we will conduct a critical, psychological review of the same texts. We will do this through a discussion that relates the Pauline keys for coping we have identified with the discoveries about hardiness, resilience and posttraumatic growth in the field of positive psychology, for the purpose of developing a theological-practical approach to coping with traumatic experiences in Paul.

II.1. Pauline Keys for Coping and Positive Coping with Trauma

As result of our analysis of the keys for coping that Paul presents in selected texts of 2 Corinthians, next we will summarize the eleven categories we uncovered, establishing a critical discussion with the contributions of psychological research about coping styles, hardiness, resilience, and posttraumatic growth. The contents will be presented, addressing: a) a summary of every key for coping found in 2 Corinthians (see next table); b) a categorization in terms of coping mechanisms; to then establish connections with three principle constructs about positive posttraumatic coping: c) hardiness; d) resilience; and e) post-traumatic growth.

Table 7: Hermeneutical Keys for Coping in 2 Corinthians Paragraph
(2 Cor 4:7-5:10; 6:3-10; 11:21b-12:1; 1:3-11)

CODE	CATEGORIES	CONCEPTS	2 Cor
A1 B1 C1 D2	1. Paradoxical identity	Fragile container of glory and significant contribution to others.	4:7, 16
		Personal identity as a medium of grace, bearer of goodness to many.	4:7
		Transcendent, not victimized identity	4:9
		Suffering Christian identity	4:10
		Paradoxical perseverance, powerful weakness Paradoxical experience of victorious impotence.	6:8-10

		Trust in what you own in an inalienable, intrinsic way, in the midst of adversity. Perception of fundamental present fullness.	6:10
		Positive self-image, with paradoxical elements associated with fulfilling his call in the midst of suffering	11:21b-29
		Use of irony to refer to himself in a paradoxical way, describing himself as "superior" to others but in sufferings.	11:21b, 23
		Dissociation between being a container of glorious and ineffable revelation, and being personally weak and impotents	12:1-6
		Definition of himself in reference to the free and empowering gift of God.	12:9-10
		Conception about himself as vulnerable and impotent, where the power of God is manifested through his freedom and support.	1:8-9
A2 B2 C2 D3	2. Experience of faith as faithfulness and perseverance	Hardiness of theological origin (faith/faithfulness, hope, and love).	4:8-9; 5:6-10
		Trust in the power of the resurrection	4:9, 13
		Coping that is ethical instead of speculative (theodicy), focus on the kingdom of God in life and his glorification as an ultimate concern.	5:1-4, 9
		Coping based on the desire to be a perseverant servant of God.	6:3-4
		Pursuit of an irreproachable character: being pleasing to God, with a clean conscience in every circumstance.	6:3-4a
		Perseverance as a central virtue of Christian experience.	6:3-10
		Perseverance as a virtue based in the power of God, through faith and hope, not as an attribute of personal merit.	6:3-4a

		(Cardinal and theological) virtues as coping mechanisms.	6:6-7
		Self-evaluation of his ministry in function of his perseverance through adverse situations.	11:23-29
		Confidence in the comfort and intervention of God in tribulations.	1:3-11
A3 B3 C3 D6	3. Resignification of death and/or traumatic events	Positive resignification of death.	4:8-9; 5:1-2
		Positive resignification of traumatic events.	4:10-12
		Appropriating and relativizing the misfortune suffered.	4:10-12; 16-18
		Not focusing on suffering.	4:16-18
		Suffering and diverse adversities as necessary secondary cost assumed to accomplish of his mission.	6:4b-5
		Adversity as corroborating instance of the purity, sincerity and character of his mission.	6:6-7a
		Suffering redefined as a positive self-care experience and an experience of deepening one's knowledge of the empowering grace of God.	12:7-10
		Interpretation of the adversities face as experiences which facilitate the development of perseverance.	1:6
A6 B4 C4 D7	4. Altruistic coping	Focusing on the well-being of others when faced with personal adversity.	4:12,15
		Focus not on himself, but on not causing others to stumble, nor defame his ministry.	6:3
		Attention focused on relational qualities that seek the well-being of others.	6:6,10

295

		Empathy and focus on the well-being of others in the midst of adversity.	11:28-29
		God's comfort as training for comforting others.	1:4, 6
		Communion and support in suffering as a communal and not individual experience.	1:6, 7, 11
A4 D4	5. Eschatological coping	Coping based on theological promises.	4:9; 5:1-5
		Hope in the resurrection as a coping mechanism.	4:10-12
		Resurrection as communal hope	4:14
		Eschatological resignification of present adversity.	5:1-4
		Confidence in the faithful liberating action of God in new adverse events.	1:9-10
A9 B6 C6 D8	6. Expression of traumatic events	Appropriating, remembering, and communicating traumatic events to others.	4:8-10
		Appropriating all the adverse events suffered and communicating them to others (not denying them).	6:8-10
		Appropriating all the adverse events suffered and communicating them to others (not denying them).	11:23b-29, 12:10
		Appropriating all the adverse events suffered and communicating them with others.	1:8-10
A8 B5 C5	7. Detachment from the material or visible	Focusing on what is permanent, and disregarding what is temporary and preliminary.	4:16-5:8
		Disregarding what is material and preliminary. Christ as his everything. Focusing on eternal and invisible things.	6:8b-10
		Focusing on needs of superior order, and not on the basic ones.	11:27

A5 D5	8. Identification with Jesus as a coping mechanism	Identification with Jesus Christ in his death and resurrection.	4:10-11
		Identification with Christ in his suffering.	1:5
A7 D9	9. Thanksgiving	Thankfulness for the positive action of God in adverse situations.	4:15
		Thankfulness for the positive action of God in adverse situations.	1:11
D1	10. Comforting presence of God	Cheerful awareness of the active, positive and permanent presence of God in the midst of adversities.	1:3-5
D10	11. Prayer	Prayer as a supportive coping mechanism.	1:11

Explanation of the table: The table summarizes the hermeneutical keys about coping found in the four passages. The first column lists the code (the capital letter indicates the passage and the number indicates the specific key); the second column lists the category of the key; the third column presents the concepts within each category; and finally, the fourth column indicates the specific biblical references.

1. Paradoxical Identity:

a) Summary of key: This corresponds to the first and most frequent key for coping observed in the selected Pauline texts. Paul presents a very particular way of perceiving himself when dealing with the subject of serious hardships. His identity is constantly described in a paradoxical way: as someone who in himself is weak and vulnerable, but who has an ability to significantly and transcendently contribute to others, through God, which also allows him to overcome even extreme afflictions (2 Cor 4:7, 16; 11:21b-29; 12:1-6; 1:8-9).

This perspective of himself allows him to see himself not as a passive victim in midst of violent events that he suffers, but as someone who can effectively and constantly overcome adversities, which are understood as expected events in function of the mission which has been entrusted, but that one day will be overcome by a future full of a vast and eternal goodness, which he is called to share with others (2 Cor 4:9-10; 6:8-10).

Along these lines, Paul also refers to himself in an ironic way, because he describes himself as "superior" to his opponents, specifically in regards to the sufferings that he had to face, and bases this understanding of himself in a way that is exclusively related to the free gift of God (grace), as a response to his impotence and fragile condition (2 Cor 11:21b, 23; 12:9-10).

It is worth mentioning, as we indicated before, that the Apostle normally talks in the first person plural (including his co-workers in the ministry). In other words, his paradoxical identity can also be understood as a communal identity, a way of understanding the people who serve Jesus as their Lord within the apostolic ministry.

b) Coping mechanism: Paradoxical identity, as a key for coping observed in Paul, could be described according to the categories established for coping strategies, focused on the representation of himself more so than on the specific situation or problem; as an active method; with characteristics of being more cognitive-affective than behavioral; temporarily anticipatory, and not just restorative; and with a reach that is more global than specific, related to particular contexts (Rodríguez Marín, 1995).

c) Hardiness: Regarding the resources associated with hardiness, this key for coping has important connections with the constructs that involve this adaptive mechanism which reduces the harmful effects of high levels of stress in people's health. We are referring to sub-constructs of commitment, control, and challenge, as we will see below (Kobasa, 1979, 1982; Kobasa, Maddi & Courington, 1981; Kobasa, Maddi & Kahn, 1982; cf. Eschleman, Bowling & Alarcón, 2010; Maddi, 2013; Singh, 2016):

With respect to commitment, Paul, through his paradoxical identity, manages to get away from an alienating perspective of himself which denies undesirable dimensions, and instead believes in the truth, importance, and value of what he himself is and of all that he can do through the grace of God. For this reason, it tends to be significantly involved in all the activities of his life, since in them he sees the fulfillment of his own new and redefined identity in Jesus Christ, which also allows him to feel useful and relevant in the community.

Control, as second central factor of hardiness, also connects with the paradoxical Pauline identity, because it involves a way of thinking, feeling, and behaving, which involves a conviction about the importance of influence and personal responsibility during adverse events. And despite his powerlessness, he is certain that the power of

298

God himself acts and allows him to foresee the final triumph over adversity.

Regarding challenge, as the third sub-construct of hardiness, through his paradoxical identity, Paul sees himself as continuously changing, constantly growing in such a way that he interprets all situations as opportunities and incentives for personal and communal development, and not as a threat. In this way he shows an important degree of cognitive flexibility and tolerance of ambiguity.

Another important factor associated with hardiness and resistance to trauma is the integration of previous adverse experiences. Paradoxical identity is a way of identifying oneself that narratively articulates one's negative dimensions with positive qualities received from God, qualities that enable Paul to incorporate various events to his personal story, especially the ones which have a disruptive potential, in such a way that they can be incorporated as an integral constitutive part and as a growth experience (Pérez Sales, 2006).

The convictions of religious faith, as a recognized resource that mediates the harmful and permanent effects of traumatic events and enables greater hardiness to them, is connected in an evident way with the paradoxical identity. For Paul faces adversity from his identifying conviction given by his Lord, an identity of theological, particularly Christological, character that mediates all experiences, including highly stressful ones (Pargament, 1997; Ganzevoort, 1998a; Prati & Pietrantoni, 2009)[135].

Finally, regarding the capacity for hardiness, we also observe the coherence of the paradoxical identity, with the perception of oneself as a survivor, typical of the processes of traumatic resistance. Paul sees himself as someone who has emerged from a traumatic experience stronger than before, and who, consequently, has a deeper experience of the divine resources he has.

d) Resilience: If we compare paradoxical identity as coping mechanism with the factors associated to the development of resilience, following several authors (Kotliarenco, et al., 1997, 1999; Munist, et al., 1998; Vanistendael & Lecomte, 2002; Cyrulnik, 2001, 2002, 2003, 2007, 2009; Yates & Luthar, 2009; Reich, Zautra & Hall, 2010; Cruz-

---

[135] This aspect will be present in a later section with more detail, because of its central relevance to the theological contribution of this work.

Villalobos, 2007, 2009, 2011, 2012; Brownlee, et al., 2013; Fletcher & Sarkar, 2013; Kent, Davis & Reich, 2014), we can highlight the following:

Among the affective resources associated with resilience, self-esteem stands out, which in the case of the paradoxical view of self seen in Paul, we can indicate that we are observing a positive, though paradoxical, self-esteem, since the Apostle regards himself in terms of the positive and unconditional affection (grace) of God manifested in Jesus Christ, despite knowing he himself is precarious and inadequate.

Paradoxical identity, especially when takes on a connotation of irony (especially at the end of 2 Cor 11 and the beginning of 12), can be connected to humor as an important factor significantly associated with resilient processes (cf. Jáuregui, 2009; Vanistendael, et al., 2013).

The basic contextual resources associated with resilience include unconditional acceptance and support with at least one person (meaningful attachment). This factor can be related to the paradoxical identity, because the Apostle sees himself as being fundamentally bonded with Jesus (resurrected), who is his Lord, has loved him unconditionally, and has given him a mission of the highest importance. In this last element, we can also observe another important factor related to the expression of high and positive expectations. Despite being aware of his fragility and vulnerability, Paul sees himself as a servant of God, who has been assigned a mission that has the potential to transform the world.

e) Posttraumatic Growth: Regarding posttraumatic growth, the paradoxical identity observed in Paul is a coping mechanism that can be linked to some of its associated factors. Particularly we see an association with one of the three categories of changes that are considered in the literature when talking about personal development after trauma, beyond the level seen prior to the traumatic event (Calhoun & Tedeschi, 1999, 2001, 2004a, 2004b, 2008; Vera, et al., 2006; Pérez Sales, 2006; Acero, 2008, 2011; Cruz-Villalobos, 2016; Eve & Kangas, 2015; Blix, et al., 2016). We are referring to the changes in the perception of oneself. Although in Paul we cannot speak of trauma as such, with the respective disruption or collapse of one's world, we can observe this tendency to feel stronger (though not in itself, but in the power of God and his grace), more reaffirmed in one's self (of course

300

paradoxically), with more experience and more capacity to face future difficulties, after having to go through traumatic circumstances.

2. Experience of Faith as Faithfulness and Perseverance:

a) Summary of key: The second most important category, given its constant in the Pauline texts, refers to an understanding of faith as faithfulness and perseverance in every event. A coping mechanism is observed where faithfulness to God in the fulfillment of the mission assigned by him, with total honesty and clear conscience, is especially manifested in the midst of suffering and opposition (2 Cor 4:8-9; 5:6-10; 6:3-4; 11:23-29; 1:3-11).

Perseverance is seen as a constitutive and fundamental part of the life of a follower of Jesus Christ, in such a way that positive coping with tribulations is understood as a virtue (*hupomoné*) which belongs to a set of qualities indicative of mature Christian character, but which are not based on practice or self-discipline[136], but on the power given by God himself, manifested in the resurrection of Jesus Christ. This power is also experienced by the disciple, in a special way, in overcoming serious afflictions (2 Cor 4:9, 13; 5:1-4, 9; 6:3-4, 8-10).

Faith, understood in this way, has a relational component that transcends a purely cognitive or dogmatic perspective and connects it with the affective dimensions of someone's faithfulness, more than with the acceptance or conviction about some particular content or discourse[137].

b) Coping mechanism: Faith understood as faithfulness and perseverance, can be considered a coping mechanism focused on the representation of oneself, but which also incorporates elements related to specific, adverse and oppositional situations or problems. It also corresponds to a resource method, with characteristics of a process that is both cognitive-affective and behavioral. It is temporarily anticipatory,

---

[136] As was the Greek perspective of that time, especially Stoic and Epicurean.

[137] As we indicated before, this conception can be seen in the systematic development made by P. Tillich (1976, 1982) about faith as *ultimate concern*, that without limiting or leaving cognitive aspects, involves affective and volitive (as well as behavioral and relational) dimensions, in other words, the complete multidimensional life experience of a person.

not restorative, and is wide in scope in that it involves the whole life of the Apostle (Rodríguez Marín, 1995).

c) Hardiness: The way that Paul understands his experience of faith is closely related with Kobasa's general conception of hardiness (Kobasa, 1979, 1982; Kobasa, Maddi & Courington, 1981; Kobasa, Maddi & Kahn, 1982; Maddi, 2013). We see this association again with the three main sub-constructs: Paul does not perceive himself as being alienated from the reality he faces, but rather he is committed to everything he does, because he knows he is an envoy (apostle) of his Lord, and believes that what he does or does not do in his daily life is of utmost importance, particularly how he responds to the suffering he must face (commitment). On the other hand, by arduously persevering, as an expression of his faith, he also acts with the conviction that his actions are relevant for himself and his environment, especially about the communities he leads, and he knows about his influence and personal responsibility in the course of the events that he experiences, despite the fact that many of them correspond to unjust acts of oppression and abuse of power by the authorities and adversaries (control). Finally, he assumes the circumstances that must be faced as opportunities and incentives for personal and community (ecclesial) growth, without emphasizing the threatening character of the serious tribulations experienced (challenge). This factor has also been conceptualized more specifically as transformational coping, characterized as the process that sets in motion adaptive strategies to take charge of the problems that arise, and which is contrary to regressive coping, associated with escape behaviors or avoidance of potentially or effectively stressful stimuli or circumstances (Maddi & Hightower, 1999; Omeri, Lennings & Raymond, 2004).

d) Resilience: Regarding resilience, understood in general terms as the ability to move forward in difficult circumstances and to get up and continue after a traumatic event (Driver, 2011), we can state that there is a fairly direct association with the conception that Paul has of faith as perseverance and fidelity, to the point that we could speak of resilience as a type of response inherent to the life of believers in Jesus Christ, according to the Pauline perspective. We can even dare to use resilience as a translation of *hupomoné*, a central virtue that Paul associates with the experience of faith (2 Cor 1:6-7; 6:4, 8; cf. 1 Tes 1:3; Rom 8:25; 12:12; 15:4-5; Stg 1:2-3).

In more specific terms (Kotliarenco, et al., 1997, 1999; Cruz-Villalobos, 2007, 2009; Brownlee, et al., 2013; Fletcher & Sarkar, 2013; Kent, Davis & Reich, 2014), we can mention some factors related to resilience that are associated with this Pauline key, such as affective factors that involve the experience of stress and coping with stress through positive subjective signification, because in the case of the Apostle, we see that he sees adversity as an opportunity to reveal the authenticity of his faith, calling, and ministry.

Among the cognitive-behavioral factors related to resilience, it is possible to associate perseverance as a constitutive virtue of Paul's conception of faith, with the command of adaptation and conflict resolution strategies. For the Apostle understands his faithfulness God as being inseparable with the way in which he copes with tribulations and adapts to circumstances of extreme adversity.

Among the resources associated with resilience that some have called spiritual or existential, we can highlight the ability to discover meaning and vital coherence, and to find a sense of transcendence, purpose, and future. Along this line, for Paul faith functions as a kind of matrix of vital coherence that helps him to incorporate traumatic events into his biographical and personal/community identity, with meaning and purpose. This allows him, on the one hand, to persevere and remain faithful to his Lord in the midst of difficulty and, on the other hand, to be free to suffer a disruption of the continuity of his experience in the face of events threatening his personal integrity. That is, traumatic events are not experienced by the Apostle as a breakage or trauma, but are integrated into his story and added up as experiences of perseverance, typical of his faith in the one who was crucified and resurrected.

e) Posttraumatic Growth: Finally, regarding posttraumatic growth, this Pauline key for coping is related to some cognitive variables that different researchers have indicated as being significant for the possibility of becoming stronger after experiencing a traumatic event, such as: the ability to evaluate a threatening situation; coping focused on the problem (instead of the emotion); and positive reinterpretation and optimism (Linley & Joseph, 2004). These types of factors can be observed, in part, within the understanding that Paul has of faith as perseverance, since he presents a clear awareness of the threats he must constantly face in his ministry, threats that he does not face from a state of excessive emotional activation but instead in a practical way with a marked positive reinterpretation of adverse events from his faith perspective.

3. Resignification of Death and Traumatic Events:

a) Summary of key: As we indicated in first section of this chapter (5.1.1), the concept of trauma in Paul is modified. In him we do not observe the contemporary notion of trauma (DSM) which involves an event of specific characteristics along with an expected response to said event (at least from his autobiographical writings that we have). We only find a description of events that meet the characteristics of a traumatic event, but the Apostle does not describe reactions that classify as traumatic responses, rather, on the contrary we only observe positive coping mechanisms (very much aligned with the positive responses to trauma associated with resistance and resilience according to contemporary psychological research). Although we recognize that our analysis and conclusions have limitations, because they are framed in the sections of the Pauline corpus chosen and in a particular perspective of approaching the texts (it is possible that from other approaches different elements could be seen).

Coping in Paul is associated in a special way with the way in which he interprets or situates himself (affective, cognitive, behavioral, and relationally) in traumatic events. In the selected passages, we find the resignification of death and events where his or personal integrity is in danger as a central key for coping in Paul.

The Apostle, by assigning a positive meaning to death and traumatic events, takes charge of his multiple experiences of suffering without denying them, and neither does he avoid them in his memory nor does he move away from circumstances that remind him of them. He relativizes the negative aspects of these disruptive events, and interprets them as events that end up contributing to his life of faith in Jesus Christ (2 Cor 4:8-12; 5:1-2).

On the other hand, despite addressing the subject of his sufferings many times, Paul does not present himself as a victim that is passive and mired under adverse circumstances. Instead, we see him give meaning to these situations from a transcendent perspective, placing its focus on an eternal and permanent reality that is approaching. The Apostle sees his sufferings, in many cases[138], as secondary costs of fulfilling the mission that has been assigned to him. He also sees them as possibility to publicly corroborate his clear conscience, his ministerial sincerity, and his purity of spirit, word, and love in service of Jesus Christ and his church, in the midst of harsh opposition, where he can also comfort those who suffer thanks to his own experiences where he was comforted (2 Cor 4:16-18; 6:4b-5, 6-7a; 1:6).

Within the resignification of death and traumatic events, Paul's hope in the resurrection (or glorious transformation) based on the resurrection of Christ plays an important role. It is from this eschatological conviction that he interprets death and vital risks (2 Cor 4:10-12; 5:1-5).[139]

b) Coping mechanism: This key for coping used by Paul, where resignifies death and traumatic events, can be considered a form of confrontation focused on the situation. It also corresponds to an asset method, which facilitates facing events and not the avoiding them. It has characteristics of both cognitive-affective and behavioral processes, is temporarily anticipatory rather than restorative, and is wide-reaching (Rodríguez Marín, 1995).

c) Hardiness: Positive resignification of death and adverse events can be associated with psychological resistance to one of their basic sub-constructs: challenge. Paul is aware of the scarcity of the life in general and especially of his own. He understands that stability only can be found in the transcendental plan, because live is characterized by instability. As we can observe in subjects with high levels of resistance, for Paul the benefit of higher cognitive flexibility and tolerance to ambiguity is that situations are resignified as opportunities for personal growth and not as threats to his own safety (even high risk circumstances), which is linked, as we can see in his letters, to the proper integration of previous sufferings (Kobasa, 1979, 1982; Kobasa,

---

[138] A redefinition of a very particular type of one of his sufferings, which for most scholars could refer to a chronic illness, as we indicated previously, is what 2 Corinthians 12: 7-10 does, where he comes to interpret the deep discomfort described there as a positive experience of self-care on the part of God, a care of his spiritual condition, which also allows him to deepen his experiential knowledge of the grace of God.

[139] We are going to talk about this in the next section about the Pauline key that we have called eschatological coping.

Maddi & Courington, 1981; Eschleman, Bowling & Alarcón, 2010; Singh, 2016).

As has been observed in studies about resistance to high stress situations, convictions of religious faith can be resources for integrating disruptive events by allowing a type of "logic" to be found that is particular to these events, allowing for better coping and greater resistance (Prati & Pietrantoni, 2009; Maddi, 2013).

Among the cognitive and behavioral resistance resources that we observe in Paul that are associated to this key for coping, we can mention the act of selectively remembering positive elements in the autobiographical memory, with a tendency to attenuate or leave out negative ones. In Paul's case, instead of omitting the events themselves (which he definitely he does not do, as evidenced by his long lists of sufferings), he positively interprets them out of his eschatological hope as a servant of Christ (Pérez Sales, 2006)[140].

d) Resilience: Regarding resilient resources, Paul's way of coping here shows several connections. In particular, the ability to discover meaning and vital coherence in the midst of the difficulties, which is characteristic of people who overcome adversity, is highlighted. In Paul's case we observe it through the assignment of meaning to traumatic events and to death itself. This is linked with the sense of transcendence, purpose and future, which is also highly correlated with resilient positive coping, which in the Apostle is also evident in this modality where he confronts afflictions by reinterpreting them or assigning from an eschatological perspective, which helps him cope adaptively (Kotliarenco, et al., 1999; Vanistendael, 1994, 2003; Cruz-Villalobos, 2007; Kent, Davis & Reich, 2014).

e) Posttraumatic Growth: Regarding posttraumatic growth, as we mentioned before, in our pauline texts studied we technically do not find the concept of trauma as such, so therefore we cannot talk specifically, but only in a general way, about "posttraumatic" growth. We can talk about growth after "traumatic events", even when these

---

[140] Though maybe is possible that he omits the emotional impact and damage. That could be considered a case of dissociation. In that case also the narrative of the mystical experience of being lifted up into the third heaven might be interpreted as posttraumatic responding.

events do not result in traumatic disruption as defined by current criteria.

In the Pauline texts studied we can observe some common elements reported by people who have experienced posttraumatic growth. If "posttraumatic growth is a consequence of attempts to reestablish some useful, basic cognitive guides for living, rather than a search for meaning or an attempt to manage the terror of mortality" (Tedeschi & Calhoun, 2004a, p. 15), in Paul we can see that traumatic events strengthen his cognitive tendencies (in mostly theological ways) which allows him to overcome adversity in an effective way.

Religiosity and spirituality, as factors which are highly correlated with posttraumatic growth, correspond to an experience that is strongly associated with the search for understanding regarding questions about life and its meaning. Narrative constructions based on healthy or adaptive perspectives can make it easier to integrate traumatic sensorial factors (mnemonic registers of traumatic events) in a new affective and cognitive synthesis, which thus decreases posttraumatic symptoms (Peres, et al., 2007). We can clearly observe this in Paul when he positively resignifies the events in which his life is at risk. His eschatological understanding (about death and himself) gives him a matrix of vital coherence that is wide and integrative enough to enable him to grow through coping with adversity and suffering.

4. Altruistic Coping:

a) Summary of key: This fourth coping mechanism employed by Paul in the sections of 2 Corinthians has a predominantly relational character. The apostle describes himself and his co-workers as people who stay focused on the welfare of the others in the midst of suffering. His attention is placed on not to being a stumbling block and not defaming his ministry for the good of the communities of faith that will be blessed through his perseverance. Paul faces adversity in consideration of the contribution that he can make to the welfare of the communities of faith, even if this has a high cost for himself in the shorter and middle run. In other words, he responds to adverse situations in an altruistic way (2 Cor 4:12,15; 6:3, 6, 10).

According to Paul, as a relational coping mechanism it involves high levels of empathy or affective resonance to the discomfort or suffering of others, as well as providing them comfort, as an extension of the same comfort received from God during his own adversities. Paul always understands coping with tough circumstances in terms of communion and solidarity with the suffering of the others, as a communal and not individual or isolated experience (2 Cor 11:28-29; 1:4, 6-7, 11).

b) Coping mechanism: In terms of the coping categories, this Pauline key can be though of as a way of coping that is focused on the situation. It is an active method, with characteristics of both a cognitive-affective as well as a behavioral (and particularly relational) process. It is more temporarily anticipatory than restorative, and it is wide-reaching (Rodríguez Marín, 1995).

c) Hardiness: Regarding resistance to traumatic events, research has shown the important role played by relational aspects. It is practically not possible to expect someone to resist or overcome extremely adverse events in a healthy way if they are isolated or lack social ties (Kobasa, Maddi & Courington, 1981; Pérez Sales, 2006).

Although the coping mechanism in Paul that we have called altruist coping does not specifically exhibit the social variables presented in studies about psychological hardiness, it is a type of relational coping that allows traumatic events to be experienced with constant feeling of community. Bibliographic references indicate that people who keep their significant bonds will have better resources for resisting the consequences of traumatic events, or even the possibility of new losses or adverse events (Pérez Sales, 2006; Singh, 2016).

On the other hand, altruistic coping, can be related to sub-construct of control. This is because when interpreting the results of adverse events from a focus on the welfare of other people, Paul tends to feel, think, and act with the conviction that his positive coping with events is relevant for the welfare of others (Kobasa, 1982; Eschleman, Bowling & Alarcón, 2010; Maddi, 2013).

d) Resilience: Cyrulnik has argued that social factors are one of the fundamental pillars of resilience, especially as it relates to the availability of significant affective bonds (2001, 2009). In altruistic coping we observe that for Paul the affective bond with the communities of faith that he founded or serves pastorally is fundamental, to such an extent that their own well-being is put aside in seeking the development of the churches.

The relationship the Apostle established with communities of faith in which he used to practice his ministry was very tight despite the conflicts that tended to arise (such the case of Corinthians). This kind of relationships turned into a network of informal contacts that was outside the nuclear family, but perhaps became even more important (cf. Mark 3:31-35). For Paul, living in community allows him to see adversity as an opportunity for participation (communion, *koinonía*) and significant contribution to the social environment (ecclesiastical where appropriate), and is an important resource for people with high levels of resilience (Kotliarenco, et al., 1997, Vanistendael, 1994, 2003; Cyrulnik, 2007; Yates & Luthar, 2009; Puig & Rubio, 2011; Fletcher & Sarkar, 2013).

e) Posttraumatic Growth: Of the three main categories of changes associated with post-traumatic growth, we highlight in a special way to positive changes in interpersonal relationships, following traumatic events (Calhoun & Tedeschi, 1999, 2008, Blix, et al., 2016). The Apostle, in interpreting adverse circumstances as opportunities to manifest their altruistic disposition and affection towards their communities of faith, tended to strengthen and deepen their bond with the communities. Traumatic events, in this way, were moments that developed mutual affection and fraternal communion.

It is worth mentioning that the literature focuses on the social support received by those who are suffer traumatic events, whereas in Paul we observe that his emphasis is on what he and his partners can contribute to others from their experience of perseverance in the midst of suffering (Calhoun & Tedeschi, 2008; Vera, et al., 2006; Eve & Kangas, 2015).

5. Eschatological Coping:

a) Summary of key: In the texts we studied in 2 Corinthians we can observe that Paul habitually based his perseverance on a theological-eschatological hope, which was sustained from his personal experience of having been a witness of the resurrected Christ. He associates this experience directly with the possibility of the future resurrection or glorious transformation of him and the community of believers (2 Cor 4:10-12, 14; 5:1-5).

A hope based on resurrection of Christ to Paul does not just point to the future, but is also connected to his experience in the present. This hope is experienced as a power that grants him the ability to tenaciously face those sufferings head-on which could have defeated him or brought him to his death. Paul, therefore, maintains full confidence in the faithful liberating action of God in new adverse events that could arise in the future (2 Cor 1:9-10).

b) Coping mechanism: This Pauline key for coping is mostly cognitive in nature, and can be thought of as a way of coping that is focused on the situation. It is an active method that makes it easier to face new events. It is also temporarily anticipatory more than restorative, and is wide-reaching (Rodríguez Marín, 1995).

c) Hardiness: Eschatological coping can be related to the tendency to interpret the stress stimuli as less threatening, which is common in people who exhibit a significant psychological resistance to high-stress events (Kobasa, Maddi & Kahn, 1982; Pérez Sales, 2006). In Paul's case, by putting his hopes on his resurrection or final glorious transformation, he tends to see traumatic events as having less disruptive (or traumatic) potential, since the things that are truly important for him are not at risk, but instead guaranteed as an eschatological promise. It is not his physical wellbeing (which is frequently threatened) that worries to Paul, but his future reality, about which he is deeply confident.

On the other hand, as we saw before, religious convictions can be resources to give integration, coherence, and meaning to high stress events, by providing a type of "logic" that enables adaptive coping and higher resistance in adversity (Prati & Pietrantoni, 2009). This is the case with Paul, where his eschatological convictions help him to deal positively with his sufferings.

Along this line, it has been observed that a higher "religious meaning" (of positive type specifically), in life softens the effects of high stress and maladapted behaviors (e.g., addictions). On the contrary, a "general meaning" of life is not significantly correlated with a similar level of stress softening (Pargament, 1997; Krause, et al., 2016).

310

d) Resilience: As Vanistendael (2003) proposed, people who see meaning and coherence in their live events exhibit more resilience than others, and certain religious beliefs facilitate resilient processes by confirming that life is always sustained by a positive fundamental reality, even amidst destructive chaos. We can observe this in this Pauline key for coping.

In this same line, the eschatological coping that we see in Paul is shown as a particular version of the spiritual factors associated with resilience, such as: the ability to find transcenddent meaning in the middle of traumatic events; and having a foundational purpose of life and a clear perspective on the future (Munist, et al., 1998; Vanistendael, 2003; Yates & Luthar, 2009; Fletcher & Sarkar, 2013).

f) Posttraumatic Growth: Even though the connections that we can establish with posttraumatic growth are complex because we do not observe in Paul's writings the typical disruptive traumatic responses, we can highlight that positive development after adverse events are clearly related to religiosity and spirituality, both in Paul as well as in cases presented in psychological studies in this field (Calhoun & Tedeschi, 2001, 2008; Patri & Pietrantoni, 2009; Denney, Aten & Leavell, 2011).

Religiosity and spirituality can promote posttraumatic growth through providing a sense of community or community support, as well as contributing beliefs that facilitates the process of creating holistic and positive meaning in the face of adversity, such as the case of eschatological coping, which can provide an important transformational contribution (Cadell, Regehr & Hemsworth, 2003). Likewise, narrative constructs that are based on positive perspectives, as the belief in a great future, allows one to integrate events with high disruptive potential, as we observed in the case of Paul (Peres, et al., 2007).

On the other hand, recent research indicates that people who have a well-established meaning to life face adversity in a more adaptive manner and with high rates of posttraumatic growth, unlike those who search for meaning after these types of events (Linley & Joseph, 2011).

6. Expression of Adverse Events:

a) Summary of key: The particular use that the Apostle makes of the lists of sufferings (which is different from how it was used in his time, as we mentioned previously), leads us to a coping mechanism that involves the practice of remembering and communicating in his letters the traumatic events that he and his co-workers experienced (2 Cor 4:8-10; 6:4-10; 11:23-33; 12:10; cf. 1 Cor 4:9-11; Phil 4:11-12; Rom 8:35-36). Paul seems to incorporate adverse events into his biographical narrative. He does not deny or resist them, he does not escape, and he does not avoid mentioning them or any allusion to them. On the contrary, he usually expresses them at opportune times, without victimizing himself but communicating them as part of his personal history, as part of his narrative identity as a servant of Jesus Christ, in such a way that these events do not seem to imply a significant disruption in the continuity of both his personal and community life.

b) Coping mechanism: The communication of adverse events experienced can be classified as a type of coping that is predominantly behavioral and focused on the situation. It is also an active method, which makes it easier to approach new events in a direct way. It is temporarily anticipatory more than restorative; and is wide-reaching. (Rodríguez Marín, 1995).

c) Hardiness: With respect to the capacity of resistance to traumatic events without major psychological alteration, it has been observed that the communication of the traumatic experience[141] is beneficial, since it enables: 1) catharsis or abreaction; 2) giving coherence and internal meaning to the experience, which facilitates its integration; 3) validation and social recognition of it; 4) sharing

---

[141] In relation to the importance of memory and commemoration, religion itself has been described as a chain of memories, that is, a form of collective memory and imagination based on a tradition regarding the sacred, which produces collective meanings (Urbaniak, 2015). The written communication of the memories, in the form of letters in this case, makes us think of the collective character of memory, which for some authors, one never remembers alone; to remember, we always need others. We are not original owners of our memories, which does not necessarily mean that we are not an authentic subject of the attribution of memories (Halbwachs, 1992). "To account for the logics of coherence presiding over our perception of the world, we must eventually turn to the side of collective memory, as it is within the frameworks of collective thought that we find the means of evoking the series and the connection of objects" (Ricoeur 2004, pp. 122-123).

experiences and coping mechanisms that are potentially useful for others[142] (Pérez Sales, 2006).

In Paul we can observe these four positive aspects, because the Apostle uses the opportunity to share his sufferings publicly with the communities (in a written way, in this case), which probably facilitated the possibility of articulating their painful experiences within a broader and more coherent story, both communal (that of his service to the churches) and personal (in his paradoxical identity as a servant of Christ).

On the other hand, for Paul it is also important to use this coping mechanism to validate himself (apologetically) to the faith communities and, specially, to his opponents, as a legitimate faithful, and perseverant apostle of the Lord.

Finally, the Apostle also shares his painful experiences pedagogically, giving examples of coping with adversity to his brothers and sisters in faith who are experiencing similar circumstances, and see in Paul a practical and inspiring example to follow.

d) Resilience: This is, as we have indicated before, a predominantly social construct (Zautra, 2014). Similarly, these kinds of coping mechanisms are very much related to social development in people.

Among the contextual resources of resilience are the networks of informal contacts, within which faith communities or churches are important, since there one can find opportunity for meaningful participation in an open and welcoming environment. This is what Paul's self-exposition presupposes. By openly and repeatedly presenting his experiences of suffering, his weakness, and his arduous difficulties, he shows that he possesses a community space that is willing to receive this type of intimate information (Kotliarenco, et al., 1997, 1999; Vanistendael, 2003; Cyrulnik, 2007; Kent, Davis & Reich, 2014).

e) Posttraumatic Growth: The practice of Paul of exposing his suffering, and giving details of both descriptive aspects and emotional

---

[142] Research also has showed that these benefits are mediated by factors, such as: that it be voluntary, and not forced; that it be at the right time for the victim of the events; that be appropriate in the socio-cultural context to which the person belongs (Pérez Sales, 2006).

aspects, is a coping mechanism that is very much aligned with findings in the field of posttraumatic growth.

Several studies have found positive relations between posttraumatic growth and self-revelation (Tedeschi & Calhoun, 2004b; Schexnaildre, 2011), as also social sharing (Páez, Martínez & Rimé, 2004; Páez, et al., 2007; Vázquez, et al., 2009; Gasparre, Bosco & Bellelli, 2010). Particularly, affective expression in writing has been observed to be a factor that makes facilitates posttraumatic growth (Ullrich & Lutgendorf, 2002; Fernández Sedano & Pennebaker, 2011).

7. Detachment from Material or Visible Things:

a) Summary of key: Another key for coping that we found in the passages studied in 2 Corinthians is the one where Paul, in order to cope with the high stress circumstances he must endure, instead of putting attention on his present condition of scarcity and discomfort, shows a marked disregard to all visible possessions (and misfortunes), because to him they are temporary, brief, and totally preliminary. In other words, he relativizes his misfortunes and the traumatic events that he has faced, seeing them in light of his glorious final destiny. He has found supreme goodness and transcendence in Christ, which for him is *his everything*, completely sufficient, both as a promise of future and eternal plenitude, as well as for the present which he lives as an advance of future glory (2 Cor 4:16-5:8; 6:10).

In Paul we can observe a marked focus on transcendent human needs, instead of physiological and basic needs that are associated to survival (2 Cor 11:27).

b) Coping mechanism: In terms of coping strategies, the detachment seen in Paul can be described as being focused on the representation of his own and the universal future, more than being a process orientated to deal with a specific problem or situation. It is also an active method, with characteristics of a process that is more cognitive-affective than behavioral. It is temporarily anticipatory, and not simply restorative; and wide-reaching, for use in broader contexts (Rodríguez Marín, 1995).

c) Hardiness: Among the factors associated with psychological resistance to high-stress events, a sense of security has been observed, which is largely based on links established with emotionally significant people (Pérez Sales, 2006).

Detachment from material or visible things that we see in the Pauline texts has its counterpart in the very close emotional bond that he feels with Christ. Paul's faith experience also involves a deep emotional and relational component towards the figure of the risen Jesus, as the only fundamental and unconditional attachment.

On the other hand, in this kind of coping we also can see aspects present in the sub-construct of hardiness. The apostle believes that change, and not stability, is the common characteristic of this life, thought of as a preliminary reality. He sees situations as opportunities and incentives for personal and community growth, not as threats to his safety, which, in its more transcendent sense, is never in play, since is it guaranteed by God, through his Spirit that is present in him as a guarantee of a grant future (Kobasa, 1982; Kobasa, Maddi & Courington, 1981; Eschleman, Bowling & Alarcón, 2010).

d) Resilience: Regarding the resilience factors that we can relate to this type of Pauline coping, we must emphasize the sense of transcendence, together with the sense of purpose and future, which has been observed in people with high levels of resilience (Kotliarenco, et al., 1997, Vanistendael, 2003, Cyrulnik, 2003, 2007). Paul faces adversity and, in general, he confronts all circumstances, both positive and negative, from a particular perspective: he is always focused on the transcendent meaning that guides him in the affective-spiritual bond with Jesus Christ who sustains him, and not on what is material or visible.

f) Posttraumatic Growth: Optimism has been shown in research on posttraumatic growth as a factor of relative importance. This type of attitude would promote growth after traumatic events through its effects on the evaluation of threats and on the facilitation of adaptive strategies, such as positive reevaluation and active coping. (Schaefer & Moos, 1998; Wagner, Knaevelsrud & Maercker, 2007).

Although we cannot equate Paul's response of detachment with optimism, we can link it to the fact that in Paul it facilitates a positive re-evaluation of adverse circumstances, in terms of perceiving them as definitive or fundamentally disruptive, despite its severity. The Apostle has an optimistic perspective of the future that awaits him, and this makes him face the sufferings of the present as events of importance and relative negativity.

8. Identification with Jesus as a Model for Coping:

a) Summary of key: Another category of coping that we can see in Paul refers to his identification with Jesus, particularly with his sufferings and resurrection. This identification allows him to understand himself as a follower of someone who experienced extreme suffering, even death, and defeated it. This kind of identification enables Paul to give meaning to his own suffering, in the way that when suffering as apostle, he himself is a concrete, physical representation of the passion of Jesus Christ. And when he overcomes extreme adversities, he is a witness and example of the power of his Savior's resurrection (2 Cor 4:10-11; 1:5; cf. Gal 3:1; 4:13; 5:11; 6:17).

b) Coping mechanism: This Pauline key for coping can be considered to be a way of coping that is focused on the situation. It is an active method that makes it easier to face adverse events and not avoid them. It has characteristics of a cognitive-affective as well as behavioral process as. It also is more temporarily anticipatory than restorative, and is wide-reaching (Rodríguez Marín, 1995).

c) Hardiness: Among the factors associated with hardiness, the ones related to the social context are among the most relevant, such as the feeling of belonging to a group of peers that have the same experiences, that is, feeling part of a community that can identify themselves under a collective narrative as being "survivors" (not passive victim). In the case of Paul, this sense of belonging, in addition to being in community, is fundamentally with Christ. He identifies himself with his suffering and resurrected Lord, which enables him to tenaciously resist the many difficulties that he experienced personally and in community (Pérez Sales, 2001, 2006).

In this Pauline strategy we can also observe elements of the construct of psychological hardiness that is associated to control, since the Apostle, by identifying with Jesus in his death and resurrection, promotes the conviction that his behavior during these events is important, such that the consequences of adverse situations become more predictable, which facilitates the execution of strategies for adaptive coping (Kobasa, 1982; Singh, 2016).

d) Resilience: Among the contextual resources linked to resilience, it has been seen that the opportunity for participation and significant contribution in the social environment, such as the availability of relationships with positive role models, are highly impactful when overcoming traumatic circumstances (Yates & Luthar, 2009; Reich, Zautra & Hall, 2010; Cruz-Villalobos, 2009; Brownlee, et al., 2013).

That Paul has Jesus as model of coping provides him with resources for coping with extremely adverse events, because the life of Jesus, especially at the end, was characterized by the suffering he voluntarily endured with courage and strength. Also, his resurrection from the dead can be understood by his followers as the maximum expression of resilience.

On the other hand, the Apostle, in identifying himself with Jesus in his way of facing and overcoming negative circumstances, perceives himself as someone who contributes significantly to his community, even to society at large, by being a minister of the good news of salvation for the whole world (cf. Rom 1:13-16).

e) Posttraumatic Growth: Paul's identification with Jesus as a model for coping can be connected with posttraumatic growth as it is a predominantly religious modality of constructively overcoming traumatic events. In fact, the same paschal message of victory over death by Jesus as the Christ is a message that we could call posttraumatic growth. The core of the Gospel, of the life, passion, death, and resurrection of Jesus, is a message that speaks of overcoming evil, injustice, adversity, and suffering, in such a way that one's condition after the traumatic event (passion and death) is better than before, because Christ assumes his glorified condition, is transformed, "grows" to a higher somatic-spiritual constitution, through extreme adversity.

Paul, by identifying himself with Jesus in his sufferings and in his resurrection, can experience traumatic events in such a way that after each one of them he is strengthened, and acquires new resources for facing future tribulations with the confidence that he will be able to always walk away victoriously. And if that were not so, and he saw his live in imminent danger, he does not lose hope either, because he knows that he has a transcendent gift which goes beyond the present temporary experience, which will be manifested later, and which involves acquiring the glorified condition of the risen Christ who changed his life by appearing to him on the road to Damascus.

In this way, we can say that Paul's experience with Jesus as the Christ and his identification with him modified the three dimensions that are observed in those who have posttraumatic growth: changes in the perception of oneself (as a paradoxical identity and imitator of Christ); changes in interpersonal relationships (marked by love and the ecclesial fraternal experience); and changes in the philosophy of life and spirituality (with the new global understanding of human existence and its transcendent meaning interpreted from Jesus Christ) (Calhoun & Tedeschi, 1999, 2001).

9. Thanksgiving:

a) Summary of key: Thankfulness is a very frequent response of Paul in his letters (Rom 1:8, 21; 6:17; 7:25; 14:6; 16:4; 1 Cor 1:4, 14; 10:30; 11:24; 14:16, 17, 18; 15:57; 2 Cor 1:11; 2:14; 4:15; 8:16; 9:11, 12, 15; Fil 1:3; 4:6; 1 Tes 1:2; 2:13; 3:9:5:18; Flm 1:4).

The Apostle uses thanksgiving broadly, normally referring to positive circumstances, but also uses it in contexts of adversity. The community connotation usually given to this practice is notable.

In adverse circumstances, Paul express his gratitude for the positive intervention of God (2 Cor 4:15). He shows himself to be grateful in advance, in other words, anticipating God's positive response in his favor on the midst of his sufferings (2 Cor 1:11).

b) Coping mechanism: As a coping response, Paul's gratitude for adverse situations could be classified as predominantly behavioral and focused on situation. It is an active method, with restorative as well as anticipatory elements, and is wide-reaching (Rodríguez Marín, 1995).

c) Hardiness: Regarding resistance to high stress events can be related to the willingness of people with higher levels of resistance to disruptive events to see positive elements in harmful events, that involves a focus on the good things ("there are worse situations", "it could be worse", "some moments we fail, but in others we respond well"), and the acceptance that discomfort is normal and will not be permanent (Pérez Sales, 2006).

318

With gratitude in the middle of the adverse, we can also associate the tendency of resistant people to see themselves as survivors, that is, as people who have come out stronger from a traumatic experience and who, consequently, have more resources to face new difficult situations.[143] We can also observe that these types of people interpret the stressing stimulus as being less threatening, therefore with positive elements, or at least having a higher degree of control. These characteristics are present in the act of thanksgiving, as we see in Paul.

d) Resilience: Similarly, among the factors associated with the recovery of traumatic events, it has been observed that it also highlights the experience, by way of the subjects who have higher levels of resilience to stress and cope with positive subjective signification. This is typical of the act of thanksgiving in adverse events. It is also related to the ability to find meaning and coherence for life in the midst of difficult circumstances, because through thanksgiving, one focuses on the positive dimensions of the events, which facilitates their biographical integration (Munist, et al., 1998; García-Vesga & Domínguez-de la Ossa, 2013).

e) Posttraumatic Growth: Reviews of various studies on the possible positive consequences of traumatic events have indicated that cognitive variables would be the most significant, among which the ability to evaluate the threat, positive reinterpretation, and optimism stand out (Linley and Joseph, 2004). These factors can be connected with thanksgiving as a posttraumatic response, since gratitude involves evaluating and analyzing the threatening events based on the positive aspects that can be found in these circumstances. In addition, this type of response also involves positive reinterpretation, either from the beneficial aspects observed or in view of a positive future that is coming, which is also related to optimism (cf. Salgado, 2009; García, Reyes & Cova, 2014; Eve & Kangas, 2015).

10. *Comforting Presence of God:*

a) Summary of key: In Paul we can observe a cheerful confidence in the active, positive and permanent presence of God in the

---

[143] Along the lines of posttraumatic growth, but does not involve a serious disruption in life as is observed in the cases of growth after traumatic experiences.

midst of adversities, both in his favor and that of his co-workers, as well as God's people in general. For the Apostle, this divine presence seems to guarantee comfort and mercy from God when his people face tribulations (2 Cor 1:3-5).

b) Coping mechanism: Confidence in the comforting presence of God in the midst of adversities, can be classified as a cognitive-affective coping mechanism that is focused on the situation. It is also an active method, with both restorative and anticipatory elements, and is wide-reaching (Rodríguez Marín, 1995).

c) Hardiness: In this way of coping we can observe the presence of three theoretical components of the construct of psychological hardiness: 1) commitment, instead of alienation in adversity, such that through his conviction of the active presence of God in his whole life, Paul involves it in an active way in every task as a relevant agent, both personally as well as collectively; 2) control, instead of feeling powerless, such that Paul has the conviction of influence and significant personal responsibility in the course of the events, thanks to the ability given to him by God; 3) and challenge instead of emphasizing the threatening character of adverse circumstances, such that when trusting in the constant support of God in his life which is always changing, situations are interpreted as opportunities and incentives for personal and community growth, and not as a true threats to his safety or well-being (Kobasa, 1979, 1982).

d) Resilience: Paul's belief in the presence of God as a comforter in the midst of his tribulations is related to several of the characteristic aspects of the people who exhibit high resilience. We observe that this disposition in the Apostle involves: 1) counting on God as a close person whom he can trust and who has an unconditional affection for him, which manifests itself as a constant willingness to help him in moments of difficulty; 2) knowing that he is a person for whom others feel appreciation and affection (in his case, God himself and many of his brothers and sisters in the faith); and 3) having the confidence that everything will turn out well in the end and that he will find support from those who appreciate him (Munist, et al., 1998).

e) Posttraumatic Growth: Finally, regarding posttrauma-tic growth, Paul's confidence in the presence of God before, during, and after traumatic events, is a coping mechanism that is particularly religious and spiritual.[144]

Cadell, Regehr, and Hemsworth (2003) affirmed that spirituality and religiosity can play an important role in the creation of meaning and transformational coping. In meta-analyses they have been considered as the most significant variables for being able to grow after traumatic events (Ano & Vasconcelles, 2005; Patri & Pietrantoni, 2009).

11. Prayer:

a) Summary of key: Prayer is a habitual practice of Paul, and he frequently requests it from the communities of faith (cf. Rom 15:30; 2 Cor 13:7, 9; Fil 4:6; 1 Tes 3:10, 5:17, 25). Specifically, in one of the texts we studied (2 Cor 1:11), we observe prayer, and asking others for prayer, as a coping mechanism.

In the Pauline texts, prayer's community connotation is predominant, since it is presented as a mode of spiritual solidarity in the face of suffering, as a type of fraternal communion, which also expects effective results in terms of divine response of comfort and mercy. It is considered to be a real action, rather than mere positive intentions for the good of others or a simple declaration of good will.

b) Coping mechanism: Prayer can also be classified as predominantly behavioral, although it also has important cognitive and affective elements. It is focused on the situation, and makes it easier to actively approach new events. It is restorative, occasionally anticipatory, and wide-reaching (Rodríguez Marín, 1995).

c) Positive coping (Hardiness, Resilience and Posttraumatic Growth): Of the connections that can be made between prayer and the factors associated with resistance, resilience, and posttraumatic growth, a few correspond to several of the Pauline coping mechanisms already described, particularly eschatological coping, expressing of traumatic events, and confidence in the consoling presence of God in adverse circumstances.

---

[144] Although, as we will see in next section, all of the coping mechanisms found in Paul can be characterized as being fundamentally religious, and with important spiritual elements. For this reason we are not going to talk about this subject in this section.

As with the previous key, this is also a fundamentally religious and spiritual way of coping. As such, it is associated with various factors related to positive coping with traumatic events, just as we have analyzed it with respect to resistance, resilience, and posttraumatic growth.

Prayer is a type of religious behavior with a wide spectrum of uses. It can particularly facilitate the experience of solidarity and dedication to a purpose. However, it is not easy to ascertain the exact influence of this practice, since it is always circumscribed to the religious lifestyle, and the spirituality of the specific person and their community in their context, that is to say, it always includes personal and social factors. Nevertheless, it has been observed the most effective prayer functions involve seeking guidance and expressing gratitude (Bade & Cook, 2008).

11.2. Trauma in Pauline Perspective

If we follow the research of Pérez Sales (2006) about the autobiographies of victims of traumatic events, such as Primo Levi, Victor Flankl, and Jean Amery, with main categories including a) elements that form the traumatic fact; b) consequences of traumatic fact; and c) hardiness elements, we encounter a very special version in the case of Paul.

The Pauline texts studied (2 Cor 4:7-5:10; 6:3-10; 11:21b-12:1; 1:3-11) explicitly address real traumatic events, which effectively correspond to situations that are very dangerous to his physical or psychological integrity. However, they do not contain most of the parameters typically found in the field that studies traumatic response, as: a) disorder and confusion during the experience, memory fragmentation, absurdity, horror, ambivalence, or turmoil; b) the indescribable character of event or the assumption that it will be incomprehensible to others; c) an experience that breaks one or more of the basic assumptions of what constitutes indicators of human safety, especially the beliefs of being invulnerable and in control of one's own life own; d) serious questioning (or disruption) of the basic structure of oneself and the world (Pérez Sales, 2006).

In this line, the psychological notion of trauma implies, on the one hand, the presence of a traumatic event or occurrence[145] and, on the other hand, the (subjective/intersubjective) traumatic experience. Without one of these elements we cannot properly speak of trauma. In the case of Paul, it is difficult to speak of trauma as such, given that his response to traumatic events, his experience, does not meet the elements described in the literature, at least based on the information that his autobiographical records give us, nor does it meet the criteria for a diagnosis of PTSD[146].

However, as we will see below, several of the events described by Paul in his lists of adversities do fall in the category of indicated traumatic event[147]:

---

145 Clearly described in A Criteria of TEPT del DSM-5 (APA, 2013, p. 271): The person was exposed to: death, threatened death, actual or threatened serious injury, or actual or threatened sexual violence, as follows: (1 required) 1. Direct exposure. 2. Witnessing, in person. 3. Indirectly, by learning that a close relative or close friend was exposed to trauma. If the event involved actual or threatened death, it must have been violent or accidental. 4. Repeated or extreme indirect exposure to aversive details of the event(s), usually in the course of professional duties (e.g., first responders, collecting body parts; professionals repeatedly exposed to details of child abuse). This does not include indirect non-professional exposure through electronic media, television, movies, or pictures.

146 Criterion B: intrusion symptoms; Criterion C: avoidance; Criterion D: negative alterations in cognitions and mood; Criterion E: alterations in arousal and reactivity (APA, 2013, pp. 271-272).

147 Specifically, several of Paul's descriptions of his adversities today fall within the concept of *torture*, as defined by Briere & Scott: "The United Nations Convention Against Torture defines torture as "any act by which severe pain or suffering, whether physical or mental, is intentionally inflicted on a person for such purposes as obtaining from him [sic] or a third person information or confession, punishing him for an act he has committed or is suspected of having committed, or intimidating him or a third person" (United Nations Treaty Collection, 1984). The current U.S. Code (Title 18, Part I, Chapter 113C, Section 2340) defines it as "an act committed by a person acting under the color of law specifically intended to inflict severe physical or mental pain or suffering (other than pain or suffering incidental to lawful sanctions) upon another person within his [sic] custody or physical control." Regardless of function or context, methods of torture involve both physical and psychological techniques, including beatings, near strangulation, electrical shock, various forms of sexual assault and rape, crushing or breaking of bones and joints, water-boarding, sensory deprivation, threats of death or mutilation, mock executions, being made to feel responsible for the death or injury of others, sleep deprivation, exposure to extreme cold or heat, stress positions, mutilation, and being forced to engage in grotesque or humiliating acts (Hooberman, Rosenfeld, Lhewa, Rasmussen, & Keller, 2007; Punamäki, Qouta, & El Sarraj, 2010; Wilson & Droždek, 2004)" (2014, p.17).

For we who are alive are always being given over to death for Jesus' sake, so that his life may also be revealed in our mortal body. (2 Cor 4:11).

[...] I have worked much harder, been in prison more frequently, been flogged more severely, and been exposed to death again and again. Five times I received from the Jews the forty lashes minus one. Three times I was beaten with rods, once I was pelted with stones, three times I was shipwrecked, I spent a night and a day in the open sea, (2 Cor 11:23b-25).

We do not want you to be uninformed, brothers and sisters,[a] about the troubles we experienced in the province of Asia. We were under great pressure, far beyond our ability to endure, so that we despaired of life itself. 9 Indeed, we felt we had received the sentence of death. But this happened that we might not rely on ourselves but on God, who raises the dead. 10 He has delivered us from such a deadly peril, and he will deliver us again. On him we have set our hope that he will continue to deliver us, (2 Cor 1:8-10).

Following the classification also done by Pérez Sales (2006), we can say that these events are considerably severe, due to the fact that they are: a) sudden (the more unpredictable a traumatic experience is, the more potential it has to destroy the life of the subject or harm them psychologically); b) prolonged (the longer one is exposed to the stimuli or adverse experiences, the more one's resistance capacity decreases without sequelae); c) repetitive (the more frequently that the same adverse event is experienced, the more its traumatic potential increases); and d) intentional in their cause (there would be a greater difficulty of psychosocial resistance to events that arise from a voluntary and deliberate human action).

It is necessary to remember that when we referring to the term trauma, in this work we made the distinction between traumatic event, traumatic experience and trauma itself. We used the concept of traumatic event, operationalizing it in the way it is established in the diagnosis for PTSD in the DSM-5 (APA, 2013, p. 274)[148], to delimit its

---

[148] "What is trauma? The Diagnostic and Statistical Manual of Mental Disorders, 5th edition (APA, 2013) defines a trauma as: Exposure to actual or threatened death, serious injury, or sexual violence in one (or more) of the following ways: (1) Directly experiencing

polysemy and limit it to particularly disruptive events, where a person is exposed, directly or as a witness, to death or the possibility of serious damage to personal integrity. We used the notion of traumatic experience to understand the disruptive response to a traumatic event. We talked on trauma itself[149] when a traumatic response or experiences occur front a traumatic event.

Paul's examples of posttraumatic coping, especially in texts of 2 Corinthians, are very striking for us psychologically, because even when he really suffers, he shows himself (at least in the records we have) to be well-intact and without major after-effects, in terms of

---

the traumatic event(s); (2) witnessing, in person, the event(s) as it occurred to others; (3) learning that the traumatic event(s) occurred to a close family member or close friend – in cases of actual or threatened death of a family member or friend, the event(s) must have been violent or accidental; (4) experiencing repeated or extreme exposure to aversive details of the traumatic event(s) (e.g., first responders collecting human remains; police officers repeatedly exposed to details of child abuse) (Note: Criterion A4 does not apply to exposure through electronic media, television, movies, or pictures, unless this exposure is work related). Although this definition is useful, some have criticized the requirement that trauma be limited to "exposure to actual or threatened death, serious injury, or sexual violence," since many events may be traumatic even if life threat or injury is not an issue (Briere, 2004; Anders, Frazier, & Frankfurt, 2011). The earlier DSM-III-R (APA, 1987) definition also included threats to psychological integrity as valid forms of trauma. Because the DSM-5 does not consider events to be traumatic if they are merely highly upsetting but not life threatening—for example, extreme emotional abuse, major losses or separations, degradation or humiliation, and coerced (but not physically violent) sexual experiences—it undoubtedly underestimates the extent of actual trauma in the general population. It also reduces the availability of a stress disorder diagnosis in some individuals who experience significant posttraumatic distress, since Criterion A is a prerequisite for the diagnosis of posttraumatic stress disorder (PTSD) and acute stress disorder (ASD). The issue of whether an event should have to satisfy current diagnostic definitions of trauma in order to be, in fact, "traumatic" is an ongoing source of discussion in the field (for example, Kubany, Ralston, & Hill, 2010; O'Donnell, Creamer, McFarlane, Silove, & Bryant, 2010). Our own conclusion is that an event is traumatic if it is extremely upsetting, at least temporarily overwhelms the individual's internal resources, and produces lasting psychological symptoms. This broader definition is used [...], since people who experience major threats to psychological integrity can suffer as much as those traumatized by physical injury or life threat, and can respond equally well, we believe, to trauma-focused therapies. This is solely a treatment issue; however the DSM-5 version of trauma should be adhered to when making a formal stress disorder diagnosis" (Briere & Scott, 2014, pp. 9-10).

[149] Following the APA Psychology Dictionary, we understand Trauma proper as: "Any disturbing experience that results in significant fear, helplessness, dissociation, confusion, or other disruptive feelings intense enough to have a longlasting negative effect on a person's attitudes, behavior, and other aspects of functioning" (VandenBos, 2015, p. 1104).

psychosocial or clinically significant unbalance. From this emerges the great interest generated by the mode of signification that the Apostle assigns to adverse events in general and particularly those of a traumatic nature.

Although, we can make several interpretative hypotheses regarding the testimonial accounts of Paul. For example, that he may be showing much better than he really was, thereby minimizing in his writings the real impact of the adverse events he had experienced, either to show himself as an approved minister of the Lord in the midst of sufferings (thus enhancing his apostolic authority questioned before his readers) or as an unconscious form of response, in the line of a posttraumatic dissociation. Here we will not dwell on this type of interpretive alternatives, because we focus on the texts and their reserve of meaning for us, rather than on Paul's intention, which we find very difficult to access beyond the purely speculative.

The importance of personal mediation in assigning meaning to the facts is a subject that has been studied in psychology and is central in the field of studying trauma and coping. Among the factors involved in this mediation, as we indicated in Chapter 2 (Pérez Sales, 2006, Cyrulnik, 2006, Kenneson, 2004, Crittenden, 2002, Guidano and Liotti, 2006, Jhonson, 2009, Arciero & Bondolfi, 2009), we can observe the following in Paul:

Personality style: Paul shows, in the classification developed by Arciero and Bondolfi (2009), and Arciero, Bondolfi, and Mazzola (2018)[150], a personality style tending toward obsessive disorders (understanding tha it not possible to make a diagnosis in this case), with a disposition of outward affection which characterizes people who orient themselves towards the world and found continuity in their experience through an abstract external reference, which in the case of Paul is God (Jesus Christ or the Holy Spirit). This modality affects the way in which the Apostle situates himself emotionally and gives meaning to events, not having an inward disposition centered on immediate bodily experience as a fundamental reference.[151]

---

[150] For a similar approach, but on the concept of personal meaning organization, cf. Guidano (1987, 1997); Guidano & Liotti (2006); Guidano & Quiñonez (2018).

[151] The study of Paul's personality based on the approaches of Guidano and Arciero, is a rich and promising field of research that we can only reference here in a very general way.

Previous events: as Paul himself says explicitly (2 Cor 1:10), his expectations that threatening and traumatic events will be positively resolved as based on previous experience, are important in his coping process[152]. The character of the autobiographical accounts (such as the Pauline texts we have studied) and their narrative identity turns out to be extremely important in the interpretation of present and future events, especially those which are traumatic.

Cultural belonging: Paul's participation in Hebrew culture is central for the way in which he interprets his life events and experiences, since the convictions, ethical principles, practices, images, and narratives that the Old Testament gives to Paul undoubtedly mark the form and meaning that he assigns to events in his life. Especially regarding adversities, the Apostle, has a rich wisdom and narrative tradition as a cultural resource to give meaning to the bad things he suffered and find positives ways to move forward. On the other hand, as a follower of Jesus, identificated as the Suffering Servant, the crucified and resurrected Christ, Paul also has a wide and coherent background through which he can integrate the traumatic events he experienced, functioning as a master narrative that gives deep meaning to the lived events, where he identifies himself with Jesus and his sufferings (cf. Lim, 2009).

Spiritual or religious beliefs: as we will discuss later, in the final section of theological-practical contributions, Paul's way of coping with and interpreting the very difficult events he went through is fundamentally marked by his faith experience, which he cares very strongly about (his ultimate concern, in the words of Tillich, 1976, 1982). In fact, we can speak of a kind of theological coping, founded in his faith convictions, especially as it relates to the person and works of Jesus Christ, and the corresponding implications for his own understanding of himself and place in community.

---

[152] Obviously, here classical, operative, direct, and vicarious conditioning processes come into play, which involve an automatic response to events of similar characteristics.

11.3. Pauline Coping Modalities as Religious Coping

As we pointed out at the end of the second chapter, one of the most common ways that people cope with adverse circumstances or traumatic events is through religious and/or spiritual practices. It is here that these types of practices appear as a factor that involves the way in which one person understands their life and develops in it, articulating meaning and coherence of their experience in relation with the things they considered as sacred and essential.

The psychological study of religion as a coping factor has been around for about twenty years (Pargament, 1997; Pargament, Koenig & Pérez, 2000; Trevino & Pargament, 2007). In other contexts, religion has been understood as a dynamic transaction between the individual and their life situations, within a wider socio-cultural context (Pargament, 1997).

Religious convictions can be seen as resources for integration and the search for coherence in life, in general terms, and especially in circumstances with high disruptive potential (Prati & Pietrantoni, 2009).

Given their structured nature, religious and spiritual practices, such as participation in individual or collective rituals, or disciplines such as reading the Scriptures and prayer among others, are behaviors that help people who have been broken by some crisis or traumatic event put their lives in order. Rituals also play an important role in the transition from one phase of life to the next, by guiding and releasing emotions, along with facilitating their integration into a wider, more legitimate, and communally shared frame of reference (Ganzevoort, 1999a).

If we consider the proposals of Pargament et al., in comparison with the coping modalities that we have seen in Paul, we can confirm that we are looking at a set of modalities that can be classified as types of religious coping, because they meet most of the elements which describe this phenomenon: 1) the Pauline keys for coping cover a wide spectrum of functions, among which we can highlight the search for meaning, close friendship, identity, feeling in control, anxiety reduction, transformation, as well as searching for the sacred or spirituality itself; 2) Paul's ways of responding to adversity are multi-modal, in that they involve behaviors, emotions, relationships, and cognitions; 3) Paul's ways of coping are dynamic processes that change over time, developing according to different contexts and circumstances; 4) they are ways of coping that are associated directly or indirectly to Paul's faith convictions and his relationship with the sacred (Pargament, Feuille & Burdzy, 2011).

The three possible interactions between religion and coping that are described by Pragament (1990) can also be observed in the Pauline coping modalities: 1) religion as part of all elements of the coping process (evaluation, activities of coping, results, support and motivation); 2) religion contributing to the coping process in preventive terms regarding future events or consequences, influencing the way the events are interpreted; 3) the religious experience being affected by the process of coping.

Diagram 2: A Multidimensional Model of Religious Coping

(Ganzevoort, 1998a)

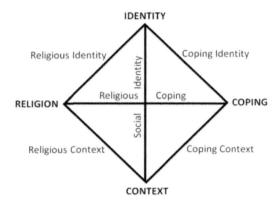

Related to this last form of interaction between religiosity and coping is R. R. Ganzevoort (1998a, 1998b) who highlighted the multidimensional and dynamic character of the phenomenon of religious coping. For this author it is extremely important for understanding this phenomenon, considering the reciprocal or bi-directional influence between coping and religion, as well as taking into account the dimensions of personal identity and social context. In addition, each of these dimensions must be conceptualized as a dynamic, biographical process that includes all aspects of human life.

Next, we will describe Paul's ways of coping as a type of religious coping, using the multidimensional model of Ganzevoort (1998a).

The basic dimensions of religious coping (religion, coping, identity and context), broken down into their emerging facets, can be summarized in Paul as follows:

Religious Coping: We can see that all the Pauline coping modalities are markedly defined by his experience of faith and his relationship with the sacred. They are ways of dealing with traumatic circumstances that always directly or indirectly involve religious and/or spirituals elements. In other words, the way that Paul deals with adverse situations, involves theological intervention. The events are always interpreted in spiritual or transcendent terms.

Religious Identity: In the Apostle, his identity, which is defined completely from his faith and his experience with the sacred, is seen as a fundamental element in his process of resisting, overcoming, and growing in response to traumatic events. Particularly, as we have seen, his identity, which is religious by definition, has a paradoxical character, by being constantly aware of his fragility and vulnerability, but also sustained by the certainty of God's unconditional affection for him, in Christ, and through the continuous work of the Holy Spirit in his life. Paul sees himself as an invincible weak person, as someone who despite experiencing the sufferings of his Lord is also witness to the power of his resurrection in his physical life, especially in the midst of traumatic events.

Religious Context: The Apostle lives in a dynamic and community religious context, the church. It is to this fraternal community of faith, made up of various human groups in different parts of the Roman Empire, that Paul feels completely connected and to which he directs his ministry, both in terms of care or edification, as well as evangelistically by seeking to grow the church through new believers in Jesus Christ added from both the Jewish people as well as the pagan world. The religious context of Paul is also marked by his Hebrew background, which is observed in his discourse and practices, but was

330

from the moment he recognized Jesus of Nazareth as the Christ. This conviction redefined his life as a Shammaite Pharisee and gave him a diametrically opposite path, from persecutor to envoy or ambassador (apostle) of the kingdom of God, in Jesus Christ.

Coping Identity: Coping with adversity in Paul is not just one more facet of the Christian life, but rather, it is seems to constitute a fundamental aspect of both his identity as well as his assigned ministerial vocation. In 2 Corinthians we observe that the Apostle bases his defense against his opponents on his perseverance in the midst of the serious tribulations that he has had to live. The integrity of his apostolate is based on the power (of God) that constantly sustains his life. Being a man that is resistant to suffering (hardiness), who manages to overcome traumatic circumstances (resilience), and has the ability to grow as a person after events that could have destroyed him (posttraumatic growth), are central aspects of Paul's identity.

Coping Context: The Apostle, is always immersed in a dual context. On one hand, he is fundamentally part of the church, the community of followers of Jesus Christ, to which he is pastorally dedicated. And on the other hand, he is always exposed to opposition, continuously struggling against his various adversaries, from which his sufferings normally come.

Social Identity: Finally, as we have already indicated, for Paul his community experience is paramount. He expresses being a servant of his Lord Jesus Christ through service to his brothers and sisters in the faith, and to those who can potentially become disciples of Christ. His paradoxical identity is also communal. Together with his co-workers and with those to whom he has dedicated his faithful service of care, they are fragile vessels of God, destined for eternal glory.

Furthermore, if we compare the coping modalities found in the Pauline texts with the categories developed by Pargament et al. for measuring religious coping (Pargament, Feuille & Burdzy, 2011), we can determine the following:

Methods related to meaning: In the Pauline texts we find a marked use of certain types of benevolent religious reevaluation, where he redefines the stressor through his perspective of faith with a positive and potentially beneficial connotation. On the contrary, we do not at any time see him re-evaluate God as a punisher in the context of adversity, question God's power to influence situations of stress, but quite the opposite (Pargament, 1997). Regarding the so-called demonic reevaluation, in Paul we do not observe him attributing stressful or traumatic circumstances to the devil, except in the specific case of 2 Corinthians 12, where Satan (or a demonic adversary) is mentioned, but only as an efficient cause, where God is still the one behind Paul with a beneficial purpose.

Methods related to control: In the Pauline texts we find collaborative religious confrontation, because the Apostle seeks control through his connectoin with God to solve the problems. We also see the method called active religious surrender, because Paul actively devotes himself to God's control in the moment of coping. We do not find any passive religious coping methods in the passages studied in 2 Corinthians, such passively waiting for God to control the situation, or the indirect search for control by means of asking God for a miracle or immediate divine intercession. On the other hand, neither do we observe self-directed religious confrontation, because the Apostle is far from seeking control directly through his individual initiative instead of seeking the help of God.

Methods related to comfort: In Paul, one frequently encounters the search for spiritual support, as a coping mechanism through which comfort and security are sought through the love and care of God. We also find a religious focus, although with certain nuances, which involves participating in religious activities so as not to focus on the stressor, which in the case of the Apostle, has more spiritual and theological connotations than rituals. We also observe coping as religious purification, that is, as the search for spiritual cleansing through religious actions in adversity contexts, more specifically in growth and sanctification through trials. The method of spiritual connection, where one experiences a sense of connection with forces that transcend the individual and the group in the midst of difficulties, is markedly present in the Pauline texts. We do not observe in Paul a spiritual discontent characterized by confusion and dissatisfaction with God's relationship in the stressful situation.

Methods related to intimacy: The search for support in clergy or members is clearly present in the paragraphs studied, since Paul seeks (and seeks to deliver) comfort and security through the love and care of the members of the congregation and the ecclesial leadership. The method of religious assistance, which we call altruistic coping, stands out in 2 Corinthians as the continuous attempt to provide spiritual support and comfort to others in the midst of adversity. In Paul we observe interpersonal religious discontent, specifically directed to his opponents, but not to the community of faith in general.

Methods related to transformation: The search for religious direction is clearly present in the Pauline texts, since Paul sees his experience of faith as a fundamental aid in his search for new directions in the face of traumatic events. We also find the so-called method of religious conversion, which refers to seeking the possibility for radical change in life through religion. Although in the case of Paul, an event of this kind would not be related to specific traumatic events but to the beginning of his path as a follower of Jesus, the Messiah. Although forgiveness is a recurrent theme in the Pauline letters, especially regarding his relationship with God (reconciliation, justification), we do not observe it as a coping mechanism in the texts studied, that is, it does not appear as an aid for achieving a state of peace through anger, pain, and fear associated with a wrongdoing.

Through all this, we can conclude that the keys for coping found in the Pauline texts fundamentally belong in the category of positive religious coping (Pargament, Feuille & Burdzy, 2011).

As we saw earlier, in Paul we observe the types of this category of coping, such as: religious purification, spiritual connection, seeking support from clergy or members, and religious conversion. On the other hand, we do not significantly observe allusions to the religious coping modalities that are significantly related with negative mental health states (negative religious coping), such as: the reassessment of God as a punisher, the negative reevaluation of God's power, request for direct intervention, and spiritual discontent (Ano & Vasconcelles, 2005).

11.4. Critical Approach to Pauline Coping

Although, in general terms, the texts we have analyzed regarding the coping of traumatic events by Paul give us plausible data that the Apostle coped adaptively to his extreme sufferings, we can also make a critical approach from the theory of trauma, psychopathology and positive psychology. However, this critical approach will be carried out only in a general way, since our focus of research, as we have shown, has to do with the resources of positive coping with trauma present in the Pauline texts.

Current research, as we have demonstrated before, shows that only a minority of people exposed to a traumatic event (cf. Criterion A, DSM-5, APA, 2013) develop PTSD (Breslau, et al., 1991; Kubany, Ralston, & Hill, 2010), although they may respond with other anxious, depressive or dissociative symptoms, depending on the risk factors present in each case.

According to what was observed in our case study, Paul could present some specific risk factors associated with victims of traumatic events, which respond with psychopathological conditions, such as: a) previous history of exposure to multiple traumatic events (Breslau, et al., 1999; Ozer, Best, Lipsey, & Weiss, 2003; Yuan, et al., 2011; Jakšić, et al., 2012), which in the case of the Apostle is a very marked factor, as we observe in the lists of adversities studied; b) peritraumatic dissociation[153], which may involve deregulation, depersonalization or cognitive disconnection at the time of or subsequent trauma (Ozer et al., 2003; Lensvelt-Mulders et al., 2008; Sugar & Ford, 2012), which in the case of Paul, although we cannot corroborate it with certainty, we can find symptomatic elements that can be interpreted in this line, especially in the account present in Paragraph C (2 Cor 11:21b-12 10). It is worth mentioning that particularly the dissociation that begins at the time of trauma and continues over time, is considered one of the most significant risk factors of posttraumatic psychopathology (Briere, Scott, & Weathers, 2005).

On the other hand, if we understand coping as the use of cognitive and behavioral strategies to handle the demands of a situation when it is considered of high demand or exceeds the resources of the person, or to reduce negative emotions and conflicts caused by stress (VandenBos, 2015), in Paul's writings we observe, in addition to the resources that can be associated with hardiness, resilience, posttraumatic growth and positive religious confrontation, also some elements of the so-called reactive coping, that is, management

---

[153] This concept can be defined as: "A transient dissociative experience that occurs at or around the time of a traumatic event. Affected individuals may feel as if they are watching the trauma occur to someone else, as if in a movie, or they may feel —spaced out and disoriented after the trauma. The occurrence of peritraumatic dissociation is a predictor for the later development of posttraumatic stress disorder" (VandenBos, 2015, p. 780).

strategies stress that involves efforts to face a past or present stressful situation through the compensation or acceptance of the associated damage or loss. Reactive coping can also involve efforts to readjust goals, find benefits or seek meaning in adverse events. We observe this repeatedly in the Apostle's texts, with a reactive emphasis focused on the problem and on social relationships, rather than a confrontation centered on emotion.

It can also be suspected in Paul what has been called a repressive coping style, that is, a pattern of stress management characterized by the search for the minimization of problems or misfortunes, by maintaining a positive outlook on life. that can become artificial or that is not consistent with immediate reality. This style is closely associated with the so-called positive illusion, which corresponds to a belief about oneself that is pleasant or positive and that remains independent of its truth. The most common positive illusions involve the exaggeration of the good traits of oneself, the overestimation of the degree of control over important events (illusion of control) and the maintenance of an unrealistic optimism (Schwarzer, Knoll, & Rieckmann, 2004; Schwarzer & Luszczynska, 2008; VandenBos, 2015).

In the Pauline texts, we observe elements in this line, which show a positive perspective of oneself and an important degree of minimization of the effects of adverse events on life, however, they are compensated with their perspective that we call Paradoxical Identity, as well as indicating personal characteristics that can be understood within the categories of repressive coping, positive illusion and illusion of control, they also emphasize (paradoxically) the characteristics of vulnerability and lack of control (cf. especially in Paragraphs B and C).

On the other hand, coping strategies correspond to actions, series of actions or a thought process that is used to face a stressful or unpleasant situation or to modify a person's reaction to such situation (VandenBos, 2015). These strategies usually involve a conscious and direct approach to the problems, in contrast to defense mechanisms, which correspond to automatic psychological processes that protect the individual against anxiety and threats of internal or external origin, mediating personal reactions against conflicts and threats that may vary in their level of adaptability (APA, 2002).

Regarding the latter, the defence mechanisms (following the DSM-IV-TR, APA, 2002)[154] possibly employed by Paul in the face of adverse situations, show a marked predominance of high level adaptive defenses, associated with optimal levels of adaptation in the management of stressful events. These defenses usually maximize gratification and allow you to be aware of feelings, ideas and their consequences. They also promote an optimal balance between conflicting options. Among these mechanisms that can be detached from the analyzed paragraphs we can highlight: a) affiliation (sharing of anxiety and gratifications, formation of work groups or problem solving, effort)[155]; b) altruism (substitution of aggression and competition for support, unconditional offer of help)[156]; c) anticipation (planning of acts and coping strategies, prediction of probable events and planning of solutions)[157]; d) self-affirmation (transformation of fear, anxiety and aggressiveness into socially acceptable expressions, expression of impulses in a socially constructive way)[158]; e) self-observation (increased awareness of feelings, impulses and thoughts, reflection on one's feelings, impulses and thoughts)[159]; f) sense of humor (convert anxiety produced by the threat of irony, comedy or exaggeration)[160]; and g) sublimation (recanalization of impulses in socially acceptable expressions, avoidance of problems, desires or painful feelings)[161].

---

[154] Although it is possible to apply these concepts to the Pauline texts, from the descriptive perspective used by the DSM-IV-TR, not from the psychoanalytic approach originating from these terms, here we do it in a very general way. A more detailed analysis, particularly of unconscious processes, would require more data than the few elements we observe in the selected texts on the coping with adversity. However, it seems important to mention possible defensive processes (which are mostly of a high adaptive level as will be indicated) in the Pauline texts we have studied.

[155] Cf. 2 Cor 4:8-10, 15; 6:8-10; 11:23b-29, 12:10; 1:7-11.

[156] Cf. 2 Cor 4:12,15; 6:3, 6,10; 11:28-29; 1:4, 6; 1:6, 7, 11.

[157] Cf. 2 Cor 4:9, 10, 12, 14; 5:1-5; 1:9-10.

[158] Cf. 2 Cor 4:7, 9, 10; 6:3-4, 8-10; 11:21b-29; 12:1-6, 9-10; 1:8-9 (although it corresponds to a type of paradoxical self-affirmation).

[159] Cf. 2 Cor 4:7-5:10; 6:3-4, 8-10; 11:21b-12:19.

[160] Cf. 2 Cor 11:21-30.

[161] The four paragraphs studied have elements that can be considered under this defensive category.

In some Pauline texts, other defence mechanisms indicative of good adaptive levels are also observed: mental inhibition or compromise formation. These mechanisms allow potentially dangerous ideas, feelings, memories, desires or fears to be kept out of the individual's conscience. In the Pauline texts we can infer the use of some of these, such as: a) abstraction (symbolic denial of an impulse, associated with compulsive behaviors) [162]; b) affective isolation (separation of content and emotion, elimination of the affective, which can be manifested through the story of emotionally intense events without showing emotional impregnation)[163]; c) dissociation (temporary alteration of consciousness, memory, perception and identity)[164]; and d) intellectualization (suppression of the emotional and personal components of the stressful event, abstract thinking, generalizations)[165].

In terms of the less adaptive levels of defense that can be observed in the Pauline texts, we can mention the following: a) within the lower level of adaptability, called image distortion, we can infer the presence of the omnipotence[166] defensive mechanism, which operates through the search for compensation of feelings of fragility, inferiority, failure or low self-esteem, turning said conflict into feelings and acts of superiority, self-assessment and/or claims of authority over others; b) at

---

[162] Here, too, the four paragraphs studied can be considered as examples, since Paul addresses the serious experiences lived in an abstract and instructive way, under an approach of total behavioural rigor.

[163] Also in all the selected paragraphs we observe a very low emotional impregnation when recounting facts that in many cases correspond to serious acts of violence, torture and violation of the physical and moral integrity of the Apostle.

[164] While the study of 2 Cor 12: 1-10 can be done from the perspective of a psychopathological dissociation event, this would require a comprehensive and detailed study. Here we only mention it as a possibility of interpretation along the lines of defensive psychodynamics.

[165] In all cases of our chosen texts describing the adversities experienced (4: 8-10; 6: 8-10; 11: 23b-29, 12:10; 1: 8-10) emotional components are omitted and associated the events to a descriptive perspective of a more abstract and instructive type.

[166] Cf. 2 Cor 4: 7-17; 6:10; 11: 21-31. Although, as we indicated in the case of the self-affirmation mechanism, here we also observe a tendency in the line of the defensive mechanism of omnipotence, however, with marked paradoxical elements that moves it away from self-exaltation.

the low adaptive level of concealment, we can observe the projection[167], where the internal conflict associated with marked hostility or other attitudes, desires or interests classified as unacceptable, tends to attribute these same feelings to other people, expressing ideas of paranoid self-reference, suspicion and perception of injustice; c) regarding the so-called level of defensive imbalance, we can infer that the use of denial might eventually be present in Paul (not of psychotic nature in his case), where the painful and overwhelming reality is handled unconsciously through the annulment of the evident facts, emphasizing a reality that is not visible (eschatological, in his case).

Finally, we will focus on a relevant aspect that attracts attention for being completely absent in the selected paragraphs. We refer to the subject of forgiveness. This topic has been a concept studied by positive psychology and which has been observed to be of great relevance within the processes of coping and posttraumatic restoration. But the Apostle completely omits it, at least in our researched material.

McCullough, Rachal, and Worthington (1997, in Pugh, 2011, p. 188), defined forgiveness as:

> The set of motivational changes whereby one becomes: a) decreasingly motivated to retaliate against an offending relationship partner, b) decreasingly motivated to maintain estrangement from the offender, and c) increasingly motivated by conciliation and goodwill for the offender, despite the offender's hurtful actions.

Forgiveness can also be considered a prosocial change in motivations to avoid or seek revenge against a transgressor (McCullough, 2000; Cerci & Colucci, 2018). Forgiveness allows us to put aside the claims of the past, so we keep in the present. Because forgiveness is both intrapersonal and intrapsychic, it becomes a choice that must be taken after careful consideration of many factors, as it is not a trivial or simple process (Thoresen, Harris, & Luskin, 2000; Pugh, 2011).

---

[167] We do not have specific texts that can be cataloged in this mechanism, but the apologetic nature of the texts gathered in 2 Corinthians in general does not suggest the possibility of the presence of projection, especially because of the recurring manifestation of paranoid self-reference ideas, suspicion and perception of injustice or discredit of the apostolic ministry.

Current research indicates an undeniable link between forgiveness and health (both physical and mental), but the size of this relationship, as well as its specific mechanisms, remains difficult to specify (Toussaint & Webb, 2005). Positive effects of forgiveness have been observed such as: decrease in negative experiences (stress, anger, rumination and depression), increase in positive experiences (affection, social support, positive spiritual experiences) and improvements in physiological responses (blood pressure, cortisol levels). Like everything worthwhile, forgiveness cannot be forced or rushed into an individual's experience, otherwise, it will mean nothing; It must be experienced intimately and through a personal process that involves effective work especially in terms of the pain of being attacked or offended (Fisher & Exline, 2006; Toussaint, Worthington, & Williams, 2015).

In consideration of these elements, it is striking that Paul, referring to his drastic experiences of punishment and torture intentionally executed by individuals, does not refer to the issue of forgiveness to them, being such a central theme in evangelical teaching (Mat 6:14-15, 18:27-35; Mr 11:26; Luk 7:42, 43). This may be because the Apostle has already resolved this issue personally, to the point that it does not seem necessary for him to even mention it. However, this argument does not seem to be very strong, as one would even expect it to raise for educational purposes for the Christian community, which at that time was permanently exposed to possible persecutions and intentional damages by third parties.

Finally, regarding this same issue, the Pauline silence regarding forgiveness is also critical, especially in the context of the story of traumatic events committed by others. The fact that Paul not only omits the importance of forgiveness towards the aggressors, but also does not refer to the injustice and reprobation that this type of received treatment meant, is a very strange point.

As some authors have stated, although forgiveness is very important to deal with a violent past, there is a need to critically transform the socio-political epistemic subjectivities that underpin the execution of evil and injustice, which includes the use of speeches, narratives or ideas that explicitly refer to and denounce acts of violence committed as completely unjustified and worthy of reprobation. If this is not worked out, the probability of the repetition of the acts committed increases and a sustainable restoration and reconciliation becomes difficult, as well as the key aspects to deal with the past, such as the search for truth, justice and responsibility in as for the facts. The lack of emphasis on justice and transformation means that forgiveness is susceptible to abuse or underutilization, and therefore may end up not being so relevant to facilitate true and sustainable reconciliation. These issues are not addressed by Paul nor do they seem to be part of his understanding (normalization of violence?), which is striking, especially if we consider the historical and socio-political aspects associated with the imperial violence of that time (Toussaint, Worthington , & Williams, 2015; Tarusarira, 2019).

Chapter 12
Conclusions

To conclude our work, we will make an integration of the contributions found in the Pauline texts and those that have arisen from the discussion made of these with the psychological investigations regarding positive coping with trauma.

First we will give some conclusions regarding the Pauline coping that we have observed, understood as a particularly theological sense of coherence, then dwell on the key theological concepts that we find at the base of the Pauline ways of coping that we have found in the paragraphs of 2 Corinthians.

We will conclude by dwelling on the implications of positive coping with traumatic events found in the Pauline texts regarding ecclesial functions. And we will indicate, finally, some of the limitations of our research and future perspectives of study in the line that we have developed here.

12.1. Pauline Coping as Sense of Theological Coherence

The general perception is that the world we occupy is significant and coherent, because we perceive a certain pattern that allows us to have the impression that harmony is around us. This sense of coherence and underlying order is at the basis of everyday life and provides a certain matrix in which our relationships, projects, pleasures, and pains occur. The usual thing for people is that the meaning of the world is intrinsic, because they normally live their lives without having reason to question it. However, there are times when the meaning and coherence of the world tends to recede. Even with all (or almost all) of the elements of our life being present, we can lose the foundation and reference point that unifies them into a harmonious whole. If life could be compared to a game of chess, in those moments it seems that the board itself has disappeared. The pieces can be kept in place, but their connection to each other becomes arbitrary and confusing. In those instances we can say that we are dealing with a traumatic experience characterized by a deep struggle with the search for meaning (and that it also includes associated neurocognitive symptomatology, as we have indicated), particularly when we are confronted drastically with our condition of personal mortality or that of people close to us (Bracken, 2002; Cruz-Villalobos, 2014b).

According to what we have observed in the Pauline texts, his way of coping with traumatic events is predominantly cognitive-affective. It is presented as a particular theological hermeneutic of the adverse, which is framed within a specific religious understanding of human existence.

Religious experience is clearly related to the interpretation of events. Within the functions of religion, described by Pargament (1997), the search for meaning and the search for oneself can be seen as part of the interpretative dimension of the religious process. Religious interpretation can influence the evaluation process during a crisis and in the way in which the crisis is faced, because in those instances, questions about meaning and identity become paramount. Religion can provide a set of meanings with a clear message about the possible interpretations of life events and situations, especially those that are difficult to assimilate. It can also reduce the threat of a crisis, since it grants certain criteria and norms that orient the evaluation and enables one to face future adverse circumstances with better resources (Ganzevoort, 1998a, Hess, Maton & Pargament, 2014).

In the literature on coping with traumatic events, there is a model that is highly relevant to the coping mechanisms that Paul uses when dealing with adversity. This is the concept of *sense of coherence*, developed by Antonovsky (1979, 1984, 1987, 1993).[168]

To Antonovsky the fundamental quality of a living organism is *heterostasis* and chaos, in such a way that human nature itself is characterized by the continued presence of stressors. Therefore, the important thing is not knowing which factors drive the person to the disorder, but those that will push the person to the positive side of the continuum, towards health and welfare. For this reason Antonovsky proposes the concept of sense of coherence (Antonovsky, 1987; Moreno-Jiménez, González & Carrosa, 1999).

---

[168] We have omitted the model presented by Antonovsky in the chapter corresponding to the positive coping of the trauma (Chap 3), of which he should have formed an important part, given that we developed it here in some detail, since it is a perspective that is very useful in our work, as an integrating model of our results.

Antonovsky was a sociologist and anthropologist from the University of Ben Gurion in Israel, and began to primarily study Jewish survivors of Nazis concentration camps, asking himself: What is the thing that keeps some people healthy, despite being subjected to the same circumstances of life, coming out of those situations unharmed? (1987).

The concept of sense of coherence arises, to Antonovsky, as the disposition that allows to people to move towards the healthy pole of the healthy-illness continuum, and is defined in this way:

> The sense of coherence is a global orientation that expresses the extent to which one has a pervasive, enduring though dynamic, feeling of confidence that 1) the stimuli deriving from one's internal and external environments in the course of living are structured, predictable and explicable [comprehensibility]; 2) the resources are available to one to meet the demands posed by these stimuli [manageability]; and 3) these demands are challenges, worthy of investment and engagement [meaning-fulness] (Antonovsky, 1987, p .19, added parentheses).

Antonovsky, based on multiple longitudinal and interdisciplinary investigations (1979, 1984, 1987, 1993; Antonovsky & Sourani, 1988; Du Plessis, 2001), considers that the sense of coherence is not a specific feature of personality, and neither is it a specific style of coping, but rather it is a *general dispositional orientation.*

In general terms, the sense of coherence alludes to an interpretation of events in such a way that the individual considers the results of what they do as an extension of who they are, giving them a sense of continuity and vital relationship with the world. It is therefore a construct that describes a way of perceiving oneself and the world that would entail a certain degree of stability and that leads one to evaluate the circumstances of life as meaningful, predictable, and manageable. These are the elements that constitute the three dimensions (theoretical and empirical) of the sense of coherence. Next, we will address each one, relating them to the way in which Paul confronts adversity (Antonovsky, 1984, 1987, Du Plessis, 2001, Hernández, Ehrenzweig & Yépez, 2010):

Comprehensibility: This corresponds to the degree of perception (or interpretation) that a person has of the order, consistency, and clarity of a particular experience, instead of evaluating the experience as chaotic or hazardous. Although the event, circumstance, or context is not necessarily pleasant, since it can be a very stressful situation for the person, comprehensibility implies the possibility of understanding what happens, not necessarily in normal cognitive terms, but rather in a narrative way, as an event in the course of the life cycle. In this way, although there may be circumstances that are presented as chaotic or absurd, the person tends to interpret the situation in such a way that it is coherent with their previous worldview, or allows them to reformulate a new perspective of their world of signification up to that point. Individuals with a high level of comprehensibility perceive the events they face within a comprehensive framework, and they consider experiences to be events to which they can find order, consistency and an increasingly clear structure, instead of persistently interpreting events as a chaotic, disordered, random, accidental, or unpredictable reality. In Paul, at least in the texts we have studied related to posttraumatic coping, we observe that he constantly attributes order, consistency, and clarity to adverse experiences, always from a theological perspective and in reference to what is sacred, transcendent, and redefined for him in Jesus Christ. Even in circumstances of extreme adversity, the Apostle exhibits a level of comprehensibility regarding what happens to him and manages to integrate it in his personal narrative in a coherent way, as a minister of God. Paul finds order and consistency in his life, and we do not observe that the traumatic events have disruptive, chaotic, accidental, or unpredictable effects on him.

Manageability: This concept refers to the extent to which the individual perceives the availability of resources necessary to meet the demands of the environment. Manageability is favored by the balance of resources made by the person, with the confidence that they will be able to effectively respond to the specific demands of the environment. It is their interpretation of the availability of resources that may be under their control or the control of others that make up the social world of the person. Paul perceives that he constantly has resources available to him that are necessary for facing the demands of his environment. These resources are also of a theological nature, that is, it is God who bestows him with resources, with power in the midst of its weakness, to effectively deal with his sufferings. The Apostle is always hopeful and confident that through his faith he will be able to adequately respond to the specific demands of the environment.

Meaningfulness: This refers to what motivates people to be actively involved in the situation and find the resources that allow them to effectively cope with it. It involves the perception that the specific events, circumstances, or context make sense, and that they are not a threat but rather a challenge that deserves commitment, emotional investment, and actions towards fulfilling the project. In the Pauline texts we observe that he is continuously involved in the situations he faces, and actively searches for the necessary resources that help him cope well anytime and anywhere. Paul interprets the specific events, circumstances, or contexts as having transcendent meaning, in such a way that they are not understood as a definitive threat but as a challenge that demands his commitment, affection, and action towards fulfilling his Christian vocation, as a follower and apostle of Jesus Christ.

From these elements we can say that the way Paul copes with adversity, can be defined by a *sense of theological coherence.* Because when Paul confronts a highly stressful and potentially disruptive situation, he tends to see it as understandable, manageable, and significance, and is able to cope with and overcome it positively, as if it were less stressful[169] (Brizzio & Carreras, 2007).

12.2. Key Theological Concepts of Coping in 2 Corinthians

Understood as expressions of a sense of theological coherence, the keys for coping found in the passages analyzed in 2 Corinthians (which have been linked to the factors associated with psychological resistance to stress, resilience, and posttraumatic growth) are linked to several

---

[169] A person with a high sense of coherence has a stronger disposition to perceive circumstances as not stressful. The sense of coherence predicts the harmful effects of stress on health, insofar as it decreases the likelihood of adverse physiological reactions and negative emotions associated with the perception of stress. The sense of coherence can be considered an ability to successfully mobilize and coordinate personal resources. To that extent, a strong sense of coherence can also be assumed as a way to compensate for the deficiencies of other sources, and thus incorporate and preserve the beneficial effects of the resources that are available during psychological development (Palacios-Espinosa & Restrepo-Espinosa, 2008; Konttinen, Haukkala & Uutela, 2008).

relevant theological concepts that are widely studied in Christian theology. Here we will briefly review them, exclusively from what we have observed in the paragraphs of 2 Corinthians related to coping with adversity, without presenting a conceptual development that involves the Pauline corpus or the broader biblical and theological developments in this regard, since that work by far exceeds the scope of our project.

Identity in Christ:

As we indicated when presenting the different Pauline keys for coping found in our passages, paradoxical identity was placed first in the list, since as a category it is found repeatedly in all the selected texts. Paul refers to himself, especially when facing intense suffering, as a fragile container of glory, a weak individual who has nevertheless been designated by Christ to be a bearer of the good news, as a medium of God's grace, that can significantly contribute to the lives of others (2 Cor 4:7, 9, 16). In the midst of intense and numerous tribulations, he never describes himself as a victim, but shows his transcendent identity as a child of God, and also as a suffering servant (2 Cor 4:9-10).

The Apostle indicates in his writings a paradoxical experience of powerful-weakness, or of victorious impotence (2 Cor 6:8-10), since he is absolutely confident in what he possesses, and more specifically in the one who possesses him, which is so inalienable and intrinsic that it constitutes his fundamental identity and allows him to effectively fulfill his calling (2 Cor 11:21b-29). When expressing his identity in Christ, Paul uses irony (for apologetic purposes) when referring to himself in a paradoxical way. He describes himself as "superior" to others, but in his suffering, weakness, and fragility in the midst of adversity, which he nonetheless faces victoriously by the power present in him, and which transcends him since it comes only from God (2 Cor 11:21b, 23; 12:1-6).

Paul defines himself in reference to the free gift of God, his grace, which supernaturally empowers him not to be defeated under any circumstances (2 Cor 12:9-10). This grace also corresponds to the permanent presence of God with him, marked by mercy and comfort in the midst of suffering (2 Cor 1:8-9).

Faith/Faithfulness:

The traditionally called theological virtues (1 Cor 13:13), are the other theological concepts within which we can frame the keys for coping that we find in the Pauline texts. The first is faith (*pistis*), which was understood by the Apostle as faithfulness and perseverance. In Paul we observe a theological understanding of resistance, resilience, or growth through adversity, that is not a specutalive ethic, but rather, it has the character of a practical theodicy, and is focused on the glorification of God in all circumstances (2 Cor 4:8-9; 5:6-10; 5:1-4, 9). Faith is described by the Apostle as a praxis, directly associated with his character, which involves being persevering, sincere, and above reproach, especially in the midst of difficulty (2 Cor 6:3-10; 11:23-29).

As we indicated in the previous point about paradoxical identity, in this case faithfulness or perseverance is also seen as a virtue which is based solely on the power of God, and not seen as an attribute of personal merit (2 Cor 6:3-4a, 6-7). Faith is presented as a real gift bestowed by God that must be actualized through its exercise, particularly during adversities. That is, it is a gift, which implies human collaboration for effective application in life.

> Knowing how to wait, while patiently enduring trials, is necessary for the believer to be able to "receive what is promised" (Hbr 10:36). In the religious context of ancient Judaism, this word was used expressly for the expectation of God which was characteristic of Israel, for their persevering faithfulness to God on the basis of the certainty of the Covenant in a world which contradicts God. Thus the word (*hupomone*) indicates a lived hope, a life based on the certainty of hope. In the New Testament this expectation of God, this standing with God, takes on a new significance: in Christ, God has revealed himself. He has already communicated to us the "substance" of things to come, and thus the expectation of God acquires a new certainty. It is the expectation of things to come from the perspective of a present that is already given. It is a looking-forward in Christ's presence, with Christ who is present, to the perfecting of his Body, to his definitive coming (Benedict XVI, 2007, p. 9).

Faith, in Paul's perspective, also involves trusting in God's merciful comfort, and merciful saving intervention in the midst of adversity (2 Cor 1:3-11).

Hope:

Within this broad concept, in the passages studied we find three important categories of Pauline coping that can be placed under its umbrella: the resignification of death and/or traumatic events, eschatological coping, and detachment from the material or visible. To maintain hope in the midst of difficult tribulations, Paul uses a fundamental cognitive-affective resource: for him, both death and traumatic events (that is, events that may involve threats to his life or integrity, or that of someone close to him), have a particular meaning, which allows him to see them not as extreme threats, but as serious events that do not put at the most important parts of his existence at risk (2 Cor 4:8-12; 5:1-2).

The Apostle thematizing traumatic events by referring to them with some frequency, and thus shows that he manages to integrate them and take charge of them, not denying them or avoiding mentioning them. We also see that he relativizes the negative power of adversity and does not show himself to be focused on his sufferings, but rather evaluates them as a secondary cost that is necessary and expected for fulfilling his assigned mission. Paul also interprets adversity as a special opportunity to corroborate the purity, sincerity, and true character of his apostolate, which also enables him to develop his character in general and his perseverance in particular (2 Cor 4:16-18; 6:4b-5, 6-7a; 1:6).

Paul also resignifies his suffering (plausibly referring to a medical problem, as we indicated previously) as a positive experience of God caring for him, who allows him to grow deeper in humility, knowledge and dependence on his empowering grace when constantly experiencing his own human weakness/sickness and vulnerability (2 Cor 12:7-10). Also closely related to the concept of Christian hope is the eschatological coping. The Pauline texts show us a way to respond to high stress circumstances by appealing to theological promises, such as the hope for the resurrection (or glorious transformation) of himself and his community (2 Cor 4:9- 12, 14; 5:1-5; 4:10-12). We also find an eschatological resignification of the adversity, which is done with confidence in the faithful liberating action of God in the face of present and future adverse events (2 Cor 5:1-4, 1:9-10).

Finally, also within the notion of hope, we find detachment with the material or visible. Paul shows in his writings to the Corinthians that he is sharply focused on the ultimate, transcendent, and definitive good. He is detached from what is temporary and preliminary, which he associates with the material and visible (2 Cor 4:16-5:8). His detachment from the material is based on the conviction that Jesus Christ is everything to him, that he is sufficient, in such a way that his basic needs, including physiological needs, take a back seat compared to the pre-eminence of his affection for Christ, the church, and the mission entrusted to him (2 Cor 6:8b-10; 11:27).

Love:

Finally, to complete the trio of theological virtues, the term love allows us to group together the broadest set of Pauline keys for coping. In direct or indirect reference to this virtue, especially when emphasizing affective and community aspects, here we can consider the following keys: altruistic coping, the expression of traumatic events, identification with Jesus as a model for coping, thanksgiving, confidence in the comforting presence of God, and prayer. Regarding what we have called altruistic coping, we observe that Paul in his writings expresses a marked focus on the good of others when facing personal adversities, particularly trying to not be a stumbling block for his brothers and sisters in the faith, nor to give an opportunity for his apostolic ministry to be defamed to be defamed (2 Cor 4:12, 15; 6:3, 6, 10).

Together with focusing on the welfare of others in the midst of adversity, he shows significant levels of empathic resonance and compassion, which is linked to God's comforting experience, as a training experience for being able to comfort others. Coping with adversity is presented in Paul as an experience of communion and solidarity with communities of faith, and not as a purely individual or isolated experience (2 Cor 11:28-29; 1:4, 6; 1:6, 7, 11). On the other hand, the expression of traumatic events, in addition to facilitating such events to be appropriated and integrated into his life narrative, enables him to recall those events in a different context, he brings the communities reading his letters to participate in them, thus developing an intimate solidarity. It also enables him to legitimately stand in front of these communities as a true, persevering, and faithful apostle of Jesus Christ (2 Cor 4:8-10; 6:8-10; 11:23b-29, 12:10; 1:8-10).

We can group Paul's identification with Jesus as a model for coping within the concept of love, by the fact that what moves him to such identification is the deep affection he feels towards his Lord, who has shown immeasurable love for him, especially through his death on the cross. The Apostle identifies himself with the passion and death of Christ in his ministry that was full of suffering, as if he were himself a simile or concrete representation of the message of sacrificial love that he proclaims. Additionally, he also identifies with the resurrection of Jesus, especially when overcoming the extremely adverse events that he has to suffer constantly (2 Cor 4:10-11; 1:5). Thanksgiving in or after traumatic circumstances is presented in Paul as a fundamentally communitarian experience, because it is centered on the welfare of others and the participation of the greatest number of people in the expression of thanksgiving to God for his compassionate work towards his people (2 Cor 4:15, 1:11).

Closely linked to thanksgiving also lies Paul's confidence in God's constant comforting presence in the midst of his difficulties. This certainty is marked by a positive and intense emotion that is associated with the joy of knowing that God accompanies him in an active, positive, and permanent way in the midst of adversity (2 Cor 1:3-5). Finally, the religious/ spiritual practice of prayer, which is so recommended in other places by the Apostle, is found here as a social coping modality, since Paul presents it as a community experience of solidarity, especially in the midst of adversity, which can have an effective response from God (2 Cor 1:11).

12.3. Positive Coping and Ecclesial Functions

Here, we will reflect on some practical-theological observations that could be relevant for the church. One way to describe the relevance of the different ways that Paul takes charge of and interprets traumatic events is by ordering them in terms of Christian community praxis, and describing how they can be applied to pastoral work, in both preventive and reparative contexts, when attending to people or groups that have experienced, are experiencing, or are at a high risk of experiencing traumatic events in the present (Floristan, 1991):

Kerygmatic or evangelistic function:

Regarding this pastoral function, the Pauline modes of coping associated with positive adaptation after traumatic events (as we saw comparing them with the factors of hardiness, resilience and posttraumatic growth), allow us to confirm the importance of emphasizing the self-understanding of one's paradoxical identity when preaching the gospel. In other words, giving a perspective of the gospel that promotes a vision of self that takes charge of the fragility and vulnerability of not just human life in general but also Christian life in particular, and that recognizes one's own limitations when faced with adversity and suffering (their own and of others), but rests in the grace of God that redefines personal and communal identity in a stable and transcendent way (as son/daughter of God, that is justified and reconciled), and provides sufficient and stable resources to effectively face the hardest moments of life.

Another important element regarding the kerygmatic function, is understanding the faith experience as faithfulness and perseverance, instead of a simple intellectual assent to a set of abstract truths. Paul describes faith as a praxis, not as a simple cognitive agreement with a correct dogma. When the faith experience is defined in this way[170,] Christian communities would develop stronger and more adaptive coping dynamics, at both the preventive and posttraumatic levels. This is because adverse circumstances are conceived as being an inherent part of the Christian experience, where overcoming them is an expression of the legitimacy and inner coherence of one's own faith.

Pastoral proclamation of the gospel should also prominently include eschatology as a way of configuring meaning and hope for the church, and as a hermeneutical resource that promotes positive, or at least adaptive, resignifications of adverse situations, both for individuals as well as for families and communities.

---

[170] Very in the line of the concept of *ultimate concern* developed by P. Tillich (1976, 1982).

With this, the message of Easter, with its emphasis on the resurrection of Christ and the final and glorious eternal life for all his people, provides an important key to interpretation used for appraising and evaluating the negative events of life, assigning them value in light of the promise of definitive good.

Diaconal or service function:

What we have called altruistic coping can be thought of as a coping modality very much associated with the function of showing mercy and giving comfort to the church, and in general with service to others, as a normative central element of a community of faith that says they follow Jesus.

In church life, it is very important to emphasize the opportunity people have to significantly contribute to the community to which they belong, which is an important factor for wellbeing after traumatic events, as we mentioned before. A community of faith that functions as an organic body, where every member serves in accordance to their gifts and according to the needs of the others, is a community formed by people who are well positioned to face high-stress events, or to recover and even grow from adverse circumstances.

Koinonia, or communion, and membership function:

Social support is one of the most important functions that a community of faith can play for its members. From the Pauline perspective observed in 2 Corinthians, we can say that communion and belonging to a reality that transcends the isolated individual is key when facing adversity.

Within this, the expression of hardship and sharing of painful events with others, in a context of acceptance and consolation, is very important for the support of people or families that find themselves in adverse circumstances. Churches, in this sense, must make appropriate space and time for the catharsis of its members, where mutual consolation can be experienced as a concrete expression of the consolation that God provides, and in turn gives us the capacity to console others.

Liturgical, or worship, and celebration function:

Instances of public and private thankfulness in an ecclesiastical setting, as a liturgical expression, are essential for facilitating better levels of recovery from disruptive events. The act of thanksgiving in communal contexts, which are not exempt of the possibility of also being combined with the expression of distress or lamentation, where damage and suffering is remembered, are very important for individual and collective health.

Another resource in the realm of liturgy that must be encouraged for the wellness of the church is corporate prayer. Especially in the context of vulnerability, adversity, or the necessary recovery from negative events, prayer in private and especially with others is very significant as a resource for positive coping.

Didactic or educational function:

Finally, within the formative function of the church, the Pauline texts encourage us to emphasize following of Christ as a model of coping. For this, ecclesial education must place sufficiently heavy emphasis on praxis, so that it is not just an abstract and irrelevant discourse about life, particularly in moments of intense ailment.

It is worth mentioning that the Christian message, on both its kerygmatic and didactic levels, describes the three psychological constructs (hardiness, resilience, and posttraumatic growth) that we have studied that are associated with positive responses to traumatic events. Jesus Christ is the prime example of resistance to adversity or *hardiness*. Not only in his passion and dead, but in his whole life, Jesus is described as one who overcomes temptation, keeps moving forward with his purpose despite the opposition, even when it comes from his own disciples. He is a model of tenaciousness, courage, and perseverance in the face of evil, against which he fights, denounces, and does not bend.

Also, in both his life and message, Jesus shows himself as a clear example of *resilience*, flexibility, and recovery in the face of adverse circumstances, conditions of vulnerability, and psycho-social disadvantage. Jesus is the resilient one, who moves forward, and emerges from geographic, social, economic, political, and religious marginality to stand as the teacher of the needy multitudes and the energetic enemy of the religious and moral powers of his time. He is the resilient one that even overcomes death itself.

Finally, if we could describe the gospel in terms of some of the positive coping models, perhaps the most precise model would be *posttraumatic growth*, since Jesus, as the Christ, is by definition the one who arises victoriously from death, the most extreme trauma. His message announces transcendent growth from the traumatic. The resurrection, which is fundamental to Paul as he faced adversity, is also central to the foundation of the good news itself. We can say that this good news which recognizes Jesus as the awaited Messiah, is the announcement of the event of him who arose gloriously from death, defeated it, and opened up a new era and possibility for the world, particularly for his followers as people who know they are fragile and vulnerable but at the same time invincible in Christ.

12.4. A Pauline Practical Theology of Posttraumatic Coping

To answer our main research question[171], in this work we have used the hermeneutical arc in the perspective of Psychological Biblical Criticism, going from our first reading, where we reviewed the current psychological literature on the positive management of trauma, and then examined selected texts from 2 Corinthians. This was the Pauline letter with more references to traumatic events and where the confrontation was addressed explicitly. We then moved on to our exegetical reading, where a critical review of 2 Corinthians was carried out, along with a general exegetical analysis of the selected passages, in order to discover Paul's hermeneutical clues regarding the coping of the traumatic events he mentions. Finally, we ended with the third part of the arc that Ricoeur poses, called hermeneutic reading, where the results found in the Pauline texts are discussed in relation to current psychological contributions on positive coping of trauma (especially with reference to hardiness, resilience, posttraumatic growth and positive religious coping), developing some ideas and reflections for a practical theology of posttraumatic coping.

---

[171] What insights regarding coping with adversity can we find in the writings of the Apostle Paul (particularly in 2 Corinthians) and in recent research on positive coping with trauma for the purposes of building a practical theology of posttraumatic coping?

To finish, we will deliver some conclusions, as a complement to our final step through the hermeneutic arc from the Psychological Biblical Criticism on our subject.

12.4.1. Positive psychology, practical theology and hermeneutical phenomenology

Positive Psychology has been defined as:
> [...] recent subfield of psychology that has focused on (a) positive emotions (Baumeister, et al, 2007; Fredrickson, 1998 , 2009), (b) happiness or subjective well-being (Seligman, 2004; Tay & Diener, 2011), and (c) character strengths or virtues (Peterson & Seligman, 2004; Snyder, Lopez, & Pedrotti, 2011) (Worthington, et al., 2014, p. 51).

Although today we speak of Positive Psychology as a relatively emerging area, in the research field it already has some consolidation. That is why it is important that studies such as the present consider the contributions of this branch of psychology to explore biblical themes, as is the case of dealing with traumatic events in Paul. Rather than looking for psychopathological features or applying theoretical models (as has been done quite a lot with psychoanalysis and analytical psychology) as an interpretive and explanatory matrix of the phenomena present in the texts, it seems relevant to join the vision of Positive Psychology and, from a descriptive perspective with a markedly phenomenological and hermeneutical character, to look for Christian factual life in the Scriptures, taking the texts (in our case the Pauline letters, in particular 2 Corinthians) not purely as doctrinal documents where theological dogmas are exposed, but as documents of the author's own life experience as a believer and follower of Christ (cf. Heidegger, 2006). Perspectives of this kind can be fully aligned with an understanding of practical theology as a "hermeneutic of Christian praxis" (Hoch, 2011, p.76) or a "hermeneutic of lived religion" (Ganzevoort, 2009a, p.1).

In this way, we could talk about a Positive Practical Theology, whose thematic object of study is Christian praxis or lived religion that correlates significantly, according to empirical research in the field of Positive Psychology, with mental, individual and mental health. community, and with its restoration and development. In other words, a theology that seeks to be a hermeneutic of positive religious or spiritual experience and is linked to well-being, positive emotions and virtues, whether in real life or in the biblical texts that testify to them.

In our case, our hermeneutic approach to Pauline texts of 2 Corinthians, from the psychology of positive trauma coping as our starting point and arrival (world versus the initial text or reading and hermeneutic reading), has allowed us to develop a particular understanding of Paul's own coping mechanisms (and probably of the first Christian communities) regarding adverse events that involved vital risk. The Apostle shows us through the clues we find in his texts related to posttraumatic coping, that the hermeneutical factor is central to human experience, especially in the results when we face suffering.

Most of us live our lives with the feeling that the world we occupy is significant, coherent, because we perceive a certain pattern that allows us to have the impression of harmony around us. This sense of coherence and underlying order is at the base of our daily life and provides a certain matrix in which our relationships, projects, pleasures and pains occur. The usual thing for people is that the meaning of the world is inherent, because they live their lives without normally having reason to question it. We tend to live in a flow assumed as natural where we face a given world of personal, family and cultural meanings. However, there are times when the meaning and coherence of the world is broken and the coordinates that unified our experience and our life is at risk of being lost. In those instances we can say that we are facing a traumatic event, characterized by a deep struggle with the search for meaning, particularly when we are drastically confronted with our mortality condition, be it personal or among people close to us.

The usual models that try to explain the trauma and its coping, are usually mostly under the Cartesian dualistic understanding of human reality, which fails to fully account for the complexity of our world as something significant. We experience the world fundamentally as an integrated set and only then do we encounter particular things within that world. Specific entities appear as meaningful to us only in contrast to a background context and not in isolation. The human being is a being constituted as a unit between his organism and his significant world in which he is always incorporated. Being-in-the-world, the person accesses the understanding of events not as a cognitive phenomenon, in the sense of capturing something thematically or theoretically, but through a primary understanding, which corresponds to a factual meeting fundamentally referred to know-how. From this perspective, the immediate effect of a traumatic experience is the confrontation with the existential fragility itself, where the previous modes of understanding and coherence of the own world collapse, are no longer reliable. The very nature of being-in-the-world and the concerns that constitute it change and become uncertain, as the continuity of the vital project is put at risk (Dreyfus, 1996; Heidegger, 1997; Bracken, 2002).

Regarding psychopathological responses to traumatic events, it has been suggested that PTSD is a "disease of the times", as it is a disorder that allows the past to live again in the present, in the form of intrusive images and thoughts, giving a kind of reproduction of ancient events compulsively. However, time is not a linear phenomenon, independent of the mind and consciousness, it is not an event "out there", where the past is a collection of different moments "stored in memory", because the memory implies something qualitatively unlike a simple storage of events, since the original experiences are experienced only once and remembering is to recover information related to what has been lived, actively reconstructing associations of synaptic traces of memory, which are reconsolidated new mnemic each time (Edelman & Tononi, 2000 ; Chan & LaPaglia, 2013; Nader, et al., 2013).

Anxiety and anguish, central today for the categorization of cadres associated with traumatic events, are very human moods linked to fear of vulnerability, damage and death, but normally we live our lives free of intense degrees of these emotions, especially in contexts where a certain social order prevails and basic human needs are met. But anguish can become a privileged revealing experience of our essential finitude, of our mortality.

However, and here we draw attention to highlight of our research, since in the Pauline texts we do not find this direct relationship between traumatic event and anguish. There is no such existential disruption described by the Apostle, there is no such break in the face of the possibility of the end, of death. As Heidegger puts it in addressing his reading of Paul, the Christians in Thessaloniki seem to want to date in an objective time the moment of the second coming of Christ (or of the end, or of death, we could consider when talking about trauma). However, the Apostle tells them that it does not matter "when" the Lord will come, but what matters is the "how" of waiting for his arrival. Paul does not interpret, according to Heidegger, the question of the Thessalonians as a question concerning knowledge, but as a question concerning existence. It is about living soberly and on alert, in the middle of the world and without eluding it, but facing adversities with hope, with the attention placed on the future. In this way, waiting is a mode of existence, a particular "how" of factual life, not a term that is shortened and accounted for as the days pass in expectation of the end (Heidegger, 2006; cf. Peña, 2019) .

This perspective is very much in line with the hermeneutical keys found in 2 Corinthians regarding the coping with trauma. They are not fundamentally about interpretative keys of adversity that focus on the "what" (specific contents or explanatory approaches) but rather on the "how" of the confrontation itself, that is, on Christian praxis. Paul does not give greater reflections or explanatory arguments about human suffering (along the lines of a theodicy), but argues in favor of the truthfulness of his apostolic ministry (and this is the main apologetic use made throughout the letter of the lists of adversities) through a life of faithfulness to the Lord in the midst of extreme adversities. The Apostle states deep down that his firm and resilient life, of continuous posttraumatic growth, is a factual testimony of his call and mission that come from God Himself.

As we indicate when referring to the theological virtues as concepts that can contain and classify the Pauline keys found, Paul's perspective acquires a lot of meaning from a reading linked to the phenomenology of temporality:

> [...] if our life consists in deciding what we are going to be, it means that in the very root of our life there is a temporary attribute: deciding what we are going to be therefore, the future. And, without stopping, we receive now, one after another, a whole fertile crop of inquiries. First: that our life is first of all bumping into the future. Here is another paradox. It is not the present or the past that we live first, no; life is an activity that runs forward, and the present or the past is discovered later, in relation to that future. Life is futurization, it is what it is not yet (Ortega-Gasset, 1964, p. 420)[172].

---

[172] In original Spanish version: "[...] si nuestra vida consiste en decidir lo que vamos a ser, quiere decirse que en la raíz misma de nuestra vida hay un atributo temporal: decidir lo

That our life is first of all bumping into the future, a constant disposition forward, towards what is not yet, and that both the past and the present are always discovered and experienced in relation to the planned future, are organized from a future that He goes ahead and consists of something that he still does not give, he gives us a fairly clear picture of the way in which Paul faces his present adversities and as he remembers those already lived.

We see this in large part in the hermeneutical keys found in 2 Corinthians: The experience of faith as faithfulness and perseverance (key 2), shows Paul before the tribulations resisting on the basis of his theological convictions (2 Cor 4:8-9; 5:6-10; 6:6-7; 11:23-29), where trust is placed in the power of the resurrection that was manifested in Jesus Christ (2 Cor 4:9, 13), thereby that his religious confrontation is ethical rather than speculative and is focused on God's reign[173] and future glorification as a fundamental concern (2 Cor 5:1-4, 9). Likewise, the resignification of death and traumatic events (key 3) as positive experiences (2 Cor 4:8-12, 16-18; 5:1-2; 6:6-7a; 12:7-10; 1:6); eschatological confrontation (key 5), as a way of dealing with tribulations based on the promised hope (2 Cor 4:9; 5:1-5), especially of resurrection or transformation (2 Cor 4:10-12, 14) it is from where Paul redefines the adverse present (2 Cor 5:1-4) and anticipates a future where God's liberating action will become manifest (2 Cor 1:9-10). This focus on the future is connected with detachment from the material or visible (key 7), where everything is relativized in its value with a view to the eternal and glorious approach (2 Cor 4:16-5:8; 6:8b-10; 11:27), and where Christ himself becomes a role model in the midst of suffering and death, for the resurrection or final transformation in his image is expected (2 Cor 4:10-11; 1:5). Thus, as Bultmann puts it, *parousia* is a "present future" in the sense that Christians must react to it right now and not be waiting

---

que vamos a ser —por tanto, el futuro. Y, sin parar, recibimos ahora, una tras otra, toda una fértil cosecha de averiguaciones. Primera: que nuestra vida es ante todo toparse con el futuro. He aquí otra paradoja. No es el presente o el pasado lo primero que vivimos, no; la vida es una actividad que se ejecuta hacia adelante, y el presente o el pasado se descubre después, en relación con ese futuro. La vida es futurición, es lo que aún no es."

[173] As Bultmann states, the kingdom of God can be understood as a future, true, but future reality, since it would not be a metaphysical entity, a concrete state, but a full and future work of God, which although not present in a sense Strictly, as the future determines the human being in his present (Bultmann & Jaspers, 1968; cf. Roldán, 2013).

passively as if it were really meaningful only when it which is announced happens (Bultmann & Jaspers, 1968).

> Dasein is authentically alongside itself, it is truly existent, whenever it maintains itself in this running ahead. This running ahead is nothing other than the authentic and singular future of one's own Dasein. In running ahead Dasein is its future, in such a way that in this being futural it comes back to its past and present [...] With regard to time, this means that the fundamental phenomenon of time is the future (Heidegger, pp. 13E-14E)

Christian existence for Paul is effectively a permanently projected, organizing life from the future that is anticipated through faith, hope and love, "whenever it maintains itself in this running ahead", as Paul expresses:

> What is more, I consider everything a loss because of the surpassing worth of knowing Christ Jesus my Lord, for whose sake I have lost all things. I consider them garbage, that I may gain Christ and be found in him, not having a righteousness of my own that comes from the law, but that which is through faith in Christ—the righteousness that comes from God on the basis of faith. I want to know Christ—yes, to know the power of his resurrection and participation in his sufferings, becoming like him in his death, and so, somehow, attaining to the resurrection from the dead. Not that I have already obtained all this, or have already arrived at my goal, but I press on to take hold of that for which Christ Jesus took hold of me. Brothers and sisters, I do not consider myself yet to have taken hold of it. But one thing I do: Forgetting what is behind and straining toward what is ahead, I press on toward the goal to win the prize for which God has called me heavenward in Christ Jesus (Phil 3:8-14).

Similarly, in 2 Corinthians 5:1ss Paul urges the community to turn its gaze to the future, after having contrasted the fullness of the glory that is expected with the brief and, therefore, bearable tribulation of this perishable world (2 Cor 4:1-18). The Apostle makes a contrast between exile within earthly life and life in the homeland of the Lord (2 Cor 5:6-8), but this eschatological communion, desired and expected, Paul connects (2 Cor 5:9) , with the constant search for the Lord's approval in everything, that is, a life that is pleasing and approved by God, here and now. In this way, eschatological hope becomes the foundation of the Christian's responsibility and daily integrity. Consequent and persevering behavior in this time of waiting and tribulation is therefore fundamental and an expression of eschatological faith and hope (Schrage, 1987).

12.4.3. Pauline writings and the psychology of posttraumatic coping

All the Pauline coping keys that we have identified and described in our 2 Corinthians texts are an important observation of Paul's factual experience as a Christian. They are a description of the way you operate in your world, in your specific circumstances. They tell us how he took charge, at least in an epistolary way (since we have no way of accessing the facts in any other way), of the adversities he had to live.

As we saw in detail above, in Paul we observe significantly many of the factors associated with hardiness, resilience and posttraumatic growth, as well as those associated with positive religious coping. This fits very well with the characteristics of their behavior in terms of positive mechanisms, strategies and coping styles that are observed in their texts.

We see in Paul the use of adaptive cognitive and behavioral strategies to handle the demands of a situation when they can be considered high stress or that exceeds personal resources, which allow him to reduce negative emotions and conflicts caused by stress. This is done through various adjustments or mechanisms of conscious or non-conscious adaptation that reduce tension and anxiety.

Paul's coping style, that is, the characteristic way in which he faced and dealt with stress, situations that caused him anxiety or emergencies, following the current definitions in the field of psychology and psychiatry (VandenBos, 2015), it could be said that it was: a) a proactive coping style, that is, the use of stress management strategies that reflect efforts to accumulate resources that facilitate promotion towards challenging goals and personal growth; motivation to face the challenges and commitment to meet their high standards; perception of demands and opportunities in the distant future and beginning of constructive ways of action towards their achievement of achievements; interpretation of stress as eustress, that is, as productive excitement and vital energy; coping becomes objective management instead of risk management; b) a coping style focused on the problem, that is, a stress management strategy in which a person directly faces a stressful factor in an attempt to reduce or eliminate it, which may involve generating possible solutions to a problem , confronting others who are responsible or associated with the stressor or other forms of instrumental action; c) a social coping style, that is, any interpersonal stress management strategy, where support from family, friends or community is sought in an event or situation; d) a coping approach style, that is, any strategy to handle a stressful event or situation in which a person actively focuses, cognitively or behaviorally, on the problematic event or situation; e) a style of assimilative coping, which involves the management of stress where the person actively tries to transform a situation in such a way that fits their goals and aspirations, which may consider acquiring a new ability to solve problems or seek help in the environment; f) a behavioural coping style, that is, any strategy in which a person handles a stressful event or situation by modifying their actions; and g) a cognitive coping style, which implies any strategy in which a person uses mental activity to handle a stressful event or situation, within which there are positive refocusing and positive reevaluation, such as those most associated with adaptive processes (see Table 8).

While we can classify Pauline praxis in the face of adverse events as we have done, it is important to note that in Paul what we observe is an ethic of resilience and posttraumatic growth. For the Apostle, as Becker (2007) puts it, the peculiarity of the Pauline ethical exhortation consisted in establishing a characteristic relationship between the new state of salvation or reconciliation of individuals and the moral norms that they had to comply, so that it is always the state of relationship with God that determines the behaviour of Christians and what is given to the believer is required as something that he must translate into practical life. It is never, then, a simple formal fulfillment of duties, but of the unity between the acts and the person, between the behaviour and the new identity in Christ. Identity that, as we saw, is paradoxical for Paul, as it is conceived as a suffering but victorious condition, defined by the free gift of God's love that transforms the

Christian into a bearer of stable glory despite his personal condition of fragility (2 Cor 4:7, 10, 16; 6:8-10; 11:21b-29; 12:1-6, 9-10; 1:8-9).

Table 8: Pauline Coping Keys and Coping Styles

COPING KEYS	COPING STYLES						
	proactive coping	focused on the problem	social coping	approach style	assimilation coping	behav coping	cognitive coping
1. Paradoxical identity	X	X		X	X		X
2. Experience of faith as faithfulness and perseverance	X	X		X	X	X	
3. Resignification of death and/or traumatic events	X	X		X	X		X
4. Altruistic coping	X	X	X	X	X	X	
5. Eschatological coping	X	X		X	X		X
6. Expression of traumatic events	X	X	X	X	X	X	
7. Detachment from the material or visible	X				X		X
8. Identification with Jesus as a coping mechanism	X	X		X	X	X	X
9. Thanksgiving	X	X	X	X	X	X	X
10. Comforting presence of God	X	X		X	X		X
11. Prayer	X	X	X	X	X	X	X

For Paul, Christian behaviour, especially in the midst of suffering, is a matter of the believer's responsibility before God, a responsibility that demands full and free surrender to the will of God, specifically expressed in the love of others, as we observe in the what we have called the key to altruistic confrontation (key 4), where the Apostle describes how important it is in the midst of adversity to focus on the good of others, rather than the focus on himself and his individual well-being (2 Cor 4:12.15; 6:3, 6, 10; 11:28-29; 1:4, 6, 7, 11). Thus, for Paul, the fundamental ethical question is, then, how the eschatological community must remain in love until the end of everything, how to promote its integration, how not to discredit the mission with scandalous behaviour, typical of the old life away of God (Brecker, 2007).

12.4.4. Towards a theology of trauma, resilience and posttraumatic growth

Our understanding of traumatic events and their coping is affected if we consider the human being as a complex, unitary entity, always constituted by its significant world and its projection to the future. Traumatic events, which are presented as a historical disruption in the person, are a hermeneutical, interpretive phenomenon, a polysemic experience; not an objective, static reality, which cannot be modified. This is how we observe it in Paul. Highly adverse events are reconnected positively and hopefully by the Apostle.

As Moltmann (1976) has put it, in true hope, man does not flee from the unbearable pressure of the present towards a better future, where he imagines a perfect comfort, but brings the future to his present and now lives from it . This does not make the present more bearable, but rather often more conflictive. In hope, the Christian opens himself to the future that is promised to him, leaving the enclosure of his life and also that of his society, which, as they lived in Paul's time, was bleak and conceived under the impending destruction.

In the Apostle's message we find the horizon of hope where God has manifested himself to the rescue of those who trust him, who are called to form an eschatological community that thanks to Christ, can escape divine judgment and can live forever. This hope of life, resurrection and final transformation renews the believer because it shows him his new possibilities. This hope disposes him to abandon himself and exist in love for others, for the fundamental, the fundamental future, is already achieved by God.

As Becker (2005) points out, Paul, when discussing the resurrection (1 Cor 15 and 2 Cor 5:1ss), shows that death appears so closely linked to the historical existence of the human being that he humans have to die integrally (since there is no platonic perspective in Paul). Only a new creative act of God can give humans perpetual existence, so that the identity of the human being is not based on himself or herself (on their self or their soul) but on God's faithfulness, which is represented in baptism as a symbol of death and resurrection in Christ. Thus the Apostle conceives death as a break, but devoid of its fundamentally destructive force, for the same God who creates from nothing, passes the believer from the zero point to the resurrected body. There is no longer fear of death or nothingness, but the end is expected as the beginning of the new life in the presence of God in Christ ("Where, O death, is your victory? Where, O death, is your sting?" 1 Cor 15:55). Thus, by redefining death, events that may imply it, that is, the traumatic events are also resigned in Paul. So that he understands the entire life of each Christian as an assimilation (progressive) of the death of Jesus; and the expected resurrection, as an assimilation of the glory of the Risen One.

From the Pauline perspective, through baptism, Christians are so involved in the event of Christ, that they irrevocably become their property. The destiny of Christ and the destiny of Christians are definitively related to each other, putting themselves in mutual correlation, so that just as Christ was resurrected, so his followers must walk in a new life, which is characterized, in one of its fundamental aspects, by overcoming adversity by overcoming it (2 Cor 6:9-10; cf. Rom 6:1ss). Thus, although Christians have obviously not yet been resurrected identically to Jesus, they do enter into a radical novelty of life that is concretized by being a new way of behaving in the world. For the Christ who acts in baptism becomes the Lord of the baptized, which shows that these, from now on, are no longer at the service of evil, as a tyrannical owner, but have been released by a new Lord most powerful and placed at your service. Thus, baptism is a gift of freedom, but also a change of sovereignty, which is expressed through voluntary and persevering obedience to Jesus as Christ and Lord (Schrage, 1987).

The concept of perseverance (*hupomone*), normally translated as patience, according to our study in connection with the current psychological concepts of positive coping with trauma, seems to us very close to the concept of resilience. In Paul we observe that this concept functions as a central virtue (as we saw it, especially in the analysis of 2 Cor 6:4b-7a), because he assigns it a fundamental place in the character of every follower of Christ. The interesting thing is that this Christian virtue can only manifest itself fully in the midst of adversity and, for the Apostle, rests on the awareness of one's own fragility, on the one hand,

and on the certainty of God's power, on the other (2 Cor 4:7-5:10; 11:21-12:10).

As we saw in the exegetic section, the term *hupomone*, in Paul, designates the attitude of firmness and faithfulness of the Christian especially in the midst of trials and sufferings, an attitude that is based on eschatological hope and the affective bond with God and the community of faith Given these characteristics of this virtue, it is very appropriate to connect it directly with the current concept of resilience.

It is Cyrulnik (2001, 2007, 2009) who has proposed link and meaning as the two fundamental pillars of resilience. On the one hand, resilience is a primarily relational phenomenon, so that it is essential for trauma to be faced in a resilient way, so that the person is linked to at least one person in a meaningful way, a link that can be of various types, even symbolic. This is so, to the point that it is difficult to distinguish whether we are talking about a personal or social phenomenon, hence the different emphasis that has been given in the study and discussion of individual, family, community and ecological resilience. On the other hand, there are many research and theoretical developments that have emphasized the importance of meaning in dealing with trauma and adversity in general. The case of the psychiatrist Victor Frankl (1989, 1991, 1994), who develops this point centrally in his work, is emblematic, even stating that finding meaning in the midst of traumatic experiences is the fundamental element for survival and overcoming of trauma.

Based on this, we can speak in Paul of an experience and a resilient perspective. For the Apostle, bond and meaning are central to his experience as a follower and servant of Christ. The emotional bond, of unconditional type (*agape*), marked by reciprocal fidelity (*pistis*) is the basis of overcoming adversities, along with the transcendent sense that there is in the midst of suffering, the eschatological hope that sustains it permanently.

In Paul the actual traumatic phenomenon, that is, the vital disruption after a traumatic event, is marked by symptoms of intrusion, avoidance, cognitive and affective negative alterations, as well as an alteration in reactivity that significantly affects performance in one or several areas of life (cf. Criteria C and D for PTSD, APA, 2013). Due to such, it seems appropriate to talk about a more resilient experience in

Paul than along the lines of post-traumatic growth, as that implies a symptomatic traumatic experience, from which something different and better can be reconstructed from the traumatic event (Calhoun & Tedeschi, 1999, 2006, Berger, 2015).

We can say, in this line, that the current concept of resilience is a notion fully compatible with the Pauline perspective of adversity, especially because the Apostle sees that difficult events and suffering are an unavoidable part of following Christ (1 Thess 2:14-16; 3:3-4; Gal 6:12; Phil 1:29-30; Rom 8:16-17), so that overcoming them in a positive way is fundamental in the experience of any Christian. Resilience, understood as a kind of eschatological perseverance, emotionally sustained, must develop and be evident in communities of faith. Adversity contexts, especially the most extreme ones, become the most appropriate instances to grow in *hupomone*, because that is where fidelity and love (bond) and hope (meaning) are put to the test (1 Thess 1:3 ; Rom 8:25; 12:12; 15:4-5; 2 Cor 1:6-7; 6:4; cf. Jas 1:2-4).

Recent historical research, based on studies on the concept and experience in the early church and on the writings of the Church's fathers, has made it clear that the concept of patience (*hupomone*) was the ferment of the first faith communities in between of a time marked by violent persecution. It has even been suggested that one of the fundamental elements in the expansion of Christianity during the Roman Empire was the practice of patience, a virtue that at that time should characterize as a priority those who made the decision to start the catechumenate process to opt to baptism (Kreider, 2017).

Making a paraphrase of Kreider's conclusion (Ibid., P. 54) of his study of patience in the abundant treatises that were written in the first centuries of Christianity on this virtue, we could speak of Christian resilience, aligned with our discoveries about the Pauline confrontation, as follows:

a) *Christian resilience has its roots in the nature of God.* God is resilient, works inexorably throughout the centuries to fulfill his mission and in the fullness of time has been revealed in Jesus Christ.

b) *The core of Christian resilience is manifested in the incarnation of Jesus Christ.* Jesus' life and teaching demonstrate what Christian resilience means, calling on those who follow him to lead a resilient lifestyle that participates in God's mission in the world.

c) *Christian resilience escapes human control.* Those who live a resilient Christian lifestyle trust God and do not try to manipulate the results; they live without excessive precautions, they risk.

d) *Christian resilience is not in a hurry.* Resilient Christians live to the rhythm of God, accepting the incomplete and waiting.

e) *Christian resilience is not conventional.* Reconfigure the behaviour according to the teachings of Jesus in many areas, especially with regard to wealth, sex and power.

f) *Christian resilience is not violent.* Accept the damage without retaliation, because God does not call violence, and it cannot produce a fundamental change.

g) *Christian resilience promotes religious freedom.* It does not impose faith or religious discipline.

h) *Christian resilience has hope.* He confidently puts the future in God's hands.

Finally, although the concept of posttraumatic growth cannot be applied directly to the modalities of Pauline confrontation, it seems to us that it can be used more broadly as a hermeneutical key to the Christian message and praxis, from a Pauline perspective:

a) *A message of passion, death and resurrection:* in Paul we observe a proclamation of the good news (*euaggelion*) as a message fundamentally focused on the event of the passion, death and resurrection of Jesus as the Messiah (more than in his life and teaching). That is, the announcement about a man who publicly experienced torture, prosecution and death, which turned out to be the Jewish Messiah awaited, because he rose from the dead, of which it Paul himself acknowledges himself witness. It is therefore a message based on an experience of posttraumatic growth, of transcendent character. Jesus of Nazareth suffers and death. Jesus of Nazareth overcomes suffering and death with his resurrection. Jesus of Nazareth reaches a state of fullness superior to the one before the trauma: he is resurrected with a glorified body. This Jesus, ends up being an archetype of posttraumatic growth for all his followers, who like him will be able to overcome, through his faithfulness and through the work of his Holy Spirit, suffering and death, reaching the final resurrection and glory in presence of God the Father. This is the annoucement of Paul.

b) *Conversion and sacraments:* Christian conversion, as Paul experienced it, is an experience of radical disruption with previous life, it is a drastic break in existence where God breaks into and takes possession of life as a new sovereign. The sacraments of baptism and the Lord's Supper function as symbols of this same character, where submerging in the waters comes to represent death and leaving them the resurrection to a new life. At the Lord's Supper the Christian participates in the body and blood of the sacrificed Christ, thus adding to the atoning event that restores life in communion with God. It is, therefore, in the conversion and participation of the sacraments, through a process of radical transformation from death to life, from condemnation to salvation, from trauma to growth.

c) *Imitation of Christ and sanctification:* as we have seen, his persistent desire to resemble his Lord, being like him implies suffering like him, suffering and overcoming evil like him, resuscitating like him, is also noticeably present in Paul. Symbolically, he every day resurrects, every time he overcomes the adverse. Sanctification, as a process of spiritual and moral growth after conversion, consists in the Pauline perspective fundamentally in growing in likeness to Christ, dying to oneself, living for him, in him, in the power of his Spirit, and through of each event, to be impelled to grow, to leave sin behind and to get stronger in faith, hope and love.

d) *Concrete eschatological hope:* finally, posttraumatic growth as a hermeneutical key to Christian faith and practice can be observed in Paul especially in the resurrection hope he possesses. It does not seem to be an abstract hope but a very concrete one, for the Apostle hoped to resurrect or be transformed (if he did not die before the return of Christ) bodily (very much in accordance with a non-dualistic Hebrew anthropological conception). The eschatological hope in Paul is therefore of posttraumatic fullness, of eternal blessing after this slight tribulation that has meant life.

12.5. Limitations of this Research, and Future Reseach Pespecctives

Our survey of the theme of positive coping with the adverse in 2 Corinthians, using the hermeneutical arc in the perspective of the Psychological Biblical Criticism, has led us to discover the particular modes of coping with traumatic events present in Paul's work, which in important aspects coincide with the discoveries of research on psychological resistance to stress, resilience, and posttraumatic growth. However, we must mention some of the limitations of our research.

In the present work we could have incorporated several pastoral and missiological applications of what we find in the Pauline texts regarding posttraumatic coping. However, given our approach that includes practical theology as "a hermeneutics of Christian praxis" (Hoch, 2011, p.76), "theological discernment in human action" (Brown, 2012, p. 113) or "hermeneutic of lived religion" (Ganzevoort, 2009a, p.1), here we have tried only to explore in a hermeneutic way, in autobiographical texts, the ways in which Paul faced the harsh adversities that he had to live. Rather than looking for patterns of pastoral or missiological action, we have privileged the understanding of the phenomenon of coping observed in the Pauline texts, interpreting them in the light of current studies on positive coping with traumatic events.

We must recognize that our approach to Pauline texts is one of many, since here we have opted to perform and exegetical overview of the selected section using some historical-critical contributions that, in our opinion, the text merited because of its strongly heterogeneous character. However, we could have employed other methods that also would have certainly produced relevant results. The same can be said about our perspective within Psychological Biblical Criticism, which in our case has allowed us to discuss the contributions of positive psychology to understanding positive coping with trauma and its concepts of stress resistance, resilience and posttraumatic growth.

A relevant aspect worth highlighting about the possible application of our results, in the field of counseling, pastoral care, or even psychotherapy and community psychosocial work, is the fact that in Paul we only find resources for coping that are exclusively associated with his dynamic of faith and his apostolic ministry, which was marked by adversity and traumatic events that occurred in the context of the cause of Christ. This makes their application limited to a religious understanding of specifically the Christian life. Therefore, it is difficult to apply these resources uncovered here to other types of circumstances and to groups that hold different beliefs about the sacred.

On the other hand, it is important to mention that the studies about the impact of the religious experience on coping with adversity have indicated that a religious system which is too tight and closed off can affect coping negatively. Extracting approaches to coping from the Pauline texts (in our case) that are too specific and prescriptive can make having a flexible religious perspective about adverse situations harder to come by. One would have to favor those approaches which have been demonstrated to be highly correlated with the wellbeing of people, i.e., the strategies of positive religious coping and the religious and/or theological approaches which present them-selves as a general framework open to a wide range of experiences (Pargament, 1997; Ganzevoort, 1998a; Pargament, Feuille & Burdzy, 2011).

Another limitation of our research, which at same time reveals a possible line of future research, is that our work has been bound to just a few sections of 2 Corinthians that explicitly refer to coping with traumatic events. Future investigations can seek to more completely integrate the contents of the whole epistle with the subject. It would also be pertinent to conduct a study along the same lines as ours but focusing on other Pauline texts (such as Philippians, for example) or with the whole Pauline corpus, as well as with the great variety of texts from Scripture that explicitly or implicitly approach the subject of adversity.

Regarding the future lines of research, for us it is important to maintain a perspective that intentionally avoids getting into the vast discussions about theodicy of theoretical type, in order to focus instead on the explicit or implicit practices of coping with adversity found in the Biblical texts. That is, to point to studies in the line of a practical theodicy (cf. Fettke & Dusing, 2016).

Finally, one concrete possibility for research line with what we have done would be to conduct empirical studies of high-stress contexts (penitentiaries, socioeconomically marginalized groups) or with populations subjected to traumatic events (earthquakes, tsunamis, terrorism, wars) with an intercultural reading of texts related to coping with adversity, such as the sections of 2 Corinthians we have analyzed. Studies of this kind could let us observe the ways that specific groups interpret and/or make use of the Scriptures to face situations of high stress, and be able to make advances in the field of the empirical theology as it relates to positive coping with traumatic events.

References

Aageson, J. W. (2007). Paul as Interpreter of the Bible. In: S. E. Porter (Ed.). *Dictionary of Biblical Criticism and Interpretation* (pp. 264-265). New York: Routledge.

Abdollahi, A., Talib, M. A., Yaacob, S. N. & Ismail, Z. (2016). Emotional Intelligence, Hardiness, and Smoking: Protective Factors Among Adolescents. *Journal of Child & Adolescent Substance Abuse*, 25(1), 11-17.

Abernathy, D. (2001). Paul's Thorn in the Flesh: A Messenger of Satan? *Neotestamentica* 35(1), 69-79.

Acero, P. D. (2008). Resistencia, resiliencia & crecimiento postraumático. Elementos para una mirada comprensiva y constructiva de la respuesta al trauma. *Intrapsiquis 1*, 2008. Online: http://www.psiquiatria.com/articulos/depresión/34054. Accessed March 15, 2010.

Acero, P. D. (2011). *La Otra Cara de la Tragedia: Resiliencia y Crecimiento Postraumático*. Bogotá: San Pablo.

Affleck, G. & Tennen, H. (1996). Construing Benefits from Adversity: Adaptational Significance and Dispositional Underpinnings. *Journal of Persobality* 64(4), 899-922.

Agamben, G. (2006). *El tiempo que resta. Comentario a la carta a los Romanos*. Madrid: Trotta.

Agnew, F. A. (1988). Paul's Theological Adversary in the Doctrine of Justification by Faith: A Contribution to Jewish Christian Dialogue. *JES*, 25, 538-54.

Agren, T. (2012). Erasing Fear. Effect of Disrupting Fear Memory Reconsolidation on Central and Peripheral Nervous System Activity. *Digital Comprehensive Summaries of Uppsala Dissertations from the Faculty of Social Sciences N° 81*.

Aguilera, C. (Coord.) (1988). *Historia del Pensamiento: Filosofía Antigua*. Madrid: Sarpe.

Ai, A. L., Peterson, C. & Huang, B. (2003). The Effect of Religious-Spiritual Coping on Positive Attitudes of Adult Muslim Refugees From Kosovo and Bosnia. *International Journal for the Psychology of Religion*, 13(1), 29-47

Akin, D. L. (1989). Triumphalism, Suffering, and Spiritual Maturity: An Exposition of 2 Corinthians 12:1-10 in its Literary, Theological, and Historical Context. *Criswell Theological Review 4*(1), 119-144.

Alberini, C.M & Leroux, J.E. (2013). Memory Reconsolidation. *Current Biology 23*(17), R746-R750.

Alberini, C.M. (Ed.) (2013). *Memory Reconsolidation.* London: Elsevier.

Alexander, P. H., Kutsko, J. F., Ernest, J. D., Decker-Lucke, S. & Petersen, D. L. (Eds.) (1999). *The SBL handbook of style: for Ancient Near Eastern, Biblical, and early Christian studies.* Peabody, MA: Hendrickson Publishers.

Alford, C. F. (2009). *After the Holocaust. The Book of Job, Primo Levi, and the Path to Affliction.* Cambridge: Cambridge University Press.

Algoe, S. B. & Stanton, A. L. (2012). Gratitude when it is needed most: social functions of gratitude in women with metastatic breast cancer. *Emotion, 12*(1), 163-168.

Allport, G. W. (1955). *Becoming.* New Haven, CT: Yale University Press.

Almedom, A. M. (2005). Resilience, hardiness, sense of coherence, and posttraumatic growth: All paths leading to "light at the end of the tunnel"? *Journal of Loss & Trauma, 10,* 253-265.

Alonso Schokel, L. (1971). *Job.* Madrid: Ediciones Cristiandad.

Alonso Schokel, L. (1996). *Biblia del Peregrino. Antiguo Testamento. Poesía.* Vol. II.2. Bilbao: Ega-Mensajero-Verbo Divino.

American Psychiatric Association (1980). *Diagnostic and Statistical manual of Mental Disorders, 3th Ed. (DSM-III).* Washington, DC: American Psychiatric Association.

American Psychiatric Association (1997). *Diagnostic and Statistical manual of Mental Disorders, 4ht Ed. (DSM-IV).* Washington, DC: American Psychiatric Association.

American Psychiatric Association (2000). *Diagnostic and Statistical manual of Mental Disorders, 4th Ed. Text Revision (DSM-IV-TR).* Washington, DC: American Psychiatric Association.

American Psychiatric Association (2013). *Diagnostic and statistical manual of mental disorders, 5th Ed. (DSM-5).* Washington, DC: American Psychiatric Association.

Améry, J. (1998). *At the Mind's Limits. Contemplations by a Survivor on Auschwitz and Its Realities.* Bloomington: Indiana University Press.

Amigo, F., Fernández, C. & Pérez, M. (1998). *Manual de psicología de la salud.* Madrid: Pirámide.

Andersen, P., Morris, R., Amaral, D., Bliss, T., & O'Keefe, J. (Ed.) (2007). *The Hippocampus Book.* Oxford: Oxford University Press.

Andriessen, P. (1959). L'impuissance de Paul en face de l'ange de Satan. *Nouveue Revue Theobgique, 81,* 462-468.

Anisman, H., Kokiinidis, L. & Sklar, L. S. (1985). Neurochemical consequences of stress-contributions of adaptative process. In: S.R. Burchfield. *Stress: psychological and physiological interactions.* Washington: Hemisphere.

Ano, G. G. & Vasconcelles, E. B. (2005). Religious coping and psychological adjustment to stress: A meta-analysis. *Journal of Clinical Psychology, 61,* 461-480.

Anthony, E. J. (1974). The syndrome of the psychologically invulnerable child. En E.J. Anthony & C. Koupernik (Eds.). *The child in his family: Children at psychiatric risk.* New York: Wiley, 3-10.

Antonovsky, A. & Sourani, T. (1988). Family sense of coherence and family sense of adaptation. *Journal of marriage and the family, 50,* 79-92.

Antonovsky, A. (1979). *Health, Stress, and Coping. New Perspectives on Mental and Physical Well-Being.* San Francisco: Jossey-Bass.

Antonovsky, A. (1984). A call for a new question—salutogenesis—and a proposed answer—the sense of coherence. *Journal of Preventive Psychiatry, 2,* 1–13.

Antonovsky, A. (1987). *Unraveling the mystery of health: How people manage stress and stay well.* San Francisco: Jossey-Bass.

Antonovsky, A. (1993). Complexity, conflict, chaos, coherence, coercion and civility. *Social Science and Medicine, 37,* 969–974.

Appelfeld, A. (1983). *Tzili: the story of a life.* New York: Schocken Books.

Apuleius, L. (2006). *The Golden Asse.* In: The Project Gutenberg eBook. *Online: http://www.gutenberg.org/files/1666/1666-h/1666-h.htm#link2H_4_0044.* Accessed February 16, 2017.

Aranda-Pérez, G., García-Martínez, F. & Pérez-Fernández, M. (1996). *Literatura Judía Intertestamentaria.* Navarra: Verbo Divino.

Arce, L. (2017). *El Infierno.* Santiago de Chile: Tajamar.

Arciero, G. & Bondolfi, G. (2009). *Selfood, Identity and Personality Styles*. Oxford: Wiley-Blackwell.

Arciero, G. (2006). *Estudio y Diálogos sobre la identidad personal: reflexiones sobre la expriencia humana*. Buenos Aires: Amorrortu.

Arciero, G. (2009). *Tras las huellas de Sí mismo*. Buenos Aires: Amorrortu.

Arciero, G. (2010). *Psicopatología y Clínica: Diálogos entre la Fenomenología-Hermenéutica, las Ciencias Cognitivo-Afectivas y la Neurociencia*. Seminario Internacional 4-6 de noviembre, 2010. Santiago de Chile: Universidad Adolfo Ibáñez / Sociedad de Terapia Cognitiva Posracionalista.

Arciero, G. (2010). Vittorio Guidano a dieci anni Della scomparsa: reflessioni sul futuro del post-razionalismo. Entervista Arciero-Liccione. Roma: IPRA. Online: ‹www.ipra.it.22-mar-2010› Accessed: 25 June 2011.

Arciero, G. (2012). *Método en Psicoterapia. Actualizaciones en psicoterapia desde el modelo Constructivista Hermenéutico*. Seminario Internacional 8-10 de noviembre, 2012. Santiago de Chile: Universidad Adolfo Ibáñez / Sociedad de Terapia Cognitiva Posracionalista.

Arciero, G., Bondolfi, G., & Mazzola, V. (2018). *The Foundations of Phenomenological Psychotherapy*. Cham: Springer.

Argue, A., Johnson, D. R. & White, L. K. (1999). Age and religiosity: Evidence from a three-wave panel analysis. *Journal for the Scientific Study of Religion, 38* (3), 423-435.

Armario, A. (2000). Estrés: aspectos psicobiológicos y significado funcional. In: C. Sandi, J.M. Calés (eds.), *Estrés: consecuencias psicológicas, fisiológicas y clínicas* (pp. 47-81). Madrid: Sanz & Torres.

Arnold, M. (2003). Fundamentos del constructivismo sociopoiético. *Cinta de Moebio 18*. Online: ‹www.facso.uchile.cl/publicaciones/moebio/18/arnold.htm› Accessed 20 July 2012.

Arteche, M., Massone, J.A. & Scarpa, R.E. (1984). *Poesía chilena contemporanea*. 2da. Ed. Santiago de Chile: Andrés Bello.

Atwoli, L., Stein, D. J., Koenen, K. C. & McLaughlin, K. A. (2015). Epidemiology of posttraumatic stress disorder: prevalence, correlates and consequences. *Current Opinion in Psychiatry, 28*(4), 307–311.

Avdi, E. & Georgaca, E. (2007). Narrative research in psychotherapy: A critical review. *Psychology and Psychotherapy: Theory, Research and Practice 80*, 407–419.

Bade, M. K., & Cook, S. W. (2008). Functions of Christian prayer in the coping process. *Journal for the Scientific Study of Religion, 47*(1), 123-133.

Badiou, A. (1999). *San Pablo: La fundación del universalismo.* Barcelona: Anthropos.

Balentine, S. (2015). *Have You Considered My Servant Job? Understanding the Biblical Archetype of Patience.* Columbia, SC: University of South Carolina Press.

Barclay, W. (1995). *1ª y 2ª de Corintios.* Barcelona: Clie.

Barclay, W. (2002). *Palabras Griegas del Nuevo Testamento.* 9ª Ed. El Paso, TX: Casa Bautista de Publicaciones.

Barnett, P. W. (1984). Opposition in Corinth. *Journal for the Study of the New Testament, 7*(22), 3-17.

Barnett, P. W. (1993). Opponents of Paul. In: G. F. Hawthorne & R. P. Martin (Ed.). *Dictionary of Paul and His Letters.* Downers Grove, IL: InterVarsity Press, 700-706.

Barré, M. L. (1980). Qumran and the" Weakness" of Paul. *The Catholic Biblical Quarterly, 42*(2), 216-227.

Barrett, C. K. (1971). Paul's Opponents in II Corinthians. *New Testament Studies, 17*(03), 233-254.

Barrett, C. K. (1973). *A Commentary on the Second Epistle to the Corinthians.* New York: Harper & Row.

Barrett, C. K. (1982). *Essays on Paul.* London: SPCK.

Barrier, J. (2005). Visions of Weakness: Apocalyptic Genre and the Identification of Paul's Opponents in 2 Corinthians 12:1-6. *Restoration Quarterly, 47*: 33-42.

Barton, S. C. (2003). Paul as Missionary and Pastor. In: J.D. Dunn (Ed.), *The Cambridge Companion to St. Paul* (pp. 34-50). Cambridge: Cambridge University Press.

Bassler, J. M. (2010). Paul and his Letters. In: D. E. Aune (Ed.). *The Blackwell Companion to the New Testament.* Oxford: John Wiley & Sons, 391-415.

Bassler, J. M. (Ed.) (1991). *Pauline theology, Vol I:* Thessalonians, Philippians, Galatians, Philemon. Minneapolis: Fortress Press.

Bassler, J. M., Hay, D. M. & Johnson, E. E. (Eds.). (1995). *Pauline Theology, Vol III: Romans.* Minneapolis: Augsburg Fortress Publishing.

Baum, A. & Contrada, R. (Eds.). (2010). *The handbook of stress science: Biology, psychology, and health.* New York: Springer.

Beale, G. K. & Carson, D. A. (Eds.) (2007). *Commentary on the New Testament use of the Old Testament.* Baker Academic.

Beck, A., Rush, A., Shaw, B. & Emery, G. (1993). *Terapia Cognitiva de la depresión.* Bilbao: Desclée de Brower.

Beck, J. (2002). *The Psychology of Paul: A Fresh Look at His Life and Teaching.* Grand Rapids, MI: Kregel.

Becker, J. (2007). *Pablo. El Apóstol de los Paganos.* Salamanca: Sígueme.

Bededict XVI (2007). *Encyclical Letter Spe Salvi.* Online: http://w2.vatican.va/ content/benedict-xvi/en/encyclicals/documents/hf_ben-xvi_enc_20071130_spe-salvi. html. Accessed: 25 January, 2018.

Behm, J. (1964). ἀρραβών. In: G. Kittel, G.W. Bromiley & G. Friedrich (Eds.) *Theological dictionary of the New Testament.* Vols. I-X (HTM Digital Version). Grand Rapids, MI: Eerdmans.

Benedict, A. L., Mancini, L. & Grodin, M.A. (2009). Struggling to meditate: Contextualising integrated treatment of traumatised Tibetan refugee monks. *Mental Health, Religion & Culture,* 12: 5, 485-499.

Benyakar, M. (1997). Definición, Diagnóstico y Clínica del Estrés & el Trauma. *Revista Electrónica de Psiquiatría,* 1 (43). Online: ‹http://www.psiquiatria. com/psiquiatria/vol1num4/art_5.htm›. Accessed January 3, 2011.

Berczi, I. & Szelenyi, J. (Eds.) (1994). *Advances in Psychoneuroimmunology.* New York: Springer.

Berger, R. & Weiss, T. (2006). Posttraumatic Growth in Latina Immigrants. *Journal of Immigrant & Refugee Studies,* 4: 3, 55-72.

Berger, R. (2015). *Stress, Trauma, and Posttraumatic Growth. Social Context, Environment, and Identities.* New York: Routledge.

Bergmann, M., Murray, M. J. & Rea, M. C. (Eds.) (2011). *Divine Evil? The Moral Character of the God of Abraham*. Oxford: Oxford University Press.

Bernard, H. R. & Ryan, G. W. (2010). *Analyzing Qualitative Data: Systematic Approaches*. California, CA: Sage Publication.

Berryman, P. (1987). *Liberation Theology. The Essential Facts about the Revolutionary Movement in Latin America and Beyond*. New York: Pantheon Books.

Berthold, F. Jr. (2004). *God, Evil, and Human Learning. A Critique and Revision of the Free Will Defense in Theodicy*. New York: State University of New York Press.

Bertram, G. (1964). κατείδωλος. In: G. Kittel, G.W. Bromiley & G. Friedrich (Eds.) *Theological dictionary of the New Testament*. Vols. I-X (HTM Digital Version). Grand Rapids, MI: Eerdmans.

Betz, H. D. (1979). *Galatians: A Commentary on Paul's Letter to the Churches in Galatia*. Philadelphia: Fortress Press.

Betz, H. D. (1985). *2 Corinthians 8 and 9: A Commentary on Two Administrative Letters of the Apostle Paul*. Philadelphia: Fortress Press.

Bianchi, U., Cheng, A., Clément, O, Cosi, D. M., Margolin, J-C, Massein, P., Paolini, L., Ries, J., Sfameni Gasparro, G. & Sironneau, J-P. (2001). *Tratado de antropología de lo sagrado 4: crisis, ruptura y cambios*. Madrid: Trotta.

Bieringer, R., Nathan, E. & Kurek-Chomycz, D. (2008). *2 Corinthians. A Bibliography*. Leuven: Peeters.

Bigbee, J. L. (1992). Family stress, hardiness, and illness: A pilot study. *Family Relations, 41*(2), 212-217.

Biggs, A., Brough, P. & Drummond, S. (2017). Lazarus and Folkman's psychological stress and coping theory. In: *The Handbook of Stress and Health: A Guide to Research and Practice*. (pp. 349-364). Oxford: John Wiley & Sons.

Bird, M. F. (2008). *A Bird's-Eye View of Paul: The Man, His Mission and His Message*. Nottingham: InterVarsity Press.

Bird, M. F. (Ed) (2012). *Four Views on the Apostle Paul. Counterpoints: Bible and Theology*. Grand Rapids: Zondervan.

Birnbaum, A. (2008). Collective trauma and post-traumatic symptoms in the biblical narrative of ancient Israel. *Mental Health, Religion & Culture, 11*(5), 533-546.

Bishop, E. F. F. (1971). Pots of Earthenware. *EvQ, 43,* 3-5.

Bisson, J. I., Ehlers, A., Matthews, R., Pilling S., Richards, D. & Turner, S. (2007). Psychological treatments for chronic post-traumatic stress disorder. *British Journal of Psychiatry 190:*97–104.

Black, D. A. (1984). Paulus Infirmus: The Pauline Concept of Weakness. *Grace Theological Journal, 5*(1), 77-93

Blix, I., Birkeland, M. S., Hansen, M. B. & Heir, T. (2016). Posttraumatic growth—An antecedent and outcome of posttraumatic stress: Cross-lagged associations among individuals exposed to terrorism. *Clinical Psychological Science, 4*(4), 620-628.

Boals, A. & Schuettler, D. (2009). PTSD symptoms in response to traumatic and nontraumatic events: The role of respondent perception and A2 criterion. *Journal of Anxiety Disorders, 23,* 458–462.

Bobele, M. (1989). A comparison of beliefs about healthy family functioning. *Family Therapy, 16*(1), 21-31.

Boeri, M. D. & Salles, R. (2014). *Los Filósofos Estoicos. Ontología, lógica, física y ética. Traducción, comentario filosófico y edición anotada de los principales textos griegos y latinos.* Santiago de Chile: Ediciones Universidad Alberto Hurtado.

Boff, L & Boff, C. (1986). *Cómo hacer teología de la liberación.* Madrid: Paulinas.

Boff, L. (1986). *Teología desde el lugar del pobre.* Santander: Sal Terrae.

Boff, L. (2002). *Experimentar a Dios. La transparencia de todas las cosas.* Santander: Sal Terrae.

Boivin, M. J. & Giordani, B. (Eds.) (2013). *Neuropsychology of Children in Africa. Perspectives on Risk and Resilience.* New York: Springer.

Bonanno, G. A. (2004). Loss, trauma and human resilience: Have we underestimated the human capacity to thrive after extremely aversive events? *American Psychologist, 59,* 20-28.

Bonanno, G. A., Pat-Horenczyk, R. & Noll, J. (2011). Coping flexibility and trauma: The Perceived Ability to Cope With Trauma (PACT) scale. *Psychological Trauma: Theory, Research, Practice, and Policy, 3*(2), 117-129.

Boniwell, I. (2006). *Positive Psychology in a Nutshell. A balanced introduction to the science of optimal functioning.* London: Personal Well-Being Centre.

Borg, M. J. & Crossan, J.D. (2009). *The First Paul. Reclaiming the Radical Visionary Behind the Church's Conservative Icon.* New York: HarperCollins.

Bornkamm, G. (1978). *Pablo de Tarso.* Salamanca: Sígueme.

Botella, L. & Herrero, O. (2001). *Pérdida y duelo desde una visión constructivista narrativa.* Barcelona: Universidad Ramon Llull.

Botella, L., Herrero, O. & Pacheco, M. (1997). *Pérdida y Reconstrucción: una aproximación constructivista al análisis del duelo.* Blanquerna: FPCEE.

Botella, L., Pacheco, M. & Herrero, O. (1999). *Pensamiento posmoderno constructivo & psicoterapia.* Barcelona: Universidad Ramon Llull.

Boudewijnse, B., Droogers, A. & Kamsteeg, F. (1991). *Algo más que opio: una lectura antropológica del pentecostalismo latinoamericano y caribeño.* San José de Costa Rica: DEI.

Bowker, J. W. (1971)."Merkabah" Visions and the Visions of Paul. *JSS, 16,* 157-173.

Bowlby, J. (1973). *Separation: Anxiety & Anger. Attachment and Loss.* Vol. 2. London: Hogarth Press.

Bowlby, J. (1980). *Loss: Sadness & Depression. Attachment and Loss.* Vol. 3. London: Hogarth Press.

Bowlby, J. (1999). *Attachment. Attachment and Loss.* Vol. 1 (2th ed). New York: Basic Books.

Bracken, P. J. (2002). *Trauma. Culture, Meaning and Philosophy.* London: Whurr Publishers.

Bradley, K. (1994). *Slavery and Society at Rome.* Cambridge: Cambridge University Press.

Breslau, N., Chilcoat, H. D., Kessler, R. C., Peterson, E. L., & Lucia, V. C. (1999). Vulnerability to assaultive violence: further specification of the sex difference in posttraumatic stress disorder. *Psychological Medicine, 29*(4), 813-821.

Breslau, N., Davis, G. C., Andreski, P. & Peterson, E. (1991). Traumatic events and posttraumatic stress disorder in an urban population of young adults. *Archives of general psychiatry, 48*(3), 216-222.

Breslau, N., Davis, G. C., Peterson, E. L. & Schultz, L. (1997). Psychiatric sequelae of posttraumatic stress disorder in women. *Archives of General Psychiatry, 54*(1), 81-87.

Breslau, N., Davis, G. C., Peterson, E. L. & Schultz, L. (1997). Psychiatric sequelae of posttraumatic stress disorder in women. *Archives of General Psychiatry, 54*(1), 81-7.

Breslau, N., Kessler, R. C., Chilcoat, H. D., Schultz, L. R., Davis, G. C. & Andreski, P. (1998). Trauma and posttraumatic stress disorder in the community: the 1996 Detroit Area Survey of Trauma. *Archives of General Psychiatry, 55*(7), 626-632.

Briere, J. N. & Scott, C. (2014). *Principles of trauma therapy: A guide to symptoms, evaluation, and treatment (DSM-5 update)*. 2nd Ed. London: Sage Publications.

Briere, J., Scott, C., & Weathers, F. (2005). Peritraumatic and persistent dissociation in the presumed etiology of PTSD. *American Journal of Psychiatry, 162*(12), 2295-2301.

Brizzio, A. & Carreras, A. (2007). Variables Salugenicas y su Relación con los Sucesos de Vida. *Revista Iberoamericana de Diagnóstico y Evaluación Psicológica, 23*(1), 83-99.

Brizzio, A. & Carreras, A. (2007). Variables salugénicas y su relación con los sucesos de vida. *RIDEP, 23*(1), 83-99.

Brody, G. H., Stoneman, Z. & Flor, D. (1996). Parental religiosity, family processes, and youth competence in rural, two-parent African American families. *Developmental Psychology, 32*, 696-706.

Brown, A. R. (1998). *The Gospel Takes Place:* Paul's Theology of Power-in Weakness in 2 Corinthians. *Interpretation, 52*(3), 271-286.

Brown, C. (Ed.) (1985). *The New International Dictionary of New Testament Theology*. Vols. I-IV (Digital version). Grand Rapids, MI: Regency.

Brown, R. E. (2002). *Introducción al Nuevo Testamento*. Tomos I - II. Madrid: Trotta.

Brown, R. E., Fitzmyer, J.A. & Murphy, R.E. (Dir.) (1972). *Comentario Bíblico "San Jerónimo", Tomo IV*. Madrid: Cristiandad.

Brown, R. E., Fitzmyer, J.A. & Murphy, R.E. (Eds.) (2004). *Nuevo Comentario Bíblico San Jerónimo. Nuevo Testamento y artículos temáticos.* Navarra: Verbo Divino.

Brown, S. A. (2012). Hermeneutical Theory. In: J.B. Miller-McLemore (Ed.). *The Wiley Blackwell Companion to Practical Theology* (pp. 112-122). Oxford: John Wiley & Sons.

Brownlee, K., Rawana, J., Franks, J., Harper, J., Bajwa, J., O'Brien, E. & Clarkson, A. (2013). A systematic review of strengths and resilience outcome literature relevant to children and adolescents. *Child and Adolescent Social Work Journal, 30*(5), 435-459.

Brudholm, T. (2008). *Resentment's virtue: Jean Améry and the refusal to forgive.* Philadelphia, PA: Temple University Press.

Brueggemann, W. & Linafelt, T. (2012). *An Introduction to the Old Testament. The Canon and Christian Imagination.* 2nd. Ed. Louisville: Westminster John Knox Press

Brueggemann, W. (1985). *The Message of the Psalms. A Theological Commentary.* Minneapolis: Fortress Press.

Brueggemann, W. (1986). *Revelation and violence. A study in contextualization.* Wisconsin: Marquette University Press.

Brueggemann, W. (2007). *Teología del Antiguo Testamento. Un juicio a Yahvé Testimonio.* Disputa. Defensa. Salamanca: Sígueme.

Brüll, F. (1969). The Trauma: theoretical considerations. *The Israel annals of psychiatry and related disciplines, 7,* 96-108.

Bruner, J. (1997). *Realidad Mental y Mundos Posibles.* Barcelona: Gedisa.

Budick, E. M. (2005). *Aharon Appelfeld's Fiction: acknowledging the Holocaust.* Bloomington: Indiana University Press.

Buitrago, X. & Restrepo, L. (2006). *Arte y Resiliencia: una propuesta política para la convivencia.* Master Thesis. Bogota: Universidad de La Salle.

Bultmann, R. & Jaspers, K. (1968). *Jesús. La Desmitologización del Nuevo Testamento.* Buenos Aires: Sur.

Bultmann, R. (1955), *Theology of New Testament. Vol. II.* New York: C. Scribner's Sons.

Bultmann, R. (1964). πιστεύω, πίστις, πιστός. In: G. Kittel, G.W. Bromiley & G. Friedrich (Eds.) *Theological dictionary of the New Testament.* Vols. I-X (HTM Digital Version). Grand Rapids, MI: Eerdmans.

Bultmann, R. (1985). *The Second Letter to the Corinthians*. Minneapolis: Augsburg.

Buzsáki, G. (2006). *Rhythms of the Brain*. Oxford: Oxford University Press.

Cacioppo, J.T., Reis, H.T. & Zautra, A.J. (2011). Social resilience: The value of social fitness with an application to the military. *American Psychologist, 66*(1), 43-51.

Cadell, S., Karabanow, J. & Sanchez, M. (2001). Community, empowerment and resilience: paths to wellness. *Canadian Journal Community Mental Health, 20*(1), 21-35.

Cadell, S., Regehr, C. & Hemsworth, D. (2003). Factors contributing to posttraumatic growth: A proposed structural equation model. *American Journal of Orthopsychiatry, 73*(3), 279-287.

Calhoun, L. G. & Tedeschi, R. (1999). *Facilitating Posttraumatic Growth: A Clinician's Guide*. Mahwah, N.J.: Lawrence Erlbaum Associates Publishers.

Calhoun, L. G. & Tedeschi, R. G. (1998). Beyond recovery from trauma: Implications for clinical practice and research. *Journal of social Issues,54*(2), 357-371.

Calhoun, L. G. & Tedeschi, R. G. (2001). Posttraumatic growth: The positive lesson of loss. In: Neimeyer, R. *Meaning Construction and the Experience of Loss*, Washington, DC: APA.

Calhoun, L. G. & Tedeschi, R. G. (2004a). Posttraumatic Growth: Conceptual Foundations and Empirical Evidence. *Psychological Inquiry, 15*(1), 1-18.

Calhoun, L. G. & Tedeschi, R. G. (2008). Crecimiento postraumático en las intervenciones clínicas cognitivo-conductuales. In: V. Caballo (Ed). *Manual para el tratamiento cognitivo-conductual de los trastornos psicológicos* (pp. 30-49). Madrid: Siglo XXI.

Calhoun, L. G. & Tedeschi, R. G. (Eds.) (2006). *The Handbook of Posttraumatic Growth: Research and Practice*. Mahwah, NJ: Lawrence Erlbaum Associates Publishers.

Calhoun, L.G. & Tedeschi, R. G. (2004b). The Foundations of Posttraumatic Growth: New Considerations. *Psychological Inquiry, 15*(1), 93-102.

Callan, T. (1990). Psychological Perspectives on the Life of Paul: An Application of the Methodology of Gerd Theissen. New York: Edwin Mellen Press.

Calvin, J. (1964). *The Second Epistle of Paul the Apostle to the Corinthians and the Epistles to Timothy, Titus, and Philemon.* Grand Rapids, MI: Eerdmans.

Cameron, R. & Miller, M. P. (Eds.) (2011). *Redescribing Paul and the Corinthians.* Atlanta: Society of Biblical Literature.

Cannon, W. B. (1932). *The wisdom of the body.* Nueva York: Norton.

Caplan, G. (1982). The family as a support system. In H. I. McCubbin, A. E. Cauble & J. M. Patterson (Eds.), *Family stress, coping, and social support* (pp. 200-220). Springfield, IL: Charles C Thomas.

Caputo, J. & Alcoff, L. M. (2009). *St. Paul among the Philosophers.* Bloomington-Indianapolis: Indiana University Press.

Cardinali, D. P. (2007). *Neurociencia Aplicada: Sus Fundamentos.* Buenos Aires: Médica Panamericana.

Carrez, M. (1986). *La segunda carta a los corintios.* Navarra: Verbo Divino.

Caruana Vañó, A. (Coord.) (2010). *Aplicaciones Educativas de la Psicología Positiva.* Valencia: CEFIRE.

Caruana, C. (2010). Picking up the pieces: Family functioning in the aftermath of natural disaster. *Family Matters, 84,* 79-88.

Cassidy, R. (1971). Paul's Attitude to Death in II Corinthians 5: 1-10. *Evangelical Quarterly, 43,* 210-217.

Castro, J. (1997). *En busca del tesoro escondido: espiritualidad cristiana & psicología junguiana.* 2ª Ed. Santiago de Chile: Ediciones Universidad Católica de Chile.

Catalano, D., Chan, F., Wilson, L., Chiu, C. & Muller, V.R. (2011). The buffering effect of resilience on depression among individuals with spinal cord injury: A structural equation model. *Rehabilitation Psychology, 56(3),* 200-211.

Cederblad, M., Dahlin, L., Hagnell, O. & Hansson, K. (1995). Coping with life span crises in a group at risk of mental and behavioral disorders: From the Lundby study. *Acta Psychiatrica Scandinavica, 91,* 322-330.

Cerci, D. & Colucci, E. (2018). Forgiveness in PTSD after man-made traumatic events. A systematic review. *Traumatology, 24(1),* 47.

Chambling, J. K. (1993). *Paul and the Self: Apostolic Teaching for Personal Wholeness.* Grand Rapids: Baker.

Chan, J. C. & LaPaglia, J. A. (2013). Impairing existing declarative memory in humans by disrupting reconsolidation. *Proceedings of the National Academy of Sciences, 110*(23), 9309-9313.

Chang, S. S. H. (2002). The Integrity of 2 Corinthians: 1980-2000. *Torch Trinity Journal, 5,* 167-202.

Cheavens, J.S. & Dreer, L.E. (2009). Coping. In: S.J. Lopez. *The Encyclopedia of Positive Psychology.* Oxford: John Wiley & Sons, 232-239.

Christensen, A. & Escobar, J. (2010). Así se gestó el megaterremoto, el más intenso en Chile desde 1960. *La Tercera.* Santiago de Chile, 28 de febrero, 2010. Online: http://diario.latercera.com/2010/02/28/01/contenido/9_25222_9.html. Accessed May 3, 2010.

Christianson, E. S. (2005). *Ecclesiastes.* Oxford: Blackwell.

Christianson, E. S. (2007). *Ecclesiastes through the centuries.* Oxford: Blackwell.

Ciccotti, E. (2005). *La Esclavitud en Grecia, Roma y el Mundo Cristiano.* Barcelona: Círculo Latino.

Coenen, L., Beyreuther, E. & Bietenhard, H. (1990). *Diccionario Teológico del Nuevo Testamento.* 3 Ed. Tomos I-VI. Salamanca: Sígueme.

Cohen, S. (1980). Aftereffects of stress on human performance and social behavior: a review of research and theory. *Psychological Bulletin, 88,* 81-108.

Colomer, E. (2002). *El Pensamiento Alemán de Kant a Heidegger. Tomo III.* 2° Ed. Barcelona: Herder.

Conrad, C. D. (Ed.). (2011). *The Handbook of Stress: Neuropsychological Effects on the Brain.* Oxford: John Wiley & Sons.

Contrada, R. J. & Baum, A. (2011). *The Handbook of Stress Science: Biology, Psychology, and Health.* New York: Springer.

Cooper, C. L. & Quick, J. C. (Eds.). (2017). *The Handbook of Stress and Health: A Guide to Research and Practice.* Oxford: John Wiley & Sons.

Copeland, K. & Gorey, C. (2012). The effects of early adverse life experiences on the HPA axis and their impact on the development of depression. *Undergraduate Journal of Psychology at Berkeley, 5,* 13-18.

Corbin, J. & Strauss, A. (1990). Grounded theory method: Procedures, canons, and evaluative criteria. *Qualitative Sociology, 13*, 3-21.

Corrales, N. (2002). *Teoría del Trauma.* Buenos Aires: Longseller.

Cortés, B.G.M. & Cruz, L.P. (2011). Resilience: is it possible to measure and influence it? *Salud Mental, 34(3)*, 237-246.

Cothenet, E. (1985). *San Pablo en su tiempo.* 4° Ed. Navarra: Verbo Divino.

Courtenay, B. C., Poon, L. W., Martin, P., Clayton, G. M. & Johnson, M. A. (1992). Religiosity and adaptation in the oldest-old. *International Journal of Aging and Human Development, 42(3)*, 249-250.

Coutsoumpos, P. (2008). Paul, the Cults in Corinth, and the Corinthian Correspondence. In: S.E. Porter (Ed.) *Paul's World* (pp. 171-180). Boston: Brill.

Cowen, E. I., Gardner, E.A. & Zax, M. (Eds.) (1967). *Emergent Approaches to Mental Health problems: An overview and directions for future work.* New York: Appleton-Century-Crofts.

Cowen, E.L. (1991). In pursuit of wellness. *American Psychologist, 46*, 404-408.

Cowen, E.L. (1994). The enhancement of psychological wellness: Challenges and opportunities. *American Journal of Community Psychology, 22*, 149-179.

Cox, T. & Mackay, C. J. (1981). A Transactional approach to occupational stress. In E.N. Corlett and J. Richardson (Eds.), *Stress, Work Design and Productivity.* Chichester: Wiley & Sons.

Crenshaw, J. L. (2005). *Defending God: Biblical Responses to the Problem of Evil.* New York: Oxford University Press.

Cristaudo, W. (2008). *Power, Love and Evil. Contribution to a Philosophy of the Damaged.* Amsterdam-New York: Rodopi.

Croatto. J. S. (1994). *Hermenéutica Bíblica. Para una teoría de la lectura como producción de sentido.* 2da Ed. Buenos Aires: Lumen.

Crook, Z. (2009). Honor, Shame, and Social Status Revisited. *Journal of Biblical Literature, 128* (3): 591-611.

Crossan, J. D. & Reed, J. L. (2006). *En busca de Pablo. El Imperio de Roma y el Reino de Dios frente a frente en una nueva visión de las palabras y el mundo del apóstol de Jesús.* Navarra: Verbo Divino.

Crossan, J. D. & Reed, J.L. (2004). *In Search of Paul: How Jesus's Apostle Opposed Rome's Empire with God's Kingdom.* San Francisco: Harper San Francisco.

Crossan, J. D. (2007). *God and Empire: Jesus Against Rome, Then and Now.* New York: HarperCollins.

Crownfield, D. R. (1979). The self beyond itself: hermeneutics and transpersonal experience. *Journal of the American Academy of Religion,47*(2), 245-267.

Cruz-Villalobos, L. (2004). *Tormenta Crisol.* Santiago de Chile: Hebel.

Cruz-Villalobos, L. (2007). Resiliencia: una novedad antigua. In: H. Santos (Ed.). *Dimensiones del cuidado y asesoramiento pastoral: aportes desde América Latina y el Caribe* (pp. 261-276). Buenos Aires: Ediciones Kairós.

Cruz-Villalobos, L. (2009). *¿Constructores de Resiliencia? Aproximaciones desde la Resiliencia al Pentecostalismo chileno.* Santiago de Chile: Ediciones CIRES.

Cruz-Villalobos, L. (2011). Resiliencia y Experiencia Pentecostal. In: M.A. Mansilla & L. Orelllana (Eds.). *La Religión en Chile del Bicentenario* (pp. 59-78). Santiago de Chile: RELEP.

Cruz-Villalobos, L. (2012). Posibles Deconstrucciones del Trauma. Una aproximación posmoderna. *Revista Sociedad & Equidad, 3,* 172-194.

Cruz-Villalobos, L. (2014a). *Hermenéuticas del Trauma. Aproximación al Trauma y su Afrontamiento Positivo como Fenómenos Hermenéuticos.* Master in Clinical Psychology Thesis. University of Chile.

Cruz-Villalobos, L. (2014b). Psicología y Hermenéutica de la Esperanza. Aportes desde una revisión crítica de los conceptos de sí-mismo y trauma. In: H.F. Bullón (Ed.) (2015). *Misión Holística, Acción Interdisciplinaria y Realidad Latinoamericana* (pp. 75-109). Grand Rapids, MI: Desafío.

Cruz-Villalobos, L. (2016). Esta leve tribulación momentanea. Afrontamientos religiosos, crecimiento postraumático y potencial eclesial/pentecostal. In: A. Fajado & D. Mesquiati de Oliveira (Org.). *FTL 45 anos. E as fronteiras teológicas na contemporaneidade: Consulta Continental 2015* (pp. 187-243). Sao Paulo: Garimpo.

Cuestas, A., Estamatti, M. & Melillo, A. (2002). Algunos fundamentos psicológicos del concepto de resiliencia. In: A. Melillo & E.

Ojeda. *Resiliencia: descubriendo las propias fortalezas* (pp. 83-102). Buenos Aires: Paidós.

Cutuli, J. J. & Masten, A.S. (2009). Resilience. In: S.J. Lopez. *The Encyclopedia of Positive Psychology* (pp. 837-843). Oxford: John Wiley & Sons.

Cyrulnik, B. (2001). *La Maravilla del Dolor.* Barcelona: Granica.

Cyrulnik, B. (2002). *Los Patitos Feos. Resiliencia: una infancia infeliz no determina la vida.* Barcelona: Gedisa.

Cyrulnik, B. (2003). *El Murmullo de los Fantasmas.* Barcelona: Gedisa.

Cyrulnik, B. (2007). *De Cuerpo y Alma.* Barcelona: Gedisa.

Cyrulnik, B. (2009). *El Amor que nos Cura.* Barcelona: Gedisa.

D'Alessio, L. (2010). *Mecanismos Neurobiológicos de la Resiliencia.* Buenos Aires: Polemos.

Dalgleish, T. (2004). Cognitive approaches to posttraumatic stress disorder: the evolution of multirepresentational theorizeng. *Psychological Bulletin,130*(2), 228-260.

Danker, F. W. (1989). *II Corinthian.* Minneapolis: Augsburg.

Davidson, J. R., Hughes, D., Blazer, D. G. & George, L. K. (1991). Post-traumatic stress disorder in the community: an epidemiological study. *Psychological Medicine, 21*(3), 713-721.

Davis, C., Nolen-Hoeksema, S. & Larson, J. (1998). Making Sense of Loss and Benefiting from the Experience: Two Construals of Meaning. *Journal of Personality and Social Psychology, 75*, 561-574.

Davis, D. E., Hook, J. N., Worthington Jr., E. L., Gartner, A. L., Jennings II, D. J., Greer, C. L., Van Tongeren, D. R., & Greer, T. W. (2011). Evil and Positive Psychology. In: J. H. Ellens (Ed.). *Explaining Evil. Vol. 3. Approaches, Responses, Solutions* (pp. 220-236). Oxford: Praeger.

De Wit, H. (2001). *En la Dispersión el Texto es Patria. Introducción a la Hermenéutica Clásica, Moderna y Posmoderna.* San José, Costa Rica: UBL.

De Wit, H. (2010). *Por un Solo Gesto de Amor. Lectura de la Biblia desde una Práctica Intercultural.* Buenos Aires: ISEDET.

Debergé, P. (2005). *Pablo, el Pastor.* Navarra: Verbo Divino.

Deębiec, J., Doyère, V., Nader, K., & LeDoux, J. E. (2006). Directly reactivated, but not indirectly reactivated, memories undergo reconsolidation in the amygdala. *Proceedings of the National Academy of Sciences, 103*(9), 3428-3433.

Delage, M. (2010). *La Resiliencia Familiar. El Nicho Familiar y la Superación de las Heridas.* Barcelona: Gedisa.

Deleuze, G. (1993). *Critique et Clinique.* París: Les Éditions de Minuit.

Dell, K. & Kynes, W. (2012). *Reading Job Intertextually.* New York-London: Bloomsbury T&T Clark.

Den Heyer, C. J. (2000). *Paul. A Man of Two Worlds.* Harrisburg: Trinity Press International.

Denney, R. M., Aten, J.D. & Leavell, K. (2011). Posttraumatic spiritual growth: a phenomenological study of cancer survivors. *Mental Health, Religion & Culture, 14*(4), 371-391.

Derks, N. A., Krugers, H. J., Hoogenraad, C. C., Joëls, M. & Sarabdjitsingh, R. A. (2017). Effects of early life stress on rodent hippocampal synaptic plasticity: a systematic review. *Current Opinion in Behavioral Sciences, 14,* 155-166.

Diehl, M. & Hay, E. L. (2010). Risk and resilience factors in coping with daily stress in adulthood: the role of age, self-concept incoherence, and personal control. *Developmental Psychology, 46* (5), 1132-1146.

Diekelmann, S., Born, J., & Wagner, U. (2010). Sleep enhances false memories depending on general memory performance. *Behavioural Brain Research, 208*(2), 425-429.

Diez-Macho, A. (Ed.) (1984). *Introducción General a los Apócrifos del Antiguo Testamento.* Vol. I. Madrid: Cristiandad.

Driver, M. (2011). *Coaching Positively. Lessons for coaches from positive psychology.* New York: McGraw-Hill.

Dreyfus, H. L. (1996). *Ser-en-el-mundo: comentários a la división I de Ser y Tiempo de Martin Heidegger.* Santiago de Chile: Cuatro Vientos.

Du Plessis, A. (2001). *Resilience Theory: A Literature Review.* Pretoria: South African Military Health Service.

Dudai, Y. (2004). The Neurobiology of Consolidations, or, How Stable is the Engram?. *Annual Review of Psychology 55,* 51-86.

Duff, P. B. (1991). Apostolic Suffering and the Language of Processions in 2 Corinthians 4: 7-10. *Biblical Theology Bulletin: A Journal of Bible and Theology, 21*(4), 158-165.

Dunn, J. D. G. (1990). *Jesus, Paul and the Law: Studies in Mark and Galatians.* London: SCM.

Dunn, J. D. G. (1998). *The Theology of Paul the Apostle.* Grand Rapids, MI: Eerdmans.

Dunn, J. D. G. (2008). *The New Perspective on Paul.* Rev. Ed. Grand Rapids, MI: Eerdmans.

Dussel, E. (1997). Teología de la liberación. Transformaciones de los supuestos epistemológicos. *Theologica Xaveriana, 47*(122), 203-214.

Edelman, G. & Tononi, G. (2000). *A Universe of Consciousness: How Matter Becomes Imagination.* New York: Basic Books.

Edmondson, D., Chaudoir, S. R., Mills, M. A., Park, C. L., Holub, J. & Bartkowiak, J. M. (2011). From Shattered Assumptions to Weakened Worldviews: Trauma Symptoms Signal Anxiety Buffer Disruption. *Journal of Loss & Trauma, 16*(4), 358-385.

Ehlers, A. & Clark, D.M. (2000). A cognitive model of posttraumtic stress disorder. *Behaviour Research and Therapy, 38,* 319-345.

Ehrman, B. D. (2009). *God's Problem. How the Bible Fails to Answer Our Most Important Question: Why We Suffer.* New York: HarperCollins.

Eichenbaum, H. (2002). *The Cognitive Neuroscience of Memory.* Oxford: Oxford University Press.

Eichrodt, W. (1975). *Teología del Antiguo Testamento. Tomo II.* Madrid: Cristiandad.

Eisen, A. & Laderman, G. (Eds.) (2007). *Science, Religion, and Society: An Encyclopedia of History, Culture, and Controversy.* New York: M.E. Sharpe.

Eisenhaum, P. (2014). *Pablo no fue Cristiano. El mensaje original de un apóstol mal entendido.* Navarra: Verbo Divino.

Elder, G. H. & Conger, R. D. (2000). *Children of the Land: Adversity and Success in Rural America.* Chicago: University of Chicago Press.

Ellens, J. H. (1997). The Bible and Psychology, an Interdisciplinary Pilgrimage. *Pastoral Psychology, 45*(3), 193-208.

Ellens, J. H. (Ed.) (2011). *Explaining Evil.* Vols. I-III. Oxford: Praeger.

Ellens, J. H. (Ed.) (2012). *Psychological Hermeneutics for Biblical Themes and Texts. A Festschrift in Honor of Wayne G. Rollins.* New York-London: Bloomsbury / T&T Clark.

Ellicott, C. J. (Ed.) (2015). *Ellicott's Bible Commentary: Volume 3.* Harrington, DE: *Delmarva Publications.*

Elliott, N. (1994). *Liberating Paul: The Justice of God and the Politics of the Apostle.* Maryknoll: Orbis Books.

Ellis, E. E. (1957). *Paul's Use of the Old Testament.* Edinburgh: Oliver & Boyd.

Ellis, E. E. (1961). *Paul and His Recent Interpreters.* Grand Rapids: Eerdmans.

Ellis, E. E. (1975). Paul and his Opponents. In: J. Neusner (Ed.). *Christianity, Judaism and Other Greco-Roman Cults* (pp. 264-298). Leiden: Brill.

Engberg-Pedersen, T. (2010). *Cosmology and Self in the Apostle Paul. The Material Spirit.* Oxford: Oxford University Press.

Epstein, N. B. & Bishop, D. S. (1981). Problem-centered systems therapy of the family. En A. S. Gurman & D. P. Kniskern (Eds.), *Handbook of Family Therapy* (pp. 444-482). New York City, NY: Brunner/Mazel.

Eschleman, K.J., Bowling, N.A. & Alarcón, G.M. (2010). A meta-analytic examination of hardiness. *International Journal of Stress Management, Vol. 17*(4), 277-307.

Esser, H.H. (1985). Mercy, Compassion. In: C. Brown (Ed.). *The New International Dictionary of New Testament Theology.* Vol. II (pp. 593-601). Grand Rapids, MI: Regency.

Esser, H.-H. (1994). Misericordia. In: L. Coenen, E. Beyreuther & H. Bieterhard (Eds). *Diccionario Teológico del Nuevo Testamento.* Vol. III (pp. 101-102). Salamanca: Sígueme.

Eve, P. & Kangas, M. (2015). Posttraumatic Growth Following Trauma: Is Growth Accelerated or a Reflection of Cognitive Maturation? *The Humanistic Psychologist, 43*(4), 354-370.

Fairhurst, R. M. & Wellems, T.E. (2015). Malaria (plasmodium species). In: J.E. Bennett, R. Dolin, M.J. Blaser (Eds.). *Mandell, Douglas, and Bennett's Principles and Practice of Infectious Diseases.* 8th ed. Philadelphia, PA: Elsevier Saunders.

Falkenroth, U. & Brown, C. (1985). Patience, Steadfastness, Endurance. In: C. Brown (Ed.). *The New International Dictionary of New Testament Theology.* Vol. II (pp. 764-776). Grand Rapids, MI: Zondervan.

Falkenroth, U. (1994). Paciencia. In: L. Coenen, E. Beyreuther & H. Bieterhard. *Diccionario Teológico del Nuevo Testamento*. Vol. IV (pp. 234-242). Salamanca: Sígueme.

Feder, A., Nestler, E. J. & Charney, D. S. (2009). Psychobiology and molecular genetics of resilience. *Nature Reviews Neuroscience*, 10(6), 446-457.

Feinmann, J. P. (2011). *La filosofía y el barro de la historia*, 9° Ed. Buenos Aires: Planeta.

Fernández Sedano, I. & Pennebaker, J. W. (2011). La superación del trauma a través de la escritura. In: D. Páez, C. Martin Beristain, J. L. González, N. Basabe & J. Rivera (Eds.). *Superando la violencia colectiva y construyendo una cultura de paz* (pp. 343-351). Madrid: Fundamentos.

Fernández-Abascal, E. (Ed.) (2007). *Las emociones positivas*. Madrid: Pirámide.

Ferrater Mora, J. (1955). *El hombre en la encrucijada*. Bueno Aires: Sudamericana.

Fettke, S. M., & Dusing, M. L. (2016). A Practical Pentecostal Theodicy? *Pneuma*, 38(1-2), 160-179.

Fiala, A. (2009). Militant atheism, pragmatism, and the God-shaped hole. International Journal for Philosophy of Religion, 65(3), 139-151.

Filipp, S. H. (1999). A three-stage model of coping with loss and trauma. In A. Maercker, M. Schützwohl & Z. Solomon (Eds.) *Posttraumatic stress disorder: A lifespan developmental perspective* (pp. 43-78). Seattle, WA: Hogrefe and Huber.

Finamore, D. (2008). Resilience. In: *Encyclopedia of Counseling*. SAGE Publications. 6 Sep. 2009. ‹http://sage-ereference.com/counseling/Article_n265.html›. Accessed May 22, 2009.

Fink, G. (Ed.) (2010). *Stress Consequences: Mental, Neuropsychological and Socioeconomic*. San Diego, CA: Elsevier.

Fisher, M. L. & Exline, J. J. (2006). Self-forgiveness versus excusing: The roles of remorse, effort, and acceptance of responsibility. *Self and Identity*, 5(2), 127–146.

Fitzgerald, J. T. (1988). *Cracks in an Earthen Vessel: An Examination of the Catalogues of Hardships in the Corinthian Correspondence*. Atlanta: Scholars Press.

Fitzgerarld, J. T. (1988). *Cracks in an Earthen Vessel: An Examination of the Catalogues of Hardships in the Corinthian Correspondence.* Atlanta, GA: Scholars.

Fitzmyer, J. A. (1972). Vida de San Pablo. In: R.E. Brown, J.A. Fitzmyer & R.E. & Murphy (Dir.). *Comentario Bíblico "San Jerónimo"*, Tomo III (pp. 547-564). Madrid: Cristiandad.

Fletcher, D. & Sarkar, M. (2013). Psychological Resilience. A Review and Critique of Definitions, Concepts, and Theory. *European Psychologist, 18*(1),12-23.

Floristán, C. (1998). *Teología Práctica. Teología y Praxis de la Acción Pastoral.* Salamanca: Sígueme.

Foa, E. B., Keane, T. M. & Friedman, M. J. (2003). *Tratamiento del estrés postraumático.* Barcelona: Ariel.

Folkman, S. & Lazarus, R. S. (1980). An analysis of coping in a middle-aged community sample. *Journal of Health and Social Behavior, 21,* 219–239.

Folkman, S., Lazarus, R. S., Gruen, R. J. & Delongis, A. (1986). Appraisal, coping, heath status and psychological symptoms. *Journal of Personality and Social Psychology, 50*(3), 571-579.

Follis, E. R. (1987). *Directions in Biblical Hebrew Poetry.* Sheffield: JSOT Press.

Forbes, C. (1983). Paul's Opponents in Corinth. *Buried History, 19:* 19-23.

Forbes, C. (2008). Paulo e a Comparação Retórica. In: J. P. Sampley (Org.). *Paulo no Mundo Greco-Romano. Um Comêndio* (pp. 113-146). Sao Paulo: Paulus.

Ford, J. D. (2009). *Posttraumatic Stress Disorder. Science and Practice.* Oxford: Elsevier.

Foster, J. K. (2009). *Memory.* Oxford: Oxford University Press.

Frankel, H., Snowden, L. R. & Nelson, L. S. (1992). Wives' adjustment to military deployment: An empirical evaluation of a family stress model. *International Journal of Sociology of the Family, 22,* 93-117.

Frankl, V. E. (1992). *Man's Search for Meaning. An Introduction to Logotherapy.* 4th Ed. Boston: Beacon.

Frankl, V. E. (2000). *Man's Search for Ultimate Meaning.* New York: MJF Books.

Fredrickson, B. L. (2001). The role of positive emotions in positive psychology: The broaden-and-build theory of positive emotions. *American Psychologist*, 56, 218-226.

Fredrickson, B. L., Tugade, M. M., Waugh, C. E. & Larkin, G. (2003). What good are positive emotions in crises?: A prospective study of resilience and emotions following the terrorist attacks on the United States on September 11th, 2001. *Journal of Personality and Social Psychology*, 84, 365-376.

Fredrickson, D.E. (2008). Paulo, as tribulações e o sofrimento. In: J. P. Sampley (Org.). *Paulo no Mundo Greco-Romano. Um Comêndio* (pp. 147-170). Sao Paulo: Paulus.

Freed, E. D. (2005). *The Apostle Paul and His Letters.* London: Equinox.

Freedman, D. N. (Ed.) (1992). *The Anchor Bible Dictionary.* Vols. 1-6. New York: Doubleday.

Freeman, J. (2001). *Terapia Narrativa para Niños.* Barcelona: Paidós.

Freud, S. & Breuer, J. (1996). Estudios sobre la histeria. In: S. Freud, *Obras Completas*, Vol. I. Buenos Aires: Amorrortu.

Freud, S. (1994). *Cartas a Wilhelm Fliess, 1887-1904.* Buenos Aires: Amorrortu.

Friberg, B., Friberg, T. & Miller, N.F. (2000). *Analytical Lexicon of Greek New Testament.* Grand Rapids, MI: Baker.

Friedman, M. J., Resick, P.A., Bryant, R.A. & Brewin, C.R. (2011). Considering PTSD for DSM-5. *Depression and Anxiety*, 28, 750-769.

Friesen, S. J., Schowalter, D.N. & Walters, J.C. (Eds.) (2010). *Corinth in Context. Comparative Studies on Religion and Society.* Leiden-Boston: Brill.

Fry, P. S. (2000). Religious involvement, spirituality, and personal meaning for life: Existential predictors of psychological well being in community-residing and institutional care elders. *Aging and Mental Health*, 4(4), 375-387.

Furnish, V. P. (1998). Paul and the Corinthians: The Letters, the Challenges of Ministry, the Gospel. *Interpretation*, 52, 229-245.

Furnish, V. P. (2007). *II Corinthians: Translated with Introduction, Notes and Commentary.* New Haven: Yale University Press.

Fuster, J. (2008). *The Prefrontal Cortex.* 4th Ed. San Diego: Elsiever.

Gadamer, H.-G. (1993). *Verdad y Método.* Salamanca: Sígueme.

Galende, E. (2004). Subjetividad y resiliencia: del azar & la complejidad. In: A. Merillo, E. Ojeda & D. Rodríguez. *Resiliencia y Subjetividad* (pp. 23-61). Buenos Aires: Paidós.

Gantman, C. A. (1980). A closer look at families that work well. *International Journal of Family Therapy, 2*(2), 106-119.

Ganzevoort, R. R. & Roeland, J. (2014). Lived religion: The praxis of practical theology. *International Journal of Practical Theology, 18*(1), 91-101.

Ganzevoort, R. R. (1998a). Religious coping reconsidered. Part one: An integrated approach. *Journal of Psychology and Theology, 26*(3), 260-275.

Ganzevoort, R. R. (1998b). Religious coping reconsidered. Part two: A narrative reformulation. *Journal of Psychology and Theology, 26*(3), 276-286.

Ganzevoort, R. R. (2004a). Van der Ven's empirical / practical theology and the theological encyclopaedia. In: C. A. M. Hermans & M. E. Moore (Eds.). *Hermeneutics and empirical research in practical theology. The contribution of empirical theology by Johannes A. van der Ven* (53-74). Leiden: Brill.

Ganzevoort, R. R. (2004b). What you see is what you get. Social construction and normativity in practical theology. In: Van der Ven, J.A. & Scherer-Rath, M.(Ed.) *Normativity and empirical research in theology* (pp. 17-34). Leiden: Brill.

Ganzevoort, R. R. (2008). Coping with tragedy and malice. In: N. van Doorn-Harder & L. Minnema. *Coping with evil in religion and culture* (pp. 247-260). Amsterdam-New York: Brill Rodopi.

Ganzevoort, R. R. (2009a). Forks in the Road when Tracing the Sacred. Practical Theology as Hermeneutics of Lived Religion. Presidential address to the International Academy of Practical Theology. Chicago, 03.08.2009. Online: http://www.ruardganze voort.nl/pdf/2009_Presidential.pdf. Accessed August 7, 2017.

Ganzevoort, R. R. (2009b). All things work together for good'? Theodicy and post- traumatic spirituality. In: W. Gräb & L. Charbonnier (Eds.). *Secularization Theories, Religious Identity, and Practical Theology* (pp. 183- 192). Münster: LIT- Verlag.

Ganzevoort, R. R. (2010). Encruzilhadas do caminho no rastro do sagrado: a teologia prática como hermenêutica da religião vivenciada. *Estudos Teológicos, 49*(2), 317-343.

Garber, D. G. (2015). Trauma Theory and Biblical Studies. *Currents in Biblical Research, 14*(1), 24-44.

García, F. E., Reyes, A. & Cova, F. (2014). Severidad del trauma, optimismo, crecimiento postraumático y bienestar en sobrevivientes de un desastre natural. *Universitas Psychologica, 13*(2), 15-24.

García, N. B. & Zea, R. M. (2012). Estrés académico. *Revista de Psicología Universidad de Antioquia, 3*(2), 55-82.

García-Coll, C. & Vásquez-García, H. A. (1995). Hispanic children and their families: On a different track from the very beginning. In H. E. Fitzgerald, B. M. Lester & B. Zuckerman (Eds.), *Children of poverty: Research, Health, and Policy Issues* (pp. 57-83). New York: Garland Publishing.

García-Vesga, M. C. & Domínguez-de la Ossa, E. (2013). Desarrollo teórico de la Resiliencia y su aplicación en situaciones adversas: Una revisión analítica. *Revista Latinoamericana de Ciencias Sociales, Niñez y Juventud, 11*(1), 63-77.

Garland, D. E. (1989). Paul's Apostolic Authority: The Power of Christ Sustaining Weakness (2 Corinthians 10-13). *Review and Expositor, 86*, 371-389.

Garmezy, N. & Masten, A. S. (1986). Stress, competence, and resilience: Common frontiers for therapist and psychopathologist. *Behavior Therapy, 17*, 500-521.

Garmezy, N. (1974). The study of competence in children at risk for severe psychopathology. In: E. J. Anthony & C. Koupernik (Eds.), *The Child in his Family: Children at Psychiatric Risk: III*. New York: Wiley.

Garmezy, N. (1987). Stress, competence, and development: Continuities in the study of schizophrenic adults, children vulnerable to psychopathology, and the search for stress-resistant children. *American Journal of Orthopsychiatry, 57*, 159-174.

Garmezy, N. (1993). Children in poverty: Resilience despite risk. *Psychiatry: Interpersonal & Biological Processes, 56*, 127-136.

Garmezy, N., Masten, A. S. & Tellegen, A. (1984). The study of stress and competence in children: A building block for developmental psychopathology. *Child Development*, 55, 97-111.

Gartner, B. (1994). Sufrimiento. In: L. Coenen, E. Beyreuther, & H. Bieterhard, *Diccionario Teológico del Nuevo Testamento*. Vol. IV (pp. 236-245). Salamanca: Sígueme.

Garzón, F., Garver, S., Kleinschi, D., Tan, E. & Hill, J. (2001). Freedom in Christ: quasi-experimental research on the Neil Anderson approach. *Journal of Psychology and Theology*, 29(1), 41-51.

Gasparre, A., Bosco, S. & Bellelli G. (2010). Cognitive and social consequences of participation in social rites: Collective coping, social support, and posttraumatic growth in the victims of Guatemala genocide. *Psicología Social*, 25, 35-46.

Gazzaniga, M. (1999). *El Pasado de la Mente*. Santiago de Chile: Andrés Bello.

Gazzaniga, M.S. (2009). *Human: The Science Behind What Makes Us Unique*. New York: Harper Perennial.

Georgi, D. (1986). *The Opponents of Paul in Second Corinthians*. Philadelphia: Fortress.

Georgi, D. (1991). *Theocracy in Paul' s Praxis and Theology*. Minneapolis: Fortress Press.

Gerald R. (2004). *Posttraumatic Stress Disorder: Issues and Controversies*. Chichester, England: Wileyy & Sons

Gerkin, C. V. (1984). The *Living Human Document*. Nashville: Abingdon.

Gerrish, N., Dyck, M.J. & Marsh, A. (2009). Posttraumatic Growth and Bereavement, *Mortality*, 14(3), 226-244.

Giallanza, J. (1978). When I Am Weak, Then I Am Strong. *Biblia Today*, 95, 1572-1577.

Gignilliat, M. S. (2007). *Paul and Isaiah's servants. Paul's theological reading of Isaiah 40-66 in 2 Corinthians 5,14-6,10*. London: T & T Clark.

Gilchrist, J. M. (1988). Paul and the Corinthians. The Sequence of Letters and Visits. *Journal for the Study of the New Testament*, 11(34), 47-69.

Gillham, J. E. & Seligman, M. E. P. (1999). Footsteps on the road to positive psychology. *Behaviour Research and Therapy*, 37, 163-173.

Gilmore, D. D. (Ed.) (1987). *Honor and shame and the unity of the Mediterranean.* Washington: American Anthropological Association.

Given, M. D. (2001). *Paul's True Rhetoric: Ambiguity, Cunning, and Deception in Greece and Rome.* Harrisville: Trinity Press International.

Glaser, B. G. & Strauss, A. (1967). *Discovery of Grounded Theory. Strategies for Qualitative Research.* New Brunswick-London: Aldine Transaction.

Glessner, J. M. (2017). Ethnomedical Anthropology and Paul's "Thorn" (2 Corinthians 12:7). *Biblical Theology Bulletin, 47*(1), 15-46.

Goldberg, M. (1981). *Theology and Narrative: A Critical Introduction.* Nashville: Abingdon.

Goldsmith, D. (2004). *Communicating Social Support.* Cambridge: Cambridge University Press.

Gómez de Silva, G. (2011). *Breve diccionario etimológico de la lengua española.* 2° Ed. México, DF: Fondo de Cultura Económica.

Gómez, E. & Kotliarenco, M. A. (2011). Resiliencia Familiar: un enfoque de investigación e intervención con familias multiproblemáticas. *Revista de Psicología, 19*(2), 103-132.

Gonçalves, O. F. (2002). *Psicoterapia Cognitiva Narrativa. Manual de Terapia Breve.* Bilbao: Desclée de Brouwer.

Gooder, R. R. (2006). *Only the Third Heaven? 2 Corinthians 12.1-10 and Heavenly Ascent.* London-New York: T&T Clark-Continuum.

Goulder, M. (1994). Vision and Knowledge. *Journal for the Study of the New Testament, 56*, 53-71.

Goulder, M. D. (2003). Visions and Revelations of the Lord (2 Corinthians 12:1-10). In: T. J. Burke & J. K. Elliott (Eds.), *Paul and the Corinthians: Studies on a Community in Conflict* (pp. 303-312). Leiden-Boston, MA: Brill.

Griez, E. J. L., Faravelli, C., Nutt, D. & Zohar, D. (Eds.) (2001). *Anxiety Disorders.* Londrés: John Wiley & Sons.

Grotberg, E. (1995). *A guide to promoting resilience in children: strengthening the human spirit. The International Resilience Project.* La Haya: Bernard Van Leer Foundation.

Grotberg, E. (1997). The International Resilience Project: Findings from the Research and the Effectiveness of Interventions. In: B. Bain, et al. (Eds.). *Psychology and Education in the 21at Century: Proceedings of the 54th Annual Convention. International Council of Psychologists* (pp. 118-128). Edmonton: ICP Press.

Grover, V. K. (2015). Cognitive Resilience as related to Hardiness across Social Value Orientation among Adolescents. *International Journal of Research in Economics and Social Sciences, 5*(5), 230-238.

Guerra, C. & Plaza, H. (2009). Tratamiento Cognitivo-Conductual del Estrés Postraumático en un caso de violación infantil. *Revista de Psicología, 18*(1),103-129.

Guidano, V. & Liotti, G. (2006). *Procesos Cognitivos y Desordenes Emocionales.* Santiago de Chile: Cuatro Vientos.

Guidano, V. (1987). *Complexity of the self.* Nueva York: Guilford Press.

Guidano, V. (1991). *The self in processes.* New York, Guilford Press.

Guidano, V. F. (1997). Un enfoque constructivista de los procesos del conocimiento humano. En: M. J. Mahoney, *Psicoterapias cognitivas y constructivistas* (pp. 115-129). Bilbao: Desclée de Brouwer.

Guidano, V. F., & Quiñonez, A. (2018). *El modelo cognitivo postracionalista. Hacia una reconceptualización teórica y clínica.* Ed. Rev. Desclée de Brouwer.

Gundry, R. H. (2005). *Soma in Biblical Theology.* With Emphasis on Pauline Anthropology. New York: Cambridge University Press.

Gunn, D. C. (1980). Family identity creation: A family strength-building role activity. In N. Stinnett, B. Chesser, J. De Frain & P. Knaub (Eds.), *Building family strengths: Positive models for family life* (pp. 17-31). Lincoln, NE: University of Nebraska.

Gunther, J. J. (1973). *St. Paul's Opponents and Their Background.* Leiden: Brill.

Guthrie, G. H. (2015). *2 Corinthians.* Grand Rapids, MI: Baker.

Gutiérrez, G. (1975). *Teología de la Liberación. Perspectivas.* Salamanca: Sígueme.

Gutiérrez, G. (1995). *Hablar de Dios desde el Sufrimiento del Inocente. Reflexiones sobre el libro de Job.* 3th Ed. Salamanca: Sígueme.

Hafstad, G., Gil Rivas, V., Kilmer, R. & Raeder, S. (2010). Posttraumatic growth among Norwegian children and adolescents following a natural disaster. *American Journal of Orthopsychiatry, 80,* 248-257.

Halbwachs, M. (1992). *On collective memory.* Chicago: The University of Chicago Press.

Hanhart, K. (1997). Hope in the face of death: preserving the original text of 2 Cor 5: 3. *Neotestamentica, 31, 77-86.*

Harding, M. (2004). Disputed and Undisputed Letters of Paul. In: S.E. Porter (Ed.). *The Pauline Canon* (pp. 129-168). Leiden-Boston: Brill.

Harker, L. & Keltner, D. (2001). Expressions of positive emotion in women's college yearbook pictures and their relationship to personality and life outcomes across adulthood. *Journal of personality and social psychology, 80*(1), 112-224.

Harris, J. I., Erbes, C. R., Engdahl, B. E., Olson, R. H. A., Winskowski, A. M. & McMahill, J. (2008), Christian religious functioning and trauma outcomes. Journal of Clinical Psychology, 64, 17-29.

Harris, M. J. (1970). *The interpretation of 2 Corinthians 5: 1-10 and its place in Pauline eschatology.* Doctoral dissertation, University of Manchester.

Harris, M. J. (1971). Corinthians 5: 1-10: Watershed in Paul's Eschatology? *Tyndale Bulletin, 22, 32-57.*

Harris, M. J. (1985). *Raised Immortal: Resurrection and Immortality in the New Testament.* Grand Rapids, MI: Eerdmans.

Harrop, J. H. (1991). Corinto. In: *Nuevo Diccionario Bíblico Certeza.* Barcelona: Certeza.

Hartman, S. & Winsler, A. (2005). Resiliency. In: *Encyclopedia of Human Development.* Online : http://sage-ereference.com/humandevelop ment/Article_n522.html. Accessed May 6, 2009.

Hauck, F. (2003). κοινός [común], κοινωνός [compañero, partícipe], κοινωνέω [tomar parte en, compartir], κοινωνία [comunión, participación]. In: G. Kittel & G. Friedrich. *Compendio del Diccionario teológico del Nuevo Testamento* (pp. 447-450). Grand Rapids, MI: Desafío.

Hauck, F.(2002). *Hupomoné.* In: G. Kittel & G. Friedrich (Eds.) (2002). *Compendio del Diccionario Teológico del Nuevo Testamento.* Grand Rapids, MI: Libros Desafío.

Hauerwas, S. (1990). *Naming the Silence. God, Medicine, and the Problem of Suffering.* Grand Rapids, MI: Eerdmans.

Hawley, D. R. & De Haan, L. (1996). Toward a definition of family resilience: Integrating life-span and family perspectives. *Family Process, 35*(3), 283-298.

Hawthorne,G. F., Martin, R. P. & Reid, D. G. (Eds.) (1993). *Dictionary of Paul and His Letters.* Downers Grove, IL: InterVarsity Press.

Hay, D. M. & Johnson, E. E. (Ed.) (1997). *Pauline Theology, Vol IV: Looking Back, Pressing On.* Atlanta: Scholars Press.

Hay, D. M. (Ed.) (1993). *Pauline theology, Vol II: 1 and 2 Corinthians.* Minneapolis: Fortress Press.

Hefferon, K. & Boniwell, I. (2011). *Positive Psychology. Theory, Research and Applications.* New York: McGraw-Hill.

Heidegger, M. (1992). *The Concept of Time.* Oxford: Blackwell.

Heidegger, M. (1997). *Ser y tiempo.* Santiago de Chile, Chile: Editorial Universitaria.

Heidegger, M. (2005). *Introducción a la fenomenología de la religión.* Madrid: Siruela.

Heil, J. P. (2005). *The Rhetorical Role of Scripture in 1 Corinthians.* Atlanta: Society of Biblical Literature.

Heil, J. P. (2010). *Philippians. Let Us Rejoice in Being Conformed to Christ.* Atlanta: Society of Biblical Literature.

Helgeson, V. S., Reynolds, K. A. & Tomich, P. L. (2006). A meta-analytic review of benefit finding and growth. *Journal of Consulting and Clinical Psychology, 74*(5), 797-816.

Helzer, J. E., Robins, L. N., & McEvoy, L. (1987). Post-traumatic Stress Disorder in the General Population. *New England Journal of Medicine, 317*(26), 1630-1634.

Herman, J. L. (1992). *Trauma and Recovery.* New York: Basic Books.

Hernández, Z.E., Ehrenzweig, Y. & Yépez, L. (2010). Sentido de coherencia y salud en personas adultas mayores autopercibidas como sanas. *Revista Costarricense de Psicología, 29*(43), 17-34.

Herranz, M. (2008). *San Pablo en sus Cartas.* Madrid: Encuentro.

Hervieu-Léger, D. (2000). *Religion as a Chain of Memory.* New Brunswick: Rutgers University Press.

Hess, R. E., Maton, K. I. & Pargament, K. (2014). *Religion and prevention in mental health: Research, vision, and action.* New York-London: Routledge.

Hessen, J. (2007). *Teoría del Conocimiento.* 17°Ed. Buenos Aires: Lossada.

Hiembrock, H.-G. (2004). Given Through the Senses. A Phenomenological Model of Empirical Theology. In: J. A. van der Ven. *Normativity and Empirical Research in Theology* (pp. 59-83). Leiden-Boston: Brill.

Hinkelammert, F. J. (2013). *La Maldición que Pesa sobre la Ley: Las raíces del Pensamiento Crítico en Pablo de Tarso.* San José, Costa Rica: Arlekín.

Hisey, A. & Beck, J.S.P. (1961). Paul's 'Thorn in the Flesh': A Paragnosis. *Journal of Bible and Religion,* 29(2), 125-129.

Hoad, J. H. (1991). Paciencia. In: *Nuevo Diccionario Bíblico Certeza.* Barcelona: Certeza.

Hobfoll, S. E., Hall, B. J., Canetti-Nisim, D., Galea, S., Johnson, R. J. & Palmieri, P. A. (2007). Refining our understanding of traumatic growth in the face of terrorism: Moving from meaning cognitions to doing what is meaningful. *Applied Psychology,* 56(3), 345-366.

Hoch, L.C. (2011). Reflexiones en torno al método de la Teología Práctica. In: C. Shneider-Harppecht & R. Zwetsch. *Teología Práctica en el Contexto de América Latina* (pp. 75-91). Sao Leopoldo/Quito: Sinodal-CLAI.

Hodgson, R. (1983). Paul the Apostle and First Century Tribulation List, *ZNTW* 74: 59–80.

Hogan, N. S. & Schmidt, L. A. (2002). Testing the grief to personal growth model using structural equation modeling. *Death Studies,* 26(8), 615-634.

Holmes, T. H. & Masuda, M. (1974). Life change and illness in community psychology. *Journal of Community Psychology,* 5, 423-33.

Holmes, T.H. & Rahe, R.H. (1967). The social readjustment rating scale. *Journal of Psychosomatic Research,* 11, 213-8.

Holmes, T.H. (1979). Development and application of a quantitative measure of life change magnitude. In: J.E. Barret, R.M. Rose & G.L. Klerman (Eds.) *Stress and Mental Disorder.* New York: Raven.

Holtz, T. H. (1998). Refugee trauma versus torture trauma: a retrospective controlled cohort study of Tibetan refugees. *Journal of Nervous and Mental Disease,* 186(1), 24-34.

Hood, R. W., Hill, P. C. & Spilka, B. (2009). *The Psychology of Religion. An Empirical Approach.* New York-London: The Guilford Press.

Horley, R.A. (Ed,) (2000). *Paul and politics: Ekklesia, Israel, Imperium, Interpretation.* Harrisburg, PA: Trinity Press International.

Horowitz M. J. (1976). *Stress Response Syndromes.* New York: Jason Aronson.

Horowitz M.J., Wilner, N., Kaltreidr, N. & Álvarez, W. (1980). Signs and symptoms of post-traumatic stress disorder. *Archives of General Psychology, 37,* 85-92.

Horsley, R.A. (1997). *Paul and Empire. Religion and Power in Roman Imperial Society.* Harrisburg, PA: Trinity Press International.

Horsley, R.A. (Ed.) (2004). *Paul and the Roman Imperial Order.* New York: Trinity Press International.

Hotze, G. (1997). *Paradoxien bei Paulus. Untersuchungen zu Einer Elementaren Denkform in Siner Theologie.* Münster: Aschendorff.

Howard, G. (1990). *Paul: Crisis in Galatia. A Study in Early Christian Theology.* 2° ed. Cambridge: Cambridge University Press.

Howard-Snyder, D. (Ed.) (1996). *The Evidential Argument from Evil.* Indianapolis: Indiana University Press.

Hughes, P. E. (1962). *Paul's Second Epistle to the Corinthians.* Grand Rapids: Eerdmans.

Huguelet, P. & Koenig, H. G (2009). *Religion and Spirituality in Psychiatry.* Cambridge: Cambridge University Press.

Hutcheon, E. & Wolbring, G. (2013). Deconstructing the Resilience Concept Using an Ableism Lens: Implications for People with Diverse Abilities. *Dilemata,* 5(11), 235-252.

Hutchison, J., Greer, J. & Ciarrocchi, J. (1999). An Empirical Exploration of Concomitants of Vossen's Theodicies in a Population of Elderly Women. *Journal of empirical theology,* 12(2), 23-34.Inbody, T. (1997). *The Transforming God: An Interpretation of Suffering and Evil.* Louisville, Kentucky: Westminster John Knox Press.

Infante, F. (2002). La resiliencia como proceso: una revisión de la literatura reciente. In: Melillo, A. & Ojeda, E. N. S. (Orgs.). *Resiliencia: descobriendo las propias fortalezas.* Buenos Aires: Paidós, 31-53.

Inwood, B. (1985). *Ethics and Human Action in Early Stoicism.* Oxford: Oxford University Press.

Jakšić, N., Brajković, L., Ivezić, E., Topić, R., & Jakovljević, M. (2012). The role of personality traits in posttraumatic stress disorder (PTSD). *Psychiatria Danubina, 24*(3.), 256-266.

Janoff-Bulman, R. (1992). *Shattered Assumptions.* New York: Free Press.

Jáuregui, E. (2009). Tomarse el humor en serio: aplicaciones positivas de la risa y el humor. In: C. Vázquez & G. Hervás (Eds.) *Psicología Positiva Aplicada.* 2º Ed. (pp. 283-309). Bilbao: Desclée de Brouwer.

Jaureguizar, J. & Espina, A. (2005). *Enfermedad física Crónica y Familia.* Online: http://www.centrodepsicoterapia.es/pdf/7-enfermedad%20cronica%20y%20familia.pdf. Accessed May 20, 2012.

Jewett, R. (1971). *Paul's Anthropological Terms: A Study of their Use in Conflict Settings.* Leiden: Brill.

Johnson, L. A. (1999). Satan talk in Corinth: the rhetoric of conflict. *Biblical Theology Bulletin: A Journal of Bible and Theology, 29*(4), 145-155.

Johnson, S. L. (2009). *Therapist's Guide to Posttraumatic Stress Disorder Intervention.* London: Elsevier.

Joseph, J. (2012). Paul's Contextual use of the Catalogue of Circumstances in 2 Cor 6:4b-10. In: *SBL Annual Meeting: Second Corinthians: Pauline Theology in the Making.* Chicago, 17-20 November, 2012.

Joseph, S. (2009). Growth Following Adversity: Positive Psychological Perspectives on Posttraumatic Stress. *Psychological Topics, 18,* 2, 335-344.

Jung, C. G. (1973). *C. G. Jung letters, 1, 1906-1950.* Princeton: Princeton University Press.

Kandel, E.R. (2007). *En Busca de la Memoria: Nacimiento de una Nueva Ciencia de la Mente.* Buenos Aires: Katz.

Kaplan, C. P., Turner, S., Norman, E. & Stillson, K. (1996). Promoting resilience strategies: A modified consultation model. *Social Work in Education, 18*(3), 158-168.

Karl, A. & Werner, A. (2006). The use of proton magnetic resonance spectroscopy in PTSD research—Meta-analyses of findings and methodological review. *Neuroscience & Biobehavioral Reviews,* 34(1),7-22.

Kee, D. (1980). Who were the 'Super-Apostles' of 2 Corinthians 10-13? *RQ, 23,* 65-76.

Keener, C. S. (2003). *Comentario del Contexto Cultural de la Biblia.Nuevo Testamento.* El Paso, TX: Mundo Hispano.

Keener, C. S. (2005). *1-2 Corinthians.* Cambridge: Cambridge University Press.

Keinan, G. (1987). Decision-making under stress: scanning of alternatives under controllable and uncontrollable threats. *Journal of Personality and Social Psychology, 52,* 639-44.

Kelley, H. H. (1972). Attribution in social interaction. In E. E. Jones, DE. Kanouse, H. H. Kelley, R. E. Nisbet, S. Valins & B. Weiner (Eds.) *Attribution: Perceiving the causes of behavior* (pp. 1-26). Morristown, NG: General Learning Press.

Keltner, D. & Bonanno, G.A. (1997). A study of laughter and dissociation: The distinct correlates of laughter and smiling during bereavement. *Journal of Personality and Social Psychology, 73,* 687-702.

Kennedy, G.A. (1984). *New Testament Interpretation through Rhetorical Criticism.* Chapelhill - London: The University of North Carolina Press.

Kenneson, P.D. (1999). *Life on the Vine: Cultivating the Fruit of the Spirit.* Illinois: InterVarsity Press.

Kent, M., Davis, M. C. & Reich, J. W. (2014). *The Resilience Handbook: Approaches to Stress and Trauma.* New York: Routledge.

Kessler, R. C., Sonnega, A., Bromet, E., Hughes, M. &, Nelson, C.B. (1995). Posttraumatic stress disorder in the National Comorbidity Survey. *Arch Gen Psychiatry, 52,* 1048-1060.

Keysers, C. & Gazzola, V. (2010). Social Neuroscience: Mirror Neurons recorded in Humans. *Current Biology, 20*(8), 353-354.

Kille, D. A. (2000). *Psychological Biblical Criticism.* Minneapolis: Fortress Press.

Kille, D. A. (2002). Psychology and the Bible: Three worlds of the text. *Pastoral Psychology, 51*(2), 125-134.

Kille, D. A. (2009). Psychology and the Bible. In: K. D. Sakenfeld (Ed.), *New Interpreter's Dictionary of the Bible* (Vol. 4, pp. 684–685). Nashville: Abingdon.

Kille, D. A. (2015). "A Degree in What?" Revisited: A Response to Psychological Hermeneutics for Biblical Themes and Texts (Ellens, 2012). *Pastoral Psychology, 64*(4), 499-505.

Kilmer, R. P. & Gil- Rivas, V. (2010). Exploring posttraumatic growth in children impacted by Hurricane Katrina: Correlates of the phenomenon and developmental considerations. *Child Development, 81*, 1211-1227.

Kittel, G., Bromiley, G. W. & Friedrich, G. (Eds.) (1964). *Theological dictionary of the New Testament.* Vols. I-X (HTM Digital Version). Grand Rapids, MI: Eerdmans.

Kittredge, C. B. (1998). *Community and Authority: The Rhetoric of Obedience in the Pauline Tradition.* Harrisburg: Trinity Press International.

Klaassens, E. R., van Veen, T. & Zitman, F. G. (2007). Does trauma cause lasting changes in HPA-axis functioning in healthy individuals?. *Progress in Brain Research, 167*, 273-275.

Kobasa, S. C. (1979). Stressful life events, personality, and health: An inquiry into hardiness. *Journal of Personality and Social Psychology, 37*(1), 1-11.

Kobasa, S. C. (1982). The hardy personality: Toward a social psychology of stress and health. In G. S. Sanders & J. Suls (Eds.), *Social Psychology of Health and Illness* (pp. 3-32). Hillsdale, NJ: Lawrence Erlbaum Assoc.

Kobasa, S. C., Maddi, S. R. & Courington, S. (1981). Personality and constitution as mediators in the stress-illness relationship. *Journal of Health and Social Behavior, 22*, 368-378.

Kobasa, S. C., Maddi, S. R. & Kahn, S. (1982). Hardiness and health: A prospective study. Journal of Personality and Social Psychology, 42(1), 168-177.

Koenig H., Nelson B., Shaw S., Zaben F., Wang Z. & Saxena S. (2015). Belief into Action Scale: A Brief but Comprehensive Measure of Religious Commitment. *Open Journal of Psychiatry, 5*, 66-77.

Koenig, H. G. & Cohen, H. J. (Eds.) (2002). *The Link between Religion and Health: Psychoneuroimmunology and the Faith Factor.* Oxford-New York: Oxford University Press.

Koenig, H. G. (2012). Religion, spirituality, and health: The research and clinical implications. *International Scholarly Research Notices Psychiatry*, 2012. Online: http://www.hindawi.com/journals/isrn/2012/278730/cta/. Accessed February 4, 2016.

Koenig, H. G. (2015). Religion, spirituality, and health: a review and update. *Advances in Mind-body Medicine, 29*(3), 19-26.

Koenig, H. G. (Ed.) (1998). *Handbook of Religion and Mental Health*. San Diego, CA: Elsiever Science.

Koenig, H. G., King, D. & Carson, V. B. (2012). *Handbook of religion and health*. 2º Ed. New York: Oxford University Press.

Konttinen, H., Haukkala, A. & Uutela, A. (2008). Comparing sense of coherence, depressive symptoms and anxiety, and their relationships with health in a population-based study. *Social Science & Medicine, 66*(12), 2401-2412.

Köster, H. (1988). *Introducción al Nuevo Testamento*. Salamanca: Sígueme.

Kotliarenco, M. A., Cáceres, I. & Álvarez, C. (1999). *Notas sobre Resiliencia*. Santiago de Chile: CEANIM.

Kotliarenco, M. A., Cáceres, I. & Álvarez, C. (Eds.) (1996). *Resiliencia: construyendo en adversidad*. Santiago de Chile: CEANIM.

Kotliarenco, M. A., Cáceres, I. & Fontecilla, M. (1997). *Estado del Arte en Resiliencia*. Washington: OPS.

Kowalski, M. (2013). *Transforming Boasting of Self Into Boasting in the Lord: The Development of the Pauline Periautologia in 2 Cor 10-13*. Landam, MD: University Press of America.

Krause, N., Pargament, K. I., Ironson, G. & Hill, P. (2016). Religious Involvement, Financial Strain, and Poly-Drug Use: Exploring the Moderating Role of Meaning in Life. *Substance Use & Misuse, 52*(3), 286-293.

Kreiner, A. (2017). *La Paciencia. El Sorprendente Fermento del Cristianismo en el Imperio Romano*. Salamanca: Sígueme.

Kruse, C. G. (1989). The Relationship between the Opposition to Paul Reflected in 2 Corinthians 1-7 and 10-13. *The Evangelical Quarterly, 61*, 195-202.

Kubany, E. S., Ralston, T. C., & Hill, E. E. (2010). Intense fear, helplessness,"and" horror? An empirical investigation of DSM-IV

PTSD Criterion A2. *Psychological Trauma: Theory, Research, Practice, and Policy, 2*(2), 77.

Kübler-Ross, E. (2006). *Sobre el duelo y el dolor.* Barcelona: Luciérnaga.

Kübler-Ross, E. (2008). *La muerte: un amanecer.* Barcelona: Luciérnaga.

Kübler-Ross, E. (2010). *Sobre la muerte y los moribundos.* Barcelona: Luciérnaga.

Küng, H. (1995). *Grandes pensadores cristianos. Una pequeña introducción a la teología.* Madrid: Trotta.

Kurt, A., Black, M., Martini, C. M., Metzger B. M. & Wikgren, A. (Eds.) (1994). *The Greek New Testament.* 4ᵗʰ Ed. Stuttgard: Deutsche Bibelgesellchaft/ United Bible Societies.

Kurz, W.S. (1996). 2 Corinthians: Implied Readers and Canonical Implications. *Journal for the Study of the New Testament, 18*(62), 43-63.

Kuss, O. (1976). *Carta a los Romanos. Cartas a los Corintios. Carta a los Gálatas.* Barcelona: Herder.

Laato, A. & de Moor, D. C. (2003). *Theodicy in the World of the Bible.* Leiden-Boston: Brill.

Labrador, F. J. (1988). Conceptualización y Tratamiento de los Trastornos Asociados al Estrés. In: A. Fierro (Coord.). *Psicología Clínica. Cuestiones Actuales.* Madrid: Pirámide.

Lacan, J. (1988). Función y campo de la palabra y del lenguaje en psicoanálisis. In: *Escritos I.* Buenos Aires: Siglo XXI.

Lalive, C. (1968). *El Refugio de las Masas: estudio sociológico sobre el protestantismo chileno.* Santiago de Chile: Editorial del Pacífico.

Lambrecht, J. (2003). Brief Anthropological Reflections on 2 Corinthians 4:6-5:10. In: T. J. Burke & J. K. Elliott (Eds.) *Paul and the Corinthians: Studies on a Community in Conflict* (pp. 259-266). Leiden-Boston, MA: Brill.

Lanius, R., Brand, B., Vermetten, E., Freewn, P. A. & Spiegel, D. (2012). The dissociative subtype of posttraumatic stress disorder: Rationale, clinical and neurobiological evidence, and implications. *Depression and Anxiety, 29*, 701-708.

Lassi, S. & Mugnaini, D. (2015). Role of Religion and Spirituality on Mental Health and Resilience: There is Enough Evidence.

International Journal of Emergency Mental Health and Human Resilience, 17(3), 661-663,

Laufer, A. & Solomon, Z. (2006). Posttraumatic symptoms and posttraumatic growth among Israeli youth exposed to terror incidents. *Journal of Social and Clinical Psychology,* 25(4), 429-447.

Lazarus, R. S. & Folkman, S. (1984). *Estrés y procesos cognitivos.* Barcelona: Martínez Roca.

Lazarus, R. S. (1966). *Psychological Stress and the Coping Process.* New York: McGraw-Hill.

Leary, T. J. (1992). A Thorn in the Flesh: 2 Corinthians 12:7. *Journal of Theological Studies,* 43, 520-522.

LeDoux, J. E. (1991). Emotion and the Limbic System Concept. *Concepts in Neuroscience,* 2, 169-199.

LeDoux, J. E. (1993). Emotional memory systems in the brain. *Behavioural brain research,* 58(1), 69-79.

Lee, P. A. & Brage, D. G. (1989). Family life education and research: Toward a more positive approach. In: M. J. Fine (Ed.), *The Second Handbook on Parent Education* (pp. 347-378). San Diego, CA: Academic Press.

Légasse, S. (2005). *Pablo Apóstol. Ensayo de biografía crítica.* Bilbao: Desclee de Brouwer.

Lehtipuu, O. (2015). *Debates over the Resurrection of the Dead. Constructing Early Christian Identity.* Oxford: Oxford University Press.

León Portilla, M. (1985). *Visión de los Vencidos: Crónicas Indígenas.* Madrid: Historia 16.

León-Dufour, X. (1974). *Resurrección de Jesús y Mensaje Pascual.* Salamanca: Sígueme.

Lesburguères, E., Gobbo, O. L., Alaux-Cantin, S., Hambucken, A., Trifilieff, P., & Bontempi, B. (2011). Early tagging of cortical networks is required for the formation of enduring associative memory. *Science,* 331(6019), 924-928.

Léveque, J. (1987). *Job. El libro y el mensaje.* 2th Ed. Navarra: Verbo Divino.

Levi, P. & De Benedetti, L. (2015). *Auschwitz Report.* London-New York: Verso.

Levi, P. (1976). *Se questo è un uomo.* Torino: Einaudi.

Levine, S., Laufer, A., Stein.E., Hamama-Raz, Y. & Solomon, Z. (2009) Examinig the relationship between resilience and posttraumatic growth. *Journal of Traumatic Stress, 22*(4), 282–286.

Libet, B. (1981). The experimental evidence for subjective referral of a sensory experience backwards in time: Reply to P. S. Churchland. *Philosophy of Science, 48*,181-197.

Libet, B. (2004). *Mind time: The temporal factor in consciousness.* Cambridge, MA: Harvard University Press.

Lim, K. Y. (2009). *The Sufferings of Christ Are Abundant in Us. A Narrative Investigation of Paul's Suffering in 2 Corinthians.* New York: T&T Clark International.

Lindstrom, C. M., Cann, A., Calhoun, L. G. & Tedeschi, R. G. (2013). The relationship of core belief challenge, rumination, disclosure, and sociocultural elements to posttraumatic growth. *Psychological Trauma: Theory, Research, Practice, and Policy, 5*(1), 50.

Linley, P. A. & Joseph, S. (2004). Positive Change Following Trauma and Adversity: A Review. *Journal of Traumatic Stress, 17*(1), 11-21.

Linley, P. A. & Joseph, S. (2011). Meaning in Life and Posttraumatic Growth. *Journal of Loss and Trauma: International Perspectives on Stress & Coping, 16*(2), 150-159.

Lipton, B. & Fosha, D. (2011). Attachment as a transformative process in AEDP: Operationalizing the intersection of attachment theory and affective neuroscience. *Journal of Psychotherapy Integration, 21*(3), 253-279.

Loiselle, K. A., Devine, K.A., Reed-Knight, B. & Blount, R.L. (2011). Posttraumatic growth associated with a relative's serious illness. *Families, Systems & Health, 29*(1), 64-72.

Løkke, H. (2015). *Knowledge and virtue in early Stoicism.* Dordrecht: Springer Netherlands.

Long, F. (2004). *Ancient Rhetoric and Paul's Apology. The Compositional Unity of 2 Corinthians.* Cambridge: Cambridge University Press.

Longenecker, R. N. (1999). *Biblical Exegesis in the Apostolic Period.* 2nd ed. Grand Rapids: Eerdmans.

López-Ibor, J., Christodoulou, G., Maj, M., Sartorius, N. & Okasha, A. (Eds.) (2005). *Disasters and Mental Health.* Chichester, England: Weley.

415

Lorente Martinez, S. (2012). Hermenéutica como Método de la Ontología Fundamental. *Revista Internacional de Filosofía, 56*, 121-137.

Lucena, N. (Ed.) (2006). *Diccionario Esencial de Física Larousse.* México, DC: Larousse.

Ludemann, G. (2002). *Paul: The Founder of Christianity.* New York: Prometheus Books.

Luhrmann, D. (1992). *Galatians.* Minneapolis: Fortress Press.

Luthar, S. & Cicchetti, D. (2000). The construct of resilience: Implications for interventions and social policies. *Development and Psychopathology, 12,* 857-885.

Luthar, S. & Cicchetti, D. (2000). The construct of resilience: Implications for interventions and social policies. *Development and Psychopathology, 12,* 857-885.

Luthar, S. (2006). Resilience in development: A synthesis of research across five decades. In: D. Cicchetti & D.Cohen (Eds.). *Developmental Psychopathology: Risk, Disorder, and Adaptation.* Vol. 3, 2th Ed. (pp. 739-795). New York: Wiley.

Luthar, S., Doernberger, C. & Zigler, E. (1993). Resilience is not a unidimensional construct: Insights from a prospective study of inner-city adolescents. *Development and Psychopathology, 5,* 703-717.

Lyon, M. (2005). Resilience and Protective Factors. *Encyclopedia of School Psychology.* Online:<http://sage-ereference.com/schoolpsychology/Article_n242.html>. Accessed October 14, 2009.

Lysne, C. J. & Wachholtz, A.B. (2011). Pain, Spirituality, and Meaning Making: What Can We Learn from the Literature? *Religions, 2,* 1-16.

MacDonald, M. (2010). 2 Corinthians. In: J. Muddiman & J. Barton. *The Pauline Epistles Oxford Bible Commentary* (pp. 126-151). Oxford: Oxford University Press.

Maddi, S. R. (2005). On hardiness and other pathways to resilience. *American Psychologist, 60*(3), 261-262.

Maddi, S. R. (2013). *Hardiness. Turning Stressful Circumstances into Resilient Growth.* Dordrecht: Springer.

Maddi, S. R., & Hightower, M. (1999). Hardiness and optimism as expressed in coping patterns. *Consulting Psychology Journal: Practice and Research, 51*(2), 95-105.

Maercker, A. & Herrle, J. (2003) Long-term effects of the Dresden bombing: Relationships to control beliefs, religious beliefs, and personal growth. *Journal of Traumatic Stress, 16*, 579-587.

Mahoney, M. J. (2005). *Psicoterapia Constructiva. Una Guía Práctica.* Barcelona: Paidós Ibérica.

Mak, W. S., Ng, I. S. & Wong, C. Y. (2011). Resilience: Enhancing well-being through the positive cognitive triad. *Journal of Counseling Psychology, 58*(4), 610-617

Malcolm, M. R. (2013). *Paul and the Rhetoric of Reversal in 1 Corinthians. The Impact of Paul's Gospel on his Macro-Rhetoric.* Cambridge: Cambridge University Press.

Mann, D. & Cunningham, V. (Eds.) (2009). *The Past in the Present. Therapy enactments and the return of trauma.* New York: Routledge.

Martin, D. B. (1990). *Slavery as Salvation: The Metaphor of Slavery in Pauline Christianity.* New Haven: Yale University Press.

Martin, R. P. (1986). *2 Corinthians.* Waco, TX: Word Publisher.

Martin, R. P. (1987). The Opponents of Paul in 2 Corinthians: An Old Issue Revisited. In: G. F. Hawthorne & O. Betz (Eds.). *Tradition and Interpretation in the New Testament* (pp. 279-289). Grand Rapids, MI: Eerdmans.

Martínez, J. M. (1984). *Hermenéutica Bíblica.* Barcelona: CLIE.

Martínez, S. L. (2012). Hermenéutica como método de la ontología fundamental. *Daímon, 56*, 121-137.

Mason, J.W. (1968). Organisation of psychoendocrine mechanisms. *Psychosomatic Medicine, 30*(5), 565-808.

Mason, S. & Robinson, T. A. (Eds.). (2004). *Early Christian Reader: Christian Texts from the First and Second Centuries in Contemporary English Translations Including the New Revised Standard Version of the New Testament.* Peabody, MA: Hendrickson.

Matthews, B. H. & Benjamin, D.C. (Eds.) (1996). *Honor and Shame in the World of the Bible.* Atlanta, GA: Society of Biblical Literature.

Maturana, H. & Varela, F. (2003). *El Árbol del Conocimiento.* Buenos Aires: Lumen.

Maturana, H. (2001). *Emoción y Lenguaje en Educación y Política.* Santiago de Chile: Dolmen.

417

Matustik, M. B. (2008). Radical Evil and the Scarcity of Hope. Postsecular Meditations. Bloomington, IN: Indiana University Press.

Mazlom Bafroe, N., Shams Esfand Abadi, H., Jalali, M. R., Afkhami Ardakani, M. & Dadgari, A. (2015). The Relationship between Resilience and Hardiness in Patients with Type 2 Diabetes in Yazd. *Journals* Shahid Sadoughi Univ Med Sci, 23(2), 1858-1865.

McCaslin, S. E., Zoysa, P., Butler, L. D., Hart, S., Marmar, C. R., Metzler, T. J. & Koopman, C. (2009).The relationship of posttraumatic growth to 162 peritraumatic reactions and posttraumatic stress symptoms among Sri Lankan University students. *Journal of Traumatic Stress, 22*, 334-339.

McCubbin, H. I. & McCubbin, M. A. (1988). Typologies of resilient families: Emerging roles of social class and ethnicity. *Family Relations, 37*, 247-254.

McCubbin, H. I. & McCubbin, M. A. (1992). Research utilization in social work practice of family treatment. In: A. J. Grasso & I. Epstein (Eds.). *Research utilization in the social sciences: Innovations for practice and administration* (pp. 149-192). New York City, NY: Haworth.

McCullough, M. E. (2000). Forgiveness as Human Strength: Theory, Measurement, and Links to Well-Being. *Journal of Social and Clinical Psychology, 19*(1), 43-55.

McEwen, B. S. & Wingfield, J. C. (2003). The concept of allostasis in biology and biomedicine. *Hormones and behavior, 43*(1), 2-15.

McEwen, B. S. (2001). Plasticity of the hippocampus: adaptation to chronic stress and allostatic load. *Annals of the New York Academy of Sciences,933*(1), 265-277.

McEwen, B. S. (2002). Sex, stress and the hippocampus: allostasis, allostatic load and the aging process. *Neurobiology of aging, 23*(5), 921-939.

McEwen, B. S. (2008). Central effects of stress hormones in health and disease: Understanding the protective and damaging effects of stress and stress mediators. *European journal of pharmacology, 583*(2), 174-185.

McIntosh, D. N., Silver, R. & Wortman, C. B. (1993). Religion's role in adjustment to a negative life event: Coping with the loss of a child. *Journal of Personality and Social Psychology, 65*, 812-821.

Mena, P. (Comp.) (2006). *Fenomenología por decir: homenaje a Paul Ricouer.* Santiago de Chile: Universidad Alberto Hurtado.

Mesters, C. (1993). *Pablo Apóstol: Un Trabajador que Anuncia el Evangelio.* San Pablo: Paulinas.

Meyer, H. A. W. (1884). *Critical and Exegetical Hand-book to the Epistles to the Corinthians.* New York: Funk & Wagnalls.

Meza, J. L. (2002). Comprensión epistemológica de la teología pastoral. *Theologica Xaveriana, 142*: 257-276.

Midali, M. (1991). *Teología Pastorale o Pratica*, 2ª ed. Roma: LAS.

Mihaila, C. (2008). *Paul-Apollos Relationship and Paul's Stance toward Greco-Roman Rhetoric. An Exegetical and Socio-historical Study of 1 Corinthians 1-4.* Sheffield: Sheffield Academic Press.

Miller, M. W., Wolf, E. J., Kilpatrick, D., Resnick, H., Marx, B. P., Holowka, D. W., & Friedman, M. J. (2013). The Prevalence and Latent Structure of Proposed DSM-5 Posttraumatic Stress Disorder Symptoms in US National and Veteran Samples. *Psychological Trauma: Theory, Research, Practice, and Policy, 5*(6), 501.

Miller-McLemore, B. J. (Ed.). (2012). *The Wiley Blackwell companion to practical theology.* Oxford: John Wiley & Sons.

Minuchin, S. (1974). *Families and Family Ttherapy.* London, UK: Tavistock.

Miró, M. T. (2005). La Reconstrucción Terapéutica de la Trama Narrativa. *Monografías de Psiquiatría, 17*(3), 8-17.

Mitchell, M. M. (1993). *Paul and the Rhetoric of Reconciliation: An Exegetical Investigation of the Language and Composition of 1 Corinthians.* Louisville: Westminster John Knox.

Mitchell, M. M. (2010). *Paul, the Corinthians and the Birth of Christian Hermeneutics.* New York: Cambridge University Press.

Mollica, M. A., Underwood III, W., Homish, G. G., Homish, D. L. & Orom, H. (2016). Spirituality is Associated with Better Prostate Cancer Treatment Decision Making Experiences. *Journal of Behavioral Medicine, 39*(1), 161-169.

Mollica, R. (2012). *Mental Health Sequelae of Extreme Violence.* Harvard Medical School Department of Continuing Medical Education. CME On-line.

Moltmann, J. (1976). *El Hombre. Antropología Cristiana en los conflictos del presente.* Salamanca: Sígueme.

Moltmann, J. (1976). *El Hombre. Antropología Cristiana en los conflictos del presente.* Salamanca: Sígueme.

Moore, R. J. (2012) (Ed.) *Handbook of Pain and Palliative Care. Biobehavioral Approaches for the Life Course.* New York-Dordrecht-Heidelberg-London: Springer.

Moreira-Almeida, A., Lotufo Neto, F. & Koenig, H. G. (2006). Religiousness and mental health: a review. *Revista Brasileira de Psiquiatria, 28*(3), 242-250.

Moreno-Jiménez, B., González, J.L. & Carrosa, E. (1999). Burnout Docente, Sentido de Coherencia y Salud Percibida. *Revista de Psicopathología y Psicología Clínica, 4*(3), 163-180.

Morray-Jones, C. R. A. (1993a). Paradise Revisited (2 Cor 12:1-12), The Jewish Mystical Background of Paul's Apostolate. Part 1: The Jewish Sources. *The Harvard Theological Review, 86*(2), 177-217.

Morris, B., Shakespeare-Finch, J., Rieck, M. & Newberry, J. (2005). Multidimensional nature of posttraumatic growth in an Australian population. *Journal of Traumatic Stress, 18*, 575-585.

Morris, D. (1970). *El Zoo Humano.* Barcelona: Plaza & James.

Morris, D. J. (1996). *La Cultura del Dolor.* 3ra Ed. Santiago de Chile: Andrés Bello.

Morris, D. J. (2015). *The Evil Hours: A Biography of Posttraumatic Stress Disorder.* New York: Houghton Mifflin Harcourt Publishing.

Morris, L. (1993). Salvation. In: G. F. Hawthorne & R. P. Martin (Ed.). *Dictionary of Paul and His Letters* (pp. 612-615). Downers Grove, IL: InterVarsity Press.

Moule, C. F. D. (1966). St. Paul and Dualism: The Pauline Conception of Resurrection, *NTS 12*(02), 106-123.

Mowrer, O. H. (1960). *Learning theory and symbolic processes.* New York: John Wiley and Sons.

Mullins, T. Y. (1957). Paul's Thorn in the Flesh. *Journal of Biblical Literature, 76* (4), 299-303.

Munist, M., Santos, H., Kotliarenco, M. A., Suárez, E., Infante, F. & Grotberg, E. (1998). *Manual de Identificación y Promoción de la Resiliencia en Niños y Adolescentes.* Washington: Organización Panamericana de la Salud (OPS).

Murphy, L. B. & Moriarty, A. (1976). *Vulnerability, coping, and growth: From infancy to adolescence.* New Haven, CT: Yale University Press.

Murphy-O'Connor, J. (1991). *The Theology of the Second Letter to the Corinthians.* Cambridge: Cambridge University Press.

Murphy-O'Connor, J. (1994). *A Antropologia Pastoral de Paulo. Tornar-se humanos juntos.* Sao Paulo: Paulus.

Murphy-O'Connor, J. (1996). *Paul: A Critical Life.* Oxford: Claredon Press.

Murphy-O'Connor, J. (2002). *St. Paul's Corinth: Texts and Archaeology,* Collegeville, MN: Liturgical Press.

Murphy-O'Connor, J. (2003). 1 and 2 Corinthians. In: J.D. Dunn (Ed.), *The Cambridge Companion to St. Paul* (pp. 74-90). Cambridge: Cambridge University Press.

Murphy-O'Connor, J. (2004). *Paul: His Story.* New York: Oxford University Press.

Murray, J. H. (2005). *The Second Epistle to the Corinthians.* Grand Rapids, MI: Eerdmans.

Nadel, L., Hupbach, A., Gomez, R. & Newman-Smith, K. (2012). Memory formation, consolidation and transformation. *Neuroscience and Biobehavioral Reviews, 36,* 1640-1645.

Nader, K., Hardt, O., Einarsson, E. Ö., & Finnie, P. S. (2013). The Dynamic Nature of Memory. In: C. Alberini (Ed.) *Memory Reconsolidation* (pp. 15-41). London: Elsevier.

Neff, L. A. & Broady, E. F. (2011). Stress resilience in early marriage: Can practice make perfect?. *Journal of Personality and Social Psychology,101*(5), 1050.-1067.

Neimeyer, R. A. & Mahoney, M. J. (Eds.) (1998). *Constructivismo en psicoterapia.* Barcelona: Paidós.

Neimeyer, R. A., Keesee, N. J. & Fortner, B. V. (1997). Loss and meaning reconstruction: Propositions and procedures. En S. Rubin, R. Malkinson and E. Wiztum (Eds.). *Traumatic and Non-traumatic loss and Bereavement: Clinical Theory and Practice.* Madison, CT: Psychosocial Press.

Neira, G. (1994). *Edificar la Iglesia hoy: Teología Práctica.* Bogotá: Pontificia Universidad Javeriana.

Neuhouser, F. (2008). *Rousseau's Theodicy of Self-Love. Evil, Rationality, and the Drive for Recognition.* Oxford: Oxford University Press.

Neusner, J. & Avery-Peck, A. J. (2003). *The Blackwell Companion to Judaism.* Oxford: Blackwell.

Newman, B. M. (1993). *A Concise Greek/English Dictionary of the New Testament.* Stuttgart: Deutsche Bibelgesellschaft/German Bible Society.

Nolen-Hoeksema, S. & Davis, C. G. (1999). "Thanks for sharing that": Ruminators and their social support networks. *Journal of Personality and Social Psychology, 77,* 801-814.

Nolen-Hoeksema, S., Wisco, B. E. & Lyubomirsky, S. (2008). Rethinking Rumination. *Perspectives on Psychological Science, 3*(5), 400-424.

Nongbri, B. (2015). 2 Corinthians and possible material evidence for composite letter in antiquity. In: B. Neil & P. Allen (Eds). *Collecting Early Christian Letters. From the Apostle Paul to Late Antiquity* (pp. 54-67). Cambridge: Cambridge University Press.

Norris, F. H. & Slone, L. B. (Eds) (2014). Epidemiology of Trauma and PTSD. In: M. J. Friedman, T. M. Keane, P. & A. Resick. Handbook of PTSD. Science and Practice. 2nd Ed. (pp. 100-140) Ney York-London: Guilford Press.

Norris, F. H. (1992). Epidemiology of trauma: frequency and impact of different potentially traumatic events on different demographic groups. *Journal of consulting and clinical psychology, 60*(3), 409-418.

Noy, S. (2004). The traumatic process: conceptualization and treatment. *Traumatology, 10*(4), 211-230.

O'Brien, P. T. (1993). Letters, Letter Forms. In: G.F. Hawthorne, R. P. Martin & D. G. Reid (Eds.). *Dictionary of Paul and His Letters.* Downers Grove, IL: InterVarsity Press.

O'Collins, G. G. (1971). Power Made Perfect in Weakness, 2 Cor 12:9-10. *CBQ, 33,* 528-537.

O'Leavy, V. E. & Ickovics, J. R. (1995). Resilience and thriving in response to challenge: An opportunity for a paradigm shift in women's health. *Women's Haelth: Research on Gender, Beahvior, and Policy, 1,* 121-142.

O'Rourke, J. J. (1972). Comentario a la Segunda Carta a los Corintios. In: R.E. Brown, J.A. Fitzmyer & R.E. Murphy (Dir.). *Comentario Bíblico "San Jerónimo", Tomo IV* (pp. 63-100). Madrid: Cristiandad.

O'Rourke, J. J. F., Tallman, B. A. & Altmaier, E. M. (2008). Measuring posttraumatic changes in spirituality/religiosity. *Mental Health, Religion & Culture, 11*(7), 719-728.

Oatley, K. & Jenkins, J. (1996). *Understanding Emotions.* Oxford: Blackwell.

Ojeda, E. N. S. (2002). Una concepción latinoamericana: la resiliencia comunitaria. In: A. Melillo, A. & Ojeda, E. N. S. (Orgs.). *Resiliencia: descubriendo las propias fortalezas* (pp. 67-82). Buenos Aires: Paidós.

Oktay, J. S. (2012) *Grounded Theory.* New York, NY: Oxford University Press.

Oliva, I. (2012). Vida, Cognición y Cultura: Cartografiando procesos de auto-eco-organización *Cinta de Moebio 43*: 40-49. Online: www.moebio.uchile.cl/43/oliva.html. Accessed July 20, 2012.

Oman, D. & Thoresen, C.E. (2005). Do Religion and Spirituality Influence Health? In: R. F. Paloutzian & C. L. Park (Eds.). *Handbook of the Psychology of Religion and Spirituality.* New York: Guilford Press, 435-459. Omeri, A., Lennings, C., & Raymond, L. (2004). Hardiness and transformational coping in asylum seekers: the Afghan experience. *Diversity in Health & Social Care, 1*(1), 21-30

Orr, P. (2016). The Comfort of God and Pastoral Ministry: An Exegetical Study of 2 Corinthians 1:3-7. In: K. G. Condie (Ed.). *Tend My Sheep: The Word of God and Pastoral Ministry* (pp. 61-78). London: Latimer Trust.

Ortega-Gasset, J. (1964). ¿Qué es Filosofía?. In: J. Ortega-Gasset, *Obras Completas. Tomo VII (1948-1958).* Madrid: Revista Occidente.

Orton, D. E. (Comp.) (2000). *Poetry in the Hebrew Bible. Selected studies from Vetus Testamentum.* Leiden, Boston, Köln: Brill.

Otto, R. (1980). *Lo santo. Lo racional y lo irracional en la idea de Dios.* Madrid: Alianza.

Ozer, E. J., Best, S. R., Lipsey, T. L., & Weiss, D. S. (2003). Predictors of posttraumatic stress disorder and symptoms in adults: a meta-analysis. *Psychological Bulletin, 129*(1), 52.

Páez, D., Basabe, N., Ubillos, S. & Gonzalez, J.L. (2007). Social sharing, participation in demonstrations, emotional climate, and coping with collective violence after the march 11th Madrid bombings. *Journal for Social Issues, 63*, 323-328.

Páez, D., Martín Beristain, C., González, J. L., Basabe, N. & de Rivera, J. (Eds.) (2011). *Superando la violencia colectiva y construyendo una cultura de paz.* Madrid: Fundamentos.

Páez, D., Martínez, F. & Rimé, B. (2004). Los efectos del compartimiento social de las emociones sobre el trauma del 11 de marzo en personas no afectadas directamente. *Ansiedad y Estrés, 10*, 219-232.

Paillard, J. (2003). *In Praise of the Inexpressible: Paul's Experience of the Divine Mystery.* Peabody, MA: Hendrickson.

Paloutzian, R. F., & Park, C. L. (Eds.) (2005). *Handbook of the Psychology of Religion and Spirituality.* New York: Guilford Press.

Pannenberg, W. (1976). *El hombre como problema. Hacia una antropología teológica.* Barcelona: Herder.

Pannenberg, W. (2004). *Systematic Theology, Vol. 2.* New York: T&T Clark International.

Pargament, K. I. (1990) God help me, toward a theoretical framework of coping for the psychology of religion. In: M.L. Lynn & D.O. Moberg (Eds.) *Research in the Social Scientific Study of Religion,* Vol. 2. (pp. 195- 224). Greenwich, CT: JAI Press.

Pargament, K. I. (1996) Religious contributions to the process of coping with stress. In: H. Grzymala- Moszczynska & B. Beit- Hallahmi (Eds.). *Religion, psychopathology and coping* (pp. 177- 196). Amsterdam: Rodopi.

Pargament, K. I. (1997) *The psychology of religion and coping. Theory, research, practice.* New York: The Guilford Press.

Pargament, K. I., Feuille, M. & Burdzy, D. (2011). The Brief RCOPE: Current Psychometric Status of a Short Measure of Religious Coping. *Religions, 2*(1), 51-76.

Pargament, K. I., Kennell, J., Hathaway, W., Grevengoed, N., Newman, J. & Jones, W. (1988). Religion and the problem-solving process: Three styles of coping. *Journal for the Scientific Study of Religion, 27*(1), 90-104.

Pargament, K. I., Koenig, H. G. & Perez, L. M. (2000). The many methods of religious coping: Development and initial validation of the RCOPE. *Journal of Clinical Psychology, 56*(4), 519-543.

Pargament, K. I., Koenig, H. G., Tarakeshwar, N. & Hahn, J. (2004). Religious coping methods as predictors of psychological, physical and spiritual outcomes among medically ill elderly patients: A two-year longitudinal study. *Journal of Health Psychology, 9*(6), 713-730.

Pargament, K. L., Koenig, H. G., Tarakeshwas, N. & Hahn, J. (2001). Religious struggle as a predictor of mortality among medically ill elderly patients. *Archives of Internal Medicine, 161*, 1881-1885.

Park, C. L. & Folkman, S. (1997). Meaning in the context of stress and coping. *Review of General Psychology, 1*, 115-144.

Patruno, N. (1995). *Understanding Primo Levi.* Columbia: University of South Carolina Press.

Patzia, A. G. (1993). Canon. In: G.F. Hawthorne, R. P. Martin & D. G. Reid (Eds.). *Dictionary of Paul and His Letters.* Downers Grove, IL: InterVarsity Press.

Paul, A. (1978). *Intertestamento.* Navarra: Verbo Divino.

Pecorino, P. A. (2001). *Philosophy of Religion.* Online: http://www.qcc.cuny.edu/SocialSciences/ppecorino/PHIL_of_RELIGION_TEXT/default.htm Accessed February 15, 2017.

Pedersen, J. (1991). *Israel. Its Life and Culture. Volume I.* Atlanta: Scholars Press of University of South Florida.

Pennebaker, J.W. & Haber, K.D. (1993). A Social Stage Model of Collective Coping: The Loma Prieta Earthquake and The Persian Gulf War. *Journal of Social Issues, 49*(4), 125-145.

Peres, J. F., Moreira-Almeida, A., Nasello, A. G. & Koenig, H. G. (2007). Spirituality and resilience in trauma victims. *Journal of religion and health, 46*(3), 343-350.

Pérez Sales, P. (2001). *Reconceptualizar de la psicología del trauma desde los recursos positivos: una visión alternativa.* Online: http://www.psicosocial.net/es/centrodedocumentacion/cat_view/8-libros-y-documentos/40-psicologia-clinica-trauma. Accessed September 21, 2010.

Pérez Sales, P. (Ed.) (2006). *Trauma, culpa y duelo: hacia una psicoterapia integradora.* Bilbao: Desclée de Brouwer.

Pérez Sales, P., Cervellon, P., Vazquez, C., Vidales, D. & Gaborit, M. (2005). Post-traumatic factors and resilience: the role of shelter management and survivours' attitudes after the earthquakes in El Salvador (2001). *Journal of Community & Applied Social Psychology*, 15(5), 368-382.

Perkonigg, A., Kessler, R. C., Storz, S., & Wittchen, H. U. (2000). Traumatic events and post-traumatic stress disorder in the community: prevalence, risk factors and comorbidity. *Acta Psychiatrica Scandinavica*, 101(1), 46-59.

Perkonnig, A., Kessler, R. C., Storz, S. & Wittchen, H. U. (2000). Traumatic events and post-traumatic stress disorder in the community: prevalence, risk factors and comorbidity. *Acta Psychiatr Scand* 101, 46-59.

Peterson, C. & Seligman, M.E.P. (2004). *Character strengths and virtues: A handbook and classification.* Washington, DC: American Psychological Association.

Phillips III, R. E., Lynn, Q. K., Crossley, C. D. & Pargament, K.I. (2004). Self-Directing Religious Coping: A Deistic God, Abandoning God, or No God at All? *Journal For The Scientific Study Of Religion*, 43(3), 409-418.

Plummer, A. (1975). *A Critical and Exegetical Commentary on the Second Epistle of St. Paul to the Corinthians.* Edimburgo: Clark.

Plummer, R. L. (2013). The Role of Suffering in the Mission of Paul and the Mission of the Church. *The Southern Baptist Journal of Theology*, 17(4), 6-19.

Polaski, S. H. (1999). *Paul and the Discourse of Power.* Sheffield: Sheffield Academic Press.

Polk, L. V. (1997). Toward middle range theory of resilience. *Advances in Nursing Science*, 19(3), 1-13.

Poma, A. (2008). *The Impossibility and Necessity of Theodicy. The "Essais" of Leibniz.* London: Springer.

Porter, S. E. & Robinson, J. C. (2011). *Hermeneutics. An introduction to interpretative theory.* Grand Rapids: Eerdmans.

Porter, S. E. (1999). *Paul in Acts.* Peabody, MA: Hendrickson.

Porter, S. E. (2006b). Paul and His Bible: His Education and Access to the Scriptures of Israel. In: *SBL 2006 Annual Meeting Seminar Papers.*

Online: http://www.westmont.edu/-fisk/paulandscripture/port
er.html. Accessed January 10, 2014.

Porter, S. E. (2009). *Paul: Jew, Greek, and Roman.* Boston: Brill.

Porter, S. E. (Ed.) (2004). *The Pauline Canon.* Leiden-Boston: Brill.

Porter, S. E. (Ed.). (2006a). *Paul and his theology* (Vol. 3). Boston-Leiden: Brill.

Porter, S.E. (2002). Exegesis of the pauline letters, including the deuteron-pauline letters. In: S.E. Porter (Ed.). *Handbook to Exegesis of the New Testament.* Boston-Leiden: Brill.

Powell, S., Rosner, R., Butollo, W., Tedeschi, R. G. & Calhoun, L. G. (2003). Posttraumatic growth after war: A study with former refugees and displaced people in Sarajevo. *Journal of Traumatic Stress, 59,* 71-83.

Prati, G. & Pietrantoni, L. (2009). Optimism, Social Support, and Coping Strategies as Factors Contributing to Posttraumatic Growth: A Meta-Analysis. *Journal of Loss and Trauma, 14*(5), 364-388.

Prentiss, C. (2008). *Debating God's Economy: Social Justice in America on the eve of Vatican II.* Pennsylvania: University Press.

Pressman, P., Lyons, J. S., Larson, D. B. & Strain, J. J. (1990). Religious belief, depression, and ambulation status in elderly women with broken hips. *American Journal of Psychiatry, 147,* 758-760.

Price, R. M. (1980). Punished in Paradise: An Exegetical Theory on II Corinthians 12:1-10. *Journal for the Study of the New Testament, 7,* 33-40.

Pruessner, J. C., Wuethrich, S. & Baldwin, M. W. (2010). Stress of Self Esteem. In: G. Fink (Ed.) (2010). *Stress Consequences: Mental, Neuropsychological and Socioeconomic* (pp. 53-57). San Diego, CA: Elsevier.

Pugh, M. (2011). How Individuals Cope with Evil Daily. In: J. H. Ellens (Ed.). *Explaining Evil. Vol. 3. Approaches, Responses, Solutions* (pp.183-202). Oxford: Praeger.

Puig, G. & Rubio, J.L. (2011). *Manual de Resiliencia Aplicada.* Barcelona: Gedisa.

Quesnel, M. (1980). *Las cartas a los corintios. (CB-22).* Navarra: Verbo Divino.

Ramognini, M. (2008). *Arte y resiliencia en niños en situación de riesgo psicosocial: Estudio de sistematización de los primeros años de actividad de la Fundación Casa Rafael: 2006 a 2008.* Buenos Aires: Fundación Casa Rafael.

Ramsay, W. M. (1898). *St. Paul the Traveller and the Roman Citizen.* New York: Putnam's Sons.

Raynier, C. (2009). *Para leer a San Pablo.* Navarra: Verbo Divino.

Reich, J. W., Zautra, A. J. & Hall, J.S. (Eds.) (2010). *Handbook of Adult Resilience.* New York and London: The Guilford Press.

Resnick, H. S., Kilpatrick, D. G., Dansky, B. S., Saunders, B. E. & Best, C. L. (1993). Prevalence of civilian trauma and posttraumatic stress disorder in a representative national sample of women. *Journal of consulting and clinical psychology, 61*(6), 984-991.

Rice, P. L. (1998). El Afrontamiento del Estrés: Estrategias cognitivo-conductuales. In: V. Caballo. *Manual para el Tratamiento Cognitivo-Conductual de los Trastornos Psicológicos. Vol. 2: Formulación Clínica, Medicina Conductual y Trastornos de Relación* (pp. 323-358). Madrid: Siglo XXI.

Rickaby, J. (1908). Cardinal Virtues. In: *The Catholic Encyclopedia.* New York: Robert Appleton Company. Online:: http://www.newadvent.org/ cathen/03343a.htm. Accessed December 14, 2016.

Ricoeur, P. (1967). *The Symbolism of Evil.* New York: Harper & Row.

Ricœur, P. (1973). The Model of the Text: Meaningful Action Considered as a Text. *New Literary History, 5*(1), 91-117.

Ricoeur, P. (1976). *Interpretation Theory. Discourse and the surplus of mining.* Fort Worth: Texas Christian Univerity Press.

Ricoeur, P. (1977). Expliquer et comprendre: sur quelques connexions remarquables entre la théorie du texte, la théorie de l'action et la théorie de l'histoire. *Revue philosophique de Louvain, 75*(25), 126-147.

Ricoeur, P. (1995). *Tiempo y narración, I, Configuración del tiempo en el relato histórico.* México: Siglo XXI.

Ricoeur, P. (1996). *Sí mismo como otro.* Madrid: Siglo XXI.

Ricoeur, P. (2002). *Del Texto a la Acción. Ensayo sobre hermenéutica II.* 2th Ed. México: Fondo de Cultura Económica.

Ricoeur, P. (2004). *Memory, History, Forgetting.* Chicago-London: The University of Chicago Press.

Ricoeur, P. (2016). *Hermeneutics and the Human Sciences. Essays on Language, Action and Interpretation.* Cambridge: Cambridge University Press.

Riggs, T. (2006). *Worldmark Encyclopedia of Religious Practices,* Vols. 1-3. New York: Thomson Gale.

Rioseco, P., Escobar, B., Vicente, B., Vielma, M., Saldivia, S. & Cruzat, M. (1994). Prevalencia de vida de algunos trastornos psiquiátricos en la provincia de Santiago. *Revista de Psiquiatría* 11(4), 186-193.

Rizzolatti, G. & Craighero, L. (2004). The Mirror-neuron Sistem. *Annual Review of Neuroscience 27,* 169-192.

Rizzolatti, G. & Fabbri-Destro, M. (2010). Mirror neurons: from discovery to autism. *Experimental Brain Research, 200*(3-4), 223-237.

Robertson, A. T. (2003). *Comentario al Texto Griego del Nuevo Testamento. Obra Completa.* Barcelona: Clie.

Roca Perara, M. A. & Torres Santos, O. (2001). Un estudio del Síndrome de Burnout y su relación con el sentido de coherencia. *Cubana de psicología, 18*(2), 120-128.

Rodríguez Marín, J. (1995). *Psicología social de la salud.* Madrid: Síntesis.

Roediger, H. L., Dudai, Y. & Fitzpatrick, S. M. (2007). *Science of Memory: Concepts.* New York, NY: Oxford University Press.

Roetzel, C. J. (2010). 2 Corinthians. In: D. E. Aune (Ed.), *The Blackwell Companion to the New Testament* (pp. 434-454). Oxford: John Wiley & Sons.

Roldán, A. F. (2013). La fe como evento existencial-escatológico en el pensamiento de Rudolf Bultmann. De la filosofía de Martín Heidegger al planteo teológico. *Franciscanum. Revista de las Ciencias del Espíritu, 55*(160), 165-194.

Rollins, W. G. & Kille, D.A. (Eds.) (2007). *Psychological Insight into the Bible: Texts and Readings.* Grand Rapids, MI: Eerdmans.

Rollins, W. G. (1983). *Jung and the Bible.* Atlanta: John Knox Press.

Rollins, W. G. (1999). *Soul and Psyche. The Bible in Psychological Perspective.* Minneapolis: Augsburg Fortress Publishers.

Rollins, W. G. (2002). The Bible in Psycho-spiritual Perspective: News from the world of biblical scholarship. *Pastoral Psychology, 51*(2), 101-118.

Rosen, G. M. & Frueh, C. (Ed.) (2010). *Clinicians Guide to Posttraumatic Stress Disorder.* Hoboken, New Jersey: Wiley.

Rosen, G. M. (Ed.) (2004). *Posttraumatic Stress Disorder. Issues and Controversies.* Chichester: Wiley & Sons.

Routledge, R. (2013). *Old Testament Theology. A Thematic Approach.* Drowners, IL: InterVarsity Press.

Royce, E. (2009). *Poverty and Power A Structural Perspective on American Inequality.* Plymouth: Rowman & Litttlefield Publishers.

Rudman, D. (2001). *Determinism in the Book of Ecclesiastes.* Sheffield: Sheffield Academic Press.

Ruiz de la Peña, J.L. (1988). *Imagen de Dios. Antropología teológica fundamental.* 3° Ed. Santander: Sal Terrae.

Russell, R. (1996). Redemptive Suffering and Paul's Thorn in the Flesh. *Journal of the Evangelical Theological Society, 39*(4), 559-570.

Rutten, B. P., Hammels, C., Geschwind, N., Menne-Lothmann, C., Pishva, E., Schruers, K., den Hove, D., Kenis, G., Os, V. J. & Wichers, M. (2013). Resilience in mental health: linking psychological and neurobiological perspectives. *Acta Psychiatrica Scandinavica, 128*(1), 3-20.

Rutter, M. (1979). Protective factors in children's responses to stress and disadvantage. In M.W. Kent and J.E. Rolf (Eds.). *Primary Prevention in Psychopathology: Social Competence in children.* Vol. 8. (pp. 49-74). Hanover, NH: University Press of New England.

Rutter, M. (1987). Psychosocial resilience and protective mechanisms. *American Journal of Orthopsychiatry, 57*, 316-331.

Saavedra, E. & Castro, A. (2009). *Escala de Resiliencia Escolar (E.R.E.), para niños entre 9 y 14 años.* Santiago de Chile: CEANIM.

Saavedra, E. & Villarta, M. (2008). *Escala de Resiliencia (SV-RES), para jóvenes y adultos.* Santiago de Chile: CEAMIN.

Sainsbury, M. (1988). *Paradoxes.* Cambridge: Cambridge University Press.

Salgado, A.C. (2009). Felicidad, resiliencia y optimismo en estudiantes de colegios nacionales de la ciudad de Lima. *Liberabit, 15*(2), 133-141.

Sampley, J. P. (Org.) (2008). *Paulo no Mundo Greco-Romano. Um Comêndio.* Sao Paulo: Paulus.

Sanchez-Bosch, J. (1998). *Escritos Paulinos*. Navarra: Verbo Divino.

Sanders, E. P. (1983). *Paul, the Law, and the Jewish People*. Philadelphia: Fortress Press.

Sandi, C. (2000). Estrés: aspectos psicobiológicos y significado funcional. In: C. Sandi, J.M. Calés (Eds.), *Estrés: consecuencias psicológicas, fisiológicas y clínicas* (pp. 13-45). Madrid: Sanz & Torres.

Sara, S. J. (2000). Retrieval and reconsolidation: toward a neurobiology of remembering. *Learning & Memory, 7*(2), 73-84.

Schaefer, J. A. & Moos, R. (1998). The context for personal growth: Life crises, individual and social resources, and coping. In: R. Tedeschi, C. Park & L.G. Calhoun (Eds.) *Posttraumatic growth: Positive changes in the aftermath of crisis* (pp. 99-125). New Jersey: Erlbaum.

Scheeringa, M. S., Zeanah, C. H. & Cohen, J. A. (2011). PTSD in children and adolescents: toward an empirically based algorithm. *Depression and Anxiety, 28*, 770-782.

Schellenberg, R. S. (2013). *Rethinking Paul's Rhetorical Education. Comparative Rhetoric and 2 Corinthians 10-13*. Atlanta: Society of Biblical Literature.

Schexnaildre, M. (2011). *Predicting posttraumatic growth: Coping, social support, and posttraumatic stress in children and adolescents after Hurricane Katrina*. Thesis of Master. Louisiana State University, USA.

Schlecker, M. & Fleischer, F. (2013). *Ethnographies of Social Support*. New York: Palgrave Macmillan.

Schnelle, U. (2003). *Apostle Paul. His Life and Theology*. Grand Rapids, MI: Baker.

Schnyder, U. & Cloitre, M. (Eds.) (2015). *Evidence Based Treatments for Trauma- Related Psychological Disorders. A Practical Guide for Clinicians*. London: Springer

Schrage, W. (1987). *Ética del Nuevo Testamento*. Salamanca: Sígueme.

Schwarzer, R., & Luszczynska, A. (2008). Reactive, anticipatory, preventive, and proactive coping: a theoretical distinction. *The Prevention Researcher, 15*(4), 22-25.

Schwarzer, R., Knoll, N., & Rieckmann, N. (2004). Social support. *Health psychology, 158*, 181.

Schweitzer, A. (1931). *The Mysticism of Paul the Apostle.* London: Adam & Charles Black.

Schweitzer, A. (1948). *The Psychiatric Study of Jesus: Exposition and Criticism.* Boston: Beacon Press.

Schweitzer, A. (2006). *O Misiticismo de Paulo, o Apóstolo.* Sao Paulo: Fonte.

Seery, M. D., Holman, E. A. & Silver, R. C. (2010). Whatever Does Not Kill Us: Cumulative Lifetime Adversity, Vulnerability, and Resilience. *Journal of Personality and Social Psychology.* Advance online publication. Online: ‹https://webfiles.uci.edu/rsilver/trash/Seery%2C%20Holman%2C%20%26%20Silver%202010%20in%20press%20JPSP.pdf› Accessed January 23, 2012.

Segundo, J. L. (1975). *Liberación de la Teología.* Buenos Aires: Lolhé.

Segundo, J. L. (1985). *Teología de la Liberación. Respuesta al Cardenal Ratzinger.* Madrid: Cristiandad.

Seifrid, M. A. (2015). *The Second Letter to the Corinthians.* Grand Rapids, MI: Eerdmans.

Seligman, M. E. P. & Csikszentmihalyi, M. (2000). Positive Psychology: An Introduction. *American Psychologist, 55*, 5-14.

Seligman, M. E. P. (1991). *Indefensión.* Madrid: Debate.

Seligman, M. E. P. (2002). Positive Psychology, Positive Prevention, and Positive Therapy. In: C. R. Snyder & S.J. Lopez (Eds.). *Handbook of Positive Psychology* (pp. 3-12). Oxford: Oxford University Press.

Seligman, M. E. P., Duckworth, A.L & Steen, T.A (2005). Positive Psychology in Clinical Practice. *Annu. Rev. Clin. Psychol. 1*, 629–651.

Selye, H. (1936). A syndrome produced by diverse nocuous agents. *Nature, 138*, 32-34.

Selye, H. (1956). *The stress of life.* Nueva York: McGraw-Hill.

Selye, H. (1976). *Stress in Health and Disease.* Boston-London: Butterworths.

Selye, H. (1980). *Selye's guide to stress research.* Nueva York: Elsevier.

Seow, C. L. (1997). *Ecclesiastes. A New Translation with Introduction and Commentary.* New Haeven-London: Yale University Press.

Sepulveda, J. (2009). Una aproximación teológica al la experiencia pentecostal. *Red Latinoamericana de Estudios Pentecostales, RELEP.*

En línea: http://www.relep.org/index.php?option=com_content &task=view&id=20&Itemid=38. Accessed October 26, 2009.

Sharp, D. S. (1914). *Epictetus and the New Testament*. London: CH Kelly.

Silliman, B. (1994). *Resiliency research review: Conceptual and research foundations*. Online: http://www.cyfernet.org/research/resil review.html. Accessed May 23, 2009.

Silver, R. C., Wortman, C. B. & Crofton, C. (1990). The role of coping in support provision: The self-representational dilemma of victims of life crises. In B. R. Sarason, I. G. Sarason & G. R. Pierce (Eds.), *Social support: An interactional view*. New York: Wiley.

Simundson, D. J. (1992). *Suffering*. In: D. N. Freedman (Ed.). *The Anchor Bible Dictionary*. Vol. 6 (pp. 219- 225). New York: Doubleday.

Singh, B. (2016). Study of Personality Hardiness in Relation to Gender, Locality, Organisational Set-Up and Marital Status. *ZENITH International Journal of Multidisciplinary Research*, 6(1), 110-115.

Sluzki, C. (1995). Transformaciones: una propuesta para cambios narrativos en psicoterapia. *Revista de psicoterapia*, 6(22-23), 53-70.

Smith, A., Joseph, S. & Nair, R. D. (2011). An Interpretative Phenomenological Analysis of Posttraumatic Growth in Adults Bereaved by Suicide, *Journal of Loss and Trauma*, 16(5), 413-430.

Smith, B. D. (1996). Suffering. In: *Baker's Evangelical Dictionary of Biblical Theology*. W. A. Elwell (Ed.). Grand Rapids, MI: Baker Books.

Smith, B. D. (2002). *Paul's Seven Explanations of the Suffering of the Righteous*. New York: Peter Lang.

Smith, N. G. (1959). The Thorn that Stayed An Exposition of II Corinthians 12: 7-9. *Interpretation*, 13(4), 409-416.

Snyder, C. R. & Ford, C. E. (Eds.). (1987). *Coping with Negative Life Events. Clinical and social psychological perspectives*. New York: Springer.

Snyder, C. R. & Lopez, S.J. (Eds) (2002). *Handbook of positive psychology*. Oxford: Oxford University Press.

Sodi, R. & Marcus, M. (2011). *New Reflections on Primo Levi. Before and After Auschwitz*. New York: Palgrave Macmillan.

Sorensens, R. (2005). *A Brief History of the Paradox. Philosophy and the Labyrinths of the Mind*. Oxford: Oxford University Press.

Southwick, S. M., Bonanno, G. A., Masten, A. S., Panter-Brick, C. & Yehuda, R. (2014). Resilience definitions, theory, and challenges: interdisciplinary perspectives. *European journal of Psychotraumatology,* 5, 25338. On line: http://dx.doi.org/10.3402 /ejpt.v5.25338. Accessed January 20, 2016.

Squire, L.R. & Kandel, E.R. (2000). *Memory: From Mind to Molecules.* Ney York: Henry Holt & Company.

Stählin, G. (2003). θλίβω [apretar, afligir], θλῖψις [aprieto, aflicción]. In: G. Kittel & G. Friedrich. *Compendio del Diccionario teológico del Nuevo Testamento* (pp. 261-263). Grand Rapids, MI: Desafío.

Stamps, D. L. (2007). Pauline Letters. In: S. E. Porter (Ed.). *Dictionary of Biblical Criticism and Interpretation* (pp. 264-265). New York: Routledge.

Stendahl, K. (1976). *Paul Among Jews and Gentiles and Other Essays.* Philadelphia: Fortress Press.

Stickgold, R. & Walker, M.P. (2013). Sleep-dependent memory triage: evolving generalization through selective processing. *Nature Neuroscience* 16, 139–145.

Stinnett, N. & De Frain, J. (1989). The healthy family: Is it possible? In M. J. Fine (Ed.), *The second handbook on parent education* (pp. 53-74). San Diego, CA: Academic Press.

Strauss, A. & Corbin, J. (1994). Grounded Theory Methodology. In: N.K. Denzin & Y.S. Lincoln (Eds.). *Handbook of Qualitative Research* (pp. 217-285). Thousand Oaks: Sage.

Summerfield, D. (1998). The social experience of war and some issues for the humanitarian field. In: P. Bracken & C. Petty (Eds.), *Rethinking the Trauma of War.* London: Free Association Press.

Sumney, J. (1990). *Identifying Paul's Opponents.* Sheffield: JSOT.

Talavera, A. F. & Beyer, H. (1991). Retrato del movimiento evangélico a la luz de las encuestas de opinión pública. *Estudios Públicos,* 44, 82-83.

Tallman, B., Shaw, K., Schultz, J. & Altmaier, E. (2010). Well-being and posttraumatic growth in unrelated donor marrow transplant survivors: A nine-year longitudinal study. *Rehabilitation Psychology,* 55(2), 204-210.

Tarusarira, J. (2019). The Anatomy of Apology and Forgiveness: Towards Transformative Apology and Forgiveness. *International Journal of Transitional Justice,* 13(2), 206-224.

Tasmuth, R. (2014). *Pauline Antropology: On the Inner Human Being and the Human "I"*. Estonian Science Foundation / Estonian Research Council Grant no. ETF8665. Online: http://usuteadus.ee/word press/wpcontent/uploads/2014_2%20(67)/UA-2014-2-5.Tasmuth.pdf. Accessed March 13, 2016.

Taubes, J. (2007). *La Teología Política de Pablo*. Madrid: Trotta.

Taylor, J. (1994). *Les Actes des Deux Apôtres. Vol. 5, Commentaire Historique (Act 9,1-18,22)*. Paris: Librairie Lecoffre.

Taylor, J. (2001). *Petra and the Lost Kingdom of the Nabataeans*. London-New York: I. B. Tauris.

Taylor, N.H. (1991). The Composition and Chronology of Second Corinthians. *JSNT 14(44)*, 67-87.

Taylor, S. E. (1983). Adjustment to threatening events: A theory of cognitive adaptation. *American Psychologist, 38*, 1161-1173.

Tedeschi, R. G. & Calhoun, L. G. (1995). *Trauma and transformation: Growing in the aftermath of suffering*. Thousand Oaks, CA: Sage.

Tedeschi, R. G. & Calhoun, L. G. (1996). The Posttraumatic Growth Inventory: Measuring the positive legacy of trauma. *Journal of Traumatic Stress, 9*, 455–472.

Tedeschi, R. G. & Calhoun, L. G. (2000). Posttraumatic growth: A new focus in psychotraumatology. Psy-talk. *Newsletter of the British Psychological Society Student Members Group, 5*.

Tedeschi, R. G. & Calhoun, L.G. (2004) Posttraumatic Growth: Conceptual Foundations and Empirical Evidence. *Psychological Inquiry, 15*(1), 1-18.

Tedeschi, R. G., Park, C. L. & Calhoun, L. G. (1998). Posttraumatic growth: Conceptual issues. In: R. G. Tedeschi, C. L. Park & L. G. Calhoun (Eds.) *Posttraumatic growth: Positive changes in the aftermath of crisis* (pp. 1-22). New Jersey: Erlbaum.

Teicher, M. H., Andersen, S. L., Polcari, A., Anderson, C. M., Navalta, C. P. & Kim, D. M. (2003). The neurobiological consequences of early stress and childhood maltreatment. *Neuroscience & Biobehavioral Reviews, 27*(1), 33-44.

Tennen, H. & Affleck, G. (2005). Benefit-finding and benefit-reminding. En C. R. Snyder & S. J. López (Eds.). *Handbook of positive psychology* (pp. 584-597). Oxford: Oxford University Press.

Thakur, M. S. & Chawla, J. (2016). Comparative Study of Psychological Hardiness among Teacher Trainees in Relation to Gender. *International Education and Research Journal*, 2(1), 112-115

Thayer, J. H. (2006). A Greek-English Lexicon of New Testament. In: *BibleWorks*, Version 7.0.012g.

Theide, W. (2008). *El Sentido Crucificado. Una Teodicea Trinitaria*. Salamanca: Sígueme.

Theissen, G. (1987). *Psychological aspects of Pauline theology*. Philadelphia: Fortress.

Thomas, J.C. (1996). An Angel From Satan': Paul's Thorn in the Flesh (2 Corinthians 12.7-10). *Journal of Pentecostal Theology*, 9, 39-52.

Thombre, A., Sherman, A.C. & Simonton, S. (2010). Religious Coping and Posttraumatic Growth Among Family Caregivers of Cancer Patients in India. *Journal of Psychosocial Oncology*, 28(2), 173-188.

Thompson, J. W. (2006). *Pastoral Ministry according to Paul. A biblical vision*. Grand Rapids, MI: Baker.

Thornton, T. C. G. (1972). Satan-God's Agent for Punishing. *ExpT*, 83, 151-152.

Thorsteinsson, R. (2010). *Roman Christianity and Roman Stoicism: a comparative study of ancient morality*. Oxford University Press.

Thrall, M.E. (1996). Paul's Journey to Paradise: Some Exegetical Issues in 2 Cor 12,2- 4. (pp. 347-363). In: R. Bieringer (Ed.), *The Corinthian Correspondence*. Leuven: Leuven University Press-Peeters.

Tillich, P. (1976). *La Dinámica de la Fe*. Buenos Aires: La Aurora.

Tillich, P. (1982). *Teología Sistemática, Tomo I*. Salamanca: Sígueme.

Toth, E., Gersner, R., Wilf-Yarkoni, A., Raizel, H., Dar, D.E., Richter-Levin, G., Levit, O. & Zangen, A. (2007). Age Dependent Effects of Chronic Stress on Brain Plasticity and Depressive Behavior. *Journal of Molecular Neuroscience*, 33(2), 201-15.

Toussaint, L. L. & Webb, J. R. (2005). Theoretical and empirical connections between forgiveness, mental health, and well-being. In: E. L. Worthington, Jr. (Ed.), *Handbook of forgiveness* (pp. 349-362). New York: Brunner-Routledge.

Toussaint, L. L., Worthington, E. L. J., & Williams, D. R. (2015). *Forgiveness and health. Scientific Evidence and Theories Relating Forgiveness to Better Health*. Dordrecht: Springer.

Trevino, K. M. & Pargament, K. I. (2007). Religious Coping with Terrorism and Natural Disaster. *Southern Medical Journal*, 100(9), 946-947.

Treynor, W., Gonzalez, R. & Nolen-Hoeksema, S. (2003). Rumination reconsidered: A psychometric analysis. *Cognitive Therapy & Research*, 27, 247–259.

Trivette, C. M., Dunst, C. J., Deal, A. G., Hamer, W. & Propst, S. (1990). Assessing family strengths and family functioning style. *Topics in Early Childhood Specialist Education*, 10(1), 16-35.

Tuggy, A. E. (1996). *Léxico Griego-Español del Nuevo Testamento*. El Paso, TX: Mundo Hispano.

Ullrich, P. M. & Lutgendorf, K. (2002). Journaling about stressful events: Effects of cognitive processing and emotional expression. *Annals of Behavioral Medicine*, 24, 244-250.

Ungar, M. (Ed.) (2012). *The Social Ecology of Resilience. A handbook of Theory and Practice*. New York: Springer.

Universidad Nacional del Noreste de Argentina – UNNA (2010). *Apuntes del Departamento de Mecánica Aplicada: Estabilidad II*. Facultad de Ingeniería. Online: http://ing.unne.edu.ar /download.htm. Accessed September 6, 2010.

Urbaniak, J. (2015). Religion as memory: How has the continuity of tradition produced collective meanings?–Part one. *HTS Teologiese Studies/Theological Studies*, 71(3), 1-8.

Valdés, M. & Flores, T. (1985). *Psicobiología del Estrés*. Barcelona: Martínez Roca.

Vallejo, C. (1996). *Hay Golpes en la Vida tan Fuertes... Antología Poética*. Santiago: Andrés Bello.

Van Aarde, A. G. (2015). Progress in Psychological Biblical Criticism. *Pastoral Psychology*, 64(4), 481-492.

Van der Lans, J. M. (2002). Implications of Social Contructionism for the Psychological Study of Religion. (pp. 23-39). In: G.A.M. Hermans, G. Immink, A. de Jong & J.M. van der Lans (Eds.). *Social Constructionism and Theology*. Leiden-Boston-Koln: Brill.

Van der Ven, J. A. & Vossen, E. (1995). *Suffering: Why For God's Sake?* Kampen: Kok Pharo Publishing House.

Van der Ven, J. A. (2004). An Empirical or a Normative Approach to Practical-Theological Research? (pp. 101-135). In: J. A. van der Ven. *Normativity and Empirical Research in Theology*. Leiden-Boston: Brill.

Van der Ven, J.A. and E. (H.J.M.) Vossen (Eds). (1995) *Suffering: Why for God's Sake? Pastoral Research in Theodicy*. Kampen: Kok Pharos.

Van Gemeren, W. A. (1991). Psalms. In: F. E. Goebelein (Ed.). *The Expositor's Bible Commentary, Vol. 5*. Grand Rapids: Zondervan.

Van Kessel, G., MacDougall, C. & Gibb, L. (2015). The Process of Rebuilding Human Resilience in the Face of the Experience of a Natural Disaster: A Multisystem Model. *International Journal of Emergency Mental Health and Human Resilience, 17*(4), 682-687.

Van Kooten, G. H. (2008). *Paul's Anthropology in Context. The Image of God, Assimilation to God, and Tripartite Man in Ancient Judaism, Ancient Philosophy and Early Christianity*. Tubingen: Mohr Siebeck.

VandenBos, G. R. (Ed.) (2015). *APA Dictionary of Psychology*. 2nd Ed. Washington, DC: American Psychological Association.

Vanistendael, S. & Lecomte, J. (2002). *La felicidad es posible*. Barcelona: Gedisa.

Vanistendael, S. (1994). *Cómo Crecer Superando los Percances: Resiliencia, Capitalizar las Fuerzas del Individuo*. Ginebra: BICE.

Vanistendael, S. (2003). *Resiliencia y Espiritualidad: el Realismo de la Fe*. Ginebra: BICE.

Vanistendael, S., Gaberan, P., Humbeeck, B., Lacomnte, J., Manil, P. & Rouyer, M. (2013). *Resiliencia y Humor*. Barcelona: Gedisa.

Vázquez, C. & Hervás, G. (Eds.) (2009). *Psicología Positiva Aplicada*. 2º Ed. (pp. 283-309). Bilbao: Desclée de Brouwer.

Vázquez, C., Castilla, C. & Hervás, G. (2009). Reacciones ante el Trauma: Resistencia y Crecimiento. In: E. Fernández-Abascal (ed.). *Las Emociones Positivas* (pp. 375-392). Madrid: Pirámide.

Vázquez, C., Crespo, M. & Ring, J.M. (2000). *Medición Clínica en Psiquiatría y Psicología*. Barcelona: Masson.

Vealey, R. S. & Perritt, N. C. (2015). Hardiness and Optimism as Predictors of the Frequency of Flow in Collegiate Athletes. *Journal of Sport Behavior,38*(3), 321.

Vegge, I. (2008). *2 Corinthians a Letter about Reconciliation: A Psychological, Epistolographical and Rhetorical Analysis.* Tubingen: Mohr Siebeck.

Veith-Flanigan, J. & Sandman, C.A. (1985). Neuroendocrine relationship with stress. In: S.R. Burohfield (Ed.), *Stress: Psychological and Physiological Interactions* (pp. 129-161). Washington: Hemisphere.

Vera, B., Carbelo, B. & Vecina, J. (2006). La Experiencia Traumática desde la Psicología Positiva: Resiliencia y Crecimiento Postraumático. *Papeles del Psicólogo, 27*(1), 40-49.

Vermeer, P., Van Der Ven, J. A. & Vossen, E. (1996). Learning Theodicy. *Journal of Empirical Theology, 9*(2), 67-85.

Vermeer, P., Van der Ven, J. A. & Vossen, E. (1997). Education for Coping With Suffering. *Journal of Empirical Theology, 10*(1), 61-83.

Vespa, A., Jacobsen, P.B., Spazzafumo, L. & Balducci, L. (2011). Evaluation of intrapsychic factors, coping styles, and spirituality of patients affected by tumors. *Psycho-Oncology, 20*(1), 5-11.

Vető, S. (2011). El Holocausto como Acontecimiento Traumático. Acerca de la Incorporacion del Concepto Freudiano de Trauma en la Historiografía del Holocausto. *Revista de Psicología, 20*(1), 127-152.

Vidal, S. (2007). *Pablo. De Tarso a Roma.* Santander: Sal Terrae.

Vidal, S. (2012). *Las Cartas Auténticas de Pablo.* Bilbao: Mensajero.

Vilchez-Lindez, J. (1995). *Eclesiastés o Qohelet.* Navarra: Verbo Divino.

Villegas Besora, M. (2006). Dolor y sufrimiento en las tradiciones sapienciales. *Revista de Psicoterapia, 17*(65), 5-43.

Volf, J. M. G. (1990). *Paul and Perseverance. Staying in and Falling Away.* Louisville, KY: Westminster/John Knox Press.

Vossen, H. E. (1993). Images of God and Coping with Suffering. *Journal of Empirical Theology, 6*(1), 19-38.

Wagner, B., Knaevelsrud, C. & Maercker, A. (2007). Post-Traumatic Growth and Optimism as Outcomes of an Internet-Based Intervention for Complicated Grief. *Cognitive Behaviour Therapy, 36*(3), 156-161.

Wallace, R. S. (1991). Sufrimiento. In: *Nuevo Diccionario Bíblico Certeza*. Barcelona: Certeza.

Walsh, F. (1996). The concept of family resilience: Crisis and challenge. *Family Process*, 35(3), 261-281.

Walsh, F. (2002). A family resilience framework: Innovative practice applications. *Family relations*, 51(2), 130-137.

Walsh, F. (2003). Family resilience: A framework for clinical practice. *Family process*, 42(1), 1-18.

Walsh, F. (2004). *Resiliencia familiar: estrategias para su fortalecimiento*. Madrid: Amorrortu.

Walsh, F. (2007). Traumatic Loss and Mayor Disasters: Strengthening Family and Community Resilience. *Family Process*, 46(2), 207-227.

Walton, J. M. (1998). 2 Corinthians 12:1–10. *Interpretation*, 52(3), 293-296.

Warfield, B. B. (1886). Some Difficult Passages in the First Chapter of 2 Corinthians. *Journal of the Society of Biblical Literature and Exegesis*, 6(2), 27-39.

Wasserman, E. (2014). Paul beyond the Judaism/Hellenism Divide? The Case of Pauline Anthropology in Romans 7 and 2 Corinthians 4-5. In: .E. Porter & A.W. Pitts (Eds.). *Christian Origins and Hellenistic Judaism. Social and Literary Contexts for the New Testament* (pp. 259-279). Leideb-Boston: Brill.

Watson, D. F. (2010). Rhetorical Criticism. In: D. E. Aune (Ed.). *The Blackwell Companion to the New Testament* (pp. 167-176). Oxford: John Wiley & Sons.

Watson, F. (1986). *Paul, Judaism, and the Gentiles*. Cambridge: Cambridge University Press.

Watson, W. G. E. (1996). *Classical Hebrew Poetry. A guide to it's techniques*. 2th Ed. Sheffield: JSOT Press.

Waugh, C. E., Thompson, R. J. & Gotlib, I. H. (2011). Flexible emotional responsiveness in trait resilience. *Emotion*, 11(5), 1059-1067.

Weindling, P. (2015). *Victims and Survivors of Nazi Human Experiments. Science and Suffering in the Holocaust*. New York-London: Bloomsbury Academic.

Weiss, J. (1993). *How Psychotherapy Works*. New York: Guilford Press.

Welborn, L. L. (1995). The Identification of 2 Corinthians 10-13 with the "Letter of Tears". *Novum Testamentum, 37*(2), 138-153.

Werner, E. & Smith, R. (1977). *Kauai's children come of age.* Honolulu: University of Hawaii Press.

Werner, E. & Smith, R. (1982). *Vulnerable but Invincible: A Study of Resilient Children.* New York: McGraw-Hill.

Werner, E. & Smith, R. (1992). *Overcoming the Odds: High Risk Children from Birth to Adulthood.* Ithaca, NY: Cornell University Press.

Werner, E. & Smith, R. (2001). *Journeys from Childhood to Midlife: Risk, Resilience, and Recovery.* Ithaca, NY: Cornell University Press.

Werner, E. (2000). Protective factors and individual resilience. In: R. Meisells & J. Shonkoff (Eds.). *Handbook of Early Intervention* (pp. 115-132). Cambridge, UK: Cambridge.

Werntz, M. (2015). The fellowship of suffering: Reading Philippians with Stanley Hauerwas. *Review and Expositor, 112*(1), 144-150.

Westphal, M. & Bonanno, G. A. (2007). Posttraumatic Growth and Resilience to Trauma: Different Sides of the Same Coin or Different Coins? *Applied Psychology, 56*(3), 417-427.

Wichert, S., Wolf, O.T., & Schwabe, L. (2013). Changing memories after reactivation: A one-time opportunity? *Neurobiology of Learning and Memory 99*, 38–49.

Witherington III, B. (1995). *Conflict and Community in Corinth. A Socio-Rhetorical Commentary on 1 and 2 Corinthians.* Grand Rapids, MI: Eerdmans.

Wolf, D. (2007). *Beyond Anne Frank: Hidden Children and Postwar Families in Holland.* London: University of California Press.

Wolff, H. W. (1975). *Antropología del Antiguo Testamento.* Salamanca: Sígueme.

Wolin, S. J. & Bennett, L. A. (1984). Family rituals. *Family Process, 23*(3), 401-420.

Worthington, E. L., Lavelock, C. R., Van Tongeren, D. R., Van OyenWitvliet, C., Griffin, B. J., Greer, C. L., & Ho, M. Y. (2014). The contributions of Christian perspectives and practices to positive psychology. In: *Religion and Spirituality Across Cultures* (pp. 47-70). Dordrecht: Springer.

Wortman, C. B. & Silver, R. C. (1989). The Myths of Coping with Loss. *Journal of Consulting and Clinical Psychology, 57*, 349–357.

Wright, N. T. (2002). *El Verdadero Pensamiento de Pablo.* Barcelona: Clie.

Wright, N. T. (2013a). *Paul and the Faithfulness of God.* Vols. I-III. Minneapolis: Fortress Press.

Wright, N.T. (2009). *Justification: God's Plan and Paul.* Downers Grove, IL: InterVarsity Press.

Wright, N.T. (2013b). *Pauline Perspectives. Essays on Paul, 1978-2013.* Minneapolis: Fortress Press.

Wu, G., Feder, A., Cohen, H., Kim, J. J., Calderon, S., Charney, D. S. & Mathé, A. A. (2013). Understanding Resilience. *Frontiers in Behavioral Neuroscience, 7* (10), 1-15. Online: http://journal.fronti ersin.org/article/10.3389/fnbeh. 2013.00010/abstract. Accessed May 22, 2014.

Yates, T. & Luthar, S. (2009). Resilience. In: *Encyclopedia of Human Relationships.* SAGE Publications online: http://sage-ereference.com/humanrelationships/Article_n445.html. Access ed September 6, 2009.

Yehuda, R. & McFarlane, A. (1995). Conflict between current knowledge about posttraumatic stress disorder and its original conceptual basis. *American Journal of Psychiatry 152,* 1705-13.

Yehuda, R. & McFarlane, A. C. (1995). Conflict between current knowledge about posttraumatic stress disorder and its original conceptual basis. *American Journal of Psychiatry, 152*(12), 1705-1713.

Yinger, K.L. (2011). *The New Perspective on Paul. An Introduction.* Ougene, OR: Cascade Books.

Yoffe, L. (2012). Beneficios de las Prácticas Religiosos/Espirituales en el Duelo. *Avances en Psicología 20*(1), 9-30.

Yoffe, L. (2013). Nuevas Concepciones sobre los Duelos por Pérdida de Seres Queridos. *Avances en Psicología, 21*(2), 129-153.

Yoo, S., Hu, P., Gujar, N., Jolesz, F., & Walker, P. (2007). A deficit in the ability to form new human memories without sleep. *Nature Neuroscience 10,* 385 – 392.

Yuan, C., Wang, Z., Inslicht, S. S., McCaslin, S. E., Metzler, T. J., Henn-Haase, C., ... & Marmar, C. R. (2011). Protective factors for posttraumatic stress disorder symptoms in a prospective study of police officers. *Psychiatry Research, 188*(1), 45-50.

Zajonc, R. B. (1984). On the Primacy of Affect. *American Psychologist, 39,* 117-123.

Zamora, Z. E. H., Sánchez, Y. E. & Olvera, L. Y. (2010). Sentido de coherencia y salud en personas adultas mayores autopercibidas como sanas. *Revista Costarricense de Psicología, 29*(43), 17-34.

Zautra, A. J. (2003). *Emotions, Stress, and Health.* Oxford: Oxford University Press.

Zautra, A. J. (2014). Resilience Is Social, After All. In: M. Kent, M. C. Davis & J. W. Reich (Eds.). *The Resilience Handbook. Approaches to Stress and Trauma* (pp. 185-196). New York: Routledge.

Žižek, S. (2001). *El Espinoso Sujeto.* Buenos Aires: Paidós.

Žižek, S. (2005). *El Títere y el Enano. El Núcleo Perverso del Cristianismo.* Buenos Aires-Barcelona-México: Paidós.

Zoellner, T. & Maercker, A. (2006). Posttraumatic Growth in Clinical Psychology. A Critical Review and Introduction of a Two Component Model. *Clinical Psychology Review, 26*(5), 626-653.

Zogbo, L. & Wendland, E. (1989). *La Poesía del Antiguo Testamento: pautas para su traducción.* Miami: Sociedades Bíblicas Unidas.

Printed in Great Britain
by Amazon